Court and Culture
in Renaissance Scotland

Court and Culture in Renaissance Scotland

Sir David Lindsay of the Mount

CAROL EDINGTON

UNIVERSITY OF MASSACHUSETTS PRESS

AMHERST

Copyright © 1994 by The University of Massachusetts Press
All rights reserved
Printed in the United States of America
LC 94-14813
ISBN 0-87023-934-1
Designed by Susan Bishop
Set in Garamond No. 3 by Keystone Typesetting, Inc.

Library of Congress Cataloging-in-Publication Data
Edington, Carol, 1965–
Court and culture in Renaissance Scotland:
Sir David Lindsay of the Mount / by Carol Edington.
p.   cm. — (Massachusetts studies in early modern culture)
Includes bibliographical references (p.   ) and index.
ISBN 0-87023-934-1 (alk. paper)
1. Lindsay, David, Sir, fl. 1490–1555.   2. Politics and literature—
Scotland—History—16th century.   3. Scotland—Court and
courtiers—History—16th century.   4. Christianity and literature—
History—16th century.   5. Scotland—Church history–16th
century.   6. Authors, Scottish—To 1700—Biography.
7. Reformers—Scotland—Biography.   8. Renaissance—Scotland.
I. Title.   II. Series.
PR2296.L6Z677   1994
821'.2—dc20
[B]   94-14813

British Library Cataloguing in Publication data are available.

CONTENTS

ILLUSTRATIONS

ACKNOWLEDGMENTS

That I have completed this book owes a great deal to very many people and, now that I have reached the oft-longed-for end, it gives me great pleasure to thank those whose help and support inspired and sustained me. My colleagues in the Scottish History Department at the University of St. Andrews have been unstinting with their advice and encouragement. In particular I must thank Norman Macdougall, Stephen Boardman, and above all, Roger Mason, who first introduced me to David Lindsay, who supervised my doctoral research, and who has had to cope with more Lindsay over these past few years than anyone deserves in a lifetime. Unfailingly generous with his time, his expertise, and his sympathy, it is no exaggeration to say that without him this book would never have been written. I am also deeply indebted to John Guy, Michael Lynch, Janet Williams, and Jenny Wormald, all of whom took the trouble to read my original thesis and to offer their typically constructive comments. Two women whom I have never even met but to whom I owe a great deal are Pam Wilkinson of the University of Massachusetts Press and Barbara Palmer. Their professionalism has saved me from many an error and inconsistency. Needless to say, any mistakes that remain are all my own. At all those libraries I used in the course of my research, most notably here at St. Andrews, the National Library of Scotland, and the British Library, the staff have been courteous and helpful. I also owe an enormous amount to the British Academy who have funded my research at both the postgraduate and postdoctoral level. This debt is more than purely financial, for at a time when career prospects and job security seem a far-off dream, to be able to pursue academic research unhindered by financial worries is an opportunity beyond price. Finally, for their support over many years, I must thank my family: my parents, my sister Shona, and my husband, Leo. To them, this book is affectionately dedicated.

CONVENTIONS

Contemporary documents are quoted in the original spelling. *Yogh* is given as "y," *thorn* as "th," and the letters i/j and u/v/w are modernized where this clarifies the sense. Contractions are expanded and modern capitalization and punctuation used.

Dates are given according to the modern calendar with the new year beginning on 1 January.

Unless otherwise stated, quotations from Lindsay's works are taken from *The Works of Sir David Lindsay of the Mount,* ed. Douglas Hamer, *1490– 1555,* 4 vols. (Edinburgh, STS, 1931–36). Quotations from *Ane Satyre of the Thrie Estatis* are taken from Charteris's 1602 edition as edited by Hamer. When citing Lindsay's works, I have given line references in parentheses immediately following the quotation.

ABBREVIATIONS

ADCP	*Acts of the Lords of Council in Public Affairs, 1501–54: Selections from the Acta Dominorum Concilii.* Edited by R. K. Hannay. Edinburgh, 1932.
APS	*The Acts of Parliament of Scotland.* Edited by T. Thomson and C. Innes. 12 vols. Edinburgh, 1814–75.
CSP Scot	*Calendar of State Papers Relating to Scotland, 1509–1603.* Edited by M. J. Thorpe. 2 vols. London, 1858.
DOST	*A Dictionary of the Older Scottish Toungue: Twelfth Century to the End of the Seventeenth.* Edited by W. A. Craigie et al. London and Aberdeen, 1937–.
EETS	Early English Text Society.
ER	*The Exchequer Rolls of Scotland.* Edited by G. Burnett et al. 23 vols. Edinburgh, 1878–1908.
Hamilton Papers	*The Hamilton Papers.* Edited by Joseph Bain. 2 vols. Edinburgh, 1890–92.
HMC	*Reports of the Royal Commission on Historical Manuscripts.* London, 1870–.
L&P Henry VIII	*Calendar of Letters and Papers, Foreign and Domestic, Henry VIII.* Edited by J. S. Brewer et al. 21 vols. London, 1864–1932.
RMS	*Registrum Magni Sigilli Regum Scotorum.* Edited by J. M. Thomson et al. 11 vols. Edinburgh, 1882–1914.
RPC	*Register of the Privy Council of Scotland.* Edited by J. H. Burton et al. 36 vols. Edinburgh, 1877–1933.
RSCHS	*Records of the Scottish Church History Society.*
RSS	*Registrum Secreti Sigilli Regum Scotorum.* Edited by M. Livingstone et al. 8 vols. Edinburgh, 1908–.
SBRS	Scottish Burgh Record Society.
SHR	*Scottish Historical Review.*

SHS	Scottish History Society.
SLJ	*Scottish Literary Journal.*
SP Henry VIII	*State Papers of Henry VIII.* 11 vols. London, 1830–52.
SRS	Scottish Record Society.
SSL	*Studies in Scottish Literature.*
STS	Scottish Text Society.
TA	*Accounts of the Lord High Treasurer of Scotland.* Edited by T. Dickon and Sir J. Balfour Paul. 12 vols. Edinburgh, 1877–1916.

Court and Culture
in Renaissance Scotland

INTRODUCTION

Faced with a piece of particularly dubious information, a Scot of the seventeenth century might well have shaken his head and muttered incredulously, "Ye'll nae find that in Davie Lindsay." As a byword for all that was considered right and proper, the work of Sir David Lindsay of the Mount held a unique place in the hearts of his countrymen. Indeed, according to the later sixteenth-century theologian James Melville, it was second only to the Good Book itself. Recalling his own childhood and the sister who read him "the Storie of the Scripture [and] David Lindsayes book," Melville explained that it was the latter which moved poor Isabel to tears and prompted her pious lamentations.[1] Although once one of Scotland's most popular authors, however, David Lindsay of the Mount has long lost his claim to be recognized as the national bard. Recent adaptations of his best-known work, *Ane Satyre of the Thrie Estatis,* may have delighted Edinburgh's Festival-going audiences, but in reviving a lost reputation they have proved only partially successful, and, *Ane Satyre* apart, Lindsay's work remains largely unread. This is a great pity. Not only is there much to enjoy in Lindsay's writing, but it also sheds important light on the religious and political culture of Renaissance Scotland.

FOR OVER thirty years, Lindsay's principal milieu was the royal court where he served both James IV and James V. Not only did the vagaries of political fortune he experienced there dictate the events of Lindsay's life, but the court was also the dominant cultural apparatus which informed his thinking and the various ways he chose—or was conditioned—to express his ideas. Recent years have seen a welcome revival of interest in the interrelated themes of court and culture stimulated by a variety of fresh approaches drawn from a range of scholarly disciplines. It has to be said though that these terms, court and culture, tend to be bandied around by historians as if, obvious to all, they can be consistently and universally applied to each and every investigation. It is clear, however, that these concepts are variously employed according to the particular interests of individual historians.

Although one might expect "culture" to prove the most difficult concept to pin down, "the court" has proved just as evasive. Echoing the views of many working in the field, R. W. J. Evans has recently referred to the early modern European court as "a protean institution and an elusive subject," at once an institution, an ethos, and a society.[2] These different ways of understanding the court have meant that even within one country and one period it has been viewed in many different lights. In Tudor England, for example, debate has focused on the division between the court and the administration and between courtiers and professional bureaucrats. Over twenty years ago, Perez Zagorin advanced a view of the court that embraced all members of the political elite whether they served their sovereign in person or sought to implement the royal will in the localities.[3] By contrast, the seminal work of Geoffrey Elton explored the institutional and administrative character of the court, stressing the growing importance of the Privy Council and Star Chamber.[4] More recently, Elton's perceived "Tudor Revolution in Government" has been challenged, most notably by David Starkey. Arguing for a more precisely conceived organization composed of those who were actually attendant on the sovereign, Starkey has shown that the development of the Privy Council was an evolutionary response to pragmatic political concerns and that the distinction between courtier and official was by no means as clear-cut as previously believed.[5]

Turning away from early Tudor England, we find less concern with this particular debate: elsewhere in Europe, the institutions of government are more readily accepted as part and parcel of what is meant by the court. Flexibility is also the key to the early seventeenth century with historians such as Malcolm Smuts, Pauline Croft, and Linda Levy Peck describing the Jacobean court as "fluid and polycentric."[6] Such words could almost have been written not about the court of James VI and I but about that of his grandfather, James V, or indeed of his great-grandfather, James IV. Like the English court of the seventeenth century, the Scottish court in the late Middle Ages was, in many respects, hard to pin down either spatially or in terms of its personnel. Enormously adaptable, the peripatetic court encompassed permanent office-bearers, irregular visitors, pivotal political figures, and itinerant hangers-on. This lack of precise boundaries and definitions can appear disconcerting to those used to dealing in perceived certainties. Nevertheless, understanding the court in this broader sense provides a meaningful framework within which to discuss the activities of a group which, apart from its common association with the king, be it intimate or remote, informal or official, was a far from homogeneous body. What is clear is that the key element linking these disparate strands was the person of the king. Calculated or capricious, the royal will was the decisive factor when it came to determining changes in policy or personnel. Equally important was the way in which the person of the king provided the focus for political and ethical discussion. The figure of the king lay at the heart of an intricate ideological web, and the representation or examination of royal authority in literary, dramatic, or visual form was a central component of sixteenth-century discourse on issues as diverse as poor relief and national identity.

Another recent development in the study of the early modern court has been the concern to stress the interpenetration of the two themes, court and culture. Instead of viewing the court as something to be studied as a political, institutional, or social organization, an ever-increasing range of activities is being seen as worthy of legitimate historical enquiry. Of course, there have always been studies of court culture, but these have been all too frequently perceived as peripheral to the "real" business of politics and patronage. However, it is becoming increasingly clear that in examining the court there are no neatly labeled packages securely occupying their allotted spot on the court–culture continuum. Even a work that categorically asserts its intention to address the issue of the court "as a centre of patronage and a forum for politics" cannot help but express a concern with the rites and symbols that articulated the ideology of court life.[7] The study of politics and culture can best be approached if the two themes are viewed not as distinct parts but as fragments in a kaleidoscope, individual pieces that engage with one another in shifting yet nevertheless discernible patterns.

As this suggests, this particular study conceives of "culture" in its broadest sense, not simply as a term reducible to the reflection of economic, social, or political activities but as a shorthand expression for the wide variety of activities through which any community defines and describes its identity. There are of course other definitions. But, as Roger Chartier comments in defense of an approach that sees culture as much more than the products and practices of economic and social forces, "Describing a culture should . . . involve the comprehension of its entire system of relations—the totality of the practices that express how it represents the physical world, society, and the sacred."[8] As he admits, such a task is an impossibly vast undertaking for the complex societies of early modern Europe. Nevertheless, focusing upon a small portion of this type of cultural representation can provide the key to a much broader analysis.

In Sir David Lindsay of the Mount we are fortunate to have a man whose career and writing offer an intriguing commentary on Scottish culture in the sixteenth century, not just at court but also within the wider community. From 1543, Lindsay was much less intimately attached to the court, and consequently the concerns of his later work are much broader in scope. In the service of the crown, Lindsay acted as a herald and later as Lyon King of Arms, Scotland's chief heraldic officer. As such he was responsible both for the production of the earliest extant Scottish armorial register and for staging many of the spectacles associated with the crown. Both of these, and

3

the latter in particular, convey something of Lindsay's response to his environment, enabling us to decode some of the ways in which sixteenth-century Scots conceived their mental and physical worlds. However, valuable though these sources are, it is Lindsay's poetry which offers the richest seam for historical investigation.

Clearly such a study has its own methodological problems. Not least of these is the validity of using what can, after all, be seen simply as the imagined constructs of one individual to gain an insight into a much broader environment. However, literature is just as much a cultural activity as fighting a war, striking a trading agreement, or enforcing a law, and it is just as open to historical examination. Like all of these activities, it operates within its own parameters according to its own set of rules; equally, it is contingent upon external pressures and responds to them. Moreover, literature should not be viewed as a static historical artifact: Like these other activities, it participates in an ongoing process, reflecting and refiguring contemporary attitudes and modes of expression. In this way it possesses a historical reality of its own at least as important—arguably more so—as the realities of political or economic life.

Although some historians still profess a reluctance—understandable perhaps—to confront the problems thrown up by literary texts, pioneers such as Lauro Martines have ensured that those who venture to cross the divide between literature and history travel much better prepared.[9] It is to be hoped that no historian now would simply use literature as a form of anecdotal evidence adduced in support of a priori assumptions. As Kevin Sharpe's sensitive study of the literature of the Caroline court has demonstrated, reading texts for the purposes of illumination rather than illustration can seriously challenge established thinking on a range of important issues.[10] Literary scholars as well as historians have helped blaze the interdisciplinary trail, and their informed approach to historical contextualization makes a welcome departure from the crude search for topical "relevance" and "background" characteristic of earlier works. In Scottish studies as in other fields, it is becoming increasingly common for historians and literary scholars to run into one another both in the conference hall and in the pursuit of complementary interests. Of enormous benefit to all concerned, this is a development which can only serve the subject well.

Of course, the relationship between language and experience is far from straightforward, and it is vital to understand the constraints and conventions of both style and language that conditioned any given text, be it poem, sermon, or political treatise. The approach adopted here owes much to the pioneering example of what has been dubbed the new contextual history of political thought. Determined to remove political texts from an ahistorical canon subject to anachronistic interpretation, scholars such as

Peter Laslett, Quentin Skinner, and J. G. A. Pocock have insisted upon the need for sensitive contextualization.[11] Stressing the essential historicity of political thought, Pocock has demonstrated some of the ways in which we can learn to decipher its various languages: retrieving once familiar mental and linguistic landscapes and identifying the various ways in which an author used the different conceptual frameworks available to him. Only in this way, argues Skinner, can we hope to recover an author's intentions and to understand his audience's response.

A somewhat different contextualizing approach is embodied in the new "cultural criticism" pioneered by literary scholars during the last decade. Drawing attention both to the historicity of texts and to the textuality of history, the work of the New Historicists has usefully questioned some traditional boundaries, such as, for example, those imposed between literary and nonliterary texts.[12] However, though the historian can have no problem with the idea that texts produce different meanings for different individuals in specific cultural contexts, there is a danger that the deconstruction of literary texts—and very often a select number of "privileged" texts at that—can be taken to a stage in which all history is viewed as a series of paradigmatic texts, each with a multiplicity of meanings or readings, a process which can serve to obscure, even to distort, the significance of a text within a very precise cultural and historical framework. After all, however healthy one's skepticism concerning the limits of our knowledge, history must in some senses be knowable or else it ceases to be open to any type of investigation. Nevertheless, the subjection of familiar texts to new methodologies and a refigured understanding of power, gender, or psychology has generated some inspirational studies of Renaissance literature, and a recent collection of essays on Scottish sources includes an intriguing "Postmodern Look at a Medieval Poet," namely William Dunbar, and the application of the Bakhtinian notion of carnival to the same author's *Fasterin's Evin*.[13]

It is not, however, the aim of this study to push any single methodology. If anything, it adopts a dual strategy which recognizes there is a place for both textual criticism and empirical research, which is conscious of the limiting—and sometimes liberating—way in which a twentieth-century academic reads a sixteenth-century text, but which is equally sensitive to the ways in which the sixteenth-century author viewed his own world, his own actions, and his own contemporary readership.[14] Just as past centuries possessed their own range of discourses, so their recovery calls for the use of a variety of methodological tools.

BY EXAMINING the works of David Lindsay, this study offers a new approach and fresh insight into the political and religious culture of Renaissance Scotland. The basic raw material for this work has long been available. Little remains of Lindsay's literary output as published during his lifetime, but it is clear that from the middle of the sixteenth century Scottish audiences could not have enough of their favorite author. Between Lindsay's death in 1555 and the end of the century, no fewer than ten editions of his work were published in Scotland, a phenomenal rate of publication matched only by the fifteen issued during the next hundred years.[15] Although Lindsay's popularity was to wane thereafter, the nineteenth century saw a revival of scholarly attention with the publication of two impressive editions of his poetry by George Chalmers and David Laing.[16] Extensively annotated and with a great deal of useful biographical information, these still command attention today. Drawing on these respected predecessors, Douglas Hamer produced a four-volume edition of Lindsay's works for the Scottish Text Society in the 1930s.[17] Hamer's publication, to which all Lindsay scholars are profoundly indebted, made a substantial contribution to our understanding of both the poet and his life. But while Lindsay has provided both ecclesiastical historians and literary critics with the material for some extremely stimulating studies, a fully comprehensive historical study of Lindsay, one looking at all aspects of his career and taking adequate account of his total cultural environment, has not yet been attempted.[18] What follows seeks to remedy this neglect.

Beginning with a detailed consideration of Lindsay's career (Chapters 1 to 3), this study then progresses to a much fuller, more thematic, examination of his work. Much of the biographical material considered in Part One is not new, but relating it more precisely to contemporary events and attitudes allows us to appreciate Lindsay's poetry that much more fully. Anyone looking for a line-by-line analysis of Lindsay's poetry will not find it here. For this reason a short summary of each of his poems is provided in Appendix 1, and those unfamiliar with them might find it helpful to read these summaries in conjunction with the main text. Although the type of thematic approach adopted here poses its own problems, it provides an essential framework for the successful integration of those aspects of history—political, religious, and cultural—which historians have a tendency to docket in their separate pigeonholes.

Although the opening, essentially chronological, section begins to suggest some of Lindsay's particular concerns, these are much more comprehensively analyzed in the two sections that follow, dealing first with what is loosely termed the art of government and second with the Church. Looking in detail at the themes of kingship, government, and service, Part Two (Chapters 4 to 6) suggests some of the ways in which these were understood and articulated by sixteenth-century Scots. Lindsay's depiction of the ideal sovereign—something which lay at the heart of his political thinking—is carefully considered with reference both to his own experiences and to the concepts and language familiar to his contemporaries. This is not an altogether straightforward business, for though in many ways Lindsay clung to a deeply conservative political outlook, in others he offered a more distinctive critique of traditional mores. Clearly, as a courtier, issues such as kingship directly impinged on Lindsay's life. He did not, however, simply respond to the various images of kingship around him. As court poet and herald, he was also involved in the occasions of pageantry and public spectacle through which such images were created and conveyed. The role of a court poet is, therefore, considered in some detail, prompting suggestions as to some of the characteristic features of Stewart court culture during the reigns of James IV and James V. Finally, Part Two moves—as did Lindsay himself—from the confines of the court to the wider community, exploring how this crucial shift influenced not only the audience he addressed but also his political thinking. Ideas of government and service articulated in Lindsay's court poetry were now recast with reference to a much wider social vision, a vision expressed in particular through the emerging ideology of the commonweal.

With Part Three (Chapters 7 to 9) and the examination of Lindsay's religious attitudes, we are on more familiar territory. Indeed, it is as a critic of the Church, even as an early Protestant, that Lindsay was best loved in the sixteenth and seventeenth centuries and is best remembered today. However, to view Lindsay's poetry simply as evidence of an ecclesiastical establishment teetering on the brink of moral and institutional collapse is very wide of the mark. Instead, his work points to a much more complex situation, one in which religious attitudes were less than clear-cut and the future direction of religious policy far from settled. Unsurprisingly, in a period of great ideological flux, Lindsay's poetry bears the stamp of a wide range of opinion. Seen like this, Lindsay offers a more intriguing study than traditionally assumed, and one which more accurately reveals the complexities of religious culture in the crucial decades immediately prior to the Scottish Reformation.

ALMOST THIRTY years ago, an early historian of the Scottish Renaissance commented on the difficulty—and the necessity—of trying "to pin down a climate of thought." "Historians who prefer tidiness to grappling with realities," he wrote, "have an understandable impatience with what they feel is a flight from footnotes and factuality. The risks are great; it may be necessary to take them."[19] With some notable exceptions, few have dared to pick up the gauntlet. What follows aims to demonstrate not only that such a history should be written but also that, by adopting the type of approach followed here, such a history can be written.

I

Sir David Lindsay of the Mount

His Life and Career

Pass vp, and schaw, in oppin audience,
Solempnitlie, with ornate eloquence,
At greit laser, the legend of my life,
How I haue stand in monie stalwart strife.
—*The Testament of Squyer Meldrum*, 165–68

ONE

Background and Beginnings

1486–1530

Investigating the court culture of Renaissance Scotland necessitates looking at a whole range of activities and a wide variety of different cultural discourses. Such a task may well be beyond the scope of any single study, but the work of an individual such as Sir David Lindsay of the Mount provides a useful starting point. For over thirty years of his life, Lindsay was intimately connected with the Scottish court, and this association profoundly influenced both the development of his thinking and the ways he chose to express himself. Not only were the majority of his poems composed for the court, but even his later works, written with different intentions and addressed to a very different audience, stemmed from his experiences there. *Ane Satyre of the Thrie Estatis,* written in 1552, is set at the court of the universal king, Rex Humanitas, and his final work, *Ane Dialogue betuix Experience and ane Courteour* (more conveniently referred to as *The Monarche*) is, as its title suggests, firmly grounded in the mental and physical worlds of a royal servant. Understanding these worlds and the various ways in which Lindsay's work enables us to decode and explain them depends to a large extent on the recovery of Lindsay's own courtly career. Although most commonly associated with James V, by the time James began his adult, independent rule in 1528, Lindsay had already spent close to two decades in royal service. These years were a formative period in Lindsay's life, and we cannot hope to understand his later career without viewing it in this wider context. Indeed, we need to extend the parameters of our investigation still further and consider too those factors in his early life that contributed to Lindsay's understanding of the society in which he lived. The lack of reliable evidence renders this no easy task. Nevertheless, intelligent speculation based upon the careful use of existing sources and the informed reading of the poems themselves offers a useful way into the significant aspects of this important period.

THE LINDSAYS had long been one of Scotland's most important families. For the Lindsays of the Mount, the family's head, the earl of Crawford, was a rather remote figure. Much more significant was their more immediate kinsman, Lord Lindsay of the Byres.[1] Although by the sixteenth century the blood relationship between these two families was distant, the proximity of their estates made for close personal ties, and the easy familiarity suggested by Lindsay's own references to the domestic routine of Lord Lindsay, his wife, and children reflects the realities of social relations in sixteenth-century Scotland.[2] The Lindsays of the Byres held lands throughout southern and central Scotland, but their family home, Ochterotherstruther, was in Fife less than eight kilometers from the Mount. Situated just outside the thriving burgh of Cupar, by the sixteenth century this land had been held by the Lindsays of the Mount for several generations.[3] In East Lothian too, the families were near neighbors, for the Byres was equally close to the lands of Garleton-Alexander, held by the Lindsays of the Mount from their noble kinsmen.[4]

Geographically, politically, and economically, Fife was an area of considerable importance in the first half of the sixteenth century. The land was rich in agricultural and mineral resources, and the sea provided fish, salt, and excellent communications: As a later sixteenth-century commentator noted, it "abound[ed] in everything necessary for the support of life."[5] At the top of the local hierarchy stood men such as the earl of Rothes, Lord Sinclair, and Lord Lindsay of the Byres, but the population also included a large number of small landowners, many of them tenants of the Church or crown, who together composed what one historian has labeled "an assertive race of small lairds and freeholders."[6] Such families included the Learmonths of Dairsie, the Melvilles of Raith, and the Woods of Largo. The Lindsays of the Mount, while not technically freeholders, certainly fit within this category, and that Lindsay viewed his position in this light is apparent when, in mock self-deprecatory tones, he dubs himself "the Anscient laird" (*The Complaynt,* 262). While historians debate the technical definition of the lairdly class—arguing that, strictly speaking, lairds were freeholders of the crown—Lindsay usefully reminds us how blurred social distinctions below the ranks of the aristocracy could be. Such ambiguity was heightened by the increasing tendency for representatives of these lairdly and quasi-lairdly families to find employment in the service of the crown be it in the localities or at court. Sir James Learmonth of Dairsie was for many years Master of Household to James V, and the Woods of Largo, father and son, served as sea captains to both James IV and James V. Within this context, the career of David Lindsay, remarkable in many respects, was not without contemporary parallels.

Evidence relating to Lindsay's early life is scanty at best. Although we know he was born the eldest of five sons, the circumstances of his birth, the exact date even, remain unclear.[7] He was probably born around the year 1486, probably in Fife.[8] Unfortunately, we know nothing concerning his education and can only assume that it followed the general pattern for those in his position. In his *History of Greater Britain,* published in 1521, the Scottish theologian John Mair lamented that "the gentry educate their children neither in letters nor morals."[9] On the other hand, he also asserted that even the meanest laird kept a household chaplain, a claim which suggests at least some educational provision for his children and probably also for the offspring of favored tenants.[10] From such a man or perhaps from the teachers of the grammar schools at Cupar or Haddington, Lindsay would have received a grounding in grammar; some instruction in the other subjects of the *trivium,* rhetoric and dialectic; and perhaps too an introduction to basic arithmetic.[11] It is unlikely that his formal education consisted of much more than this. By 1508, "one called Lindsay" was already at the royal court "in the stable of the late prince," a reference to the elder Prince James who died in infancy in February 1508.[12] Although this is not necessarily a reference to the poet, the nature of Lindsay's subsequent career makes it highly probable. If so, it invalidates the suggestion that at this stage of his life Lindsay was a student at the University of St. Andrews. The name "Da. Lindesay" which appears among the incorporated students of St. Salvator's College for the year 1508 or 1509, and which gives rise to this particular hypothesis, is after all a common one.[13] However, given the entry in the court records and the fact that, throughout his long career, Lindsay was very rarely referred to as "master," the common title for those with a university degree, the identification seems unlikely.[14] Indeed, writing in his old age, Lindsay himself alludes to the deficiencies of his education:

> Nochtwithstanding, I thynk it gret plesour,
> Quhare cunnyng men hes languagis anew,
> That, in thare youth, be deligent labour,
> Hes leirnit Latyne, Greik, and old Hebrew.
> That I am nocht of that sorte sore I rew:
>
> (*The Monarche,* 594–98)

There is, however, more to this than meets the eye for, while it is quite likely that Lindsay knew neither Greek nor Hebrew, the sources cited in his works reveal him to be a reasonably competent Latinist. Warning us against the dangers of reading Lindsay's work as straightforward autobiography, the passage nevertheless offers an intriguing comment on education in Renaissance Scotland. The reference to the "New Learning" and in particular to the study of Hebrew and Greek reinforces recent conclusions concerning the existence of humanist thought in Scotland, suggesting too Lindsay's interest in this development.[15] But in this respect, as in many others, it was the royal court rather than Scotland's schools or universities which was to prove the formative influence on his thinking.

Just how Lindsay arrived at the court of James IV and secured a position there remains unclear. Living at the Mount, just outside Cupar, the young Lindsay would have been familiar with the court as it traveled its regular path between Edinburgh, Falkland, and St. Andrews, but it is impossible to tell how or even when Lindsay first became formally associated with it. The *Treasurer's Accounts* for the period August 1508 to August 1511 no longer survive, and the details of Lindsay's early career—so far as they can be gleaned from such sources—are lost. The reference to a Lindsay at court in 1508 has already been noted, and although this is shaky ground upon which to construct a career it is surely significant that it was around this time that Lindsay may have received Garleton-Alexander in East Lothian. The charter confirming him in these lands reveals that they were formerly in the possession of his grandfather, who must have died some time before this. [16] The fact that his son, Lindsay's father, was probably still alive until around the year 1524 (when Lindsay and his wife received the Mount) gives the settlement of Garleton upon Lindsay at this stage of his life the look of family provision for an elder son, recently come of age and embarked upon an independent life. [17] It may well mark the point at which Lindsay left home to begin his career at court.

Certainly we are on firmer ground when tracing Lindsay in the following decade. Three years after his possible arrival at court, a David Lindsay is recorded as receiving a pension of forty pounds. [18] It was probably also Lindsay who that same year received "ii ½ elnis blew taffatis and vi quartaris yallow taffatis to be ane play coit . . . for the play playt in the King and Quenis presence in the Abbay." [19] Clearly, from the earliest years of his career, Lindsay was involved in the drama and pageantry that characterized an increasingly self-confident political administration. More specifically, it seems likely that he continued to be associated with the king's sons during this period, and he probably served the short-lived Prince Arthur as he had the elder Prince James and would his younger brother. His next recorded appearance is as "ischar to the Prince," the prince in question being the future James V, born in April 1512. [20] Lindsay would later describe himself serving James since "The day of [his] Natyuitie" (*The Complaynt*, 16), and this chronology, albeit designed to stress the fidelity of an old servant, seems approximately accurate. A notarial document of 22 March 1513, illustrating that Lindsay was making arrangements to reside in Edinburgh, provides further confirmation that he was settling in to a life at court. [21]

As a servant of the young princes, Lindsay was closely associated with the household of the queen, Margaret Tudor. [22] This probably explains his friendship with Sir James Inglis and, perhaps too, his introduction to the literary and dramatic aspects of court life. Clerk to the Closet of James IV, Chaplain to Prince James, Chancellor of the Chapel Royal, and, after 1515, Secretary to the queen, Inglis is mentioned by Lindsay in *The Testament of the*

Papyngo as a fellow poet.[23] Sir James, the author of "ballatts, farses, and . . . plesand playis" (40–42), might well have fired the young Lindsay's enthusiasm, and it is tempting to speculate that, given Lindsay's involvement in the performance at Holyrood Abbey the previous year, he was one of Inglis's "collegis" who in 1512 received money for "play cottis."[24]

Although it is difficult to reconstruct anything like a full picture from such fragmentary evidence, it is clear that his early years at court represented an enormously important and influential period of Lindsay's life. Certainly, his later poetry vividly reveals how his experiences shaped his ideas concerning kingship, government, and princely majesty. Recollecting his early career, Lindsay viewed the reign of James IV as something of a golden age, notable for the virtue of the sovereign, the strength of his justice, and the glittering splendor of his court:

> Allace, quhare bene that rycht redoutit Roye,
> That Potent prince, gentyll king Iames the feird?
> I pray to Christe his Saule for to conuoye;
> Ane greater noble rang nocht in to the eird.
> O Atropus, warye we may thy weird,
> For he wes myrrour of humilitie,
> Lode sterne and lampe of libiralytie.
>
> During his tyme so iustice did preuaill,
> The Sauage Iles trymblit for terrour;
> Eskdale, Euisdale, Liddisdale, and Annerdale
> Durste nocht rebell, doutyng his dyntis dour,
> And of his Lordis had sic perfyte fauour:
> So, for to schaw that he aferit no one,
> Out throuch his realme he wald ryde hym alone.
>
> And of his court, throuch Europe sprang the fame
> Off lustie Lordis and lufesum Ladyis ying,
> Triumphand tornayis, iusting & knychtly game,
> With all pastyme according for one kyng.
> He wes the glore of princelie gouernyng,
>
> (*The Testament of the Papyngo*, 486–504)

Written in 1530, close on the heels of a long and troubled minority, this may represent an exaggeration born of nostalgia for what in retrospect seemed halcyon days of untroubled government. The extravagance of Lindsay's panegyric is also partially explained by the need to provide a contrast to the dismal events of 1513 and to set before James's son a stirring example of the ideals of kingship. Nevertheless, Lindsay's assessment of the reign (Flodden apart) has been endorsed by James's most recent biographer.[25] Like more recent historians, Lindsay stresses not only the success of

James's domestic policies but also the colorful chivalric spectacle associated with his court. An enthusiastic devotee of the cult of chivalry, James IV was a notable patron of the tournaments regularly held throughout the reign. Perhaps none of these carefully staged spectacles gilded the royal image with knightly glory as splendidly as that of 1508, a three-day-long *pas d'armes* held at Holyrood in defense of the "Black Lady."[26] Involving champions from France, England, and Denmark, it was James himself, the mysterious "Wild Knight," who won the day. Whether Lindsay was associated with such occasions can only be a matter for speculation—although his position in the stable certainly supports such an idea. Indeed, the extravagant festivities may even have been the reason for his appointment in the first place. Certainly, participation in such events would have helped him acquire the skills needed for a future heraldic career. Perhaps too Lindsay's involvement in these occasions extended beyond the lists to the accompanying spectacles, the most magnificent of which was the "gret triumphe and bancat" held in 1508.[27] On this occasion, the feasting was interrupted with farces and plays such as the Black Lady's descent from a cloud, a spectacle which prefigures similar entertainments arranged by Lindsay himself later in life.

Lindsay responded not only to the representations of royal identity formulated within the confines of the court but also to specific actions taken by the crown in the wider community. As his description of James IV suggests, the firm demonstration of royal authority earned his respect. This was to be an important thematic ideal in Lindsay's poetry and, although later events provided a more immediate stimulus, earlier experiences offered both an ideological and historical context for his work. This is particularly true with regard to Lindsay's attitude to the traditional role of the king as the defender of his people. Here, the events surrounding the disastrous Scottish defeat inflicted by the English at Flodden in 1513 exercised an important influence on his thinking. Lindsay's response to the war is perhaps suggested by his involvement in a mysterious episode that supposedly occurred on the battle's eve. According to a later chronicler, Lindsay's kinsman, Robert Lindsay of Pitscottie, James IV arrived at Linlithgow and, while praying in the Church of St. Michael, was visited by a man in a blue gown with loose fair hair who warned him against women and war alike.

I hard say Schir David Lyndsay Lyoun harrott and Iohne Inglische the mairchall quho war at that tyme young men and spetiall servandis to the kingis grace war standand presentlis besyde the king quho thocht to have layit handis on this man that they might have speirit forder tydingis at him bot all for nocht; they could not tueiche him ffor he wanishit away betuix them and was no more seen.[28]

The story was later repeated by George Buchanan who cites Lindsay himself, "a man of unsuspected probity and veracity," as his authority.[29] Though it is probably true that Lindsay was with the king (more specifically with Margaret and her son) at Linlithgow on this occasion, it is unlikely that the truth of the matter will ever be known.[30] It has been suggested that the affair was an elaborate charade concocted by those opposed to the war in order to deter the king from taking to the field.[31] However, whether such a faction even existed is highly doubtful, the Flodden campaign being remarkable for the large numbers who turned out to follow their monarch into battle.[32] It may be, therefore, that this story (circulated, it should be noted, after 1513) represents wisdom only after the event—for if Buchanan did hear the story from Lindsay's lips, it could only have been in the mid 1530s when both were at court. The legend was surely a creation of later years, born out of Flodden but fostered by subsequent—abortive—attempts to rouse the country against England in the 1520s. Although Lindsay may have had a hand in the tale of the unearthly apparition, it was designed to deter not James IV but his son from the vices of the flesh and the adoption of a bellicose foreign policy. Whether inspired by ghostly visions or not, Lindsay's response to the Flodden campaign, the Scottish defeat, and James IV's own death in battle, sowed the seeds of what would become a profound unease with the military identity of the king and nourished his growing concern with the whole question of war.

In the short term, however, the events of 1513 had little immediate effect on Lindsay's life. James V was crowned at Stirling shortly after Flodden, and it seems as if Lindsay continued in his service. Between 1517 and 1523 he is variously described as Keeper of the King's Grace, Usher, Master Usher, and Gentleman of the Bedchamber or Household of the king.[33] In 1517, he is referred to as Master of the Household, but it seems improbable that he actually occupied this influential position which was held, in 1516 at least, by the earl of Argyll.[34] Unfortunately, the picture is somewhat muddied as the accounts are once more missing for the period September 1518 to June 1522. When they resume, Lindsay is again described as Master Usher or *hostario domini regis,* and it is hard to say how he was employed in the intervening period.[35]

A somewhat more detailed, certainly more colorful, picture of Lindsay's duties emerges from his poetry. In his first extant work, *The Dreme,* Lindsay reminds James how he acted as "seware, Coppare, and Caruoure, / Thy purs maister, and secreit Thesaurare, / Thy Yshare, . . . / And of thy chamber cheiffe Cubiculare" (21–24). This snapshot of the king's household is confirmed by a document outlining arrangements made in August 1522 which provided for "ane Master of Household, ane coppar, ane carver, pantreman, verlotts of his chalmer, ane prest to say him mess, his ushar, cuke, clerk of the expenss."[36] The litany of household offices related by Lindsay is obviously not a precise reference to his own duties, but it usefully brings out how closely Lindsay was involved with James's upbringing. *The Dreme,* like

17

the very similar *Complaynt,* is obviously constrained by generic convention, and both poems take pains to stress the loyal service of the "wracheit worme" (*The Dreme,* 27), a mock humility which is made all the more effective by the descriptions of the undignified games the poet played with his young master. Yet Lindsay adroitly undercuts this conventional self-deprecation with expressions of genuine tenderness, reminding James:

> Quhen thow wes young, I bure the in myne arme
> Full tenderlie, tyll thow begouth to gang,
> And in thy bed oft happit the full warme,
> With lute in hand, syne, sweitlie to the sang:
> Sometyme, in dansing, feiralie I flang;
> And, sumtyme, playand fairsis on the flure;
>
> (*The Dreme,* 8–13)

Lindsay's responsibilities gave him a practical insight into the upbringing and education of one destined to rule. This issue greatly concerned Lindsay, as it did a large number of Renaissance thinkers, and his personal experiences led him to consider it with more than the theoretician's academic interest. From the age of six, James was tutored by Gavin Dunbar, dean of Moray, prior of Whithorn, and future archbishop of Glasgow.[37] Described as a man with "an incredible affection towards the votaries of learning," Dunbar is among those called upon by Lindsay to testify to the latter's close relationship with the king (*The Complaynt,* 82).[38] The day-to-day contact Lindsay must have enjoyed with the king's preceptor may help explain how it was that Lindsay, a relatively uneducated man, acquired the type of knowledge evident in his works. This in turn reveals the extent to which the court—even in times of political instability—could act as a medium for the transmission of learning. Unfortunately, little is known of the king's education. In *The Complaynt,* Lindsay describes James as "lernand vertew and science" (134), a meager account supplemented by a sketchy outline of the preceptor's duties found in the "Ordinance for the Keeping of James V" when, with Dunbar temporarily absent, James was placed under the supervision of Lord Erskine:

He [Erskine] sall be his scule master that sall wait on his Grace and instruct him in all gude vertuis, to reid and write and to speke Latin and Fransh; and the said master to ly in the Kingis chalmer and the usher togidder with the verletts of the chalmer.[39]

Although the curriculum is far from detailed, it is interesting to see such a close association between the king, his tutor, and his usher. In 1522 when this document was drawn up, it was Lindsay who would have spent his nights with Dunbar and his young charge.[40] This marks the point at which James was deemed old enough to dispense with the services of his nurse,

Marion Douglas, but not, it seems, of Lindsay himself.[41] It is tempting to speculate that Marion was related to Lindsay's future wife, Janet Douglas, but Janet's origins remain stubbornly obscure.[42] The accounts covering the period immediately prior to Janet's first recorded appearance (when she is already described as Lindsay's wife) no longer survive, but it seems probable that the pair were married sometime around the year 1522.[43]

Given that the king's education leaves so little trace in the records, it is perhaps unsurprising that its caliber has been widely questioned. While Dunbar and Lindsay provided a certain continuity, the troubled circumstances of the minority were educationally disruptive. This point is made by Lindsay himself in *The Complaynt* where he scornfully condemns those who, "Imprudentile, lyk wytles fullis, / . . . tuke that young Prince from the sculis" (130–31). Lindsay is referring here to the events of 1524, events which resulted in the loss of his own position, and his acerbic commentary is inspired, partly at least, by personal disappointment. It seems that Dunbar, unlike Lindsay, remained in service at least until the earl of Angus assumed power a couple of years later.[44] Nevertheless, Lindsay's concern was not without foundation. According to the English ambassador, the twelve-year-old James was unable even to "rede an Einglisshe letter" without the help of his Council.[45] Although this is more probably a measure of the government's anxiety to supervise diplomatic relations rather than of James's intellectual capabilities, his education does seem to have suffered, and contemporaries would later suggest that both his Latin and his French left something to be desired. The English ambassador's report also conveys a more personal glimpse of James's education. Gratitude to his uncle, Henry VIII, for various hunting gifts and his eager request for an English buckler—a full-sized version and not one designed for a child—vividly suggest which aspects of the young king's education most appealed to him. Certainly, alongside his tuition in philosophy and languages, James was fully trained in knightly accomplishments both martial and courtly. Some six months previously the English ambassador had dispatched a much more flattering description of the Scottish king which, albeit conventional and idealized, confirms his training in these traditional aristocratic pursuits:

His said Grace stirre[d] his horses, and renne with a speare, amongges other his Lordes and servantes, at a gloove. And also . . . we have seen His saide Grace use hym self otherwise pleasauntely, both in singging, and daunsing, and shewing familiaritye amonges his Lordes. All whiche his princely actes and doinges be soe excellent for his age, not yet of 13 yeres till Eister next, that in our oppynnyons it is not possible thay shulde be amended.[46]

Lindsay claimed to have entertained James (at a slightly younger age) by singing, playing the lute, and dancing (*The Dreme*, 11–12), and he may well have helped instruct the young king in those skills which so delighted the visiting ambassador. Nevertheless, Lindsay placed the greatest emphasis upon educating the mind, condemning an exclusively martial training and lamenting the interruptions to James's own schooling. Lindsay's works portray a cherished ideal rather than the reality of royal education in early-sixteenth-century Scotland. But aspirations—even unrealized ones—represent an important clue to contemporary attitudes, and it may well be that a program for the royal education was devised although never successfully carried through.

LINDSAY'S earliest extant works, *The Dreme* and *The Complaynt,* combine a highly traditional moral condemnation of the woes of minority government with a relatively accurate narrative, ably charting the various shifts in authority that characterized Scottish politics following the death of James IV.[47] With the infant king's accession in 1513, the heir presumptive to the Scottish throne was John, duke of Albany, son of the exiled uncle of James IV. Despite the fact that he was a permanent resident in France, it was to Albany that the political community turned in the autumn of 1514, inviting him to assume the governorship of Scotland. In so doing, they were deliberately setting aside the Queen Mother, Margaret Tudor, who by the terms of her late husband's will was named tutrix to her son during her widowhood. Margaret's exclusion, partly arising from reluctance to entrust the government to Henry VIII's sister, was made possible by her marriage to Archibald Douglas, sixth earl of Angus, less than a year after her husband's death. Personally and politically, the union proved disastrous. In particular it alarmed the powerful Hamilton family whose head, the earl of Arran, stood next in line to the throne after Albany. Her hastily contracted marriage provided the Council with the pretext they required to strip Margaret of her authority, and the assumption of effective power by Albany's supporters paved the way for his arrival in Scotland in May 1515. Albany's first visit to Scotland (1515–17), notable for the firm action taken against his opponents, initiated a period of strong, relatively stable government. In the last analysis, however, his administration was dangerously dependent upon his own personality and presence: His departure and the subsequent murder of his lieutenant inaugurated a period of factional anarchy. With the earls of Arran and Angus struggling for political control, the stalemate was broken only with Albany's return to Scotland in November 1521.

Albany's second period of personal rule witnessed continued success in domestic policy although, with regard to foreign affairs, his attempts to engage Scotland in war against England—perceived as being fought only in the interests of an ungenerous and ungrateful French king—were not so successful. Scottish reluctance to engage in further conflict was also a feature of Albany's third sojourn in Scotland (September 1523–May 1524). As we have seen, this attitude is later reflected in Lindsay's poetry and possibly also in the story of the Linlithgow ghost. In other respects, however, Lindsay appears to have approved of Albany's government, referring, for example, to "the prudent Duke of Albanie" (*The Testament of the Papyngo*, 534) and equating him with Scotland's prosperity. In *The Dreme*, the character of John the Commonweal laments his plight with the words, "My tender friendis ar all put to the flycht / For polecey [surely an allegorized Albany] is fled agane in France" (946–47). Although he was left mourning Albany's departure, the political lessons of his government were not lost upon Lindsay. Hereafter, his principal concerns would be for the maintenance of order, the welfare of the commonweal, and the reinforcement of the type of strong monarchical authority able to achieve these goals.

Albany's final departure in May 1524 once again left a power vacuum in Scotland. In a bid to seize control, Margaret Tudor had Albany's authority overthrown by Parliament and her son declared of age:

> The kyng was bot twelf yeiris of aige,
> Quhen new rewlaris come, in thare raige,
> For commoun weill makand no care
> Bot for thare proffeit singulair,
> Imprudentlie, lyk wytles fullis,
> Thay tuke that young Prince from the sculis,
> Quhare he, vnder obedience
> Was lernand vertew and science,
> And haistelie plat in his hand
> The gouernance of all Scotland.   (*The Complaynt*, 127–36)

This passage represents rather more than a comment on the minority government. Beneath Lindsay's undoubtedly sincere concern for James's education there runs a subtext of personal disappointment, venomously expressed. One of the traditional methods of demonstrating that the king was of age was the revocation of the principal offices of state, a move symbolizing that the authority of the original granter was no longer recognized. This device was employed by Margaret shortly after she assumed control of the government, and the autumn of 1524 saw the enthusiastic distribution of grants, particularly of household offices, among her supporters.[48] Lindsay was a casualty of this process. In August 1524, the position of Master Usher—previously held by Lindsay—with all its attendant "feis, privilegis, fredomes and dewties aucht and wount thairfor" was granted to Andrew, Lord Avondale, the brother of Margaret's future third husband, Henry Stewart, whom she married in March 1526.[49] It is unlikely that Lindsay's loss of the position sprang from any personal animosity; rather it seems that depriving James of one of his closest companions was part of a strategy designed to isolate him politically. However, Margaret's bid for power proved unsuccessful. Her overdependence upon a select group of supporters, combined with her administration's failure to effect a restitution of good government, resulted in the political initiative passing to her former husband, the earl of Angus. Various attempts to resolve the political stalemate and find a compromise solution culminated in the decision to rule through a council of rotating membership which would have control of the king. However, when in October 1525 the time came for Angus to hand over power, belief in impending annihilation at the hands of his enemies prompted him to chance what was, in effect, a coup d'état, and he refused to relinquish the king, a situation which was ultimately accepted and finally legitimated by Parliament in June 1526.[50]

Exactly what happened to Lindsay during this period is difficult to ascertain, the task being complicated by the fact that the accounts for the crucial period April 1524 to August 1525 are again missing. We know that Lindsay fell victim to Margaret's revocation in 1524. Thereafter (in 1525 and 1526) he is referred to as an erstwhile usher of the king.[51] At Christmas 1526, however, he received a gown and velvet for a doublet.[52] The accounts are then lost for a period and, on their resumption, Lindsay is reinstated, described as usher but never again as Master Usher.[53] Lindsay's own narrative vividly illustrates the personal disappointment he felt on being "trampit doun in to the douste" (*The Complaynt*, 255). He describes how at that time, he "durst nocht be sene / In oppin court" (289–90), but whether this means, as some commentators have claimed, that he was obliged to flee the court altogether is not clear.[54] It may be simply the indignation of a formerly important figure pushed to the periphery of court life. Indeed, the receipt of his Yuletime livery and pension (albeit paid to a former servant of the king) suggests the overdramatization of a fall from grace which was, in reality, little more than a slight tumble.[55] Nevertheless, the experience certainly marked Lindsay's thinking, intensifying his awareness of the precarious nature of service at court and prompting thoughts as to how that service might best be rewarded.

While brutal in his castigation of Margaret's administration, Lindsay's most bitter criticisms were reserved for Angus's usurpation of authority in 1525–26. "And vtheris tuke the gouernyng," he wrote, "Weill wors than thay in alkin thyng" (*The Complaynt*, 299–300). The Douglas administration, however, proved short-lived. Like his predecessors, Angus found it impossible to create a power base sufficiently broad to guarantee political survival. His failure to distribute patronage on a wide scale weakened any general willingness to prop up his unstable regime, and his position was seriously undermined when he lost control of the person of the king.

Isolated from the maelstrom of events, Lindsay appears to have known little of James's dramatic escape from the Douglases in 1528. His detachment possibly explains why, when James rewarded those who had supported him in the difficult and dangerous summer of 1528, Lindsay was not among them.[56] In view of this, the vehemence of Lindsay's criticisms might well be interpreted as an eager and, in view of his Douglas wife, perhaps even a desperate bid to establish his anti-Douglas credentials and hence his claim to a place in the new administration. How Lindsay fared in the circumstances of James's adult rule is the subject of later chapters. For now it is important to examine briefly those of his poems associated with the minority and its immediate aftermath.

INTENSELY concerned with the failure of government, with the relationship between ruler and commonweal, and with the nature of service, Lindsay's earliest extant compositions, *The Dreme* (1526), *The Complaynt* (1530), and *The Testament of the Papyngo* (1530) were clearly informed by his experiences during this period. It is perhaps surprising that Lindsay's first known poem was not written until he was around forty years of age. It has been argued that the tales with which Lindsay entertained the young James V were, in fact, actual poems now lost.[57] However, it is unlikely that Lindsay was doing anything more than reciting well-worn stories from memory. Certainly, the subject matter— stories of classical and chivalric heroes, prophecies and folk tales—is very different from that of Lindsay's later works.[58] Indeed, after cataloguing these more traditional tales, Lindsay introduces his own poem as "ane storye of the new" (*The Dreme,* 48), an obvious declaration of at least a major change in thematic direction if not a first composition. A highly accomplished maiden effort, *The Dreme* is also extremely traditional, relying heavily upon such well-established genres and motifs as the dream vision, the cosmological journey, poetic complaint, and mirror-for-princes type exhortation. Additionally, Lindsay clearly draws on several well-known authorities.[59] This too is a highly conventional poetic device but, significantly, it is one little used in other works (*The Monarche* excepted). *The Dreme* also resonates with the work of earlier Scottish poets, notably Robert Henryson. There are several striking similarities between Lindsay's poem and Henryson's *Orpheus and Eurydice,* particularly with regard to the two poets' depiction of Hell. The line "In haly kirk quhilk dois abusion" appears unaltered in both poems, and Lindsay's phrases, "mony cairful kingis," "in flame of fyre," "And Archebischopis in thare pontificall," compare remarkably closely with Henryson's "mony carefull king & quene," "In flambe of fyre," "and bischopis in thair pontificall."[60] Parallels can also be found between *The Dreme* and *The Testament of Cresseid.* Both include a description of a barren winter environment, and there are similarities also in the description of the planets.[61] The publication of Henryson's *Orpheus and Eurydice* by the Scottish printers Chepman and Millar in 1508 suggests the poet's popularity, and it may have been this which influenced Lindsay's first serious composition. Similarly, the description of how the narrator was awakened from his reverie by the sound of cannons firing from a passing ship recalls an identical incident in William Dunbar's *Golden Targe,* also an early Chepman and Millar publication.[62] The unusual citation of authorities, the heavy use of traditional *topi,* and the reliance upon the language of respected and popular predecessors support the argument that *The Dreme* was in fact Lindsay's first major composition.

The Dreme is traditionally believed to have been written in 1528, a dating first suggested by George Chalmers and later endorsed by Douglas Hamer.[63] Supporting his case, Chalmers cites Lindsay's descriptions of minority misrule and of lawlessness on the Border (before James V's attempts to restore royal authority there in 1529) while Hamer uses the same argument with relation to the Western Isles, also noting that the king is, as yet, unmarried. None of these points seems conclusive. Of more significance is the final exhortation to the king urging upon him the precepts of good government. Yet this passage stands independent of the main body of the poem, which could just as easily have been written sometime before 1528. Indeed, Lindsay pointedly refers to "The Cieule weir [which] misgydis euerilk oist" (992), surely a reference to the earl of Lennox's rebellion in 1526.[64] There is, therefore, no real reason to suggest that Lindsay was not writing in the latter days of the minority. His use of the present tense not only in relation to the civil war but also in ascribing Scotland's plight to "our infatuate heidis Insolent" (905)—a description which can only apply to the various regency administrations or, collectively, to the Douglases— adds weight to this argument. It is surely significant too that John the Commonweal flees Scotland pledging not to return "tyll that I see the cuntre gydit / Be wysedome of ane gude auld prudent king" (1004–5)— hardly appropriate if James had already embarked upon independent, adult rule. John also says that the question of whether he will return or not "sall be sone desydit" (1002), which again suggests that the young king was nearing an age when he might be expected to assume full authority over his government. Although the exhortation to James could have been added to the earlier composition at a later date, it seems more likely that it represents Lindsay's attempt to conform to the fiction that the king was of age while simultaneously and adroitly exposing the fact that in reality his education in the business of kingship was not yet complete.[65] Such an interpretation is strengthened when we consider the closely related composition, *The Complaynt.* Clearly exercising his own authority, James is depicted ruling with the cardinal virtues having already begun to restore order to the kingdom.

Now he is offered specific advice (on patronage and Church reform) more suited to the altered political circumstances. The dating of many of Lindsay's poems is very speculative, but it seems clear that the hitherto accepted date of 1528 for *The Dreme* requires qualification if not revision.

There is less room for debate concerning the dating of *The Complaynt*. Lindsay here is much more specific concerning the fact of James V's personal rule, thanking God that the king is "to no man . . . subiectit / Nor to sic counsalouris coactit" (377–78). Secure in his own position and aware of James's attitude toward the Douglases, he is much more vitriolic in his denunciation of those who kept James in their control. Finally, Lindsay also refers to an old servant, Willie Dye, as being no longer alive. Since Dye is recorded as receiving his Christmas livery in 1529, the poem must have been written sometime after this date yet, in order to retain its topicality, surely not too long after James's assumption of personal power.[66] The poem represents an important (if amusing) look at service at court, in the tradition of William Dunbar, which develops the themes of the precarious— often dangerous—nature of royal service, of patronage, advancement, and the value placed upon differing aspects of these.

Dealing with many similar themes, *The Testament of the Papyngo* was also written during the early part of Lindsay's career (sometime before December 1530).[67] In this poem, Lindsay uses a Papyngo (parrot) within the fall-of-princes genre to offer an examination of ambition and fortune which is simultaneously humorous and serious in intent. Through the mouthpiece of the dying bird, he offers both James V and his court a powerful moral exhortation, strongly humanist in tone. The second part of the poem deals with the parrot's experiences at the hands of three rapacious bird-clerics, the traditional beast fable being adapted to launch a mordant attack upon clerical abuses. Taken together, these three poems represent a succinct declaration of Lindsay's intent regarding both style and subject matter; exploring in a powerful, yet often humorous, manner the issues of kingship, government, and the Church. These themes are more fully analyzed in later chapters. Meanwhile, it is to Lindsay's career in the 1530s and 1540s that we most turn our attention, beginning first of all with a look at his role as a herald of the Scottish court.

TWO

A Heraldic Career

1530–1555

In his poem *The Complaynt,* Lindsay recalls his early service at court, requesting James V to "mak me recompense" (502). If this traditional enough petition provoked any response other than an amused smile, then it probably came in the form of elevation to the office of Snowdon Herald. This was not simply a question of placating an old retainer, "Quhilk hes so lang in seruyce bene" (13), for Lindsay's career up to this point rendered the move entirely suitable. Not only would his employment in the stable have involved working alongside heralds in the course of jousts and tournaments, but he had also been connected with at least one court entertainment—valuable experience for a position that involved the supervision of public and royal spectacle beyond the confines of the tournament arena. The 1530s would see Lindsay closely engaged in both these areas of heraldic activity. Additionally, as a royal herald charged with the delivery of messages both in Scotland and abroad, Lindsay was dispatched on official business to the courts of Flanders, England, France, and Denmark. Exerting a decisive influence upon his thinking, Lindsay's travels provide a striking example of the type of cultural cross-fertilization that ensured Scottish participation in the intellectual developments of the Renaissance.

IT HAS BEEN argued that Lindsay began his heraldic career as a pursuivant, for it was common—although apparently not mandatory—to perform the one office before the other. The suggestion is, therefore, that he occupied this position in the 1520s during the period when he apparently lost office yet remained in receipt of his pension.[1] However, if we consider the evidence of *The Complaynt* and of the *Exchequer Rolls* (which explicitly refer to him as a former household servant), this seems implausible.[2] Rather, Lindsay's new career was underway swiftly after, but only after, his return to favor. At the beginning of 1530, he is mentioned as acting with Marchmont, Ross, and Islay heralds; and three months later, the *Treasurer's Accounts* note the payment of fifteen pounds to a "David Lindesay" who "passed with" a servant of the earl of Northumberland.[3] Whether Lindsay was actually a herald at this stage is not clear, although he certainly was by the end of the year when, described as such for the first time, he received livery and an annual fee of forty pounds.[4] It has often been claimed that it was at this point that Lindsay became Scotland's chief heraldic officer, Lyon King of Arms. Such swift advancement is extremely improbable, however, for there already was a Lyon King, one Thomas Pettigrew, named as such in 1529 and again in 1542.[5] At this stage in his career, Lindsay was most often described simply as a herald (sometimes as Snowdon Herald). But the dearth of recorded appearances of Thomas Pettigrew does suggest an incapacity, which renders it quite likely that during the 1530s Lindsay acted as a form of Lyon deputy.[6] It is significant that the two occasions before 1542 when Lindsay was referred to as Lyon Herald were during an embassy to England and at the funeral of Queen Madelaine, important events which demanded the dignified presence of Scotland's chief officer of arms.[7] Clearly, Lindsay could—and did—act as Lyon King when the situation demanded.

Before we examine Lindsay's heraldic duties, it is helpful to consider the officers of arms themselves. Although their numbers fluctuated quite dramatically in the course of the fifteenth century, by the middle of the sixteenth there were six royal heralds—Islay, Snowdon, Marchmont, Albany, Ross, and Rothesay—and the same number of pursuivants—Carrick, Dingwall, Bute, Unicorn, Kintyre, and Ormond.[8] At the apex of the heraldic hierarchy stood the Lyon King of Arms, first found in the records in 1377 but generally believed to have much older antecedents.[9] Theoretically, final authority over the officers of arms rested in the Constable, but while it is clear that the royal Council exercised a certain degree of control over these important royal servants, in practice the Lyon King seems to have been the key figure.[10] It was the Lyon King who took "gude ordour and maid reformatione" of the officers in 1569 and who was responsible for their discipline.[11] In 1555, for example, Lindsay together with the Constable and earl of Angus convened a chapter of heralds to consider the case against one William Crawford, a messenger accused of various acts of extortion and oppression.[12] Finding him guilty, the chapter stripped him of his office and delivered him up for punishment. This represents the forerunner of a procedure regularized by Parliament in 1587 whereby the Lyon King was vested with the authority to appoint and remove all officers of arms, to convene a biannual court in Edinburgh to hear complaints against them and to fine and dismiss the guilty.[13] Minor officers, messengers, and macers (of which there were eighty-odd) were recruited from the localities—the act of 1587 laments the prevalence of unaccredited officers and calls for the burghs to submit the names of suitable candidates to the Lords of Session.[14] Pursuivants and heralds, however, appear to have remained permanently at court, the king's "familiar daylie servitors."[15] The importance of Lindsay's continued association with the court cannot be overemphasized. Not only did his observation of kingship sustain his interest in this and related issues, but he was able to view at first hand, and from a unique vantage point, how the chivalrous ideology so intimately linked to his own office actually related to courtly life and to the practical business of government.

Although their early history remains obscure, heralds were probably first employed in warfare, charged with the tasks of recording ennoblements and the deaths of knights and also acting as messengers between opposing camps.[16] However, the key to the emergence of the office was the heralds' participation in tournaments. Again, their early attendance was in a lowly capacity, very often in association with wandering minstrels, but their growing expertise in recording the chivalric prowess of those participating in the tournament gradually rendered the heralds' position more secure and, increasingly, they came to be identified as chivalry's technical experts, wise in its history, its ideology, and the conventions according to which it operated. Additionally, as the literary tastes of the court grew more sophisticated, heralds were expected to produce elaborate, highly polished accounts of their business—be it records of valor in the lists or their visits to foreign courts—which spread their master's fame abroad and fostered his majesty at home.[17] This increasingly important aspect of a herald's duties is attested to by the old Scottish proverb concerning braggarts who "neid no lyon heraulds to sound [their] prais."[18]

Heralds constituted a specialized branch of the lay intelligentsia. A knowledge of genealogy and blazon, of the laws of nobility and inheritance, a command of the literature and historic culture of chivalry and its associated symbolism, were all necessary requisites of the sixteenth-century herald. Something of the range of a herald's erudition can be seen from the texts they possessed and the manuscripts they compiled. An English herald contemporary with Lindsay, Thomas Benolt, Clarenceaux King of Arms, owned, inter alia, rolls recording pedigrees, accounts of ceremonies such as coronations and funerals, several bestiaries, Froissart's *Chroniques,* the *Livre de Tresor* of Brunetto Latini, a translation of Giles of Rome's *De Regimine Principum,* a book of the Nine Worthies, a history of Troy, a book of Galahad, Geoffrey de Charnay's *Livre de Chevalrie,* Vegetius, and Honoré Bonet's *Tree of Battles.*[19] Of course, it is by no means certain that Lindsay enjoyed access to anything like such a collection, but such evidence as we have suggests his familiarity with a similar range of sources. *The Tree of Battles,* for example, had been translated into Scots in the fifteenth century by Sir Gilbert Hay, one of the authors mentioned by Lindsay in *The Testament of the Papyngo* whose "libells bene leuand" (20).[20] In addition, there exist several Scottish heraldic manuscripts possibly known to Lindsay which include such items as a treatise on tournaments, a description of the office of

Marshall and Constable, an account of the art of blazon, a history of arms, a tract entitled "How Gentilmen salbe Knawin Frome Churles," military material drawn from Vegetius, accounts of coronations, and a version of the classic text, *The Buke of the Ordre of Chevalrie*.[21]

Heraldic duties in Scotland, as elsewhere in Europe, represented the logical extension of the office's original functions: the delivery of royal messages both within Scotland and abroad, participation in royal and public ceremonies, the supervision of matters genealogical, and the regulation of grants of arms. Also, as mentioned above, heralds were increasingly expected to produce literature aimed at the glorification of the chivalrous court. What have been termed "the journalists of the middle ages" graduated as eloquent mouthpieces for an ever more elaborate court literature.[22] Although it would be wrong to view Lindsay simply as a glorified heraldic commentator, it is important to view his poetic development within this context for, though Lindsay's attitude to the cult of chivalry was far from straightforward, his heraldic position renders his exploration of the issue extremely pertinent and highly intriguing. It also informs his work in somewhat more obvious fashion, and the references to heraldic duties found in Lindsay's poems help flesh out our account of the office. Unsurprisingly, we find heralds in *The Historie of Squyer Meldrum,* where they supervise the joust between the Squire and Sir Talbart, ordering the crowd and giving the signal for the fight to begin. Of greater interest though is the reference in *The Deploration of the Deith of Quene Magdalene* to the macers and heralds who, "with thare awfull Vestimentis" (137), direct the crowd during the entry celebrations (see Fig. 1).[23]

The most basic and frequently performed of a herald's duties was the delivery of royal communications. Officers of arms were charged with proclaiming forthcoming parliaments at mercat crosses throughout the kingdom, and heralds bearing the king's letters were used to summon individuals to appear before Parliament.[24] In *Ane Satyre of the Thrie Estatis,* it is the herald, Diligence, who performs these offices and who also, as a herald should, proclaims the legislative action of the play. It is tempting to think that when *Ane Satyre* was first staged in Cupar in 1552 Lindsay himself played this role. It would certainly make sense, given that Diligence, adopting an almost authorial stance, both introduces and wraps up the action. He it is who delivers the bulk of the play's specific political message while at the same time claiming—somewhat disingenuously—that it is only a play and not to be taken too seriously. Moreover, Diligence's pecuniary grumbles—echoing those made by Lindsay in *The Complaynt,* the very poem which may have secured his position—doubtless raised a wry smile from those who knew that the 1540s had seen the virtual cessation of Lindsay's official pension.

Lindsay's *Satyre* is also informed by another aspect of his heraldic back-

Figure 1. "Habit of a Herald." From the Seton Armorial, NLS, ACC. 9309, fol. after 23. Courtesy of Sir Francis Ogilvy Bart.

30

ground, namely his role in the administration of the law of arms. Although heraldic authority in this area was not formally recognized until 1592, the parliamentary legislation of that year probably represents the attempted regularization of the status quo rather than the introduction of innovations. Certainly, Lindsay as Lyon King performed many of the duties it describes.[25] The legal enforcement of the law of arms possessed important implications concerning the nature of nobility and social status in Renaissance Scotland. The statute of 1592 granted the Lyon King and heralds "full power and comissioun" to inspect the arms of all "noblemen, baronis and gentlemen," to distinguish them with proper differences and to matriculate them in their books and registers, to prohibit "the common sort of people" from bearing arms and to impose harsh penalties on any who attempted to bear arms inappropriate to their status. The act claimed the abuse of arms was such that "it can nocht be distinguischit be thair armes quha ar gentlemen of blude be thair antecessors."[26] From this piece of legislation alone it is not clear whether such attitudes were long-standing or whether they expressed the reactions of a newly sensitive armigerous class. Lindsay's work makes clear, however, that status was a pertinent issue at least by the mid sixteenth century. In *Ane Satyre of the Thrie Estatis,* he attacks those members of the nobility who marry their children to the illegitimate offspring of churchmen—Temporalitie bitterly complains that, because he cannot match the dowries offered by clerics, his daughters remain unmarried (3180–96). Lindsay's solution to the problem expressed in the legislative action of the play is the prohibition of intermarriage between the first and second estates. He argues that those contravening the act should be stripped of their noble status, a reference to the type of action taken against convicted traitors, enforced by the Lyon King and, after 1592, the civil magistrates. In *Ane Satyre,* Lindsay commended a process—possibly suggested by one already in place and certainly foreshadowing the 1592 legislation—whereby nobility was subject to consideration and confirmation by the civil authorities:

> Gif Nobils marie with the Spiritualitie,
> From thyre subject thay salbe, and all
> Sall be degraithit of thair Nobilitie,
> And from the Nobils cancellit.
> Vnto the tyme that by thair libertie,
> Rehabilit be the ciuill magistrate.   (3933–38)

Based on Bartolus's *De Insignia et Armis,* a copy of which was in the possession of John Meldrum, Marchmont Herald, in the first half of the sixteenth century, there existed important links between heraldry and the civil law.[27] William Cumming of Inverallochy, Lyon King of Arms, 1512–19, was a frequent procurator before the Lords of Council and, though himself not a lawyer, Lindsay's works offer ample evidence of his interest in legal affairs.[28]

AS ROYAL messengers, heralds were frequently expected to travel outside Scotland, and in the course of his career Lindsay undertook a number of missions to foreign courts. His diplomatic activities are significant for a number of reasons. First, they shed more light on heraldic office during this period, especially in relation to that of ambassador; second, they ensured that Lindsay remained very much involved with the major political issues of day; and third, they provided him with an insight into the court cultures and political and religious affairs of a number of countries not his own.

Lindsay's first overseas journey was a seven-week visit to Flanders made in the summer of 1531.[29] In addition to being involved in the mutual confirmation of a long-standing trade agreement, Lindsay was also instructed to press for reparation in connection with an incident of piracy committed against a Scottish ship.[30] He seems too to have become embroiled in negotiations concerning James V's proposed marriage when the emperor, Charles V, asked him to persuade the Scottish king of the advantages of a match with Dorothea of Denmark.[31] Although Lindsay seems to have done no more than carry home a couple of portraits for James's consideration, the episode provided a useful introduction to the problematic business of royal matchmaking, an issue which would concern him further in the coming years.

Having proved himself on this relatively low-key mission, Lindsay subsequently became involved in a series of embassies concerning the major diplomatic issue of the first part of the decade, securing a bride for the Scottish king. As early as 1517, the Treaty of Rouen had secured a marriage with a French princess. However, Francis I's reluctance to fulfill his part of the bargain periodically spurred the Scots to look elsewhere. Though James occasionally contemplated a match with one of his many mistresses, the need to augment royal finances with a hefty dowry combined with the opportunity for participation in European affairs meant that he generally sought a foreign alliance and invariably returned to the prospect of a French match. It was in an effort to implement the Treaty of Rouen that in 1532 the Scottish government commissioned an embassy consisting of the duke of Albany, the bishop of Ross, and Sir Thomas Erskine of Brechin, Chief Secretary.[32] Having first secured safe-conduct through England for the party traveling from north of the border, Lindsay accompanied this embassy.[33] Not among those empowered to conclude the negotiations on James's behalf, Lindsay's role was probably largely ceremonial, the presence of Scotland's acting chief officer of arms lending a symbolic dignity to the proceedings.[34] He was also useful as an on-the-spot envoy entrusted with the task of informing James of the progress of the mission. Thus, in the course of the embassy, Lindsay returned to Scotland and, with stormy weather forcing his ship to turn back from Brittany, a difficult journey was completed only after some four weeks. Eventually, however, he was able to present his report to James who promptly dispatched him back to France with a letter for the French king.[35] Thereafter Lindsay remained with the embassy for another couple of months before returning home—again via England—in November 1532.[36]

Two years later, Erskine was again commissioned to travel to France to negotiate the proposed marriage with Francis's daughter, Madelaine, "to the fynale ending"—or so it was optimistically hoped.[37] Once more Lindsay was a member of the Scottish party, received by Francis at Compiègne before being sent on to Paris.[38] From the records it is not entirely clear when Lindsay returned to Scotland, but he was probably with David Beaton, another member of the delegation, when the latter returned home toward the end of the year.[39] Unfortunately, Scottish hopes for a speedy conclusion to the negotiations proved vain, and Francis continued to delay proceedings. In 1534, however, he put forward an alternative candidate for James's hand in the person of a more remote kinswoman, Marie de Vendôme. The following year, a Scottish embassy was appointed to treat for this marriage and, on 29 March 1536, a marriage settlement was drawn up.[40] A month later, James began preparations for the journey to France.

Although Lindsay continued to be involved with the French marriage during this period, he was also required to travel to England with Lord Erskine who was to act as proxy for James V at the latter's installation in the Order of the Garter.[41] The imperial ambassador at the English court states that after the installation on 23 August 1535 the delegation of "about thirty horses" traveled to France to join the envoies already there and to await the arrival of the Scottish king.[42] It is unclear whether Lindsay accompanied Erskine's party or whether, returning to Scotland, he sailed with James in September 1536. But the accounts for the period following clearly prove Lindsay to have been in France for the royal marriage.[43]

On arriving in France, the Scottish king, indulging his taste for chivalric adventure, disguised himself as a servant in order that he might view his prospective bride incognito.[44] However, the quixotic gesture backfired spectacularly when, finding Marie ugly, hunchbacked, and not at all to his taste, James reasserted his determination to marry the oft-refused Madelaine. Her father, swayed by the collapse of Anglo-French amity and the outbreak of hostilities with the emperor, was now inclined to secure Scottish support and, on 6 November 1536, a marriage contract was drawn up at Blois, followed ten days later by the religious ceremony of betrothal.

Amid an atmosphere of rejoicing, the court departed for Fontainebleau prior to James's arrival in Paris, there to be married on New Year's Day.[45] Shortly after this, Lindsay received twenty crowns "to pass in Scotland," which suggests that he returned home some three months before the main party.[46] This may have been to announce the marriage officially in his capacity as acting chief herald, or it may have been to initiate preparations for Madelaine's reception in Scotland. Given the details concerning these preparations found in Lindsay's poem, *The Deploratioun of the Deith of Quene Magdalene*, this is the most likely explanation. Indeed, *The Deploratioun* looks very much like an epithalmium turned elegy, for as Lindsay himself acknowledged, "Our *Alleluya* hes turnit in allace" (161).

Detailed scrutiny of Lindsay's participation in these embassies sheds important light on the diplomatic functions performed by heralds and in particular on their association with the emerging office of ambassador. It has been argued that during this period the title ambassador was not a specific, technical term but rather referred simply to "one sent on a mission."[47] If we employ this definition, Lindsay can certainly be classed as such. However, it appears that by this date the title in Scotland was more precise in its application, referring specifically to a senior diplomatic representative, one possessing procuratorial authority (that is the ability to negotiate without reference to one's principal) and generally one of high social status. To judge by these criteria, Lindsay was no ambassador, and in fact the only occasion when he is so described is probably best seen as the misconception of an ill-informed English observer.[48] A more accurate impression is conveyed by the entry in the *Treasurer's Accounts* recording payment "to my lordis, bishop of Ros, and Secretar, Ambassatouris in France, and to the lard of Gawistoune, and David Lyndesay, herald, being with them." Significantly, the two named as ambassadors received expenses of 600 francs each whereas Gaviston and Lindsay received only 200 and 100 francs respectively.[49]

This assessment of Lindsay's position is borne out by what is known of how he spent his time while abroad, particularly in connection with the Flanders expedition of 1531. His instructions reveal Lindsay's role to have been largely that of a letter-bearer, carrying confirmation of a treaty, a demand for reparation, and even the portraits of possible brides for the Scottish king. He did not, however, fail to take the opportunity to pass on such general information as he could regarding affairs in the Low Countries.[50] Reporting—much exaggerated—rumors of James V's death, the emperor's intended expedition against the German Lutherans, and the confirmation of Mary of Hungary as regent, he also referred to other dispatches, presumably containing similar material, which again suggests that his diplomatic function was somewhat wider in scope than the simple delivery of messages. Nevertheless, Lindsay's position as herald meant that he was largely used for the purposes of communication rather than of negotiation. In addition, as demonstrated by Lindsay's presence at Windsor for James's installation as a Knight of the Garter, the chivalric and ceremonial aspects of heraldic office represented an important facet of any diplomatic embassy. In short, the office of herald, as exercised by Lindsay and as utilized by the Scottish government, possessed important diplomatic functions that complemented and occasionally coincided with the emergent office of ambassador.

Following his return to Scotland in January 1537, Lindsay was not to leave the country for the remainder of the reign. After a period of such intense diplomatic activity in the first half of the decade, we might wonder why he was no longer employed in this capacity. The answer is elusive. It may simply be that the type of embassy on which his presence was appropriate was less frequently undertaken, for while the chief herald added to the prestige of a delegation seeking the hand of a foreign princess, his presence was not necessarily suited to the embassies of the latter part of the reign dealing primarily with increasingly strained Anglo-Scottish relations. This having been said, however, Lindsay was not associated with the embassy dispatched to France following the death of Madelaine, James's bride of just seven months. The king's choice for a second wife was the recently widowed Mary of Guise-Lorraine, a match which would firmly commit him to the French interest and would link him with one of the most powerful and most orthodox Catholic families at the French court. After some delay in the negotiations, the marriage contract was drawn up in January 1538. The marriage by proxy was solemnized on 4 May 1538, and on 10 June the new bride landed at Balcomie near Crail, Fife.[51] Lindsay was almost certainly present at the ceremony confirming the marriage shortly after Mary's arrival, for although he had not been party to the negotiations in France, he was very much involved in the preparations for the new queen's reception. This explains his absence from the French embassy for, without doubt, James V was anxious to prepare for his French wife (and, more especially, for the important kinsfolk who accompanied her) a display comparable to that which he had himself received in France. Heralds played an important part in royal marriage celebrations. Called upon to "cry largesse," they distributed among the court the gifts that symbolized the king's wealth and generosity.[52] Moreover, Lindsay, with his experience of French spectacle and with his flair for the dramatic, was the ideal person to arrange the festivities greeting the new queen on her arrival in St. Andrews:

And first scho was ressavit at the New Abbay geit. Wpon the eist syde thair was maid to hir ane trieumphant frais be Schir Dawid Lyndsay of the Mount, lyoun harrot, quhilk causit ane great clude come out of the heavins done abone the yeit quhair the quene come in, and oppin in two halffis instantlie and thair appeirit ane fair lady most lyke ane angell havand the keyis of haill Scotland in hir handis deliuerand thame into the quens grace in signe and taikin that the heartis of Scottland was opinit to the ressawing of hir grace, witht certane wriosouns and exortatiouns maid be the said Schir Dawid Lyndsay into the quens grace instructioun quhilk teichit hir to serue her god, obey hir husband, and keep hir body clene according to godis will and commandement.[53]

The author of this account, Lindsay of Pitscottie, goes on to describe the festivities following the wedding: the "great merrienes and game and iusting and ryoting at the listis, archorie, huntting and halking, with singing and danceing, menstrelling and playing, with wther princlie game and pastyme according to king and quein."[54] Such celebrations may have inspired Lindsay to write *The Iusting betuix Iames Watsoun and Ihone Barbour.* The comical joust it describes was supposed to have taken place at St. Andrews on Whitmonday and, as Mary arrived on Whitsunday, this is not unfeasible. However, the court was habitually in St. Andrews at this time of year and jousting was not uncommon.[55] The poem could have been written at any time between 1538 and 1540 and, given Lindsay's heavy involvement in the preparations for the reception of Mary of Guise, a later composition date seems more likely.

Lindsay was not only in charge of the pageantry at St. Andrews, he was also responsible for the arrangements made for Mary's entry into Edinburgh the following month. There the new queen received a welcome, in French, delivered by one Henry Lawder and "devysit with avyse of Maister Adame Otterburne, Maister James Foulis, and Dauid Lyndsay."[56] Both Otterburn and Foulis were accomplished poets. Foulis, the probable author of the anonymous Latin composition *Strena,* had also published a volume of Latin verse dedicated to Alexander Stewart, James V's half-brother and archbishop of St. Andrews, which urged his countrymen to embrace literature as a profession. Although described by the Italian humanist, Giovanni Ferrerio, as a "poet to the tips of his fingers," Foulis did not confine his energies to verse; he was also a practicing lawyer, becoming a Lord of Session in 1526 and Clerk Register in 1532.[57] Otterburn too was a lawyer, acting as King's Advocate between the years 1524 and 1538. Less is known of his poetic achievements, but it appears that he wrote a set of hexameters used by Buchanan as the basis of a Latin epigram. Buchanan also commemorated Otterburn's achievements in verse.[58] The careers of men such as Foulis and Otterburn clearly point to a flourishing court culture which, as we shall see, owed much to the influence of Renaissance humanism. Lindsay's association with Foulis and Otterburn is highly significant, suggesting perhaps that their joint composition owed something to humanist thinking. In *The Deploratioun,* Lindsay refers to the "ornate Oratouris" (a common contemporary term for humanists) who were to have greeted Madelaine (162). We shall never know the exact nature of the oration delivered in Edinburgh, but it does seem to have impressed the woman to whom it was addressed. Mary's mother (who felt her daughter would have done better to marry her other suitor, Henry VIII) wrote expressing her joy—and relief—at receiving Mary's account of her fine reception in Scotland.[59]

IT IS NOT until the very end of James V's reign that Lindsay is regularly found using the title of Lyon King of Arms. His official appointment was marked in October 1542 with the receipt of "twa chalderis of aittis [oats]" per annum for the maintenance of his stable as well as by his knighthood.[60] In many respects official recognition would have made little difference to Lindsay's duties for he had acted as Lyon King before this. However, he did now begin to assume some of the duties more specific to the chief officer of arms, particularly as described in the Act of 1592, and we find him exercising his authority with regard both to the administration of the law of arms and to the governing of the heralds. Sir George Mackenzie, writing in 1680, reports a case of 1550 brought before Lindsay by Burnet of Burnetland against Burnet of Leys requesting that the latter change his motto and, as we have already seen, Lindsay was also involved in the disciplining of errant messengers.[61] In 1542 Lindsay fulfilled his responsibility to matriculate all grants of arms (a responsibility specified in the 1592 legislation) by completing his Armorial Register, the earliest known extant official Register of Arms in Scotland.[62] This splendid Armorial contains the arms of Scotland, of various foreign princes, of John Balliol, of St. Margaret and the Stewart queens, of the nobility, of the principal families of Scotland, and of Sir David Lindsay himself (see Figs. 2 and 3). In addition, it illustrates the arms of the three kings who attended Christ's nativity and "the Armys off the nyne maist nobill," that is, of the Nine Worthies of chivalric historiography: David, Joshua, Judas Maccabeus, Julius Caesar, Alexander the Great, Hector of Troy, Charlemagne, Arthur, and Godfrey of Bouillon.

The Armorial also possesses several rather less conventional features well worthy of more detailed consideration. Perhaps the most interesting of these is the prefatory verse which offers an introduction to the work, celebrating the nobility of those whose arms are recorded within. Whether or not this is Lindsay's work is unclear. If it is, it is the only example we have of his Latin composition. The fact that this and the passage accompanying the particularly splendid arms of the sole clerical representative, Cardinal Beaton, are the only Latin texts found in the Armorial provides testimony to the growing importance of the vernacular and recognition of its status as the language of the court.[63]

Unusually, Lindsay's Armorial includes the arms of forfeited traitors.

Figure 2. "Royal Arms of Scotland." From Lindsay's Armorial Manuscript (*Facsimile of an Ancient Heraldic Manuscript Emblazoned by Sir David Lyndsay of the Mount, Lyon King of Armes, 1542* [Edinburgh, 1822]). Courtesy of the Trustees of the National Library of Scotland.

This flew in the face of accepted thinking, which held that a traitor was like "the dry and rotten tree" whose memory should be "abolished and extinguished."[64] Lindsay justified his unorthodox approach on the grounds that it honored their noble predecessors, shamed the guilty, and set an example deterring others from such heinous crimes.[65] This passage clearly echoes the 1540 parliamentary Act for Ordering of Process of Forfeiture, which arranged for all such sentences passed either in Parliament or in the justice courts to be authentically copied and gathered together in one book, partly because they might otherwise be lost or destroyed and partly because "the memor of tratouris suld remane to the schame and sclander of thame that ar cummin of thame and to the terror of all vthirs to comit siclik in tymes cumming."[66] The fact that the majority of those named by the statute are included in the Armorial suggests that Lindsay knew of the act and may, indeed, have fashioned his work partly to satisfy its requirements.

Another passage of interest is found on the final leaf of the manuscript. This offers a brief analysis of various Scottish names, noting those that arrived in Scotland from England with St. Margaret (including Lindsay), those that derived from France (including Beaton), and those of Hungarian origin.[67] Lindsay attributes this analysis to "the cronikillis of Scotland," a reference to John Bellenden's translation of Hector Boece's *Scotorum Historiae*.[68] In addition to illustrating the influence and currency of Bellenden's work (particularly in a chivalric context) this link between Bellenden and Lindsay may also add weight to the suggestion that the latter was responsible for designing the woodcut depicting the arms of Scotland that was used for Thomas Davidson's edition of the *Chronicles* and also for the same printer's publication of James V's *Acts of Parliament*.[69] The idea that arms were originally taken for the purposes of identification and distinction, as were names and surnames, is a familiar one, and it may well explain why Lindsay felt the reference appropriate in an armorial register. However, it may also be that drawing attention to the origins of some of the principal families of Scotland in this way—at a time when Scotland and England stood on the brink of war—was an attempt to defuse aggressive nationalist sentiments. Clearly, Lindsay for one was not unhappy with this reminder of a supposed English ancestry.

That Lindsay bore the symbolic office of Lyon King during this period is of considerable significance for his position at court. Granted the right to bestow arms, the Lyon King was a special delegate of royal authority and, while in theory at least he remained subordinate to the Constable, in symbolic terms he stood at the apex of the heraldic hierarchy. This was signified in a number of ways. For example, he was permitted—as was no other subject—to wear the king's own armorial coat, thereby emphasizing the relationship between the Lyon King and his sovereign.[70] The bond was

Figure 3. "Arms of Sir David Lindsay of the Mount." From Lindsay's Armorial Manuscript (*Facsimile of an Ancient Heraldic Manuscript Emblazoned by Sir David Lyndsay of the Mount, Lyon King of Armes, 1542* [Edinburgh, 1822]). Courtesy of the Trustees of the National Library of Scotland.

further enhanced by the coronation ritual. Although Lindsay himself was involved only in the coronation of Mary of Guise (February 1540) and not that of an actual sovereign, the Lyon King played a significant role in the ceremony, affirming the king's willingness to accept the crown, bearing one of the jugs of oil with which he was anointed, rehearsing the royal genealogy, and announcing the king's arrival to his people.[71] The Lyon King himself was also crowned.[72] A near contemporary description of Lindsay refers to his "Orange Tawnie" tunic emblazoned with a lion and to "a Croune of riche golde on his hedde."[73] It may be, therefore, that the office was imbued with a quasi-royal aura. To strike the Lyon King was to commit a particularly heinous offense. In 1515, for example, when Lord Drummond was found guilty of "the putting of violent handis in lioun king of armis," he was forfeited in Parliament, being lucky not to pay for his crime with his life.[74]

In the sixteenth century, the office of Lyon King was probably held for life. Although Lindsay's successor, Sir Robert Forman of Luthrie, appears to have resigned his position, it was not until the seventeenth century that retirement for reasons of age or ill health became common.[75] The fate of Forman's successor, William Stewart, is perhaps instructive. Stewart was in office only six months before being deprived. Imprisoned for necromancy and conspiracy to kill the regent, it was his opposition to the latter that lay behind his execution in August 1569. Perhaps this extreme measure was deemed necessary to shift a political opponent who, by virtue of his office, would have otherwise proved difficult to challenge. This may help explain what has appeared so puzzling to so many commentators, including Lindsay's first general editor, Henry Charteris. "How cummis it than," he pondered, "that this our Author being sa plane aganis thame [churchmen] . . . culd eschaip thair snairis, quhen vtheris, in doing les, hes cruellie perischit?"[76] With the certainty of a good Calvinist, Charteris ascribed it to "the prouydence, the Iudgement, the power, and the inmensible fauor and mercie of God towartis his sanctis and elect." Perhaps, however, the answer lies—in part at least—with this perception of the quasi-royal nature of his heraldic position. Moreover, in Lindsay's case, the symbolic significance of his office was complemented, perhaps enhanced, by his well-known personal association with the king. As we shall see, this fusion of official and personal bonds may have offered further protection not only during the reign of James V but also in the dangerous decades that followed.

THREE

Success and Survival

1530–1555

By the year 1530, Lindsay had been closely associated with the court for almost twenty years. Already he had experienced the highs and lows of a life spent in the service of the crown and seen too the difference between a strong, self-confident administration and one characterized by factional struggle and the breakdown of government. It was a cycle he would see repeated in the decades ahead for, though the 1530s saw Lindsay enjoying considerable success, after 1543 he found himself in an increasingly difficult position, beset by political dangers and personal anguish.

BEFORE THIS, however, Lindsay's fortunes continued to prosper. Following the traumas of the minority, the 1530s saw the emergence of a more stable administration. The dynasty seemed secure; Stewart application and ingenuity combined to replenish the depleted royal coffers; and with James V playing the royal marriage market for all it was worth, Scotland once again claimed a place on the European stage. A burgeoning self-confidence was reflected in ostentatious displays of royal authority. Two royal progresses around the north of the country in 1540 and 1541, increased expenditure on lavish ceremonial, and most stunningly of all, the elaborate reconstruction of the royal residences at Falkland, Linlithgow, and Stirling, all spoke of an increasingly self-assured administration. In 1528, however, this lay in the future. On his assumption of personal authority in the summer of that year, the young James V was confronted with a daunting array of problems. Many of these were part and parcel of the traditional legacy bequeathed by a minority administration, and dealing with them was a baptism of fire endured by an unusually high number of Scottish monarchs. Unlike his predecessors, however, James V faced more than the familiar problems of financial impoverishment and administrative collapse.

In Scotland, as elsewhere in western Europe, the first half of the sixteenth century was a period of intellectual and ideological innovation as many of the ideas, values, and long-held beliefs shaping both secular and spiritual life found themselves challenged on a number of fronts. Arguably, the most significant area affected by this sense of change was religious life. Here, the ideas embodied in an emergent humanist culture and the gradual infiltration of Protestant doctrine prompted men to question both their faith and the Church that served it. Looking for a renewed sense of certainty in their spiritual lives, they became enmeshed in what were often intense debates concerning personal salvation and ecclesiastical politics alike. It is hardly surprising that the discussions conducted in the universities, marketplaces, and royal palaces of Europe reverberated through the Scottish court. The royal correspondence with Erasmus, more especially with the Catholic controversialist Cochlaeus and his opponent the exiled Scot Alesius, must have been important talking points, and the latters' heated debate over the question of vernacular Scripture undoubtedly echoed throughout the court.[1]

The notion of the court as a hotbed of religious intrigue is hardly novel, but in Scotland at least it is an idea which has been discussed primarily in terms of events after 1560, less commonly after 1542, and before this date hardly at all.[2] Historians of the English Reformation have long argued that the court and its personnel played a significant role in the advancement of evangelical opinion, and, as demonstrated by the careers of Scots such as David Lindsay, the Scottish court also provided an important forum for the discussion of religious change.[3] Of course, as both an arena in which other battles could be fought and of itself a cause worth fighting for, religious policy had always played a part in court politics. In the 1530s, however, there was a great deal more at stake than securing a favorable place in the ecclesiastical pecking order for oneself or one's supporters. Now, questions of theological difference could have far-reaching implications which, in certain circumstances, might crystallize in factional division and political conflict.

At this stage, a lack of research into the political dynamics of the 1530s cautions against overemphasizing this process, for although questions of faith could and did determine political alignments, the evolution of distinct factions operating along an ideological divide is, at best, hazy. What is clear, however, is that the discussion of religious affairs represented one of the key discourses of the reign. Influenced most notably by humanist scholarship on the one hand and by the emerging doctrines of the Protestant Reformation on the other, the religious debate encompassed a wide variety of opinion: Those involved included religious conservatives (a group not exclusively clerical in composition but one nevertheless anxious to preserve the existing institutions of the Church), humanist critics of abuse and corruption, and also out-and-out Lutherans. At a time when confessions of faith were far from clear-cut, definitions of heresy and orthodoxy are extremely problematic. In the eventful years following the appearance of Martin Luther's *Ninety-five Theses,* an often bewildering variety of beliefs and practices could be found lurking beneath the blanket term "Lutheranism." Moreover, not only was the Church uncertain about what it was fighting against but, until the Council of Trent formulated a coherent response to the Protestant Reformation, men were equally uncertain about what it was they were fighting for. Against such a background, it is unsurprising that the precise vocabulary to use when describing early advocates of religious reform has proved a contentious issue. It is, however, a subject over which rather too much academic ink has been spilled for, given the fluidity of the situation, dogmatic attempts to define ideology and theological allegiance are inappropriate.[4] If the picture is not to be unacceptably distorted, a relatively flexible approach is required, one which acknowledges the existence of a shared basic outlook yet allows for considerable diversity of opinion.

In a Scottish context, it is useful to think of those who were—to whatever extent—challenging the established position of the Church as "evangelicals," a broad yet helpful classification which can, if necessary, be subdivided into evangelical humanists on the one hand and evangelical Protestants on the other. But does this mean that we can talk of an "evangelical party"? At this stage, probably not. Though the 1530s undoubtedly witnessed the emergence of an influential group of royal servants and officials who, in a variety of ways, posed a challenge to the status quo, it would be wrong to view this group as a party or "faction" in the strict sense of the word. Lacking a powerful patron, it developed neither a recognizable identity nor a coherently articulated purpose. Nevertheless, it made a significant—if at times contradictory—contribution to the religious discourse conducted at court during the reign of James V.

Of enormous importance to the religious debate, and by no means only within a court context, was the impact of humanist ideas. As most commonly employed today, the term "humanism" evokes a set of beliefs which stresses the dignity of man and the importance of the human as opposed to the divine or supernatural world. Scholars, however, have been increasingly concerned to establish a more precise definition with greater meaning for the intellectual framework of Renaissance thought. To this end, they have emphasized the importance attached to the recovery and interpretation of classical texts and highlighted the influence of classical models on Renaissance scholarship. More strictly still, humanism has been viewed as a scholarly discipline firmly located within the rhetorical tradition: Humanists were first and foremost teachers and students of the *studia humanitatis* (grammar, rhetoric, ethics, poetry, and history), concerned above all with eloquence of expression and clarity of communication.[5] This definition has been quite widely accepted but, while the move away from vague discussions of humanism as "philosophical outlook" or "attitude to life" has proved helpful in some respects, such an approach is not altogether satisfactory. Attention has rightly been drawn to the fact that, particularly in northern Europe, humanism also possessed a discernible cultural impact. No educational program can exist in a moral vacuum, and concern for the *studia humanitatis* inevitably spilled over into such areas as personal morality, politics, government, and social relations. Not only did the classical texts of the humanist canon carry implicit moral and cultural messages, but the humanist ethos was powerfully geared toward the enhanced participation of man (specifically of the layman) in a wider sphere of activity, in the service of the Church and the Prince, in the pursuit of Christian truth and the public good.

As such, humanism touched the lives of men who may not have possessed expertise in classical scholarship but who were clearly—sometimes profoundly—influenced by the social and cultural values it promoted. Men might well be attracted to Erasmus's evangelical program of personal piety without necessarily having toiled with him in the fields of Greek and New Testament scholarship. Arguably, it is the existence of these individuals which makes humanism such an important phenomenon. The importance of what may be termed "vernacular humanism"—the attachment to humanist ideals shown by those who were not strictly speaking humanists themselves—must not be underestimated.[6] David Lindsay, for example, was obviously familiar with some of the key figures and central tenets of an emergent humanistic court culture and, though not a classical scholar himself, he represents an important example of a Scottish vernacular humanist.[7]

Scholars of humanism in England and on the Continent have long accepted its profound influence upon the artistic, intellectual, social, and political mores of Renaissance society. Although Scottish humanism remains comparatively underresearched, recent scholarship suggests that it exercised a significant and enduring impact.[8] Such a conclusion is hardly surprising. There was a considerable degree of cultural cross-fertilization between Scotland and the Continent, the exchange of ideas being facilitated by the prevalence of literature printed abroad, especially in France, and by the Scottish taste for study in Europe, again notably in France. Inspired by the New Learning, many Scottish students subsequently returned to their native land, several becoming teachers. The newly founded University of Aberdeen, for example, swiftly acquired a reputation for humanist study under the guidance of its first principal, Hector Boece, who, while studying in Paris, had been a companion of the celebrated Dutch humanist, Erasmus.[9] But it was not just within the universities that humanist ideas took hold. By the 1530s, humanist influences can already be associated with the royal Secretariat where a distinguished line of royal secretaries included Archibald Whitelaw, Patrick Paniter, and, in the reign of James V, Lindsay's associate, James Foulis. All were men with impeccable humanist credentials.[10] Outwith the Secretariat also, increasing numbers of Scots were, by a variety of means, coming into contact with humanist learning. Often a result of studying abroad, it could equally work the other way. For example, the Italian humanist, Giovanni Ferrerio, visited Scotland twice (1528–37 and 1540–45) and was enormously influential in transmitting humanist ideas to the monastic community of Kinloss.[11] Moreover, during this time Ferrerio also spent some three years at the Scottish court (1528–31) where his companions included Sir James Foulis and Sir Walter Lindsay of Torphichen, Knight of Rhodes and kinsman of the poet. Ferrerio's stay suggests that the intellectual atmosphere he found there was, to some extent, receptive to his ideas and to humanism in general.

This impression is reinforced by a more detailed analysis of some of the personnel of James's court. That men such as James Foulis, Adam Otterburn, Robert Galbraith, and Thomas Erskine of Brechin were all exponents of the New Learning can be supported by an examination of their education, their associates, and their writing. Many of them can also be directly linked to David Lindsay. The two neo-Latinists, Foulis and Otterburn, collaborated with him in the preparation of the orations delivered to Mary of Guise in 1538, while another lawyer probably influenced by humanism, the Pavia-trained Sir Thomas Erskine of Brechin, was thrown into Lindsay's company on the French embassy of 1532 in which they traveled together. Robert Galbraith, a Parisian-trained lawyer, later Queen's Advocate and Lord of Session, was also a neo-Latin poet and probably closely associated with Foulis.[12] It has been suggested that Galbraith was among those writers listed by Lindsay in his literary encomium in *The Testament of the Papyngo* (47).[13] As the majority of the identifiable poets cited by Lindsay were vernacular authors working at court, this identification is not altogether likely. Nevertheless, *The Testament of the Papyngo* may contain another clue to the value placed on humanism within court circles for, significantly enough, in extolling his fellow poets Lindsay reserves his highest praise for those involved in that most humanist-inspired business, translation.[14] Among his contemporaries, he makes particular mention of John Bellenden, translator of Boece's *Scotorum Historiae* and of the first five books of Livy's *History of Rome,* while the acknowledged master, "Off Eloquence the flowand balmy strand, / And, in our Inglis rethorik, the rose" (23–24), is Gavin Douglas, honored in particular for his "trew Translatioun" (33) of Virgil's *Aeneid.*[15]

The work of John Bellenden, commissioned and paid for by the crown, suggests a certain royal enthusiasm for humanist scholarship or at least that James V was determined to emulate the kind of patronage increasingly associated with European monarchs such as Francis I and Henry VIII.[16] In support of this, we might also note the Scottish king's interest in the career of Scotland's greatest humanist scholar, George Buchanan, employed to tutor one of James's illegitimate brood. Indeed, following Buchanan's flight from court in 1539, the position was offered to his brother, Patrick, another Scot well versed in the New Learning. Such royal patronage of humanist teachers was not unprecedented. James V's own half-brothers, James Stewart, earl of Moray, and, more famously, Alexander Stewart, the gifted young archbishop of St. Andrews killed at Flodden, had both been pupils of Erasmus. Erasmian humanism appears to have exercised a significant attraction for many Scots, and the king's own correspondence with the Dutch humanist, albeit limited and somewhat cryptic, indicates a moderate, if erratic, degree of support.[17] The evidence relating to James's patronage of humanism is too fragmentary to be other than intriguing. But while it is undoubtedly wrong to view the court culture of his reign as exclusively, or even predominantly, humanistic, it is clear that such influences were making themselves felt.

Less clear is the tangible effect humanism had on court politics. By fostering the education of laymen, humanism certainly made possible their careers in the royal administration. Not only did it provide the practical skills that allowed laymen to participate in government in a way hitherto the preserve of the clergy, more importantly it also offered an important ideological framework within which ideas concerning the attributes, role, and status of this new lay elite might be refigured. Beyond this, however, there seems to have been no precise political agenda associated with humanist scholarship.[18] Grouping together all those with a humanist background may provide a telling index of the penetration of humanist ideas, but it does not necessarily reveal a group acting as such in the pursuit of a common cause. With respect to the religious life, for example, not all with a humanist training can be described as evangelical humanists. Some combined their humanism with very conservative inclinations. Sir Thomas Erskine, for instance, was deeply hostile to George Buchanan's Erasmian-inspired satire of the Franciscans.[19] Similarly, there were those who, lacking a strictly humanist education, were nevertheless profoundly influenced by humanistic ideas, especially as they related to spiritual concerns.

As elsewhere in Europe, humanist scholarship exerted a significant influence on religious life in Renaissance Scotland. With its demands for a return *ad fontes* and its insistence on the need for textual integrity, it held out the hope that ignorance and mistaken teaching might be overcome, that the perceived pristine purity of the early Church might be restored, and that, thus instructed and inspired, men could turn once again to the active Christian life. Striving for spiritual integrity at both an individual and an institutional level, evangelical humanism generated an often intensely critical discussion of the Church together with heated calls for its reform. It is hardly surprising, therefore, that humanism underpinned much of the Church's own drive for ecclesiastical renewal. Reform-minded bishops such as Robert Reid, bishop of Orkney, and, even before the reign of James V, William Elphinstone of Aberdeen were profoundly influenced by humanist ideas, and the measures taken by the provincial Church councils of 1549, 1552, and 1559 all bear the stamp of a reforming humanist ethos.

Although by no means initiating a train of events leading inexorably to the Reformation of 1560, it is fair to say that several decades of religious debate exposed the Church's vulnerability on a number of fronts: political, economic, social, and intellectual. Given the king's determination to raise royal revenue, there was inevitable conflict between Church and crown over the latter's aggressive fiscal demands. Less specifically but equally worryingly, as a newly discovered lay confidence found increasing opportunities for expression, the Church found itself facing a challenge to its social position as the patron and provider of, for example, charity, education, and the Arts. Lastly, and most damagingly, questions were being asked about the Church's status as sole interpreter of Christian doctrine. Inspired partly by humanist scholarship, these were also rooted in the emerging doctrines of the Protestant Reformation which, since the early 1520s, had been filtering into Scotland. Taken together, these problems created a climate of uncertainty further troubled—or in some cases inspired—by the knowledge that, elsewhere in Europe, challenges to ecclesiastical authority had not always proved resistible. As the duke of Norfolk reported to Thomas Cromwell in 1539,

By divers other waies I am advertised that the clergie of Scotlande be in such feare that their king shold do theire, as the kinges highnes hath done in this realme, that they do their best to bring their Master to the warr; and by many waies I am advertised that a great part of the temporalitie there wold their king shold followe our insample, which I pray God geve hym grace to come vnto.[20]

Though it is true that the majority of Scotland's first Protestants were clerics, it is important to recognize the significant role played by a small number of influential laymen at the royal court who, in the course of the 1530s, came to espouse the cause of evangelical Protestantism.[21] Of course, there were some whose new faith was rooted in an earlier attachment to evangelical humanism (thus fueling the usual clerical suspicion that humanism and heresy were one and the same). One such was Sir John Borthwick, who made Lutheran contacts while in France and whose conversion seems to date from the mid 1530s.[22] A more problematic case is that of George Buchanan. While at court during the 1530s, Buchanan composed at least three savage satires on the Franciscans; he may have attended the marriage of a heretical priest; he certainly condoned such unorthodox behavior as eating meat during Lent.[23] Whether, at this stage in his career, his commitment was to anything more than an Erasmian-inspired evangelical humanism is doubtful, but he would in time adopt a more radical position.

There were also evangelical Protestants who do not seem to have drunk first at the humanist well, although by the mid sixteenth century it is extremely difficult to identify anyone as completely untouched by humanistic influences.[24] If nothing else, such men had benefited from the laicization of government associated with an increasingly humanistic court culture. Men in this group included James Kirkcaldy of Grange, the royal Treasurer, reputed to have "becom ane heretik and [to have] had alwayes a New Testament in his poutch"; James Learmonth of Dairsie, the Master of the Household; and Henry Balnaves.[25] Appointed earlier in his career as procurator and spokesman in the consistorial courts (an appointment made by David Beaton), Balnaves was later made Treasurer's Clerk by Kirkcaldy of Grange. Such an appointment offers a tantalizing glimpse into the ways in which like-minded men supported one another in a social and political context, suggesting at least the beginnings of a factionalized court politics. Balnaves also acted as advocate and Lord of Session, his service receiving recognition and reward when, in 1538, he was created Lord Halhill, receiving the estate of Halhill near Collessie, Fife, the following year.[26]

In later years, Balnaves would be a prominent Protestant, and there is reason to believe that he was sympathetic to the Reformed religion even before the 1540s, being one of the principal players in a significant episode indicative of a more overt attempt to advance the evangelical cause at court. In January 1540, the English commissioner on the Border, William Eure, reported to Cromwell the results of "diuers communings" between himself on the one hand and Balnaves and Thomas Bellenden, another evangelical Protestant, on the other, "especially touching the stay of the spiritualitie in Scotland."[27] Eure's report leaves many questions unanswered, but what seems clear is that he was in touch with a group of men sympathetic to England and in particular to the type of religious settlement established there during the 1530s. Bellenden, also a lawyer (he was created Director of Chancery in 1538 and Justice Clerk the following year), was described by Eure as a man "of gentle and sage conversation . . . inclyned to the soorte [of religion] used in our Soverain's Realme of England." In support of this, Eure described how Bellenden had requested abstracts of acts, constitutions, and proclamations passed in England "touching the suppression of religion, and gathering unto the kinges majestie suche other proffettes as before haithe been sp——, with the reformation of the mysdemeanors of the clergye." These he required for the enlightenment of the king of Scots.

Clearly Bellenden hoped to persuade James to adopt a religious policy in line with that followed in England, that is, a Cromwellian-type solution based on the establishment of a royal supremacy through parliamentary legislation. Although Bellenden painted an overly optimistic picture of James's enthusiasm for reform, the episode does demonstrate Scottish interest in the issue. Significantly, in attempting to emphasize this interest, Bellenden referred to a vehemently anticlerical interlude performed before James and Mary at Linlithgow as part of the Epiphany celebrations. Although entries in the *Treasurer's Accounts* support his contention that a play was in fact performed at this time, little is known of the actual performance.[28] It is not even clear whether this was a work commissioned by the crown or a more impetuous attempt to influence religious policy staged by a group of court evangelicals. According to Bellenden, "thay" had it staged, which, although ambiguous, has been taken to refer to the king and Council. Though there is no real evidence to support this, surely Bellenden and his associates had grounds for thinking that their entertainment would find favor in James's eyes. After all, Buchanan insisted that his savagely anticlerical poem, *Franciscanus,* was written at the instigation of the king.[29] Yet the details of Buchanan's quarrel with the Franciscans are obscure, and James's status as patron of anticlerical literature remains unproven. Indeed, nothing is known of the Epiphany performance bar Eure's notes of the play, obtained significantly enough from "a scotts man of oure sorte." But these describe a drama sufficiently similar to Lindsay's *Ane Satyre of the Thrie Estatis* as known from the texts of 1568 and 1602 for it to have been taken as his work. There are many differences between the two, but the fact that the interlude introduces similar characters and presents (as Lindsay does) a humanistic critique of the Church allied with a potentially powerful political suggestion for reform has meant that his authorship of the work has never been seriously challenged.[30] Even if the provenance of the play must remain dubious, the fact of its performance suggests that the court was an important forum for the discussion of religious issues. Several of Lindsay's other works operate on a similar level, and though Lindsay's association with the play and thus by extension with Balnaves and Bellenden cannot be proven, it does seem that this was the case. Moreover, as we shall see, both men were, like Lindsay himself, victims of a conservative backlash in 1543, and it does not seem unreasonable to suppose that the evangelical connection between the three originated in the previous decade.

In seeking to win the heart and mind of the Scottish king, the religious debate conducted at court possessed a very serious objective. Events elsewhere in Europe, particularly in England, had demonstrated that for any reform program to succeed the cooperation of the secular authorities was vital, and this lesson was not lost on those Scottish evangelicals at court.

James's own religious attitude is, however, hard to pin down. While his actions suggest a conventional enough piety, his correspondence expresses a modest, if erratically offered, sympathy with the humanist call for spiritual and ecclesiastical regeneration. Proposals for monastic reform were discussed in the early 1530s, and on at least one occasion Erasmus received an encouraging—if obscure—response.[31] Such evidence, however, is far from conclusive. Undeniably the last Stewart king to fret about standards in the cloisters, James V was hardly the first. James I, for example, had harbored very similar reforming ambitions.[32] Indeed, there is much in James's behavior, his patronage of the Hermit of Loretto for instance, that suggests a fond attachment to some of the traditional expressions of faith increasingly subjected to humanist attack. Certainly, when dealing with potential continental allies, James was anxious to be viewed as a stalwart guardian of Catholic orthodoxy, the antithesis of the schismatic king of England. But, when policy required, he was prepared to dangle the hope that he might yet follow his uncle's path to antipapal revolution. "We have presently directit . . . our traist and familiar servitor to pass to Rome," he wrote when courting English amity in 1536, "for sic impretatonis to be gottin as tuichis reformation of sic enormities as pertenis to the singular weill of this our realme, and abone all to the plesour of God, and in especiall anent the ordouring of the grete and mony possessiounis and temporal landis geuin to the kyrk be our noble predecessouris."[33] This opportunism offers an important clue to James's religious policy. Certainly no convert to the evangelical cause, he nevertheless acknowledged occasions on which it was expedient to volunteer limited royal support. This was equally true of domestic politics for, if James could successfully divide and rule an ideologically riven court, there were significant political and financial rewards to be won. As George Buchanan was later to report, "The different factions pointed out the riches of their opponents, as a booty ready for him when ever he chose: and he, by agreeing alternately with either kept both in a state of suspense between hope and fear."[34]

A revealing description of the divisions at court—and the king's role in fostering them—is provided by Sir William Eure writing to Henry VIII in July 1541:

The spiritualitie and the grete lordes of Scotlande, the Bordourers, and the Out Isles, is desirous to have werre, [with England] but the kinges graces and his privy counsalie, as the treasourer [Kirkcaldy of Grange] and countroller [David Wood of Craig], and *suche as are aboute hym self of his oune making,* is desirous to have peax.[35]

Although such evidence is, to some extent, colored by the polarization of political opinion occasioned by the growing threat of war, the anxieties expressed at the end of the reign serve to highlight the increasingly entrenched political and religious attitudes dividing the Scottish polity. What is more, the emergence of this influential group of officials owing their position in part at least to royal patronage was, as this passage makes clear, deliberate policy.

Further confirmation of ideological discord is provided by Sir Ralph Sadler, the English ambassador, who visited Edinburgh in 1540. Describing his stay at the Scottish court, Sadler related how he was entertained and welcomed by most of the noblemen and gentlemen, favorers of Christ's doctrine, "whereof be a great number, but the noblemen be young."[36] Although Sadler considered them and others about the king well-minded, he saw no potential leader "to take in hand the direction of things" and concluded that James was forced to rely upon churchmen. Observing that the conservatives were "yet too strong for the other side," Sadler opined that the evangelicals lacked the guidance of mature nobles but depended instead upon the influential lesser laity. He lamented the absence of a figure such as his own master, Thomas Cromwell, and expressed the wish that the king of Scots possessed "one such servant and counsellor," continuing, "and, I dare say, so would many thousands in Scotland, for some of the honest men of the court here and well esteemed, have wished the same before me since my coming hither." Eager to tell his political masters what they so desperately wanted to hear, Sadler is an unreliable source and his testimony should not be accepted uncritically. However, adding a little weight to a suspiciously optimistic account is the fact that those of the court with whom Sadler had spent some considerable time between his arrival and the dispatch of this particular communication included both John Borthwick and David Lindsay. Responsible for conducting the English ambassador into James's presence, they also dined with him on at least one occasion.[37] It is tempting to suggest that Lindsay was one of those "well esteemed" men advocating an evangelical reform program.

To speak of a "reform program" is perhaps misleading. As already suggested, any reform party at court represented a coalition of diverse interests rather than the vehicle for the expression and furtherance of any one particular position. The range of religious opinion found at court, together with a more detailed analysis of the various strategies used to advance evangelical opinion there, is more fully discussed in later chapters. Nevertheless, something should be said here regarding its general complexion. While it is hard to distinguish subtle nuances of theological thought—and whether those at court did so is, in any case, doubtful—it is clear that a small yet significant number espoused recognizably Protestant beliefs. Additionally, as demonstrated by both the Epiphany drama and the clashes over foreign policy, there was at least some support for the type of religious settlement established south of the border. This was attractive not only to religious radicals such as John Borthwick but also to the more conservative, humanist-inspired reformers such as David Lindsay.

From the very beginning of James's personal rule, Lindsay was a passionate agitator for the humanist cause. His three earliest extant works, *The Dreme, The Complaynt,* and *The Testament of the Papyngo,* all incorporate a vigorous attack on clerical abuses (particularly among the prelacy), on worldliness, political interference, corruption, and financial exploitation at a parish level. His satire, like that of George Buchanan, is typically Erasmian in character. Hardly touching on matters of doctrine, it focuses instead on questions of moral abuse. When Lindsay does deal with religious belief, as in the attack on images and pilgrimage found in *The Complaynt,* he echoes current humanist criticism of this mechanical type of faith. It is also in typical humanist fashion that he addresses his complaints to the king urging him to attend to the spiritual estate. As developed in his later works, this added a vital politicized tone to Lindsay's critique and, though never one of their number, Lindsay found himself ranged alongside those evangelical Protestants such as Balnaves and Bellenden who wanted a Henrician—firmly schismatic—settlement for Scotland.

It is not to be expected that the Church was insensible to the challenges it faced. Arguably, the most effective action it could take was against those suspected of heretical sympathies. Even before 1539 and his elevation to the metropolitan see of St. Andrews, David Beaton began the vigorous prosecution of suspected heretics. However, as his most recent biographer has shown, circumstances rendered him unable to follow this up and limited him to the prosecution of the relatively humble. As she comments, it must have been a source of extreme personal frustration "that he rubbed shoulders daily at the royal court and in the law courts with those whose favour with the King and their public office made it difficult to accuse . . . but whose presence in public life gave Protestantism a measure of *de facto* acceptability."[38] Whether the term "Protestantism" is valid here given the heterogeneous nature of the group in question is debatable. Lindsay for one, although a vigorous critic of the Church, was never a confessed Protestant. Nevertheless, this identification of the tensions that existed during the 1530s appears largely accurate.

In 1540, only a few months after the evangelicals had—quite literally—seized center stage with the production of the Epiphany interlude, Beaton was driven to launch a more overt attack upon the suspected heretics at court. His target was John Borthwick, a man who more than most highlighted the dangers of a politicized evangelical position. However, with suspicious good fortune, Borthwick escaped arrest and fled to England. Tried and convicted in absentia, his effigy was burned in the marketplace at St. Andrews. One modern commentator judges this flamboyant yet farcical episode to have been "stage-managed by the Cardinal as a warning to Lutherans in high places and by the king in order to let David Beaton have his own way without doing any real damage."[39] Certainly, the similarity to Buchanan's equally fortuitous flight from prosecution the previous year arouses suspicion. Beaton may, however, have attempted more decisive action, producing a list of suspected heretics and hinting that their prosecution could result in financial gains for the crown. John Knox was later to refer to such a "Black List" which, he claimed, included heretics, anglophiles, and Douglas supporters, and in 1543 Ralph Sadler maintained that Arran had told him of a document listing some eighteen-score names "all minded to God's Word which then they durst not avow."[40] Whether such a list was compiled or not (and, if it was, it no longer survives), the religious views of many at court seem to have been something of an open secret emerging into the public gaze only at moments of high political tension. Thus the show trial of John Borthwick may be seen as a concession granted by the king in the face of growing clerical intransigence. That no further measures were taken has been attributed to the intervention of Kirkcaldy of Grange who, according to John Knox, dissuaded James from heeding Beaton's list.[41] Again, this points to the way in which ideological difference informed the fight for the king's ear and drew up the battle lines of political confrontation.

Similar tensions are apparent from another episode which may also be connected with the Black List. According to the chronicler Lindsay of Pitscottie, the clergy requested the appointment of a temporal judge to prosecute suspected heretics such as those accused in the list. Designated "iudge criminall" was Sir James Hamilton of Finnart, the powerful Master of Works who had benefited from royal favor throughout the reign.[42] However, if it were the case that he was so appointed (and he does seem to have received a sheriffship, possibly for this reason), his execution on 16 August 1540 averted any such purge.[43] Finnart's fall has often been seen as a royal ploy designed not to punish one who had plotted against the king but to curb the erstwhile favorite's ambition and to seize his considerable wealth. Whether or not Finnart was guilty as charged, it is surely significant that the action taken against him called into play not only tensions within the Hamilton family but also the religious divisions at court.[44] It seems that James was first alerted to the alleged intrigue (which dated back to 1528) by the son of Sir James Hamilton of Kincavil, sent by his father to tell the king of the plot against his life. Kincavil, the half-brother of the martyr Patrick Hamilton, had himself been delated for heresy in 1532 and, despite recanting, had been forced to flee south two years later.[45] Repeated petitioning secured his return to Scotland and to royal favor, but by 1540 his position was once again insecure—hence the preemptive strike against Finnart.

Upon hearing the accusations against the Master of Works, James instructed Kincavil's son to present his information to the Secretary, Thomas Erskine, and Master of the Household, James Learmonth, who, along with the Treasurer, James Kirkcaldy, imprisoned Finnart. However, fearful lest their prisoner's petitioning might successfully sway the king, they undertook his vigorous denunciation, thereby securing his execution. Although frequently unreliable, Pitscottie's account on this occasion should perhaps be taken seriously. His probable source for the episode was his kinsman, David Lindsay, who, as Lyon King of Arms, was involved in Finnart's arrest.[46] Certainly, the actions of Kincavil, Learmonth, and Kirkcaldy fit in with the emerging picture of evangelicals nervously petitioning the king. And, with the hardening of attitudes seen in the last years of the reign, they were perhaps right to fear that this was more than a question of political survival.

By the 1540s, the complicating factor of international diplomacy, specifically the breakdown in Anglo-Scottish relations that occurred at the end of the reign, was tipping the scales in the conservatives' favor. The direction taken by Scottish foreign policy at this time was of vital importance to the development of evangelical opinion as closer ties with England would bring many of the evangelicals' most cherished aims one step nearer. James's two French marriages had made it plain that, notwithstanding a certain willingness to tolerate religious debate at home, he remained fully committed to the Catholic cause. From 1538, however, English alarm over the threats posed by Franco-imperial concord prompted overtures of friendship which served to raise evangelical hopes in Scotland. In 1541, the idea of a personal meeting between Henry VIII and his nephew—first broached in 1536— was revived. It was to prove a contentious issue. In September of that year, Wharton informed the English Privy Council:

There are sundry argumentes amongest his [James V's] councell about this affare. And of the Councell Oliver Synkler,———— Synkler, brether and the Larde of Crage husher of the chambre, ar of the Cardinall and bushoppes sect and oppynion, that there kynge shulde not comme in Ingland; and there er of the other sect and oppynyon the Larde of Grange treasourer, Maister Thomas Bellynden, and Maister Henry Banese a man of lawe, and as myn espiall saith many of the barons of that side.[47]

Another name which could be added to this list is that of James Learmonth of Dairsie. A member of the embassy conducting a last-ditch attempt to salvage Anglo-Scottish relations, his efforts moved Henry VIII to declare, "We have as good an opinion of him as ever we conceyved of any man that cam furth of Scotlande," and Learmonth appears to have been genuinely sorry at the failure of negotiations.[48] It is difficult to assess the extent of such pro-English sentiment, but that it existed—at least in pockets—is clear. Obviously those named here were motivated by religious considerations, yet anglophile sympathies could exist along with a variety of other attitudes and cannot be simply equated with Protestantism. The earl of Angus and his brother, George Douglas, sought English support to further their own political and dynastic ambitions, and the earl of Bothwell was twice accused of conducting secret negotiations with the English, again for personal ends. There were some like Adam Otterburn, the humanist lawyer, who combined a reasoned support of closer Anglo-Scottish relations with a vigorous denunciation of English heresies.[49] Although he would later change his position, Otterburn blamed his fall from grace in 1538 on the belief that he was "over good an Englishe man."[50]

The traditional hostility felt by Scotland toward its southern neighbor provided religious conservatives with an important political advantage, for revived fears of English aggression made it comparatively easy to portray the evangelicals in an unfavorable light. By March 1541, the clerical party felt sufficiently strong to ensure the passage through Parliament of further antiheresy legislation.[51] This has been judged "a comment on the increase in the level of heretical activity since the act of 1525."[52] However, with Protestantism at the grass-roots level still relatively thin-spread, it is more likely that the acts forbidding abjured heretics to hold office or "to be of our counsalle," imposing penalties for the sheltering of heretics, and offering rewards as an incentive to inform were specifically targeted at the type of influential evangelical Protestant found at court.

Ultimately, those who looked sympathetically toward England lost the day. James failed to meet Henry VIII at York, relations between the two countries became increasingly strained, and border skirmishes gave way to out-and-out war. On 24 November 1542, a Scottish army led by the royal favorite, Oliver Sinclair, was ignominiously routed at Solway Moss. Within the month, the king was dead, broken, according to Lindsay, by news of the Scottish defeat (*The Tragedie of the Cardinal*, 113–19). For Lindsay, this was a serious blow. James had been a feature of the poet's life for thirty years, and his premature death terminated a close personal relationship. Moreover, at a time when Lindsay seems to have been prospering and ordering his affairs to his personal satisfaction, he was faced yet again with the prospect of a lengthy minority government, a situation which could, as past experience had taught, jeopardize all he had achieved.[53]

> Quhen I beleif to be best easit,
> Most suddantlye I am displiasit;
>
> (*The Monarche*, 342–43)

The sense of unpredictability associated with political life is a recurrent theme in Lindsay's work, and lines such as these were clearly inspired by personal experience. Moreover, it was probably around this time that Lindsay had to face the death of his wife and perhaps too that of his younger brother, John.[54] Such personal misfortune intensified his world-weariness, prompting the gloomy introspection that surfaces in his later works. However, despite the inauspicious end to James's reign, the evangelicals must have felt that there were yet grounds for optimism. Unfortunately for Lindsay, the months that followed would offer him no more than the briefest glimpse of how some of his most cherished hopes might be realized.

THE UNEXPECTED death of James V threw Scotland into confusion. The new queen, Mary Stewart, was barely a week old, and no arrangements appeared to have been made for a minority government. The best constitutional claim to regency authority lay with the Hamilton earl of Arran, heir presumptive to the throne. Arran, however, was notoriously unreliable, and it was soon obvious that as a figurehead he could be manipulated by whichever faction successfully assumed control. Following James's death, it was widely believed that power was to lie with four governors, the principal magnates Arran, Moray, Argyll, and Huntly, together with the cardinal acting as "governor of the Prencys and cheyff rewler of the cownsell."[55] However, it was not long before Arran and Beaton were at loggerheads, with the former claiming that the cardinal "hathe tolde to the counsaill many thinges in the kinges name, which he thinketh ys all lyes and so wyll prove."[56] At the beginning of 1543, Arran succeeded in having himself proclaimed sole governor with Beaton becoming chancellor shortly afterwards.

The explanation for this turn of affairs remains unclear. It has been suggested that the situation was engineered by Beaton who, by bringing pressure to bear upon Arran, arranged the compromise. This pressure could conceivably have been the threat posed by long-standing doubts concerning Arran's legitimacy, an issue which Beaton, by virtue of his ecclesiastical office, could investigate with a view to debarring Arran from the succession and hence from his premier claim to the regency. However, this was not a new threat, and it is unlikely that it held any serious terrors. Much more significant would have been a will drawn up by the late king which laid out arrangements for his daughter's minority and which excluded Arran. A notarial instrument purporting to be just such a document does exist and— fraudulent or not—it may well have been used by Beaton to purchase the Great Seal.[57] If so, this was something of a miscalculation for, with the document in his hands, Arran felt sufficiently confident to order the cardinal's imprisonment, simultaneously protecting his own position by circulating rumors that "the Cardinal did counterfeit the late king's testament; and when the king was even almost dead he took his hand and so caused him to suscribe a blank paper."[58] Most modern commentators note the persistence of this story, ascribing its acceptance to Knox, but it was in fact Lindsay who, as early as 1547 but nonetheless after the cardinal's death, first set forth the allegation in print (*The Tragedie of the Cardinal*, 120–23). The appearance of the rumor in Lindsay's work suggests its currency at court and his own position at the heart of affairs. He was perhaps fortunate that as Lyon King of Arms he was responsible for the organization of the royal funeral and, consequently, remained at the center of court life. In the uncertain and potentially dangerous days following James V's death, Lindsay—like many around him—had his ear very close to the ground.

Following Arran's assumption of authority, it seemed as if the way was open for the implementation of a more pro-Reform, anglophile policy. Nurturing ambitions to marry his son to Elizabeth Tudor, Arran evidently considered this the best way of furthering his own dynastic interests, but it was also encouraged by other factors, notably the return of the earl of Angus and his brother, George Douglas, from exile in England as well as the activities of the so-called Assured Lords.[59] Even before James's death it had been apparent that some of those captured at Solway Moss were likely to be used in the English interest, being released on the condition that they undertook to further a proposed marriage between the infant Queen of Scots and the young Edward Tudor, some even swearing to support Henry VIII's bid to assert English sovereignty over Scotland in the event of Mary's death. Against this background and with the cardinal imprisoned, the way was clear for the Parliament of March 1543 to ratify Arran's governorship, to reverse the attainder on the Douglases, and to authorize the reading of Scripture "in the vulgar toung in Inglis or Scottis . . . Provyding that na man alwayis despute or hald oppunyionis under the panis contenit in the actes of parliament."[60] That such a policy could be adopted so swiftly after James's death is a comment on the progress of evangelical opinion at court in the previous decade. As suggested by the important qualification designed to curb any potential heresies, this probably owed more to evangelical humanists than to confessed Protestants. At any rate, those Protestants prominent in the new administration such as Henry Balnaves, Secretary of State and one of the sponsors of the bill, felt obliged to adopt the more moderate, humanist-inspired line.

This Parliament, described by George Douglas as "the maist substanciall Parliament, that evir was sene in Scotland in ony mannis rememberance," and which Lindsay almost certainly attended, was enormously important for him.[61] It represented the implementation of one of his most vigorously urged reforming ideals suggesting the way in which a Henrician-type reformation could be enacted within Scotland. The idea of the secular authority working through the estates (yet overriding the clergy) had received dramatic representation in the 1540 Epiphany play and was to find powerful expression in *Ane Satyre of the Thrie Estatis* written almost a decade later.

Lindsay swiftly became associated with the new administration serving under Arran. In March 1543, the earl requested credence for Lindsay to travel to England in order to return the Order of the Garter bestowed upon the late king.[62] However, it seems likely that his departure was deferred for some weeks—possibly in order that he might attend Parliament—and he may well have traveled south with the Scottish commissioners, Learmonth, Balnaves, and Hamilton of Sanquhar, dispatched to undertake negotiations for the marriage of Mary and Edward.[63] That he did eventually make the journey is evidenced by a letter from Henry VIII to Arran in which the English king expressed his satisfaction with the Scottish Lyon who "vsed himself right Discretelye and much to our contentacioun."[64] Of course, as Lyon King of Arms, it was Lindsay's duty to return the insignia of his late master, but it is significant that Arran chose to dispatch him south at this time. Indeed, the fact that the Order of the Golden Fleece was not returned for more than another year suggests an unusual degree of alacrity in the matter.[65] This is less surprising when we recall that the spring of 1543 saw Arran eager to foster English goodwill and bent on a diplomacy designed to shore up the proposed marriage alliance. In such circumstances, emissaries sent to London would be chosen with the utmost care. Hence, the preference for the evangelicals, Balnaves and Learmonth, as well as the conservative opposition to such a choice.[66] The decision to send Lindsay south with this high-powered delegation, together with the favorable reception he received in England, seemed to presage an important future in the new administration.

The foundations of the new government were, however, far from stable. Beaton swiftly procured a move to his own castle at St. Andrews, thereby paving the way for the recovery of his political and physical freedom.[67] Further pressure was placed upon the government's already crumbling pro-English policy with the arrival from France of Arran's natural brother, John Hamilton, abbot of Paisley and future archbishop of St. Andrews, and of Matthew, earl of Lennox. Lennox offered a pointed reminder of Arran's questionable legitimacy for, if this were successfully disputed, then Lennox became heir presumptive to the Scottish throne. Moreover, being a bachelor of only twenty-six, he was not an implausible candidate for the hand of the queen dowager or even of the queen herself. Hamilton's presence in Scotland was equally worrying for Arran, and it was probably this which led him to dismiss his Protestant preachers, John Rough and Thomas Guillame. It was obvious to all that the Anglo-Scottish peace and marriage treaties, eventually concluded at Greenwich on 1 July 1543, rested upon extremely precarious foundations. Within the month the cardinal and his supporters had signed a mutual bond—dubbed the Linlithgow Bond—pledging themselves to defend the realm and to protect the queen from

English ambitions.[68] As a result, something of a compromise was reached, which focused on agreement regarding custody of the royal infant. However, further pressure on Arran resulted in his total capitulation and realignment with Beaton, a move symbolized by the former's public recantation of his association with heresy for which he received absolution at the hands of the cardinal. At the Parliament of December 1543, the treaty with England was declared broken, support for the antiheresy legislation was reaffirmed, Beaton became Chancellor, and Hamilton assumed the Privy Seal. The cardinal appeared to have the upper hand.

Obviously Lindsay's position at court—indeed his personal security—was seriously threatened by Arran's volte-face. Determined to emphasize the power of his new position, Beaton had begun to move against those who had been associated with Arran in the early months of the minority and who had openly flaunted their unorthodoxy.[69] The Protestant lords, Maxwell and Somerville, were imprisoned and, in November 1543, the earl of Rothes, Lord Gray, and Henry Balnaves suffered the same fate, with the latter detained in Beaton's personal custody "bicause he [Beaton] loved hym worst of all."[70] According to John Knox,

The men of counsall, judgement, and godlynes, that had travailled to promote the Governour, and that gave him faythfull counsall in all dowtfull materis war eyther craftely conveyed from him, or ellis, by threatnyng to be hanged, war compelled to leave him. Of the one number war the Lard of Grange foirsaid, Maister Henry Balnavis, Maister Thomas Ballentyne, and Schir Dauid Lyndesay of the Mount; men by whose lauboris he was promoted to honour.[71]

Although there is no record of Lindsay being formally dismissed, he does seem to have numbered himself among the political casualties, deeming it prudent to withdraw to his estates in the winter following Beaton's rapprochement with the governor. Lindsay was not alone in adopting such a course. Despite frantic English efforts to rouse potential sympathizers against the new regime, a disappointed Suffolk was obliged to report:

They count themselves not of force sufficient to doo any thinge ageynst the contrarye partie by force, but intendeth to kepe them selves in their countreis and to do the best they can to resiste the contrary parte that shall come agaynst them . . . and in the meane seasone to speik feire and give gentill wordes to the contrarye parte to gett out their frendes that be in presone, if they canne.[72]

This atmosphere is recalled by Lindsay in *The Tragedie of the Cardinal* where he describes how "Gret Lordis, dreidyng . . . [Beaton] shulde do thame deir / Thay durst nocht cum tyll court but assurance" (220–21). Such fear was by no means exclusive to the nobility but was shared by the poet who, in similar fashion, kept himself "in his country." In October 1543, he was certainly at Cupar where he and a servant witnessed a summons, and in March 1544 he was again—perhaps still—at the Mount.[73]

Following the immediate crisis period in the winter of 1543–44, Lindsay gradually assumed a higher profile, attending Parliament in November 1544 and October 1545, although not apparently regaining the kind of influence enjoyed during the previous decade and perhaps not even attending court on a regular basis. Evidence supporting this is provided by the virtual cessation of any type of activity undertaken in an official capacity. Although rumored to be sailing to Europe, possibly in order to return the Golden Fleece, he was not called upon on this occasion.[74] Obviously, the administration no longer placed any confidence in Lindsay, nor was it prepared to continue payment of his pension. In 1543 he received twenty pounds in part payment of his annual fee and oats for his horses, but regular payments seem to have stopped thereafter.[75] There is only one further payment (in August 1545) before money is allocated for his embassy to Denmark undertaken in the late 1540s.[76]

Forced to spend more time on his estates, Lindsay was conscious not only of personal misfortune but also of the difficulties Scotland faced on a national scale. The 1540s saw the country's internal problems aggravated by the intervention of both England and France. In May 1545, French troops arrived in support of the ruling administration while Henry VIII, thwarted in his attempt to secure the English marriage through the mediation of the Assured Lords and determined to ensure Scottish quiescence in the event of a projected assault upon France, instructed the earl of Hertford to mount a savage attack north of the border. Lindsay was well placed to appreciate the devastation caused by this so-called Rough Wooing.[77] The siege of Haddington in 1548 conducted by Hertford, now earl of Somerset and regent for the young Edward VI, must have impoverished Lindsay's own East Lothian lands, and, coming at a time when he no longer received an official pension, this surely represented an exceptionally bitter blow. Lindsay's concern for the problems thrown up by the Rough Wooing extended beyond his own affairs. His poetry reflects the fact that for the first time in some thirty years he was no longer intimately attached to the court. Focusing instead upon the wider community, poems such as *The Tragedie of the Cardinal* express a very real sorrow over Scotland's plight.

Another result of spending more time in his local community was to heighten Lindsay's awareness of growing Protestant support within the region. This is hinted at in *The Tragedie of the Cardinal* in which Beaton is condemned for his harsh treatment of heretics, "In speciale mony gentyll men of fyfe" (215). The gradual spread of Reformed opinion in Scotland is also reflected in the reception accorded the mission of the Protestant preacher George Wishart. Returning to Scotland from Germany, Switzerland, and England, Wishart preached a more radical, Zwinglian-inspired message than Scots had hitherto heard. During the autumn of 1545, Wishart ministered to the plague victims of Dundee, following this up with visits to East Lothian, notably Tranent, and Lindsay may well have heard this evangelical message in person. Certainly, he could hardly have been unaware of it. Though it would be difficult to claim Lindsay shared Wishart's views (despite his undeniable sympathy for some of them), both men brought a similar energetic, evangelical approach to their calling. Wishart's determination to speak out before a wide social audience must have struck a chord with the poet and may have encouraged the composition of later works intended to press home his message to as many as possible.

Anxious to rob the nascent Protestant movement of a potential spiritual leader, the authorities arrested Wishart in March 1546. Although the preacher's execution has been linked to the assassination of David Beaton some two months later, it is clear that plots involving Sir James Kirkcaldy of Grange (superseded as Treasurer by John Hamilton), Norman Leslie, Crichton of Brunstane, the Earl Marischal, and the earl of Cassillis had been circulating as early as April 1544.[78] Nothing was to come of these conspiracies, but on 29 May 1546 a band of men including Norman Leslie, John Leslie of Parkhill, and William Kirkcaldy, the son of the former Treasurer, broke into St. Andrews Castle and murdered the archbishop. Lindsay would have been familiar with this group of Fife lairds—Norman Leslie was the son-in-law of Lord Lindsay of the Byres—and may even have felt some sympathy for their cause.[79]

The description of the treatment of Beaton's corpse and the rumors circulating in the district found in *The Tragedie of the Cardinal* reveal that, while not in the confidence of those who perpetrated the attack, Lindsay was very much the alert local spectator. The fact that the assassins planned not only to kill Beaton but also to hold the castle in anticipation of English intervention illustrates that the episode was an intended coup, an attempt to implement by violence what had failed to survive in 1543.[80] Another link with the heady days of 1543 (and later with the English government) was provided when the Castilians were joined by Henry Balnaves. John Borthwick, another 1530s evangelical and, following his escape in 1540, a servant of Henry VIII, was also associated with the siege.[81] However, the situation in the 1540s was very different from that of the previous decade. Now, ideas of persuasion and reform through the agencies of king, governor, and Parliament were abandoned by the Castilians and, although themselves a tiny minority, their actions powerfully articulated an alternative approach to the problem of reformation.

The assassination and subsequent siege swiftly became the focus of international concern, with English intervention seemingly imminent. The cardinal's murder, though it restored a degree of political independence to Arran, nevertheless left him in an almost impossible situation. Capitulation to the murderers would earn him only universal condemnation; the resumption of friendly overtures to England would seriously damage his own dynastic interests; and to call upon French aid would pave the way for increased French domination. Neither was Arran in a position to crush the Castilians by brute force. Fear of reprisals (both from England and within Scotland) and fear for his son (whom Beaton had held to secure his father's loyalty and who was now a prisoner of the rebels) precluded this option. Obliged for appearances' sake to conduct an ineffective siege of the castle, Arran's only realistic hope lay with a negotiated solution. Significantly, he turned—as he had in 1543—to David Lindsay. Shortly after the assassination, Arran had summoned "all and sindry Baronis, Landit men, and utheris Gentilmen dwelland within the shereffdome of Fiff," to seek their "avise and counsel."[82] Presumably among this group, Lindsay was called on more specifically when, six months later, his services were again solicited. Reporting the siege for the English king, Henry Balnaves described how on 16 December 1546

Lyone heralde witht one trumpatt was send to ws frome the Governour and Counsale at 11 houris before noune, and desyred speaking; to whome we maide no ansure. Then he departid, and tolde to the Governour and Counsale he coulde have no speaking of us. Notwithstanding, he was send agane at tuo houris efter noune, and desyred that one of our servandis wolde schew to us, the Governour haithe convenit the nobill men of the realme, and by thare advise wolde send to speake us. To the whiche we condescendit and granted.[83]

Lindsay's actions here are only to be expected of an officer of arms, but after such a marked period of inactivity his employment is striking. It suggests that Arran's choice was the deliberate selection of one who, himself a Fife laird and with known evangelical sympathies, may have served to break the deadlock rather than inflame the situation.

Lindsay's limited success suggests that he was in fact able to appeal to the Castilians, several of whom he had known for some years. However, it seems as if Lindsay's sympathies were more fully committed than Arran had appreciated. Although at the start of the siege any communication with the rebels had been expressly forbidden, Lindsay, having played his part in the negotiations, maintained both a keen interest in the situation and, like Borthwick, a channel of communication with those holed up in the castle.[84] When two of its occupants, Balnaves and John Rough, the Protestant preacher who had served Arran in 1543, called upon Knox to preach, they did so after much consideration, "having with thame in counsall Schir David Lyndesay of the Mount."[85] Although Knox (our source for this episode) may have been keen to associate an event of such importance with a man later claimed by Scottish Protestants as one of their own, it is perhaps significant that, this apart, Lindsay hardly figures in Knox's account of the Reformation. Arguing from negative evidence is a dubious business, but the parallels between Knox's first sermon and Lindsay's *Monarche* provide a more convincing demonstration of contact between the two.[86] This was probably limited, with Lindsay making sporadic visits from the Mount rather than joining the occupation. He was not with the Castilians when St. Andrews fell to the French on 31 July 1547, and he escaped the fate that awaited Balnaves and Knox. Although he had some sympathy with the Reformers, Lindsay did not embrace their faith, nor did he endorse their confrontational approach. Instead, he maintained the vision of evangelical reform stimulated by an appeal to the authorities and enacted by the king in conjunction with the estates. Although Lindsay's association with the Castilians could not have passed unnoticed by the administration, the government's most pressing concern was renewed English aggression culminating in the disastrous Scottish defeat at Pinkie in September 1547 which opened the way for the semioccupation of the country. In the face of military disaster, Arran seems to have been content to dispatch Lindsay to Denmark, thereby removing from the country a man whose political and religious sympathies were not in line with government policy but whose long service and symbolic status rendered him difficult to deal with in any other manner.

Thus the end of 1548 saw Lindsay en route to Denmark charged with presenting his country's position regarding recent incidences of piracy and enlisting Danish assistance in the struggle against England.[87] Although the Danish government refused to send a fleet to Scotland, Lindsay's mission was, in other respects, relatively successful. He succeeded in extracting a conciliatory response regarding the piracies, and Christian III agreed that Scots might trade and buy arms in his country. Delayed by wintry conditions, Lindsay spent several months in Denmark, and in the course of his enforced stay he probably gravitated toward the sizable Scottish community living there.[88] This included a significant number of religious dissidents, men like John MacAlpine and John Gau, who had been forced to flee Scotland on account of their beliefs. Just how closely Lindsay associated with such men is almost impossible to ascertain, but his visit was surely important in exposing him to the Lutheran faith of the Danish Church.[89] Leaving Denmark in February 1549, Lindsay encountered treacherous conditions. His ship foundered and, fortunate to escape with his life, it was only in the spring that he was finally able to depart.[90] Undeniably, Lindsay's narrow escape from death prompted thoughts of his own mortality, inspiring the contemplation of the human condition found in his last work, *The Monarche*. In the final analysis, the poem offers comfort, holding out the promise of heavenly salvation. However, it was also the result of Lindsay's morbid speculation upon death and its meaning:

> Gretlye it doith perturbe my mynde,
> Off dolent Deith the diuers kynd
> . . . .
> . . . and quhwo mony ane man
> Apone the see doith lose thare lyuis,

(5094–95, 5133–34)

The Danish visit was to be Lindsay's last voyage outside Scotland and his final major undertaking as Lyon King. The accounts detailing "The expensis debursit upoun officiaris of armes and utheris travelland in my lord governouris affairis" for the year 1552 make no mention of Lindsay; Islay Herald was dispatched to England, and it was Lindsay's eventual successor, Robert Forman, who was sent to the French king and the emperor.[91] There are in fact no payments at all recorded to Lindsay during the 1550s. However, if these years saw no official activity, in terms of his poetry the last years of Lindsay's life were his most productive. While it may simply be that he had more time for writing during this period, it does seem as if Lindsay made a conscious decision to readdress questions of religious and political reform. A pointed rejection of the type of violent action adopted by the Castilians, this owed much to the evangelical zeal of George Wishart. Lindsay was probably also encouraged by the fact that after some eight years of intermittent warfare Anglo-Scottish hostilities ceased and most French troops withdrew from Scotland. With the restoration of peace, the reformation of the body politic seemed in order. Additionally, by the 1550s Lindsay had become interested in apocalyptic interpretations of world history. In the firm belief that the end of the world was imminent, the need to call his fellow countrymen to repentance and reform possessed a new and added urgency.

In June 1552, *Ane Satyre of the Thrie Estatis* was performed at Cupar.[92] Unfortunately, very little is known concerning the staging of this play. The lack of any reference to it in the burgh records suggests that it was staged by a very informal group of players who provided their own props and equipment.[93] A more semiprofessional setup is hinted at by Diligence's reference to a future performance the following year (4615), but this seems little more than a pleasing phrase with which to bring the action to a close, and if, as it is tempting to think, Lindsay did indeed play the part of the herald, this supports the idea that the performance (certainly as staged in Cupar) was an irregular event. At the same time as he was writing *Ane Satyre,* Lindsay was also engaged in *Ane Dialog betuix Experience and Ane Courteour, Off the Miserabyll Estait of the Warld* (commonly known as *The Monarche*), a scholarly world history which serves to answer a courtier's questions concerning the nature of personal fulfillment and spiritual salvation.

Two years after the Cupar performance of *Ane Satyre,* the play was re-staged on the newly built Greenside playfield on Calton Hill, Edinburgh.[94] Evidence for the dating of this production (12 August 1554) derives from several sources. *The Bannatyne Manuscript,* compiled in 1565–66, refers to an Edinburgh performance in the 1550s, and Henrie Charteris's preface to *The Warkis* recalls a play staged "in presence of the Quene Regent, and ane greit part of the Nobilitie, with ane exeding greit nowmer of pepil."[95] Most convincing of all, however, are the entries in the burgh records relating to a play on this date and to the props—the eight "play hattis," the crown, miter, fool's hood, scepter, angel wings, angel headdresses, "chaplet of tryvmphe," and gibbet—which were required.[96] Whether Lindsay himself was involved with this performance is unknown. If so, it was one of his last actions in this world. Exactly when he died is, like so many of the details of his life, unclear, but that he was dead by March 1555 is apparent from a charter of that date.[97]

IN THE COURSE of a poetic career spanning almost three decades, Lindsay presented his audience with a vivid picture of his environment, both physical and mental, both at court and within the wider community. However, his work does much more than passively reflect unfolding events. Crucially involved with the moral, social, and religious concerns of Renaissance Scotland, it provides a highly suggestive framework for examining the ways in which sixteenth-century Scots visualized their world and voiced their own experiences and expectations. Just how Lindsay chose to convey his perceptions of government, society, and the Church—and how these engaged with contemporary attitudes—is the concern of the chapters that follow.

II

The Art of Government

Kingship and Commonweal

Sir, gif ye please for to vse my counsall,
Your fame and name shall be perpetuall.
—*Ane Satyre of the Thrie Estatis,* 1900–1

FOUR

Kings and Kingship

Ane Dialog betuix Experience and ane Courteour (or The Monarche) is surely
Lindsay's magnus opus as, in a work of over 6,000 lines, he offers a
scholarly account of world history, the lessons of which point the way to
human enlightenment and spiritual salvation. The poem's message is at
once universal in its appeal and very specifically directed to one particular
courtier. "I haif . . . bene to this hour," the narrator tells Experience, "Sen I
could ryde, one Courtiour" (328–29) (see Fig. 4). The relationship between
the subject "I" and poetic subjectivity is of course highly problematic, but
it would be perverse to deny that the Experience who counsels the Courtiour
was born, in part at least, out of Lindsay's own experiences of courtly life.[1]
While we should be wary of any direct autobiographical reading, The
Monarche provides an intriguing insight into contemporary thinking on
many themes central to the existence of a courtier in Renaissance Scotland,
kingship, government, and service being three of the most important.
Indeed, this is true for all Lindsay's work, the entire corpus of which is
profoundly political in its concerns. Every one of his extant compositions
makes mention of a king figure—albeit only passingly in Squyer Meldrum.
Of the eight clearly court poems, over half are directly addressed to James V.
Among the remainder, The Tragedie of the Cardinal contains a passage delivered "To the Prencis," and The Monarche is dedicated, among others, to the
regent and includes a prayer for the absent queen. Three of Lindsay's court
poems (The Dreme, The Complaynt, and The Testament of the Papyngo) deal
explicitly with kingship and the same number embody more oblique messages (The Complaint of Bagsche, The Flyting, and The Deploratioun). Even
Lindsay's noncourt works make important statements on the subject, and
arguably the most cogent of all is presented in the form of a publicly
performed drama.

LINDSAY'S discussion of kingship and government was inevitably conditioned by personal experience. In the course of his life, four Stewart monarchs sat upon the Scottish throne. Two exercised a direct influence upon his
career, and James III and Mary, each in different ways, also contributed to

the development of his thinking. In addition, encounters with the rulers of England, France, Denmark, and the Empire acted as a benchmark against which to set traditional Scottish expectations. Arguably, however, it was not the experience of any one particular king but more the experience of no king at all which was the truly formative influence on Lindsay's perceptions of kingship. For some twenty-eight years of his life, Scotland was without a ruling monarch. The absence of the traditional figurehead threw into relief as nothing else could the role the king was expected to play and the qualities he had to possess. The vicissitudes of Lindsay's career—the low points all the result of minority politics—made him particularly sensitive to the problems associated with regency administrations, emphasizing the need for strong adult rule, intensifying its attraction as a political ideal, and rendering it all the more eagerly sought after.

Lindsay's preoccupation with the figure of the ideal prince was far from unusual during this period but, in his case, it was as much the result of personal experience as it was the expression of conventional political expectation. This does not necessarily mean, however, that Lindsay's work should be understood as a personal and specific critique of Scottish kingship. Certainly, with careful treatment, it yields significant biographical information. The assessment of James IV and the various regency administrations of 1513–28 is basically accurate and, when it comes to the personal rule of James V, there is some quite specific material: the reference to

Figure 4. "Experience and ane Courtiour." Woodcut from *A Dialogue betweene Experience and a Courtier, of the miserable estate of the worlde, first compiled in the Schottishe tongue by Sir Dauid Lyndesay, Knight, (a man of great learning and science) now newly corrected, and made perfit Englishe.* London, 1566. Courtesy of the Trustees of the National Library of Scotland.

Bagsche the royal hound, the wedding celebrations in Paris, possibly even James's unedifying romp with a "duddroun" or slut in the kitchens.[2] All bear the stamp of events actually witnessed. But this is not to deny that Lindsay dealt equally in archetypal figures. Unsurprisingly, though, these figures articulated deeply held political beliefs and, even allowing for the highly conventional and rather limited political vocabulary at his disposal, Lindsay was able to relate them to the real world. This is most clearly illustrated in *Ane Satyre of the Thrie Estatis*. It has been argued that Rex Humanitas, the young king who falls prey to evil counsel and the lures of a loose woman, is a portrait of James V. On this occasion, however, such a straightforward reading is inappropriate.[3] Clearly, *Ane Satyre* is an allegorical and not a mimetic drama, deriving its impact and strength from a lucid presentation of thematic material in a manner readily understood by a sixteenth-century audience. Given recent events, these themes may have been peculiarly apt, but they were not uniquely so. Rex Humanitas is, as his name suggests, the paradigmatic peg upon which Lindsay hangs his discussion of kingship. If this discussion looks at times like the simple adumbration of time-honored platitudes, that does not make it any less relevant to Lindsay's own experiences. Indeed, *Ane Satyre* reveals Lindsay's faith in the ability of this conventional vision to describe a process of real political reformation. This then helps answer the question of how Lindsay's treatment of kingship should be understood. Certainly, it was more often typological than topical, but, at the same time, such an approach could provide a pertinent commentary on Scottish kings and what was expected of them.

Lindsay's thinking was conditioned by the dominant political ideology of late-medieval Scotland, and his work forms part of a long tradition devoted to the discussion of kingship. Drawing not only upon familiar classical and European authorities but also on a rich fund of native kingship literature, this was a discussion with which sixteenth-century Scots were thoroughly familiar.[4] Firmly rooted in the philosophies of Aristotle and Augustine (the former in particular as filtered through the writing of Thomas Aquinas), the traditional kingship literature of western Europe with its stress upon the interdependence of virtue and government promoted a culture in which, to a large extent, politics became a branch of Christian ethics and political discussion was conducted within a moral matrix. This trend was reinforced by Platonic ideas of kingship and tyranny, defined in moral and psychological rather than legal terms; whereas the tyrant gave rein to his base passions, true kingship was the sovereignty of reason.[5] That only the virtuous are capable of truly virtuous government—and that only they deserve such an honor—was, in theory at least, universally accepted. Less universal yet extremely widespread was the belief that, of the six basic forms

of government identified by Aristotle, monarchy represented the best constitution. "It is," Erasmus declared, "the consensus of nearly all wise-
thinking men that the best form [of government] is monarchy."[6] Certainly,
this provided a suitable ideological foundation for most European experience, buttressing a feudal system in which the king naturally sat at the head
of a hierarchical structure. Divinely sanctioned kingship represented the
linchpin of most systems of government, and the person of the prince was
the key to good—or bad—government.

> So I conclude, the causis principall
> Off all the trubyll of the Natioun
> Ar in to Prencis, in to speciall   (*The Dreme,* 883–85)

As a result of the association between governance and theology, political
discussion was largely couched in the language of moral exhortation. To
modern ears, such homilies can sound at best unsophisticated, at worst
irrelevant. However, the fundamental importance of the principle cannot
be overemphasized. The portrayal of the virtuous Christian prince that lay
at the heart of much medieval kingship literature was not simply paying lip
service to a time-honored convention; on the contrary, it evoked a set of very
real, extremely serious, political aspirations. Grasping this allows us to
appreciate just how political Lindsay's works actually are, for while it is the
ethical drama which most forcibly hits the modern reader, it was surely the
political message which struck home to a sixteenth-century audience.

Without question or qualification, Lindsay accepted kingship as the
natural system of government. There is nothing in his work that attempts
to define the precise source of sovereign authority, nor does he, even in-
advertently, provide material for such an analysis. Unlike his contemporary
John Mair, for example, Lindsay was unconcerned with the historical origins of kingship. With an ethicopolitical rather than constitutional vision,
he focused upon its practical implications. Regarding the institution of
kingship, Lindsay simply reiterated the traditional belief in monarchy as
divinely ordained and patterned. In *The Dreme,* he tells James V, "God, of
his preordinance, / Haith grantit the to have the gouernance, / Off his
peple, and create the one King" (1037–39). This assumption also shapes
the imagery Lindsay employed when portraying the king variously as God's
"Instrument," "Governour," "Officiar," and in familiar feudal parlance, as
his "wassal."[7]

Viewing the king in his kingdom as a microcosm of God in the universe
emphasized royal power and authority to a point that, at times, seemed
awesomely vast in scope. In *The Testament of the Papyngo,* the dying bird
reminds the king how

> . . . in the erth [God] maid sic ordinance,
> Under thy feit all thyng terrestryall
> Ar subiect to thy plesour and pastance:
> Boithe fowle, and fysche, and bestis pastorall,
> Men to thy seruyce, and wemen, thay bene thrall: (269–73)

Royal power, however, could never be exercised untrammeled, for then it became tyranny. Geared as it was toward Christian salvation, it was circumscribed by the framework of natural and divine law within which all political authority functioned. The crown brought with it regal responsibility. As stated in *The Buke of the Governaunce of Princis* (Gilbert Hay's fifteenth-century translation of the pseudo-Aristotelian *Secretum Secretorum*),

And tharfore is a king lyknyt to God, for he is as depute and minister to God, and shuld follow him and be lyke him, and conforme him tyll hym in all his dedis of justice, vertu and veritee.[8]

In similar fashion, Lindsay exhorts James:

> Quharefor, dres the, abone all vther thyng,
> Off his [God's] laws to kepe the observance.
>
> *(The Dreme,* 1043–44)

God, he sternly reminds him, "wyll nocht excuse thyne Ignorance, / Geue thow be rekles in thy gouernyng" (1041–42).

The king owed an obligation not only to God but also to his subjects.[9] This dual responsibility is most evocatively conveyed in *Ane Satyre,* where it is immediately set before the audience in Rex Humanitas's important opening speech in which he praises God and asks his help in ruling according to divine will. This speech is cleverly balanced by Divyne Correctioun's opening words. Entering the stage at a point when these royal obligations appear forgotten, he reasserts them in uncompromising fashion. The very dramatization of Divyne Correctioun, the Scripture-quoting emissary of God, brings to life the bond that ought properly to exist between God and king, and the moment when Rex Humanitas "imbraces Correctioun with a humbil countenance" is one of the play's most dramatic climaxes.

When Rex Humanitas asked God for grace "till vse my diademe / To thy plesour, and to my great comfort" (100–101), what exactly did he mean? What precisely were the expectations surrounding kingship in this period? Sanctioned by classical, biblical, and legal authority, the ideals of kingship described by Lindsay and indeed common to most late-medieval literature on the subject were extremely traditional: A king's primary duty was the defense of his realm and the administration of justice within it. Justice in particular occupied a central position in Scottish thinking, a fact illustrated not only by traditional kingship literature but also, for example, by the coinage. That issued by James V in 1539 bore the inscription, "Honor regis iudicium" (from Psalm 99), the 1553 coinage proclaimed "Diligite Iusticiam," and that of 1555, 1557, and 1558 carried the motto, "Iustus fide vivit."[10] Certainly, it was the concept of justice—as opposed to defense—which most closely engaged Lindsay's attention, and his preoccupation with the theme runs throughout the corpus of his work. In *The Dreme,* John the Commonweal anticipates a time when Scotland shall be ruled by a king "Quhilk sall delyte hym maist, abone all thyng, / To put Iustice tyll executioun" (1006–7), and in *Ane Satyre,* written some twenty-six years later, the cry is the same. "The principall point, Sir of ane kings office," Gude-Counsall instructs Rex Humanitas, "Is for to do euerilk man iustice" (1882). One of the major purposes of the play is to illustrate this principle in action. It is a highly charged moment when, at the height of his infatuation with Dame Sensualitie and at the nadir of his kingship, Rex Humanitas renders up to her his judicial authority. "Dispone hir [Chastitie] as ye think expedient," he instructs his mistress, "Evin as ye list to let hir liue or die, / I will refer that thing to your Iudgement" (1429–31). This single action symbolizes not simply the abrogation of judicial authority but the surrender of Rex Humanitas's kingship itself. Fittingly, when Rex Humanitas is finally united with Divyne Correctioun, this is signaled by another, this time entirely appropriate, transference of his judicial authority. "And heir I gif you full commissioun," he tells Correctioun, "To puniche faults and gif remissioun" (1772–73).[11]

Recent scholarship has emphasized that "justice" cannot be understood simply in a legal/judicial context.[12] Rather, it was a highly emotive term referring not so much to the practical administration of justice as to the ideals of a just administration. As one of the cardinal virtues, it occupied an important position in traditional ethicopolitical discourse and was used as an effective shorthand for more general ideals of good government. In late-medieval Scotland, as elsewhere in Europe, this central concept of justice was naturally indispensable to any discussion of kingship. "Quhat is ane King?" asks Divyne Correctioun,

> . . . nocht but ane officiar,
> To caus his Leigis liue in equitie:
> And under God to be ane punisher
> Of trespassours against his Maiestie.   (1605–8)

This is reinforced when Veritie instructs Rex Humanitas to

> Fear God, do law and Iustice equally
> Tyll everie man: se that na puir opprest
> Vp to the heuin on yow ane vengence cry.   (1040–42)

Before looking in any detail at the other virtues possessed by Lindsay's ideal prince, it is as well to ponder some of his other, most basic, characteristics. Self-evidently he was a man, fit to rule by virtue of his years and his sex. Age and gender were frequently identified by medieval commentators as the criteria for sovereign rule and, again, Lindsay was no exception to this. By the sixteenth century, Scotland had become peculiarly accustomed to royal minorities with the period 1406–1528 witnessing over fifty years of regency government. The frequency of minority administrations was in many ways indicative of the strength of the Stewart dynasty and what has been termed the "patriotic conservatism" of the nobility that supported it.[13] Yet, as Lindsay's poetry forcefully illustrates, minority rule, so often tolerated for the sake of political stability, was a prospect that aroused grave disquiet.[14] Obviously, Lindsay's opinion was shaped by his own experiences. Personal bitterness undoubtedly infuses the caustic descriptions of minority rule in *The Dreme* and *The Complaynt*. However, Lindsay's principal concern lay less with his own grievances than with the neglect shown to the commonweal by the various regency governments. The character of John the Commonweal stresses the truth of the biblical proverb, "Wo to the realme that hes ouir young ane king" (*The Dreme*, 1011), and vows not to return until Scotland is ruled "Be wysedome of ane gude auld prudent king" (1005). While bemoaning periods of minority rule, Lindsay did not offer any real solution to the problem. After all, he judged the duke of Albany a successful regent, and he must have had high hopes of the earl of Arran. These might have appeared dashed after 1543, but Lindsay retained a dogged, not so say desperate, faith in the governor. After 1547 and Beaton's assassination, he used *The Tragedie of the Cardinal* to portray "our rychteous Gouernour" (127) as the guileless victim of Beaton's machinations, seduced with "sweit and subtell wordis" (205), frustrated at every turn, and finally, his son in Beaton's hands, forced to accede to his wishes. When, six years later, he wrote *The Monarche*, Lindsay dedicated it, among others, to Arran, "our Prince, and Protectour" (28). However, despite the epithet, Arran was not a true king-figure in Lindsay's eyes. As had John the Commonweal in *The Dreme*, so Lindsay too held out for "ane gude auld prudent king."

When it came to the problem of female rule, Lindsay's attitude was somewhat less straightforward. In traditional enough fashion he affirmed the widely held view that sovereign authority could only be wielded by men:

> Ladyis no way I can commend
> Presumptuouslye quhilk doith pretend
> Tyll vse the office of ane kyng,
> Or Realmes tak in gouernyng,   (*The Monarche*, 3247–50)

He took care, however, not to allow this belief to draw him into dangerous political waters, waters muddied by ideas of resistance to female rule and, ultimately, of deposition. Indeed, when politically expedient, he was prepared to grant that Margaret Tudor's regency authority "was to hir appropriate" (*The Testament of the Papyngo*, 544). Admittedly, Margaret was only a female regent acting on behalf of a male king, and this considerably predates the hostility toward gynecocracy found in *The Monarche*. But, despite his belief that "all wemen, in thare degre, / Suld to thare men subiectit be" (*The Monarche*, 1069–70), Lindsay's endorsement of the traditional patriarchal response—even later in his career—was not entirely unambivalent. True, in the infant Mary Stewart he generally saw a queen rather than a sovereign, one unable to fulfill any of the functions of a male monarch. "I traist to see gude reformatione," he wrote, "From tyme we gett ane faithfull prudent kinge" (2605–6). Yet, that Mary was "our Quene, of Scotland Heretour" (12) he accepted without question, and his choice of the word "Heretour" seems a significant recognition of her claims to sovereign authority. Mary's reign was simply an unfortunate aberration to be endured in the expectation of future male rule. Whether that male rule would be provided by any future husband is not however entirely clear. Although the young queen's primary duty was to "Bring home tyll ws ane Kyng and Governour" (16), Lindsay does not necessarily see this as a solution to the situation. The problem of reconciling a queen's sovereign political authority with a wife's natural subjugation to her husband was one of which Lindsay was not unaware.[15] In *The Monarche*, finding his belief in the natural subjection of women confirmed by history, he notes

> Quhow Quenis of moste hie degre
> Ar vnder moste subiectioun
> And sufferis moste correctioun.
> For thay, like birdis in tyll ane cage,
> Ar kepit ay vnder thirlage. (1064–68)

Surely Lindsay could not have countenanced the idea of his "Quene, of Scotland Heretour" finding herself in such a position. However, just what examples, if any, he had in mind here is not clear, and the idea is developed no further. Indeed, there were several very good reasons why Lindsay should be reluctant to press the issue. If married queenship had significant political importance, virgin queenship had serious dynastic implications which Scotland was anxious to avoid. The example of the ill-fated Maid of Norway, whose untimely death without issue in 1290 had plunged the country into arguably the most traumatic period of its history, surely haunted the imagination of later generations. James V's reported despair on hearing the news of his daughter's birth must have been shared by the entire nation when, only six days later, the infant became Queen of Scots. Despite the fact that it was likely to create as many problems as it solved, a marriage settlement—be it French or English—seemed to offer the only solution and, as such, it was enthusiastically pursued almost from the day of Mary's birth.

Over and above satisfying requirements of age and gender, the ideal prince was also expected to be a paragon of personal virtue. Examples *ad nauseam* could be produced to demonstrate how conventional a vision this was, but perhaps one of the most interesting is *The Bannatyne Manuscript* compiled by George Bannatyne in the mid 1560s. Divided into five parts, the second, described as "conteneand verry singular ballatis full of wisdome and moralitie," contains a significant section of works all addressing this point.[16] It is hardly surprising that Lindsay subscribed wholeheartedly to this enormously conventional ideal or that he articulated it in the time-honored terminology, relying almost exclusively on abstract moral concepts. He refers to few specific examples of "good government" (exceptions being James IV's pacification of the Isles and the Borders and the similar policies of his son) but instead views policy and personality as one and the same.[17]

There were two important aspects to this relationship between individual morality and public prosperity. On the one hand, it represented an extension of the universally accepted maxim that "ane man of vicious lyfe has ane vicious ending."[18] This quotation is taken from Bellenden's preface to the *Chronicles of Scotland,* a work which, with its colorful account of Scotland's kings and their—often grisly—fates, vividly illustrates the truth of the saying, but it was a commonplace of kingship literature. However, the actions of a king, unlike those of other men, determined not only his own destiny but also that of his kingdom. In *The Monarche,* Lindsay uses the histories of the Assyrian rulers Nimrod, Ninus, Semiramis, and Sardanapalus to show that royal viciousness leads equally to personal disaster and national misfortune.[19] On the other hand, there is also a more precisely defined bond between the personal morality of the king and the welfare of the realm with the former being viewed as an example and inspiration to the population at large. This is a theme dealt with, at some length, in *Ane Satyre:*

> For quhy subiects do follow day and nicht
> Thair governours in vertew and vyce.
> Ye ar the lamps that sould schaw them the light
> To leid them on this sliddrie rone of yce.
> *Mobile mutatur semper cum principe vulgus.*
> And gif ye wald your subiectis war weill geuin,
> Then verteouslie begin the dance your sell;

Going befoir, then they anone I wein,
Sall follow you, eyther till heuin or hell:
Kings suld of gude exempils be the well.
Bot gif that your strands be intoxicate,
In steid of wyne thay drink the poyson fell:
Thus pepill follows ay thair principate.
Sic luceat lux vestra coram hominibus vt
videant opera vestra bona.   (1047–60)

The traditional canon of virtue, applicable to all humanity, was centered on the four cardinal and three theological virtues: justice, temperance, fortitude, prudence or wisdom, faith, hope, and charity. Much kingship literature consists of an exposition of these qualities, generally but not always with reference to government. A good example of this in a Scottish context is Book VII of John Ireland's *Meroure of Wyssdome.*[20] Lindsay too follows this highly conventional pattern. Combining a commendation of virtue with the usual charge to rule with counsel (in itself often classified as a virtue), he urges James V to

Tak Manlie curage, and leif thyne Insolence,
And vse counsale of nobyll dame Prudence.
Founde the fermelie on faith and fortytude:
Drawe to thy courte Iustice and Temporance;
And to the commoun weill haue attendance.
And, also, I beseik thy Celestitude,
Hait vicious men, and lufe thame that ar gude;
And ilk flatterer thow fleme from thy presence,
And fals reporte out of thy courte exclude.

(*The Dreme,* 1064–72)

In *The Complaynt,* Lindsay suggests that this hope has been realized, and he rejoices to see James free of evil counselors and ruling with the support of "The foure gret verteous Cardinalis" (379). The enduring appeal of such political imagery can be seen from Alexander Scott's 1562 New Year address to James's daughter, Mary, which in similar fashion urges her, "Found on the first four vertewus cardinall."[21] This standard repertoire was frequently extended. For example, the poem, *This Hindir Nicht,* lists no less than twenty-one virtues to be pressed into royal service.[22] In *The Testament of the Papyngo,* Lindsay too elaborates on the basic theme, describing the qualities of James's Stewart ancestors. Obviously, the portraits of Scottish kings penned in this poem are intended as moral exemplars which tell us more about expectations of kingship than about actual monarchs. Nevertheless, they are in line with what is known of the rulers in question. Thus, in addition to some standard praise of James I's prudence and justice, Lindsay also applauds his "Ingyne" (431) and "Eloquence" (432)—a reference to the king's literary talent. Lindsay's sketch of James IV, "the glore of princelie gouernyng" (504), has already been discussed in some detail, and it has been suggested that while specific circumstances encouraged this particularly laudatory epithet Lindsay was not too wide of the mark. This evocative account of a Scottish court renowned throughout Europe for its knightly accomplishments occurs, significantly enough, in a poem written at the very outset of Lindsay's heraldic career. Later he would become increasingly uneasy with at least some aspects of the chivalric ideology. He is, for example, extremely unusual in the attention—or lack of it—he pays to that most chivalrous of virtues, largesse. Gilbert Hay's *Governaunce of Princis,* for instance, commences with a long and detailed discussion of this particular virtue.[23] However, apart from proclaiming James IV the "lampe of li-biralytie" (492), Lindsay make no mention of this trait in his discussion of kingship—particularly striking when we remember that, as a herald, he would have been required to cry largesse on occasions of royal show. Noting that all earthly courts, even those as splendid as that of James IV, are tawdry in comparison to the court of Christ, Lindsay deftly subverts the notion of a royal virtue grounded in knightly achievement and worldly fame.

THE DEVALUATION of chivalric, specifically martial, accomplishment that we see in Lindsay's works was partially fostered by the spirit of Christian humanism with its stress upon scholarship and spiritual virtue. Lindsay's response to such ideas is readily apparent from his attitude to the education of the prince. Within the conventional ethical framework of political discussion, the principal purpose of a prince's education was the inculcation of regal virtue. This idea is forcibly expressed in *Ane Satyre of the Thrie Estatis.* Beginning by depicting Rex Humanitas as *"Tanquam tabula rasa"* (224), the remainder of the play (particularly its first section) functions as a kind of moral curriculum, a dramatized description of a prince's education in the virtues appropriate to his position. *Ane Satyre* is far from unique in this respect. The popularity of this type of instructional literature and its currency at the Scottish court are strongly conveyed in Lindsay's own poem, *The Testament of the Papyngo:*

> I grant, thy grace gettis mony one document,
> Be famous Fatheris predicatioun,
> With mony notabyll Narratioun
> Be plesande Poetis, in style Heroycall,
> Quhow thow suld gyde thy Seait Imperiall.   (236–40)

The Papyngo's almost apologetic tone gives the impression that James was heartily sick of such exhortations! However, these lines demonstrate quite conclusively that the parrot's lecture, albeit delivered in "barbour rusticall" (246), was intended to stand alongside such other works. The "Epystyl of the Papyngo directit to kyng Iames the Fyft" is Lindsay's own "mini-mirror-for-princes" providing a more detailed account of the education he considered suitable for a king. Utilizing the well-understood shorthand, Lindsay was able to proclaim "vertew" as that to which, "abufe all vther thyng" (292), James must turn his attention. In particular, he was urged to honor God, to work with counsel, to rule with justice and mercy, and to treat his nobles with fraternal solicitude.

Lindsay also entreated James to study: "Wald thow, ilk day studie, bot half one hour, / The Regiment of princelie gouernyng, / To thy peple it war ane plesand thyng" (304–6). Compared with the rigorous timetable devised by George Buchanan for the young James VI (Greek before breakfast, Cicero, Livy, and history before lunch, to be followed by composition, arithmetic, cosmography, logic, and rhetoric), thirty minutes' daily study does not seem too arduous a program. But at least the passage serves to indicate Lindsay's support for an academic education.[24] Unfortunately, Lindsay provides no list of books suitable for the schoolroom and, given the numerous works within the *De Regimine Principum* genre, it is impossible to decide which—if any—he had in mind at this point.[25] This is also true with respect to historical chronicles, and a possible reference to Hector Boece's *Scotorum Historiae:*

> The Cronecklis to knaw I the exhorte
> Quhilk may be myrrour to thy Maiestie:
> Thare sall thov fynd boith gude & euyll reporte
> Off euerilk Prince, efter his qualytie: (311–14)[26]

As these lines suggest, the importance of historical example as instruction was a fundamental tenet of the *speculum principis* genre, and in both *The Testament of the Papyngo* and *The Monarche,* Lindsay employs history for didactic purposes. Despite the fact that, in the former, his declared aim is the illustration of the fickleness of fortune and the transience of worldly fame, his depiction of the fate of Scottish kings from Robert III to James IV offers their descendant a compelling pattern on which to model his own behavior.

One effect of prescribing a humanist-oriented education for the prince (and by extension for the aristocracy) was the promotion of what has been described as the secularization of wisdom and the erosion of the traditional boundaries between a lay education on the one hand and a clerical education on the other. Of course, the differences had never been quite as precise as this somewhat oversimplified statement suggests, for the education of the chivalric hero, the cultivation of mind and body in preparation for worldly adventure, was an indispensable element of medieval romance. Moreover, the derivation of the favored curriculum from the *speculum principis* literature of the period ensured that it included instruction in the liberal arts alongside physical and military training.[27] Nevertheless, the English humanist Richard Pace's well-known anecdote about the old man who would rather see his son hang than study letters contains an element of truth concerning aristocratic expectations in Scotland as well as England.[28] John Mair, for example, criticized both the Scottish nobility who educated their sons in neither letters nor morals and the farmers who trained their offspring only to serve some great lord.[29] Such ideas, however, were not widely held. Although Aberdeen University was established in part with an eye to the education of the laity, in general the influence of educationalists remained patchy. Increasing numbers of literate, nonnoble laymen entering government made some impact but really did little to challenge the entrenched sociopolitical position of the aristocracy. The erosion of traditional values was an extremely slow process, and it would be wrong to think of the Renaissance as presaging any sort of decisive break in educational culture. New ideas were certainly introduced (being picked up by men such as Lindsay), but it is the coexistence of different attitudes rather than the replacement of one by another that really distinguishes the period.

Though the antimartial thrust of humanist (and indeed scholastic) scholarship rendered it potentially antagonistic to the chivalric code, in practice many educationalists accepted the traditionally lauded skills so long as they were not a cause of vainglorious pride and they ranged alongside, even subordinate to, the inculcation of virtue through study. Lindsay fitted into this general pattern. As illustrated above, he was highly critical of those who set martial skill above intellectual—and hence ethical—development. Into the mouths of the Douglases and their supporters he put a scornful parody of their words:

> We think thame verray naturail fulis,
> That lernis ovir mekle at the sculis,
> Schir, ye mon leir to ryn and speir,
> And gyde yow lyke ane man of weir.
>
> (*The Complaynt*, 165–68)

Such lines might encourage the belief that Lindsay endorsed Mair's opinion that military training was "in nowise essential for the constitution of a true king" were it not for the fact that elsewhere he refuses to reject out of hand the idea that the king ought to be trained in the martial arts.[30] Indeed, in *Ane Satyre*, Divyne Correctioun echoes the very words of the irresponsible Douglases. The king must, he declares,

> . . . leirne to rin ane heavie spear,
> That he into the tyme of wear,
> May follow at the cheace.   (1848–50)

In the same speech, Correctioun also commends hunting and hawking to Rex Humanitas, declaring them "honest pastimes for ane king" (1845). These words echo those in *The Testament of the Papyngo* where James IV's "knightly game" (502) is described as "pastyme accordyng for ane kyng" (503). That the courtly arts owed so much to the traditional pursuits of knighthood points to a flourishing chivalric court culture which, Lindsay apart, held the knightly virtues of bravery and largesse in high esteem.

Lindsay's response to the martial elements of this courtly ethos had important implications for his treatment of the second traditionally accepted purpose of kingship, namely the defense of the realm. Here, it is interesting to consider a contemporary poem by William Stewart which in many ways sounds like Lindsay but which gives primary place to this second aspect of kingship:

> I the beseik againis thy lust to stryue
> And loufe thy God aboife all maner of thing,
> And him imploir, now in thy yeiris ying,
> To grant the grace thy folk to defend,
> Quhilk he hes geven the in gouerning
> In peax and honour to thy lyvis end.[31]

Although justice, with all its connotations, was Lindsay's principal theme, he could not entirely dismiss the idea of king as defender of his people. Indeed, Scotland was peculiarly attuned to this aspect of kingship. The conventional belief in a king's duty to defend his realm was necessarily strong in a country that comparatively recently had come perilously close to conquest by an external power. The continuing threat posed by English claims to suzerainty only served to strengthen this conviction, and Scottish political expectations demanded not only a king who was wise and virtuous but a kingdom that was independent and free. While this was powerfully articulated by the great chronicles of the Middle Ages, we should beware of viewing this as a purely medieval phenomenon. Acclaimed humanists such as Hector Boece and John Bellenden were equally capable of producing a stirring epic of valor in the cause of liberty, the "maist dulce tresoure and heavinly gift in erde."[32] However, as Lindsay was all too aware, one of the factors most often responsible for Scotland's social and political problems was incessant warfare. Martial endeavor, therefore, represented an incongruous blueprint for virtue. Furthermore, Boece's vision gave rise to several contradictions which could not easily be reconciled. The principal of these, frequently recognized yet never resolved by Boece himself, focused on the vicious circle whereby "Peace ingeneris riches, and ryches insolence, and insolence werre."[33] The solution, according to Boece, was a program of disciplined austerity calculated to maintain the population's moral and physical integrity. Although by no means universally endorsed, this assessment appears to have enjoyed some considerable popularity in the 1530s.[34] But, in the last analysis, it proved too illusory a framework to sustain a conceptualization of either kingship or national identity. This became painfully obvious to the Scots after 1542 when the death of the king, ignominious defeat, and virtual semioccupation by an enemy army all imparted a hollow ring to Boece's self-confident exposition of Scottish independence.

It is not surprising, therefore, that when Lindsay wrote *Ane Satyre of the Thrie Estatis* in 1552 he virtually ignored the theme of "king-as-commander" and concentrated instead upon his favorite leitmotif, justice. But that he was unable to accept as the essence of kingship the symbolization of armed struggle in the name of political independence is also discernible in Lindsay's earlier works. When, in *The Dreme,* he urged his king to "Tak Manlie curage, and leif thyne Insolence" (1064), it was not in order to don his battle armor but rather to "Drawe to thy courte Iustice and Temporance / And to the commoun weill haue attendance" (1067–68). In Lindsay's mind, the ideal king was armed with the sword of justice rather than that of war. In *The Monarche,* some of his fiercest opprobrium is reserved for Ninus who not only was the first idolater but, driven by his "Pryde, Couatyce, and vaine glore" (2013), was also the first to engage in war. By duplicating this line to explain the bellicosity of contemporary princes, Lindsay affiliates the morality of Francis I, Charles V, and Henry VIII with that of the pagan Ninus (5395). The spectacle of war waged among Christians represented a particularly offensive violation of Christian sensibilities, and Lindsay was especially sensitive to the problem. Not only was it considered at some length in *The Monarche,* but in *Ane Satyre* Folly awards one of his caps to kings whose worldly pride and ambition clearly mark them out as one of his own. There are two distinct yet interrelated aspects to Lindsay's pacificism. First, it was an extremely conservative expression of faith in the medieval ideal of Christendom united under the cross and the papacy. Second, as we shall see, it was a recognition of the political problems and social dislocation thrown up by war. This was not in itself particularly novel—others, notably John Mair, were engaged in a similar debate—but for Lindsay it was refashioned in what one commentator has called "the new language which linked peace and the commonweal."[35]

Yet Lindsay was unable completely to shake off traditional chivalric assumptions relating to the martial character of the king.[36] Fully attuned to conventional attitudes, he did on occasion flatter James in chivalric terms, referring to his "Merciall dedis dyng of memorie" (*The Testament of the*

Papyngo, 238) and wishing him "Glore, honour, laude, tryumphe, & victorie" (228).[37] Such endorsements of chivalric values date from the late 1520s, but even when he wrote *The Monarche* in 1553, Lindsay was still failing fully to demythologize the concept of the glorious warrior. Stabrobates, it is true, is engaged in the legitimate defense of his realm against the "ambitious, wyckit" Semiramis, and yet the description of his battle preparations evoke the spirit of medieval romance rather than of sober humanist treatise:

> Than Stawrobates, wyse and wycht,
> Come fordwart, lyke ane nobyll knycht,
> With mony one thousand speir and scheild,
> Arrayit Royallie on the feild,
> Thinkand he wald his land defend,
> Or in the Battle mak ane end.   (3089–94)

The account of mass slaughter and suffering that follows only serves to confound this stirring depiction of military heroism. Lindsay, however, gives no indication of deliberate irony and seems to have been unaware of the paradox.

Even the most pacifist of authors could not, however, deny the right of the king to muster the nation in legitimate self-defense. Given recent history and the politics of the mid sixteenth century, this was particularly relevant to Scotland. Here, it proved impossible to dismiss the notion that war was an adjunct of statecraft and, as such, it was necessary for Gude-Counsall to teach Rex Humanitas how "in peace ye sould provyde for weirs" (2557). Political circumstances after 1542 meant that it was impossible for Lindsay to identify the king with the struggle for national security but, in any case, the evidence of his work suggests that this was not an identification that he was keen to make. In fact, in *The Monarche,* Lindsay goes on to consider that the only solution to interminable Anglo-Scottish warfare was some form of union (5410–11).[38] Clearly, neither Lindsay's patriotism nor his conception of kingship was inextricably bound up with the Stewart dynasty—particularly as a symbol of Scottish freedom—and his views, therefore, offered a potent corrective to the conceptualization of the armed king as symbol of the political autonomy of the kingdom.

IF THE ADMINISTRATION of justice and defense of the realm represented the twin pillars of good kingship, they were strongly supported by the notion of good counsel. "Nothing in government is more fitting for a king than to have good counsellors," wrote one fifteenth-century Scottish chronicler, but such words could have graced the pages of any work on the subject.[39] Lindsay emphatically endorsed the traditional axiom:[40]

> But gude counsale, may no Prince lang indure:
> Wyrk with counsale, than sall thy work be sure.
>
> (*The Testament of the Papyngo*, 300–301)

This idea is more expansively treated in *Ane Satyre* where Rex Humanitas identifies it as one of the play's principal themes, declaring in his opening speech, "Be I nocht rewlit by counsall and ressoun / In dignitie I may nocht lang indure" (88–89). It is not long before the action of the play asserts the truth of his words. While Dame Sensualitie's ensnarement of the king symbolizes the subjugation of his reason, the introduction of the Vices, "thrie knaves in cleithing counterfeit" (1634), signifies the subversion of good counsel. Underlining the point, these false servants expressly banish Gude-Counsall from the king's presence. The dramatic representation of Gude-Counsall brings to life its importance as a guiding political principle:

> Princis or Potestatis ar nocht worth ane leik,
> Be thay nocht gydit by my gude governing.   (564–65)

Gude-Counsall's long exile from Scotland is explicitly equated with the country's misfortunes, and it is only when he is reinstated that the political problems of the realm can be rectified. As Divyne Correctioun proclaims in his opening speech (again recalling and reinforcing that of Rex Humanitas),

> . . . quhen the King stands at his counsell sound,
> Then welth sall wax and plentie as he list
> And policie sall in his Realme abound.   (1586–88)

The concept of counsel offered an attractive and arguably realistic mechanism for bridging the gulf between what was expected of the king and what he actually did. This ideal of consensus government operating within an ethical framework (rather than a constitutional or legal argument) was the most frequently offered corrective to the abuse of power in Scotland during this period. Even the sensational catalogue of tyrannicide and deposition found in Boece's *Scotorum Historiae* forms part of this tradition. In the preface to his translation, Bellenden makes it clear that later writers who see the work as evidence of the contractual nature of Scottish kingship miss the point, that point being the illustration of

how this realme salbe gouernit in iustice, and quhat personis ar necessair to bere auctoritie or office within this realme, and . . . throcht quhais corruppit counsale thi nobill anticessouris sum tymes wer abusit, and broucht to sik miserie that thai tynt nocht onlye thair lyiff and triumphand dominioun, bot remanis in memory to thair lamentabill regraitt.[41]

As we shall see, Lindsay was not wholly successful in uniting the traditional ideal of counsel—powerful yet hard to enforce—with a more rigorous program of political and social reform. In *Ane Satyre,* Rex Humanitas's position in the second part of the play, especially with regard to his counselors, becomes ill defined to the point of ambiguity. Clearly, Lindsay was attempting some formalization, even redefinition, of the traditional relationship between king and counselor. However, his reluctance—inability may not be too strong a word—to detract in any way from the central importance of the king effectively reveals the powerful and continuing attraction of the traditional ideal.

When the king in the fifteenth-century poem *The Thrie Prestis of Peblis* asked, "Quhat man in hous war meit with him to dwell / Of wisdome for to gif him counsell," the answer turned upon the ideal of virtue.[42] Likewise, Lindsay advises James V to "Hait vicious men, and lufe thame that ar gude" (*The Dreme,* 1070). Again, such words represent more than simple platitudes. Rather, they are an integral part of a political vocabulary which, although limited by modern standards, sought to express a complex reality. Although in an ideal world all courtiers would possess the moral qualities to enhance the virtuous rule of their sovereign, in practice this was not the case. It was, therefore, vital for the king to choose his counsel wisely and guard against the "barnes of Baliall" (*Testament of the Papyngo,* 160). The court was, after all, the natural haunt of a whole host of fools and flatterers, procurers and panderers, beggars and blasphemers. Such villains were the stock characters of a traditional anticourt literature which, as demonstrated by poems like *The Complaynt,* did much to inform Lindsay's work.[43] A less caustic, more amusing example of the genre is provided by *The Complaint of Bagsche* in which a dog renowned for his "wickitnes" (47) can "In Court . . . gat gret audience" (48). There his career is characterized by arrogance, brutality, and ingratitude to former protectors. Even when finally brought to account, Bagsche is pardoned his crimes by an overindulgent king. The old hound is made to confess his past with an engaging frankness which not only prompts sympathy for his present plight but smiles at the bloody shirts that were the result of many an antic. Our indulgence, however, like that of the king, is misplaced as, in this way, Lindsay illustrates the dangerous and superficial nature of courtly charm and the responsibility of the king to ensure that the ideal virtue of the sovereign is replicated throughout his court.

Virtue might guarantee good service, but what guaranteed virtue? Traditionally, nobility of blood was perceived as the distinguishing mark of the virtuous, the nobility having been originally instituted as a means whereby its members might govern the unruly postlapsarian population.[44] However, the difficulties of reconciling noble virtue on the one hand and noble blood on the other were often too severe to be ignored. Moralists and theologians frequently adopted an uncompromising stand on the issue. For example, Mair declared, "There is absolutely no true nobility but virtue and the evidence of virtue. That which is commonly called nobility is naught but a windy thing of human devising."[45] Others, however, were less dogmatic, and the relationship between virtue and nobility was more widely viewed as one of association rather than direct causation. Those who were nobly born were more likely to be virtuous—indeed, they were obliged by their birth so to be:

> It is contrair the lawis of nature
> A gentill man to be degenerate,
> Nocht following of his progenitoure
> The worthy reule, and the lordly estate.
>
> (Henryson, *Orpheus and Eurydice*, 8–11)

The two views operated in tension: On the one hand nobility was the reward of the virtuous, and on the other virtue was the obligation of the noble. Noble lineage could even be perceived as a virtue in itself. As Bellenden explained, Fergus was chosen the first king of Scots "for his nobill blude & vther excellent vertews."[46] The conflation of ideas that served to bind virtue and nobility together effectively neutralized the radical implications of a doctrine that upheld the right of the virtuous to social leadership, and Lindsay's work illustrates how apparently contradictory ideas could be held in tandem without any apparent difficulty. While in *The Dreme* he exhorted James V to "Use counsall of thy prudent Lordis trew" (1110), in *The Testament of the Papyngo* he averred that the king's council should comprise "the moste Sapient / Without regard to blude, ryches or rent" (302–303). This should not be seen as a radical shift of opinion on Lindsay's part. The fundamental—if idealistic—conviction cannot be directly equated with a rejection of the—more realistic—justification of the aristocratic right to counsel and service.

This discussion was particularly pertinent for men such as Lindsay, themselves not of noble blood, for the conclusions they reached served to justify their role in the royal administration and at court. For such men, service in both capacities was inspired by a similar ideological ethos. Indeed, the distinction between councillor and courtier was by no means straightforward; theoretically the ideal courtier had always counseled his king in virtue while, practically speaking, serving the physical and emotional needs of the king at court was never incompatible with serving on his Council.[47] The doctrine of service so important to men such as Lindsay was crucially enhanced by a nascent humanist culture. Stimulated particularly by the rediscovery and reinterpretation of Ciceronian texts, civic humanism, as it has been termed, furnished a culture and philosophy attractive to those engaged in the political life.[48] The works of many northern humanists reveal them to be self-appointed royal counselors, physicians to the body politic, and there were many who, like Lindsay, considered themselves well suited to serve their king.[49]

AS FORCEFULLY demonstrated by the works of Boece, Bellenden, and Lindsay himself, the humanist commitment to royal or public service frequently received expression in a wider concern for the affairs of Scotland as a whole and the promotion of moral reform throughout the realm. That the strongly didactic thrust of Scottish humanism so readily complemented the conventionally articulated relationship between the affairs of men and universal ethics, between the precepts of good government and the moral qualities of the prince, explains the strength of its appeal and renders its rapid absorption into the vernacular tradition unsurprising. The moralizing, reforming tone at the heart of Lindsay's work also reflects the traditionally recognized relationship between poetry and rhetoric, both of which were considered powerful agents of ethical persuasion.[50] As court poet, Lindsay drew together the concerns of an increasingly self-conscious humanist court and the traditional themes of Scottish court culture. But, as we shall see, this was never an entirely straightforward business.

FIVE

Courtly Visions

Court Poet and Pageant Master

I f poetic texts are to serve as a useful guide to contemporary attitudes, it is necessary to engage in more than an analysis of the words on the page (important though those words are). As asserted by recent criticism, literature does not embody some universal idea of "history" passively awaiting extraction. Rather, it must be understood as a complex cultural construct contingent upon the circumstances of both composition and reception. With this in mind, we have to ask what Lindsay tells us not just about Renaissance attitudes expressed through poetry but about the poets themselves. What exactly was a court poet during this period? Who was he writing for, and why? An examination of Lindsay's work and career goes some way toward answering these questions. By virtue of his heraldic office, Lindsay was also closely involved in the production of what might be termed the unwritten texts of court celebration and public spectacle. As evidenced by a thriving scholarly literature on the subject, the symbolic manifestations of power reified in the elaborate rituals of Renaissance monarchy were enormously important for ideas of kingship, and Lindsay's activities in this sphere provide a useful introduction to some powerful nonliterary discourses which, like his poetry, offer a revealing commentary on contemporary attitudes.

AS SUGGESTED in the Introduction, any discussion of court culture immediately begs the question of what exactly is meant by that frequently invoked and variously applied term. In his analysis of English court culture in the Middle Ages, J. W. Sherborne focuses on that "enlightenment and excellence of taste in the arts and in the humanities among those who through interest, experience, observation and commitment had learned to value and promote beauty and distinction."[1] This seems unnecessarily limited. To speak of a court culture is to speak not simply of aesthetics but of the wider artistic, intellectual, ethical, literary, social, and visual life of a group of people bound together by a common association with the monarch. The cultured court was that same court which, day in, day out, busied itself with affairs of state and political intrigue. As we have already seen, political considerations, ideological and factional, very often made their way into the cultural arena, and culture became in turn the articulation of a complex mesh of social, political, and ethical concerns.

Chapter 1 briefly considered the court of James IV. Unlike that of his son, his reign is fortunate to have received a comparatively large amount of scholarly attention.[2] This has highlighted several key features, perhaps the most striking of which is the dynamism, what has been termed "the sheer exuberance," of Scottish cultural and intellectual life in the late fifteenth and early sixteenth centuries.[3] As famously illustrated by the work of William Dunbar, this was reflected in all branches of the court arts and in every sphere of courtly activity:

> Schir, ye have mony servitours
> And officiaris of dyvers curis
> Kirkmen, courtmen and craftismen fyne,
> Doctouris in jure and medicyne
> Divinouris, rethoris and philosophouris,
> Men of armes and vailyeant knychtis,
> And mony other gudis wichtis:
> Chevalouris, cawanderis and flingaris:
> Cunyouris, carvouris and carpentaris,
> Beildaris of barkis and ballingaris:
> Masounis lyand upoun the land
> And schipwrichtis hewand upone the strand:
> Glasing wrichtis, goldsmithis and lapidaris
> Pryntouris, payntouris and potingaris.
>
> (*Remonstrance to the King*, 1–16)[4]

By piling on the alliterative couplets, Dunbar evocatively suggests an atmosphere of color and action fostered by a kaleidoscopic range of artistic talents. This was not mere literary bravura. The more sober evidence of the *Treasurer's Accounts* recording payment to all of these "servitours" and "officiaris" amply supports Dunbar's words.[5] But this is by no means an exhaustive description of the artistic life of the court. For example, the accounts testify to a remarkable level of musical activity, and although actual compositions no longer survive it is clear that, by any standards, the Scottish court employed large numbers of musicians. Additionally, as Dunbar's work itself makes clear, poetry made a significant contribution to the cultural life of the court, even if it is one which remains hard to quantify.[6]

Another activity not mentioned by Dunbar but central to cultural life were the revels in which the young Lindsay played a part. As evidenced by the records, much effort went into devising entertainments pleasing to king and courtier alike. Employed for this purpose was a whole host of musicians, minstrels and singers, tale-tellers, jesters and fools, players, guisers, and dancers. Special days were marked by the appearance of the King of Bean, Abbot of Unreason, Queen of the May, or St. Nicholas and, as the reign progressed, a burgeoning self-confidence manifested itself in ever more extravagant activities.

The death of James IV in 1513 rent a large hole in the cultural fabric of the Scottish court. The focus for court ceremonial and source of potential patronage was replaced (initially at least) by the unsatisfactory figure of a semiresident governor; defeat in battle and the ensuing political turmoil seriously undermined the vibrant self-confidence that had characterized previous years. With the situation compounded by plunging revenues and chronic financial problems, elegant affirmations of courtly values fell into abeyance.[7] Nevertheless, Hughes and Ramson are surely correct to refer to "a court culture which was, despite the political conflicts with which it was racked, stable and profoundly conscious of its own traditions."[8] Obviously there were periods of dislocation, but traditional court culture was strong enough to withstand hard times, emerging and flourishing when circumstances improved. Indeed, it may not have been simply a question of cultural and artistic hibernation. As Lindsay's tribute to poets such as Inglis (whose *floruit* can be dated to some time before the end of the 1520s) and as poems in *The Bannatyne Manuscript* testify, troubled circumstances did not necessarily extinguish poetic activity. At least three poems in the manuscript take the minority as their principal theme.[9] (Although vehement criticism of the regime may indicate a later composition, such poems nevertheless indicate the profound effect these years had on the court consciousness.) Literary activity also seems to have marked the start of James's personal rule. Lindsay's *Complaynt* was not the only work to celebrate the occasion, and a Latin verse addressed to James V and generally known as the *Strena* was also written at this time, possibly by Lindsay's future associate, James Foulis.[10] It is hard to believe that these accomplished works were created ex nihilo in a climate of poetic sterility. On the contrary, both were written within an existing tradition and, although in many respects very different, by celebrating the accession of a new ruler and anticipating his virtuous rule both performed similar poetic and political functions.

As with James IV, so too James V's personal and political confidence increased as his reign progressed. The delicate and dangerous game of power politics, the arrogant taxation of the Church, the unprecedented French visit, the obsessive tinkering with his royal regalia, all suggest an aggressive self-assurance. This received physical expression as household expenditure soared and vast sums were lavished on extravagant building programs owing much to a humanist-inspired approach to the visual arts.[11]

There was too a return to grand spectacle complemented by the revival of the artistic and literary activity of the court and, while the records do not suggest anything quite comparable with the heady days of the previous reign, there was a renewed upsurge of revelry. Fools and jugglers, guisers and musicians, Robin Hood and the Queen of Bean were all reinstated. [12]

James himself seems to have taken a keen interest in these activities, and his personal lead and participation are important factors explaining the renewed enthusiasm. According to one later sixteenth-century source, the king was an accomplished musician. Able to sight-read, he possessed a good ear but an unfortunate voice, "rawky and harsh." [13] However, he clearly appreciated fine musicianship; on one occasion he requested the service of the musician Thomas de Avarencia from the duke of Milan, and what has been termed the "Golden Age" of Scottish music culminated in his reign with the work of Scotland's most famous composer, the Augustinian canon Robert Carver. [14]

That James was described by Lindsay as the "Prince of Poetry" (*The Flyting,* 21) suggests too a personal interest in literary composition. Various works have been attributed—for no very good reason—to the royal pen, but although we do not know exactly what James wrote, Lindsay's *Answer . . . to the Kingis Flyting* proves that write he did. "Redoutit Roy," Lindsay addresses James, "your ragement I haue red" (1). Unfortunately, this "ragement" no longer survives, but it is clearly a vigorous example of poetic flyting, a literary attack of an individual relying upon the techniques of invective and alliteration. Lindsay's reply illustrates the subject of James's taunts, the poet's prowess as a lover, suggesting too the bawdy style in which they were couched. We are obviously dealing here with written texts. Lindsay refers to James's "prunyeand pen" (6) and his "wennemous wryting" (21), but it seems equally obvious that these were poems designed to be read aloud, a poetic duel for the entertainment of the court. Similarly, *In Contemptioun of Syde Tallis* sees Lindsay urging James "To heir . . . with greit Pacience" (10) his appeal against the latest female fashions, and it is easy to imagine the mock petition being read in front of an amused court audience.

More elaborately staged plays represent a further element of courtly entertainment. This too was a communal activity, this time involving the interaction of courtiers and the semiprofessional players and guisers. Again, James took a personal lead, and we find payments for "certane play gounis to the Kingis grace to pas in maskerie." [15] Drawing on the traditional appointment of a King of Bean for the Twelfth Night or Uphaliday celebrations, the idea of the court as dramatis personae was deftly exploited by the Epiphany drama staged in 1540. Before their eyes, the king and his court see their own mirror image as another king and court assume center stage. Indeed, there is a multiplicity of kings. When the poor man enters, he asks to see the monarch but repudiates the actor playing the part, for there is but one king, "whiche made all and gouernethe all, whoe is eternall."[16] Neither is the actor the king of Scotland, "for ther was an other king in Scotlande that hanged John Armestrang with his fellowes." This confusion of royal identity cleverly underscores the play's politicoreligious message. As the surviving "nootes" on the play make clear, the Player-King is there only to observe the action (the complaint of the poor man and the deliberations of the estates), thereafter to ratify, approve, and confirm "all that was rehearsed." The very act of play watching blurs the royal personas. James's attendance at the performance is mimicked by the role of the Player-King—the silent watcher—and his applause at the end must echo the latter's approval of the proposed legislation. The bold juxtaposition of real and staged kingship invites the audience to approve of the play's evangelical message. As the Epiphany drama so forcefully illustrates, the often complex interaction of message, medium, and social context demands a more subtle interpretation than the overt political and religious statements articulated by the text. Context informs text as allegorical points were made more forceful by blurring the distinction between what was seen and what was staged. This is also true of *Ane Satyre* where the universal Rex Humanitas recalls—but does not represent—James V and where other characters undoubtedly evoke the existence of a real Wantonnes who, with "hir twa marrowis," entertained James IV, and too of a real Diligence Pursuivant active in the previous reign.[17]

When *Ane Satyre* sees Solace given license "to sing, / To dance, to play at Chesse and Tabillis, / To reid Stories and mirrie fablis, / For plesour of our King" (1835–38), we are powerfully reminded that, as well as being highly visual, Scottish court culture was also extremely aural. In addition to the musicians and singers, there was a strong tradition of tale-telling, poetry, and recitation. Identifying the tellers of such "Stories and mirrie fablis" is, however, far from easy. While payments to minstrels, musicians, and fools appear frequently in the accounts, references to tale-tellers and the like are far more sparsely scattered. The name of James Widderspune, fiddler and tale-teller, is unusual for being regularly recorded.[18] This apart, the accounts note only spasmodic payments for a relatively small group of largely anonymous "tale-tellers," "bards," and "bard wives," many of whom, like the "pure man [who] tald tales to the king" in 1507, appear to have been of low social status.[19] The nature of these tales is as uncertain as the identity of the tellers, but it seems probable that, like the ballads commonly sung to the king, many were part of a traditional oral culture. Clearly, though, this is not the whole story. Surviving poetry of the period, not least Lindsay's own, points to a thriving literature firmly grounded in the twin traditions of verbal and written communication. The exponents of this tradition experienced a different status at court and enjoyed a very different sort of recognition. Their position was at once more elevated yet more ambiguous than that of the poor tale-tellers, the "commoun bardis" contemptuously referred to by Lindsay in *The Testament of the Papyngo* (392). It has been suggested that this disparity was a result of developments in the business of court entertainment, for as the artistic tastes of the court grew at once more diverse and more sophisticated, the preeminent position hitherto enjoyed by minstrels was challenged by the appearance of more specialized entertainers; on the one hand, by a more precisely defined company of musicians, jugglers, and fools, and on the other by "men of letters."[20]

For these educated men, literary composition was generally combined with practical service in the household or secretariat. Undertaken over and above official duties, literary composition received no specific pecuniary reward; rather, it was simply another aspect of the totally committed service demanded by the medieval household. As John Bellenden explained,

> I was in service with the king;
> Put to his grace in yeiris tenderest
> Clerk of his comptis, thocht I was inding
> With hert and hand, and evry othir thing
> That micht him pleis in any maner best.
> (*The Proheme to the Cosmographe*, 29–34)[21]

The payments Bellenden received for his translations of Boece and Livy were something of the exception that proves the rule even Dunbar was attached to the court in the vaguest of terms with no reference to his prolific creativity.[22] Lindsay, of course, provides another example of courtier-poets in this position. His life was certainly that of a working courtier, and it was as such that he received his annual pensions and liveries. Bar the entry in the *Treasurer's Accounts* noting payment for his blue and yellow "play coit" in 1511, there is nothing in the financial records of the court to connect him with literary or dramatic pursuits.[23] Admittedly, Lindsay's position was somewhat different in that, as a herald, he was part of a rich chivalric culture, occupying a position increasingly associated with literary accomplishment. Building upon this aspect of his heraldic duties, he did not simply record James's valor in the lists or praise his name on diplomatic embassies, he also celebrated his kingship in his verse. A work such as *The Deploratioun,* for example, may be seen as a more elaborate version of the type of accounts heralds were expected to produce recording their business. In general, however, heralds tended to be less creative, focusing primarily on the composition of formal descriptions, technical treatises, and the translation of standard texts. While his background clearly provided Lindsay with a rich source of imagery and ideas and to some extent inspired his compositions, the explanation as to why Lindsay wrote as he did is not to be found in his office alone.

Literary composition, particularly that in the advice-to-princes tradition, was to some extent inspired by a very real sense of moral, spiritual, and indeed political duty. As John Ireland explained to James IV, his own work was penned for "luf and seruice of thi hienes and proffit of thi pepil and realme."[24] Such pious declarations can sound affected to modern ears, but to seek, as Ireland did, the "eternal saluacioun" of the king and his people was a goal as sincere as it was serious. A less altruistic motive for the composition of court poetry was of course the hope of reward. Although court poets enjoyed a rather ambiguous status, rarely accorded recognition as poets, they did expect their work to draw the attention and material gratitude of an approving patron-monarch. Lindsay, whose own petition for royal favor, *The Complaynt,* has striking affinities with the more well-known precatory poems of William Dunbar, is unusually explicit in stating that it is for his poetry, inter alia, that he expects reward.[25] Although he recalls his practical service in the household of the young James V, he makes the point that it is his failure to flyte or flatter, to indulge in base poetic techniques, which is responsible for his lack of advancement. Although he mocks his talent in conventional self-deprecatory terms, Lindsay makes clear that it deserves recognition:

> Althocht I beir nocht lyke ane baird,
> Lang seruyce, yarnis, ay, rewaird.   (49–50)

Stressing the link that ought properly to exist between poet and patron, he hopes that James "sall anis rewarde me, or I de, / And rube the ruste of my ingyne" (47–48). Significantly, perhaps, when Lindsay reminds James of the moral obligations of patronage and his own final judgment before God, he cites the example of David, "the gret Propheit Royall" (488) and also, of course, Old Testament poet.

In addition to fulfilling a sense of moral obligation and perhaps too as a way of reaping financial reward, poetry offered a means of participating more fully in court life, of tendering a service over and above that normally expected, of securing a unique position that anchored the poet to the court while simultaneously setting him apart from his fellow courtiers. This sense of a dual existence is powerfully conveyed by Lindsay's *Testament of the Papyngo* in which the poem's narrator is both courtier and poet, both participant and observer. Although identified simply as the king's "simpyll seruetour" (85) and keeper of his parrot, his fashionably alliterative treatment of the parrot's song and aureate description of the balmy morning mark him out as a poet of some distinction. Not only the narrator but the parrot too adopts this binary function, entertaining her fellow courtiers like "ane menstrall agane yule" (98) while at the same time acting as both mirror and critic.

Given the circumstances described above, it is clear that any search for the poets of the Stewart court has to go beyond the financial records. An obvious, if not entirely unproblematic, source is the evidence provided by the poems themselves. Dunbar's *Lament for the Makaris* contains a famous depiction of the wealth of Scottish literary culture during this period and a poignant illustration of its transience.[26] The same is true of Lindsay's *Testament of the Papyngo,* which opens with a catalogue of distinguished writers Lindsay himself hardly dares emulate. Like Dunbar, Lindsay introduces his litany of famous poets with reference to the revered triumvirate of Chaucer, Gower, and Lydgate before turning to a consideration of Scottish poets past and present. Dealing first with respected predecessors, Lindsay refers to Kennedy, Dunbar, Quintin, Mersar, Rowle, Henryson, Hay, Holland, and Gavin Douglas: "Thocht they be ded, thair libells bene leuand / Quhilkis to reheirs makeith redaris to reiose" (20–21).[27] Given that this is so clearly a court poem, it seems safe to assume that the literary tastes indicated by these lines reflect the tastes of the court. Obviously, then, the court was extremely catholic in its choice of literature. The authors listed here were responsible for an extraordinarily heterogeneous collection of work: the translation of classical and chivalric texts, romances, *moralitas,* allegorical beast fables, love poetry, religious verse. Aureate and blunt, elevated and profane, the stylistic range is equally broad.[28]

A similar range of literary activity and style is suggested by Lindsay's references to poets writing in the 1520s. Seven poets are specifically named: Inglis (already noted as an acquaintance of Lindsay), Kidd, Stewart, Stewart of Lorne, Galbraith, Kynloch, and Bellenden. Of the majority of these writers we remain sadly ignorant, able only to pluck names from the records and hazard a connection. Kynloch, for example, described by one commentator as "not otherwise known," could plausibly be Paul Kynloch, a household servant who in 1527 received "ane lettre . . . makand him court stewart to the kingis grace of his household, for his lifetyme," and the following year a grant of land in Freuchie, Fife.[29] Kidd's identity is equally obscure, but at least we may have an extant example of his work, *The Rich Fontane of Hailfull Sapience,* credited by Bannatyne to one "Alexander Kidd."[30] This may be the same Alexander Kidd who in 1534 was succentor of Aberdeen. It seems less likely that he was the burgess of Dundee of that name but, in truth, there is no real evidence to pin down this shadowy figure.[31]

The sixteenth-century manuscript collections, *Bannatyne* and *Maitland,* offer helpful clues to these poets, although with a name like Stewart positive identification remains elusive. No less than fourteen poems in these collections are ascribed to an author called Stewart.[32] Two of these appear to have been later compositions of Henry Stewart, Lord Darnley, but ten are attributed simply to "Stewart." Some may be by Lindsay's Stewart of Lorne, an apparent reference to Alan Stewart of Lorne, captain of the King's Guard.[33] Equally, perhaps more likely, some may be the work of William Stewart, the probable author of the remaining two Stewart poems, *Precelland Prince* and *This Hindir Nicht*.[34] This is probably that same William Stewart who sometime between 1531 and 1535 composed a verse translation of Boece's *Scotorum Historiae* which, according to the prologue, was written at the behest of a lady of the court, possibly Margaret Tudor. From the text we know that Stewart was a descendant of Alexander Stewart, first earl of Buchan, and he appears to have been a graduate of St. Andrews and to have been educated for the Church. The *Treasurer's Accounts* record various fees and liveries granted to Stewart, but precise identification is tricky and complicated by the existence of at least one other William Stewart, James V's treasurer, the bishop of Aberdeen.[35]

Among his contemporaries, Lindsay's highest praise is reserved for John Bellenden, famous for his translations of Boece and Livy and the author of four surviving poems: *The Proheme to the Cosmographe, Ballat vpone the Translatione, The Proheme to the History,* and *The Baner of Peetie.* The first three of these are prefatory works written to accompany the two translations, the fourth an interpretation of the popular Parliament of Heaven theme.[36] Lindsay, writing in 1530, describes Bellenden as a new arrival on the literary scene and, given that he had not yet begun his celebrated translations, this seems accurate enough. Three payments recorded in the *Treasurer's Accounts* reveal that it was in 1531 that Bellenden was commissioned to translate the *Scotorum Historiae,* and it is a comment upon the impact of Boece's work at court that it was at the same time that Stewart began his metrical translation. Two years later, Bellenden received payment for "ane new cornikle," a probable reference to his translation of Livy, payment for which is recorded immediately after.[37]

It has been suggested that Lindsay's Galbraith is the humanist lawyer and neo-Latin poet of that name.[38] However, given Lindsay's interest in and own commitment to his "vulgare toung" (*Testament of the Papyngo,* 10), this is perhaps questionable. Various Galbraiths are recorded at court in the first decades of the sixteenth century, and a far more plausible candidate is Thomas Galbraith, a chaplain of the Chapel Royal. Also an artist and illuminator of some repute, Galbraith is recorded as singing ballads to the king during the New Year celebrations of January 1491, on which occasion he was accompanied by Jock Goldsmith, a future King of Bean.[39] Even if this is the more likely identification, the work of neo-Latinists such as Robert Galbraith should not be overlooked. We have already noted the existence of the *Strena,* and other neo-Latinists were certainly at work, notably George Buchanan. In addition to playing its part in the cultural life of the Scottish court, neo-Latin verse also occupied an important position within a more mainstream European intellectual culture. However, while acknowledging the existence and importance of such literature, this study is limited to the vernacular. Not only was this the language used by Lindsay himself (with the possible exception of the short verse in the Armorial Manuscript), it was also the everyday language of the court. If William Stewart is to be believed, James was an uncomfortable Latinist:

> The Kingis grace I knaw is nocht perfite
> In Latin toung, and namelie in sic dyte
> It wilbe tedious, that dar I tak in hand,
> To reid the thing he can not understand.[40]

James's disrupted education seems to have been equally disastrous for his French, and on the occasion of his marriage a French observer was moved to comment that the king of Scots "savoit peu de langage françois."[41] Even allowing for exaggeration, it seems that, while the king set the lead, court culture was decidedly vernacular in tone. The emergence of Lindsay, Stewart, and Bellenden as the principal court poets of the reign reinforced this trend, encouraging too the lay character of court culture. Bellenden and Stewart were both clerics but, as the former explained, he composed his translation "mair for lawit men than ony curious clerkis."[42]

Although not nearly comparable in value to Lindsay's *Papyngo,* there is another poetic source which sheds at least some light on court poets writing in the 1530s. This is John Rolland's *Seuin Seages,* the prologue to which describes how

> In court that time was gude Dauid Lyndsay,
> In vulgar toung he bure the bell that day
> To mak meter, richt cunnynyng and expart,
> And maister Iohn Ballentyne suith to say
> Mak him marrow to Dauid well we may.
> And for the third, Maister William Stewart,
> To mak in Scottis, richt weill he knew that Art,
> Bischop Durie, sum tyme of Galloway,
> For his plesure sum tyme wald tak thair part.   (19–27)[43]

Rolland portrays himself as a student of these illustrious masters and, though this may be more metaphorical than literal (references in *The Seuin Seages* clearly date the poem to 1560), he certainly conveys the respect in which they were held. If Rolland is correct, Lindsay, Stewart, and Bellenden were the principal court poets of James V's reign. In addition, he introduces Andrew Dury, a more occasional versifier. (Previously abbot of Melrose, Dury was bishop of Galloway, 1541–58). Nothing of Dury's work remains, but his literary reputation is remarked upon by Knox, who recalled how Dury, "sometymes called for his filthines Abbot Stottikin . . . left his rymyng, wharewith he was accustomed, and departed this lyef."[44] This may be the same individual referred to in (William?) Stewart's poem, *Lerges of this New Yeirday:*

> Off galloway the bishop new
> Furth of my hand ane ballat drew   (15–16)[45]

This work also reveals something of the circumstances in which court poetry was composed. Here Stewart describes the creation of poems for a specific day, one traditionally associated with the dispensation of patronage, and for specific individuals—the king, his mother, churchmen, lords, and officials such as the Secretary and Treasurer—who respond with varying degrees of generosity. *The Testament of the Papyngo* can be read in a similar way as Lindsay describes how poets carve out a place at court, regularly offering compositions to the king. Indeed, Stewart, displaying the productivity that might be expected of the author of the *Metrical Translation,* is even described as turning out work on a daily basis. Patronage is crucial to success, and Bellenden's future glory as a poet depends upon his "auctoritie" (53) at court. The short staccato phrasing of such lines as "Bot, now, of lait, is starte upe, haistellie, / One cunnyng Clerk, quhilk wrytith craftelie" (49–50), perfectly conveys an undignified scramble for position.[46] Impressions of this babble are made all the more vivid by the portrayal of the barking, cawing, screeching, whistling parrot, who like Lindsay himself must strive to find an individual poetic voice able to be heard above the multitude.

Identifying individual court poets is arguably less important than recognizing the various ways in which they helped define the culture of the court. Like all literature, court poetry is fundamentally concerned with the affirmation, questioning, and subversion of its audience's preconceptions and values, often more than one of these elements being present in a single poem. An important aspect of this is the creation—or at least the fortification—of images of identity, a good example of which is found in *The Complaynt* where James is explicitly and extravagantly portrayed as a virtuous monarch who has brought peace and prosperity to his realm. However, this poem also provides an example of the way in which an image could be simultaneously enhanced and embarrassed, for the paean of praise sits uneasily between two rather more ambiguous discussions of aspects of James's kingship. First, although Lindsay carefully employs a traditional and amusing petitionary format and constantly affirms his own unworthiness, to criticize the monarch's patronage and his choice of counselors was, in fact, to lay a very serious charge against his kingship. For, as stated by Gilbert Hay, "honour and rewarde suld be ay geuin to worthy personis; and to extole folk that ar worthy to hye honouris, that is the honoure of princis."[47] Although Lindsay suggests that James was simply slow to action in this respect, it is clear that such behavior failed to measure up to the paradigmatic good kingship traditionally expounded in such works. *The Complaynt* further undermines James's reputation by suggesting that, if unrewarded, Lindsay will withdraw his petition (a threat that subtly intimates the withdrawal of feudal fealty) and redirect it to "the Kyng of blys" (484). This allows Lindsay to remind James not only of his power but also of his obligations:

> For thow art bot ane Instrument
> To that gret kyng Omnipotent.   (499–500)

This is particularly apt, as Lindsay's second criticism is of James's failure to deal with problems in the Church. Again this is presented simply as something James has yet to begin but, given that this is his second such offense, the audience is left questioning Lindsay's earlier encomium.

As discussed in the previous chapter, issues of patronage and reward also underlie *The Complaint of Bagsche* in which the misdeeds of a vicious and bullying hound gain him advancement at court. Again Lindsay obliquely criticizes James with a tale that recalls *The Thrie Prestis of Peblis* where the king who pardons a murderer is deemed responsible for his subsequent crimes; Bagsche may applaud James's determination to hang all transgressors but, as his own experiences show, miscreants were as likely to end up in the royal chamber as on the gallows. *The Complaint of Bagsche* embodies a message for its audience which is rendered all the more effective by that audience's knowledge of the poet's position within the royal household. The use of the first-person narrative conflates author and narrator, suggesting too a parallel between the court and the poem's canine community. Like the royal dogs, the members of the court are dependent upon James's— somewhat capricious—favor and, as Bagsche instructs his fellow hounds, so Lindsay is instructing his fellow courtiers. The domestic tone of both language and imagery together with references to actual persons of the court effectively turn this universal morality tale into a uniquely personal insight into one very specific household. It is possible that the apparently simple beast fable also worked at a deeper level within the context of the court intrigues of the 1530s. The tale of the dog who enjoys advancement at court and then turns on his former friends—Huntly, Bagsche's former guardian, becomes his "mortall Enemie" (58)—may contain a coded warning to the earl.[48] Although the evidence for such an interpretation is extremely slight (relying on references in the poem itself), this type of reading does alert us to the importance of court poetry as a vehicle for the discussion of factional politics, perhaps even the endorsement of one particular position.

The poem that most obviously fashions James's image according to his own taste is *The Deploratioun of the Deith of Quene Magdalene.* This is one of Lindsay's most formal works, written with deliberate reference to French poetic traditions and possibly intended, in part at least, for a French audience. The French deploration, "the genre of high ritual," was a common choice for obituary verse.[49] An elaborate composition structured according to rigid convention, it made heavy use of elevated, often highly latinized, language. Lindsay's *Deploratioun,* in acknowledgment of Scottish tastes, was much more secularized, more flexible, and less aureate than was common in France. As we shall see, James V was an enthusiastic devotee of the cult of chivalry and, in this poem, Lindsay drew heavily upon his own chivalric background to fashion a work calculated to appeal to his royal master. Throughout the poem, the imagery resonates with the spirit of the romance. The work opens with Lindsay's apostrophe to the villain of the piece and immediately the audience is put in mind of the battlefield:

> O Cruell Deith, to greit is thy puissance,
> Deuorar of all earthlie leuyng thingis.   (1–2)

Death is depicted as a "dreidfull Dragoun" which, with "dulefull dart" (15) failed to spare the young bride, "of Feminine the flour" (16). Such highly conventional imagery immediately conjures up the world of romance literature; this is a tale of doomed passion which falls strictly within the courtly love tradition. The marriage of James and Madelaine, in reality the culmination of a long-standing diplomatic arrangement precipitated by strategic concerns, is eulogized as the union of such "leill luffars" (39) as are without equal in the court of Venus. In order to heighten this impression, James V is compared to Leander who swam the Hellespont for love of Hero (a not wholly inappropriate reference given the difficulties of the royal visit to France and the various attempted sea crossings), and Madelaine is praised for the constancy of Penelope (a reference to the twenty years taken for the implementation of the Treaty of Rouen). The quixotic mission to view Marie de Vendôme unobserved strongly suggests James's enthusiasm for knightly adventure, and to cast the king in the role of quintessential romantic hero represented a calculated appeal to his tastes.

Shadows, however, cloud this glittering knightly ideal. Souring the atmosphere of courtly love, Lindsay introduces an earthly realism to his lament, berating Death not so much for parting Madelaine and "hir Prince and Paramour" (19) but for snatching the young bride before "we some fruct had of hir bodie sene" (28). The idealized *amour courtois* is more brutally undermined by *The Flyting,* in which the real world of the court is exposed as a place where love is allied not to noble ideals and chaste passion but to fornication, humiliation, and venereal disease. Shunning the picture of James as heroic lover in the knightly tradition, Lindsay describes him instead as "ane rude rubeator" (48) and "ane Furious Fornicatour" (49). Battle themes, focused particularly upon artillery, provide much of the poem's imagery: James must keep his powder dry and not shoot his bolt indiscriminately. "Be war with lawbouring of your lance" (67), Lindsay tells him. Instead of recalling the undoubted royal achievements in this field, the crude double entendre only debases the king's involvement further. Subverting images of battle and tournament to undercut James's reputation again reveals Lindsay's curiously ambivalent attitude to chivalric ideology. This is particularly surprising given both his own position and its popularity at court. Arguably, perhaps, it is these two factors—and his audience's appreciation of them—which make his unorthodox use of chivalric ideology such an effective device for questioning the values of the court.

MUCH INK has been spilled debating the extent to which chivalry animated lay culture in this period, but it seems clear that, in Scotland at least, the ethos exerted a powerful hold.[50] Within this context, the royal court was the prime focus for the most elaborate and impressive expressions of chivalric mores. It was also an area in which Lindsay as herald and Lyon King of Arms was heavily involved. Possibly the most immediate and spectacular exhibition of the court's commitment to the chivalric spirit was the tournament. By the sixteenth century, tournaments generally consisted of a series of individual jousts rather than the earlier *tournai* (team fights or mock battles), and it was not uncommon for combat to be undertaken in the guise of some traditional chivalric adventure, the details of which were frequently drawn from the pages of romantic literature. Certainly, such spectacle was familiar enough in Scotland. Tournaments organized in June 1507 and May 1508 involved the construction of a "Tree of Esperance" bearing carefully crafted leaves, flowers, and pears. The dramatis personae of the first tournament included beasts and "wild men" dressed in goatskins, and on both occasions competition centered around a black woman, the "Black Lady" of the *Treasurer's Accounts*. Other such events organized in the course of the reign (for example, to mark both the marriage of James IV and that of the English pretender, Perkin Warbeck, in 1496) were only the most splendid examples of a form of courtly entertainment regularly undertaken (most notably on Fastern's Eve, or Shrove Tuesday).[51] Lindsay's assessment of the court of James IV must have struck a chord with many who remembered the pageantry of the previous reign:

> And of his court, throuch Europe sprang the fame
> Off lustie Lordis and lufesum Ladyis ying,
> Tryumphand tornayis, iusting and knychtly game,
> With all pastyme accordyng for one kyng.
> *(The Testament of the Papyngo, 500—503)*

Although James IV is traditionally lauded as the acme of Scottish chivalry, his son was no less enthusiastic and his personal rule witnessed the continuation of royal patronage. Again the king was an ardent participant, and arrangements had to be made for his "harnes, speris and uther justing geir" to be transported around the country in the wake of the royal household.[52] In addition, tournaments were often arranged for important state occasions. Lindsay refers to the "aufull Tornamentis / On hors and fute" (*The Deploratioun,* 169–70) planned as part of the celebrations to welcome Madelaine to Scotland in 1537, and jousting took place the following year to mark the arrival of Mary of Guise.[53] Lindsay, responsible for the preparation of such events, would have been thoroughly familiar with all aspects of them. His expertise is finely demonstrated in *The Historie of Squyer Meldrum,* which relates at considerable length the arrangements surrounding the joust between the English champion, Sir Talbart, and the eponymous Squire. Although this particular encounter is set in France, it is probably fair to say that the passage offers a pertinent commentary on the Scottish tourney. Chivalry was a cosmopolitan creed, and its pursuits were universally practiced throughout western Europe. Lindsay himself recalled the "martial tournamentis" (*The Deploratioun,* 61) arranged for the Scottish court in France, and during his visit to the Low Countries in 1531 he witnessed "triwmphand Iustynis, . . . terribill turnememtis . . . feychtyn of fut in barras."[54] Writing from Antwerp, Lindsay told the Scottish Secretary that he had dealt with these events "at lenth, in articles, to schaw the Kyngis grace at my haym cumin." Unfortunately, Lindsay's account no longer survives, but that he thought to offer it in the first instance is powerful testimony both to James's well-known predilection for the pursuits of chivalry and his eagerness to ensure that he was *au fait* with the latest in European spectacle.

Arguably the most impressive statement of commitment to the chivalric code, the tournament was by no means the only token of allegiance to the values it upheld. The popular literature of the period and indeed that specifically commissioned by James V (the translations of Bellenden) were decidedly chivalric in character. Books of instruction, again essentially chivalric in tone, such as *The Buke of Gude Counsall to the King* and *The Porteous of Nobleness* and works such as *The Knightly Tale of Golagros and Gawane, Sir Eglamoure of Artoys* and *The ballad of . . . lord Barnard Stewart* (all among Chepman and Millar's first publications) testify to the appeal of this particular literary genre.[55]

Lindsay's poem *The Testament of the Papyngo* may offer a further clue to the chivalric ethos prevalent at court. When the dying bird casts her mind back to the various homes in which she has spent her life, she bids farewell to Stirling Castle with the words, "Adew, fair Snawdoun, with thy touris hie /

Thy Chapell royall, Park, and tabyll rounde" (633–34). The Round Table was the name formerly given to the King's Knot, an ornamental garden sited close to the tiltyard.[56] It was additionally a permanent reminder of the old legend recalling king Arthur's preservation of his Round Table in Stirling Castle.[57] This long-standing Arthurian association may well have inspired chivalric pageantry for although the phrase "round table" should not be taken to refer to an actual table, the reenactment of scenes from Arthurian romance was a popular theme, and a highly formalized type of tournament, itself called a Round Table, had been common at least until the end of the fourteenth century. Even if this had fallen into abeyance, it is likely that the basic motif remained popular.[58] This supposition is reinforced by the possibility that the court of James IV also saw such "counterfutting of the round tabill of King Arthour of Ingland," specifically during the great tournament of 1508.[59] Certainly, there were jousts held at Stirling on more than one occasion during the 1530s, and it is possible that the "tabyll rounde" fondly remembered by the Papyngo, herself a heraldic bird, was not simply a physical feature but rather a potent chivalric symbol of Stewart court culture.[60]

A further typical manifestation of chivalric culture at courts throughout Europe during the later Middle Ages and beyond was the existence of a lay order of knighthood identified with the sovereign. Such orders often did more than proclaim allegiance to the knightly cult, they also possessed the potential to engage chivalric values in the pursuit of political aims, binding the aristocracy together in the service of the sovereign.[61] The lay orders of Europe varied considerably from loose assemblies lacking any formal constitution to the much more formally structured, tightly controlled organizations generally described as monarchical orders. Two of the most renowned monarchical orders were those of the Golden Fleece (Burgundian) and of the Garter (English). For reasons of international diplomacy, both numbered James V among their members. Chivalric zeal coupled with European ambition rendered the Scottish king appreciative of such honors; he was keen to display his regalia before an admiring court, and in 1538 a goldsmith received payment for the repair of "the Kingis ordour and target."[62] It may even be that the "ordour" referred to here was not one which James had received from any foreign prince but the Scottish Order of the Thistle.

Although it has been suggested that it was founded by James III as early as 1470, little is known of the early history of the Thistle before its revival by James VII in 1687. It has been argued that until its reorganization in the seventeenth century, the Thistle was probably no more than a glorified retinue bearing the misnomer "order" on account of the misdirected enthusiasm of a ruler bent on emulating his European counterparts.[63] Indeed, given Scottish determination to pilot the court firmly within the mainstream of fashionable European culture, it is unlikely that there would not have been some attempt to imitate the great monarchical orders, potent symbols of the chivalric virtue and political authority of their founders. Fragmentary evidence suggests that Stewart kings at least entertained such notions, although the fact that the evidence is so patchy is in itself somewhat suspicious. Perhaps the most intriguing clue to Scottish aspirations in this respect is the observation of Chapuys, imperial ambassador at the English court, reporting on the decision to offer James the Order of the Garter in 1535.[64] "I am told by a Scotch doctor of theology," he wrote, "that the king [James V] declined to any oath, putting it off till he should have got ready his Order, so that he and Henry might take reciprocal oaths at the same time."[65] If Chapuys's Scotch doctor is to be believed, James V certainly hoped to compete with his uncle in what was almost a game of chivalric one-upmanship. (It may also be that James's desire for reciprocal oaths was not simply a matter of chivalric pride but the product of painfully acquired knowledge regarding the exploitation of ambiguous oaths to suit English imperial ambitions.) Chapuys's phraseology is open to interpretation: James must "dressé son ordre," and it is not altogether clear whether he had simply to make arrangements for the installation or whether more drastic action was required. At best, this exiguous scrap points to Scottish ambitions if not to an existing Scottish order.

If, however, we are looking for something more akin to a retinue or even just for the chivalric insignia associated with such an organization however loosely conceived, then we are on much firmer ground. The beginning of the sixteenth century witnessed an explosion of what might be termed thistle iconography associated with the crown, and the Book of Hours painted around 1503 by two Flemish painters, thought to be a wedding gift from James IV to his wife, includes an illustration of the royal arms which, for the first time, incorporates the collar of thistles characteristic of the Order as it is known today.[66] The insignia is also found on seals from the year 1512, and in 1539 it makes its first appearance on the coinage.[67] It may perhaps be no coincidence that the emergence of the chain of thistles coincides with the adoption of a collar by the Order of the Garter during the reign of Henry VII. Whether indicative of an order, a pseudo-order, or nothing more than Scottish pretensions, the thistle collar was an important element of the iconography associated with James V. (This trend was possibly enhanced by his second marriage as the thistle had also been appropriated as an emblem of Lorraine.)[68] For example, the south gate of Linlithgow Palace, constructed by James in the 1530s, bears four panels depicting not only the insignia of the Golden Fleece, the Garter, and St. Michael but also that of the Thistle. While these appear to date from the nineteenth century, it has been suggested that they are replicas of previous designs, although

Figure 5. "Portrait of James V." Courtesy of the Scottish National Portrait Gallery.

ignorance regarding the Thistle's early history has thrown the whole issue into confusion.[69] Additionally, there is the late-sixteenth-century portrait of James V which depicts him wearing the collar of the Thistle (see Fig. 5). Obviously this is not painted from life, yet other portraits in the same set suggest that, where possible, the artist used available likenesses. More convincing contemporary evidence is provided by the magnificent illustration of the royal arms in Lindsay's own Armorial Manuscript (reproduced by Davidson for *The Acts of Parliament* and Bellenden's *Chronicles*) which proudly displays the collar of thistles hung with the St. Andrew medallion (see Fig. 2). The profusion of thistle iconography suggestively presented as chivalric insignia clearly points to Stewart self-confidence and, in particular, to James V's determination to match his involvement in European politics with an appropriate symbol of Scottish kingship. The thistle was the visible emblem of a cult of Stewart kingship which, in the first half of the sixteenth century, was climbing toward its zenith.

HERALDS such as Lindsay were involved not only in the staging of tournaments and chivalric pageantry but also in what might be termed the state occasions of public ceremony: royal coronations, funerals, and, above all, royal entries. Here, the interaction between text and audience noted with regard to courtly literature now operated in a broader social context. Not only did the "text"—the staged tableaux and dramas—have a much larger, socially more diverse, audience; but, financed and organized by the burgh councils, it voiced the expectations of the crown's citizens rather than those of the crown itself.[70]

The ritualized acknowledgment of both change and continuity, the entry possessed important political symbols for both ruler and ruled. On the one hand, it betokened a reaffirmation of fealty coupled with reminders of how the new king was expected to behave; on the other, it represented an opportunity for the crown to confirm the town in its rights and privileges. Additionally, a royal entry provided the burgh with the opportunity to demonstrate its wealth and importance. Lavish gifts were made, the streets rang with music, and fountains flowed with wine; it must have been a day eagerly awaited by the ordinary townsfolk. The earliest detailed account of a Scottish royal entry was, in fact, penned by an Englishman, the herald who accompanied Margaret Tudor north in 1503.[71] He describes how, even before Edinburgh was reached, the party was delayed by the spectacle of one knight robbing another of his paramour, an event which allowed James to appear in his dual role as knightly defender and wise judge, restoring harmony by breaking up the brawl and ordering "a varey fayr Torney" to determine the issue. Once in Edinburgh, the royal couple was met by a procession which accompanied them past various tableaux and finally into church. The handing over of keys signified the welcome of the new queen while the kissing of holy relics sanctified the occasion, drawing Margaret into the spiritual life of the city. Three tableaux depicting the judgment of Paris, the Annunciation, and the marriage of the Virgin juxtaposed the physical and holy aspects of matrimony, while that showing the four cardinal Virtues, each with her foot on the neck of some reprobate (Nero, Holofernes, Epicurus, and Sardanapalus), may have expressed the hope that Margaret's influence would suppress any immoral tendencies in her wayward husband.

William Dunbar's poem, *Blyth Aberdein,* also illustrates something of the circumstances surrounding Margaret's entry to that city in May 1511.[72] Dunbar describes the queen's reception by the burgesses and her passage through the town beneath a red velvet canopy. The various tableaux that greeted her included depictions of the Virgin Mary, of Christ's Nativity, and of the expulsion of Adam and Eve from Paradise. The allegorical messages conveyed by these scenes were complemented by more concrete tokens, and the Nativity offering made by the three kings probably corresponded to an actual gift presented by the town. As these actor-kings were "schawand him [Christ] king with most magnificence" (28), so too the burgesses acknowledged Margaret's sovereignty. In addition to these biblical scenes (derived almost certainly from the traditional municipal miracle plays), the theme of legitimacy was underlined with representations of Robert Bruce, "nobill, dreidfull, michtie campioun" (35), and of the "nobill Stewarts" (36) bearing green leafy branches. Thus Margaret was tacitly reminded both of her husband's noble lineage and of her part in the dynasty's future. Whether Lindsay was part of the royal visitation is not clear. He was almost certainly at court at this date and associated with the queen's household. Unfortunately, the accounts covering the period are missing, and details of the trip are scanty. Nevertheless, even if not actually present himself, both Lindsay's position and Dunbar's poem assuredly guaranteed his familiarity with the proceedings.

Evidence for Lindsay's own involvement in the preparation of royal entries relates to three occasions: the abortive arrangements made for the 1537 reception of Madelaine and those for the entries of Mary of Guise to St. Andrews and Edinburgh the following year. *The Deploratioun of the Deith of Quene Magdalene* is more than a lament for James V's young bride. With its magnificent descriptions of James's own reception in Paris and of the preparations planned in Edinburgh, it represents a powerful evocation of the splendor of the king and the type of ceremony that surrounded his office. It is the detailed nature of this description that suggests Lindsay's close involvement in the preparations, confirming what might have been expected given his position. Many of the arrangements planned for Madelaine's entry duplicate those made over twenty-five years earlier in Aberdeen. The queen was to have been met by the city's burgesses; she would have passed through the streets beneath a canopy (this time of gold cloth) and witnessed vari-ous—unspecified—tableaux. The air was to have been filled with music, and once again the fountains should have run with wine.

The Deploratioun also demonstrates that Lindsay was not unaware of contemporary developments in European court pageantry. The increasing employment of imperial imagery derived largely from humanist scholar-ship has been well documented, particularly in connection with the French royal entries of the sixteenth century.[73] This trend, stunningly exemplified by Charles IX's Parisian entry in 1571, also influenced the celebrations for James's marriage on 1 January 1537 when, according to Lindsay, the king of Scots entered Paris "throw Arkis triumphall" (73).[74] Underlining the point and making absolutely clear the cultural frame of reference, Lindsay continues:

> For as Pompey, efter his Uictorie,
> Was in to Rome resauit with greit Ioy,
> So thou [Paris] resauit our richt redoutit Roy. (75–77)

Although there is little to suggest anything comparable in the Scottish entry celebrations, it is surely significant that alongside the traditional elements of Madelaine's entry outlined above,

> [They] suld have hard the ornate Oratouris
> Makand hir hienes Salutatioun,
> Boith of the Clergy, toun, and counsalouris,
> With mony Notable Narratioun. (162–65)

The employment of "Oratouris" (a contemporary term for humanists) again points to an identification with Renaissance-style ceremony. Details con-cerning the speeches planned for this occasion no longer survive, but we do know that when Mary of Guise entered Edinburgh in July 1538 the wel-come address was "devysit with avyse of Maister Adame Otterburn, Maister James Foulis and Dauid Lyndsay."[75] In tribute to Mary, this was delivered in French, but the fact that Otterburn and Foulis were both accomplished neo-Latin poets suggests that traditional motifs received a humanist-inspired gloss. Although Michael Lynch is probably correct to consider the baptism of James VI in 1566 the first full-blown Renaissance spectacle seen in Scotland, *The Deploratioun* demonstrates that the foundations for such pag-eantry had been laid several decades previously.[76]

Mary's Edinburgh entry staged, significantly perhaps, on St. Margaret's Day, 1538, and made "with gret triumphe, and als with ordour of the haill nobillis," was clearly the occasion for immense civic pride: Orders were issued for the cleaning of the streets and the banishment of beggars, all citizens were to wear their best clothes, and strict instructions were set down as to who was to seek the queen's company.[77] It is interesting to note that when afforded this traditional opportunity for urban self-expression, the burgesses turned to Lindsay, seeking his advice "anent all ordour and furnesing."[78] As illustrated by *The Deploratioun,* Lindsay was skilled in articulating the type of communal emotion appropriate to such public spectacle but, as this poem also reminds us, he also wrote with one eye upon the expectations of the crown. Exactly what Lindsay contributed to the "greit sportis playit . . . throw all the pairtis of the toun" is unknown, but his involvement effectively conveys the way in which such ceremony sought to bind ruler and ruled in a carefully constructed web of well-controlled ritual.[79] Unfortunately, nothing is known of the actual entry tableaux that greeted Mary on this occasion for there is no source comparable to Pitscottie's description of her earlier entry into St. Andrews:

And first scho was ressavit at the New Abbay geit. Wpon the eist syde thair was maid to hir ane trieumphant frais be Schir Dawid Lyndsay of the Mount, lyoun harrot, quhilk causit ane gret clude come out of the heavins done abone the yeit quhair the quene come in, and oppin in two halffis instantlie and thair apperit ane fair lady most lyke ane angell havand the keyis of haill Scotland in hir handis deliuerand thame into the quens grace in signe and taikin that the heartis of Scottland was opinit to the ressawing of hir grace; witht certane wriesouns and exortatiouns maid be the said Dawid Lyndsay into the quens grace instructioun quhilk teichit hir to serue her god, obey hir husband, and keep hir body clene according to godis will and commandement.[80]

This device was a common one. Appearing as part of the festivities associated with the 1507 tournament, it had featured in previous entries and would do so again in future celebrations.[81] Long-established ritual, confirming existing relationships and countering the threat of the new, was extremely important on these occasions.

The increasing recourse to the imagery of classical Rome found in royal pageantry and noted in *The Deploratioun* has led one historian to pronounce the imperial ideal "a necessary preliminary to the study of the ethos and symbolism of the national monarchies of Europe as they developed in the Renaissance period."[82] Articulated through the medium of court spectacle, this ideal was embodied not simply in the proliferation of classical imagery but more importantly in the concept of empire as it related to the authority exercised by the temporal ruler within his realm. References to "empire" and matters "imperial," therefore, assume special significance, reinforcing ideas of national autonomy and identity. This was certainly true in England where the concept of empire was an integral element of the Henrician

Reformation. However, though Lindsay did on occasion refer to James V in imperial terms, it is clear that this was not designed to make a specific political point.[83] Although Lindsay was no doubt aware of the political implications of imperial imagery and indeed was sympathetic to it, his use of such language is highly conventional (usually to flatter) and, if there is anything novel here, it is the self-conscious adoption of a fashionable nomenclature designed primarily in this case to evoke the triumph and glory which was ancient Rome (perhaps only subconsciously reinforcing the national identity of the realm). Significantly perhaps, when in *Ane Satyre* Divyne Correctioun urges Rex Humanitas to replace his corrupt clerics, the image he uses is not one of empire but of congregation:

> Ye ar the head sir of this congregatioun,
> Preordinat be God omnipotent.   (3329–30)

Symbolic expressions of kingship were also transmitted through the two most solemn ceremonies surrounding the office: the coronation and the royal funeral. As previously discussed, officers of arms played an important part in the coronation ritual, the Lyon King affirming the king's willingness to accept the crown, bearing one of the jugs of oil with which he was anointed, rehearsing the royal genealogy, and announcing the king's arrival to his people. Lindsay himself was not involved in such a ceremony, for James V was crowned at Stirling shortly after his father's death, and the coronation of Mary, like her father an infant in arms, was a muted affair. However, he probably played a role in the coronation of Mary of Guise in February 1540. Preparations for the event date from what was probably the announcement of Mary's pregnancy the previous October when John Mosman received payment "for making of the Quenis crowne and furnesing of stanis thairto." Payments are also recorded for the gilding of her silver scepter, for the hanging of tapestries, for the transportation of "the chapell gair" from the Chapel Royal and the expenses of eleven chaplains, for boards erected in Holyrood Abbey, for munitions transported to Edinburgh Castle, and for summoning "the dammes" and "ladyis."[84] Little is known of the actual ceremony (which presumably differed quite considerably from that of the sovereign himself) although we do know that the occasion was celebrated in the traditional fashion with jousts and tournaments.[85]

The 1530s saw new regalia prepared not only for Mary of Guise but also for James V. Indeed, James appears to have nursed a peculiar obsession with this particular symbol of his authority. The early 1530s saw various repairs to it, and in February 1540, in time for his wife's coronation, he took delivery of a new crown, fashioned of Scottish gold and encrusted with twenty-three jewels including three great garnets and an emerald.[86] In this respect, it seems that imperial connotations were being more consciously evoked for it is surely significant that this new crown was crafted after the imperial fashion with a closed diadem. Imperial crowns had become popular in Europe during the late fifteenth century, and although James was probably the first Stewart monarch to have one actually made, coins issued by his grandfather depict a closed crown. The emergence and gradual acceptance of the idea of an imperial Scottish crown can also be seen in the evolution of the royal arms. A late-fifteenth-century roll of arms (incorporated into an English collection and probably compiled in England) depicts the traditional open crown. By the beginning of the sixteenth century, however, the closed crown appears in the Book of Hours commissioned by James IV in 1503.[87] It clearly took some time for the idea to take hold, and a sketch made in the Exchequer records by a royal official in 1538 still pictures the traditional open crown.[88] Significantly, however, when Lindsay drew up his Armorial Register four years later (and after James had refashioned his regalia), the crown of Scotland he depicts is closed; the Scottish imperial crown had been firmly installed in Stewart iconography.[89] Although no doubt partly inspired by the desire to follow continental fashion, the adoption of the imperial crown seems a much clearer indication that the Stewarts, James V in particular, were both aware of the political messages implicit in such imperial imagery and prepared to use it.

One crucial symbolic expression of kingship beyond James's control was his own funeral. Scholarly studies, particularly of the French Renaissance funeral ceremony, have highlighted the implications such an occasion had for perception of kings and kingship.[90] Unfortunately, evidence relating to Scotland remains patchy, and a fully comprehensive analysis is unlikely. Nevertheless, the royal funeral merits attention, especially as it represented another sphere of public spectacle in which Lindsay as Lyon King was involved. The heraldic funeral accorded aristocratic and royal families was a complex and extravagant affair.[91] Like the entry, it countered potential disruption with a rigorous adherence to a prescribed formula stressing the essential continuity of the noble house or royal dynasty and, by glorifying the ideal of the chivalric knight, heaping honor on the departed and his lineage. Lindsay's poem *The Testament of Squyer Meldrum* incorporates a detailed description of a typical heraldic funeral, organized in this instance by the eponymous squire's old friend, Lindsay himself. The wishes of Squire Meldrum include a costly embalmment (his heart and tongue to rest in separate jeweled caskets), an expensively carved cedar or cypress coffin, a carved marble tomb, and an elaborate funeral procession, the mourners to comprise thousands of armed soldiers and footmen and 100 mounted knights. In time-honored fashion, the Squire's arms and weapons were to be borne before the altar. Fond memories of an old friend together with the demands of Lindsay's chosen genre may have led him to depict a more lavish internment than might be expected for the relatively humble squire, and the royal funeral of James V in 1542 would have been a similar, only slightly more splendid, affair.

Royal funerals, particularly those in England and France, were impressive manifestations of the dignity, power, and splendor of the royal estate, and one would venture that the close cultural links the self-consciously European Scots enjoyed with both these countries would have engendered a fierce desire to emulate, as far as more limited means allowed, the ceremonies of their neighbors.[92] The meager evidence relating to Scottish funerals is, however, frustrating. James V's immediate predecessors all died unexpectedly and in violent circumstances, and the hurried arrangements made for their interment are far from satisfactorily recorded. Even when we come to that of James V, the evidence is sparse (two pages of the *Treasurers' Accounts* covering the crucial period are missing), but what there is does tend to support the view that the Scots sought to model their ceremonial on continental patterns. The scene that emerges is very similar to the illustration of the dirge for the king of Scots (James III) found in the Vienna Book of Hours. Significantly, the picture of the black-draped coffin, the black hangings, and the royal arms appears in other manuscripts illuminated by the same artists which, bar the Scottish heraldry, are identical in every detail.[93] Clearly the continental artists were working to a standard model, a model which almost seems to have been used again in December 1542. Then, payments were recorded for the "clayth of stait," which seems to have been of black velvet with a white satin cross, lined with black buckram and fringed with black silk. The "Dolorous Chapell" was painted with clubs and spears "all of blak collouris" and payment made for the timber needed to prepare the church. This was authorized by Lindsay, who in his capacity as Lyon King also arranged payment for sixteen foot of cast lead (presumably for the coffin) and for the masonry on the tomb. He also ordered gold cloth, purple taffeta, red cord, and red and gold silk for the royal coat of arms. In addition, a banner was painted with "gold and fyne collouris," the same artist also being employed for the coloring and painting of an effigy, crown, scepter, and shield.

The reference to an effigy is particularly noteworthy. Royal funeral effigies seem to have appeared first in England in 1327, thereafter becoming a regular feature of English, and after 1422 of French, royal obsequies. It has been suggested that the display of the effigy represented an inversion of the natural order whereby the normally invisible body politic of the king was, for once, on display, while his visible natural body lay hidden in the coffin.[94] Symbolically—and constitutionally—the king never dies. The significance of the effigy in England and France was not, however, the same. In the former it played a more pragmatic role as the focus of attention during the lengthy internment arrangements and did not, as in France, possess the profound symbolic meaning that leads one historian to describe it as "the chief actor in a full-fledged ritual of state."[95] The origins of this veneration of the effigy were classical rather than ecclesiastical in character, reinforcing the emergence of a new triumphal element into the proceedings analogous to that noted earlier in the pageantry associated with the living sovereign.[96] The extent to which the Scottish royal funeral effigy symbolized such ideas remains debatable, but its introduction into Scotland certainly suggests the attempted emulation of European Renaissance ceremony. (A manuscript illustration of the funeral of Alexander III—admittedly almost 250 years earlier—depicts a much simpler affair; the royal coffin is modestly covered, there is no regalia and no effigy.)[97]

THROUGH the literature of the court and the pageantry of state occasion, a range of kingship images was created. The reign of James V in particular witnessed a diversity of contrasting images with the king being variously presented as ideal prince, glorious knight, courtly lover, patron of art and learning, and even the enthusiastic participant in more undignified romps. It is a comment on the talent and flexibility of the part-time poets and pageant masters that such variety existed within a recognizably coherent court culture. This is not to suggest that these images were necessarily bound together harmoniously. Representations of kingship frequently expressed political aspirations which, given the nature of all aspirations, frequently went unrealized. This left the poet with two basic options: Either he could paper over the cracks, his poetry suggesting that what should be is, or he could expose the gulf between the ideal and the real, calling—subtly or otherwise—for reform. As this discussion has shown, both stratagems were adopted by Lindsay, although even apparently laudatory works were undercut by a more realistic, less encomiastic approach. As Lindsay himself commented, poetry conquers mortality and reputation defeats death (*The Deploratioun*, 194–96). But while this is certainly true, the work of court poets, not least his own, served to render this a more dubious legacy than might otherwise be expected.

SIX

Community and Commonweal

Although the dominant figure in Lindsay's political analysis was the king, and the chief cultural apparatus that shaped his thinking was the court, it would be wrong to consider Lindsay solely a "court poet." Changes in the political status quo together with his own withdrawal from court life heralded a critical shift in his work. For while the twin themes of government and kingship retained their commanding position in Lindsay's thinking, later works saw his most indispensable ideas and images lifted from the intimate environment of the court and set in a much broader sociopolitical context. Of course, the transition in Lindsay's thought was not as abrupt as this might suggest. The figure of the king had never existed in conceptual isolation and, however central he was to political discourse in the sixteenth century, he had always engaged with other ideas and constructs. After all, the paradigmatic monarch was tightly bound by a perceived double obligation to God on the one hand and to his subjects on the other. Examining this sovereign—subject bond and the various ways in which it was discussed during the sixteenth century sheds important light on changing social and political attitudes in Renaissance Scotland. In this respect, the work of David Lindsay was enormously influential as, drawing on traditional notions of good government, he refashioned some thoroughly familiar ideas with reference to the rather more novel concept of the commonweal. This was the cornerstone of Lindsay's sociopolitical vision, and as such it provided him with an essential framework for monarchical government. The king, "Quha tyll the Commoun-weil hes ay bene kynd" (*Ane Satyre*, 2554), is its protector and guardian. King and commonweal enjoy a symbiotic relationship, and the maintenance of the commonweal is synonymous with good kingship. Gradually, however, this paternalistic view is displaced by one in which the idea of the commonweal, dynamic rather than passive, emerges as the dominant element of the discussion. This subtle shift in the equation, epitomized in *Ane Satyre of the Thrie Estatis*, is hardly surprising given the fact that after 1542 Scotland had neither an adult king nor the prospect of one for some time to come. Indeed, it is testimony to the enduring importance of the king that, despite Lindsay's attempts to modify his political analysis, he remained such a prominent feature of his thinking.

LINDSAY'S conceptualization of society was shaped and articulated by two basic ideas, one extremely conventional, the other a relative newcomer to Scottish political thought. First, he utilized the ultratraditional framework of a divinely ordained, strictly hierarchical society bound together by a mutual concern for the common good on earth and spiritual salvation in the hereafter. Here it should perhaps be stressed that an undeniable sympathy for the plight of the oppressed makes Lindsay neither a democrat nor a revolutionary.[1] In traditional fashion he stressed the interdependence of society's members, rich and poor; he called for an improvement in the lives of the latter but offered no redefinition of the social status quo. Divyne Correctioun's reforming mission operates strictly within the established social hierarchy. "To rich and pure I beir ane equall band," he cries, "That thay may liue into thair awin degrie" (*Ane Satyre*, 1599–600). A telling example of Lindsay's social conservatism is the scurrilous description of two humble household servants found in *The Iusting betuix Iames Watsoun and Ihone Barbour*. Lindsay's amusing mock-tournament poem forms part of a well-established literary tradition and, although his use of two recognizable contemporary figures may have had a personal, even malicious, purpose, the basic joke was against the stereotypical lower classes attempting— and ludicrously failing—to overturn the natural social order. This type of humor was extremely popular and was used by Lindsay on more than one occasion, notably in the comic scenes in *Ane Satyre*. His attitude, however, was not as simplistic as this might suggest, and the crude stock characters so beloved of medieval audiences existed alongside a more thoughtful analysis.

The traditional tripartite division of society differentiated according to function (those who fight, those who pray, and those who labor) was powerfully ingrained in Scotland's political consciousness. Indeed, even after 1587 and the introduction into Parliament of the shire commissioners or lairds, the old estate terminology still prevailed.[2] Nevertheless, exactly what this tells us about conceptions of society is not altogether straightforward, especially when it appears in a literary context. Very often what is common knowledge is left unsaid or else is expressed through well-worn but hardly realistic social stereotypes—an easy shorthand method of describing a more complex reality. This is particularly true with respect to drama where stock characters have a function beyond that of social description and, although the traditional estate terminology provided Lindsay with a useful and readily understood means of representing the collective and individual aspects of Scottish society, it was the idea of the commonweal which shaped both his analysis and the language in which it was framed. Etymologically connected to such Latin expressions as *bonum commune* and *utilitas publica,* the term "commonweal" refers essentially to a state of universal well-being.[3] First appearing in Scotland at the beginning of the sixteenth century (probably entering the language via English sources), it had a swift yet enduring impact on political discourse in Renaissance Scotland. Though it occurs only once in the works of Dunbar and of Douglas, by the late 1520s the term could be comfortably appropriated as a character in Lindsay's *Dreme.* Rooted in the Aristotelian view of the *bonum commune* as the true end of good government, the development of the idea was also fostered by humanist-inspired notions of public service and civic responsibility.[4] The literary emergence of the term—it appears frequently in Bellenden's *Chronicles,* for example—was paralleled in official sources. References to the commonweal in *The Acts of Parliament,* only sporadic before the 1520s, occur much more frequently thereafter, being used for such important legislation as the 1540 confirmation of James V's Act of Revocation.[5] Lindsay draws on these connotations in his own mock petition *In Contemptioun of Syde Tallis,* and when he declares that long gowns trail through the dust, "Expres agane all Commoun weillis" (16), the serious parliamentary language ensures the effectiveness of his poetic exaggeration.

The early decades of the sixteenth century saw the commonweal firmly installed in the political vocabulary of sixteenth-century Scots. As Roger Mason has commented, the term was "a highly effective rhetorical shorthand for both the community's sense of collective identity and the public responsibilities of its members."[6] Rallying the community in the defense of the commonweal could encompass both an emotive plea for good government and a clarion cry for national defense. As such, the idea was readily appropriated to the patriotic cause. Certainly by the late 1540s, the commonweal carried with it those connotations of freedom and independence which traditionally conditioned Scottish thinking about kingdom and kingship alike.[7] Bellenden's *Chronicles* and Wedderburn's *Complaynt of Scotland* both use the term in this way, and such examples are easily multiplied. One example we cannot cite in this context, however, is that of David Lindsay whose work, ironically enough, did so much to establish the term in popular consciousness. Just as he eschews the idea of king as military commander and knightly hero, so in his discussion of the commonweal, Lindsay ignores the term's undeniably aggressive connotations and instead uses it as a vehicle for the discussion of good government.

This is not to suggest that Lindsay was in some sense unpatriotic. On the contrary, he was profoundly concerned for Scottish peace and prosperity but, at the same time, he did not care to foster a strong sense of national identity based upon armed conflict in the cause of political autonomy.

Indeed, like that similarly nonnationalistic patriot, John Mair, Lindsay believed that Scottish peace and prosperity depended upon union between England and Scotland. His position was neither as forcefully nor as comprehensively articulated as Mair's, but he would assuredly have joined him in praying "that one of its [Britain's] kings in a union of marriage may by just title gain both kingdoms for any other way of reaching an assured peace I hardly see."[8] *The Tragedie of the Cardinal* expresses Lindsay's deep regret at the failure of proposals for just such a dynastic union (197–98), while *The Monarche* echoes Mair's words still more explicitly:

> I dreid that weir makis none endyng,
> Tyll thay be, boith onder ane kyng.   (5410–11)

This is not to suggest that Mair was the source for this idea; the latter's *History* was published in 1521, and Lindsay's stance can only be dated to the mid 1540s. Moreover, although not widespread, there was at least some Scottish support for ideas of dynastic union in the mid sixteenth century. James Henrisoun, for example, albeit living and writing in England, also advocated such a step as a remedy for social dislocation.[9] Though the two examples cited above represent Lindsay's only categorical statements on the subject of union, Dr. William Bullein's intriguing *Dialogue against the Feuer Pestilence,* written less than ten years after the poet's death, suggests a more substantial unionist reputation.[10] The beginning of the *Dialogue* describes a vision of various poets—Gower, Skelton, Chaucer, Lydgate, Barclay, and Lindsay—each of whom delivers a characteristic speech (for example, Skelton pokes fun at Wolsey, Lydgate describes the slippery fortunes of princes). Lindsay then steps forward to proclaim British unity in opposition to the curse of Rome and the power of France:

> *Habitare fratres in unum*
> Is a blesfull thyng,
> One God, one faith, one baptism pure,
> One lawe, one lande, and one kyng.

Obviously, this stirring speech has a polemical purpose, and it is equally obvious that Lindsay could have been posthumously coopted to the unionist cause in the same way that he was marshaled into the Protestant ranks—his credentials dubious on both counts. Nevertheless, it is tempting to conclude that Lindsay's enthusiasm for union between England and Scotland was more familiar to his contemporaries than the evidence of his surviving works suggests.

In the first half of the sixteenth century such views were held by a minority of Scots only. Far more representative of contemporary thinking was the erstwhile anglophile, Adam Otterburn, whose English sympathies evaporated in the face of the proposed dynastic alliance of 1543. Lamenting the fact that Scotland had the "lass" and England the "lad," he declared to Sadler that "Our nacyon, being a stout nacyon, will never agree to have an Englishman to be a king of Scotland. And though the hole nobilitie of the realme wolde consent unto it, yet our comen people and the stones in the strete wolde ryse and rebelle agenst it."[11] It was, however, unlikely that the "hole nobilitie" would countenance such a dynastic union. George Douglas expressed the fears of many when he claimed that the marriage would lead to the economic debilitation of Scotland, "for then both the realmes shuld be as one, and Skotland clerely undone." The Scots, he asserted, "do desire to have a king amonges theym selves for their owne wealthe as they have alweys had."[12] For Lindsay, however, the question of national identity was not irrevocably bound up with the Stewart dynasty and the ideal of political independence. The pursuit of peace in the name of the commonweal was infinitely more important than rallying the nation to its armed defense.

Lindsay's work makes clear his belief that good government was crucially dependent upon peaceful conditions for, as expressed by Dame Rememberance in *The Dreme,* "Iustice may nocht have Dominatioun, / Bot quhare Peace makis habitatioun" (867–68). This attitude, already evident in the late 1520s, was reinforced by Lindsay's own experiences during the Rough Wooing:

> Had we with Ingland kepit our contrackis,
> Our nobyll men had leuit in peace and rest,
> Our merchandis had nocht lost so mony packis,
> Our commoun peple had nocht bene opprest;
> (*The Tragedie of the Cardinal,* 197–200)

Of course there was nothing new in the realization that war was the cause of much social and economic hardship, but demands that this consideration should determine policy decisions were now being expressed with a new brand of conviction. While no less than twelve "gret proffitis [and] vtiliteis of peace" are listed in Ireland's *Meroure of Wyssdome,* for example, less than half relate, even vaguely, to matters of statecraft.[13] The way of peace is the way of Christ, it honors God and defies the Devil, Christian worship requires peace: These are more typical of Ireland's arguments. What has been dubbed "a transformed peace discourse" offered an alternative approach to the problem, one which hammered home the antiwar message by stressing the benefits that peace bought of and for itself.[14] It has been suggested that in England at least a new approach to questions of war and peace (influenced both by English experiences in France and by Christian humanism) became increasingly linked with the idea of the commonweal.[15]

The powerful peace ethic advanced in Lindsay's work and in particular the association between peace and the maintenance of the commonweal illustrate similar developments north of the border. Certainly the belief that yoked peace and the commonweal so firmly together was particularly important for thinkers such as Mair and Lindsay, enabling them to adopt a position that was at once both pacifist and patriotic.

Such a stance was also made possible by adopting another approach to the question of war and by viewing it as God's punishment of a wicked people. His commitment to the idea of the commonweal notwithstanding, Lindsay also interpreted war in this way (*The Monarche*, 46–54, 415–25). But while other authors writing in this vein combined demands for spiritual and moral rehabilitation with a vigorous call to arms,[16] Lindsay remained content to plead the cause of reform: "quhen that the peple doith repent, / Than god sall slak his bow, quhilk yit is bent" (*The Monarche*, 70–71). Even though he chose not to rouse his fellow Scots in the armed defense of their nation, by suggesting that repentance and subsequent divine reward would enable Scotland to operate independently of France, Lindsay could still lay claim to patriotic credentials:

> Pray thame that thay putt nocht thare esperance
> In mortall Men onelye, thame tyll aduance,
> Bot principallye in God omnipotent.
> Than neid thai not to charge the realm of France
> With Gounnis, Gallayis, nor vther Ordinance.
>
> (*The Monarche*, 91–95)

As much psychological as political, the ideal of the commonweal conveyed very real feelings of organic unity, physical dynamism, and a very emotive patriotism. Nowhere is this more vividly conveyed than in Lindsay's dramatization of John the Commonweal. It should perhaps be stressed at this point that the character of John, despite his often hungry and ragged appearance, was not a symbolic representation of "the poor" or even, more specifically, of the rural poor. When Lindsay required such a figure he introduced the Pauper or the traditional "John Upland."[17] John the Commonweal on the other hand represents the universal and public good of the entire community and not the interests of any single element. He is the dramatic embodiment of a principle, not a party, an ideal and not an individual.

The collective ideal articulated through the characterization of the commonweal was a fundamental principal of political theorizing throughout the Middle Ages. The distinction between common and singular profit had long been utilized to define what constituted acceptable social—and indeed political—behavior.[18] Unsurprisingly, the theme appears frequently in Lindsay's work, in particular in his discussion of the commonweal.[19] For example, in *The Dreme,* the victory of self-interest is portrayed as the root cause of the failures of the various regency administrations, John the Commonweal being abused and finally banished by the personified concept of "singulare proffect" (969–73). Over twenty-five years later, Lindsay uses the notion of singular profit in *Ane Satyre,* once more invoking it to explain the miseries experienced by John the Commonweal:

> With singular profeit he hes bene sa supprysit,
> That he is baith cauld, naikit and disgysit.   (3767–68)

The twin concepts of singular and common profit so deeply embedded in medieval thinking also received frequent expression in a chivalric context. They can be found, for example, in the works of Gilbert Hay, particularly his translation of *The Buke of Knychthede,* which it should be noted displays a much greater concern for this theme than its French source.[20] This stress upon responsibility to the community lay at the heart of the mythical foundations of knighthood: As Hay puts it, "The office is foundit ay on gude and proffitable werkis that ar spedefull to the commoun proffit."[21] In the same type of chivalric context, we also find the appearance of the actual phrase "commonweal":

To ane knycht appertenys that he be lover of the comyn weil. For by the comynalte of the peple wes the cheualry fundin and stablissed. And the comyn wele is grettar & mair necessary than propir gud and speciale.[22]

This passage is taken from the Loutfut Manuscript, which includes a transcript of Caxton's translation of *The Ordre of Chyvalry,* made in 1494 by Adam Loutfut, Kintyre Pursuivant, at the direction of William Cumming of Inverallochy, Marchmont Herald and later Lyon King of Arms. A further copy was made around the year 1530 by John Scrymgeour, and another in 1591 by Lindsay's brother, also Lyon King.[23] Both versions use the same commonweal terminology.[24] That the text was well known to Lyon Kings previous and subsequent to Lindsay suggests that he too was acquainted with it and, if this is so, then it probably contributed to the development of his commonweal thinking. Interestingly, in the corresponding passage of Hay's manuscript, the latter refers to a knight's obligation "tobe amorous of the commoun prouffit and of the commouns."[25] This cumbersome phraseology is typical of Hay, and it illustrates that, while the concepts fundamental to the commonweal ideal and the duties of civic responsibility it entailed were well established in fifteenth-century Scotland, the language used to articulate them had yet to emerge. The work of David Lindsay—drawing indirectly on English chivalric sources—clearly contributed to the process by which it did so.

Lindsay, uncomfortable about many aspects of the chivalric ideology, was profoundly appreciative of the stress it laid upon common profit. He therefore sought to isolate and to elevate this particular tenet of the knightly code, thereby providing a revised pattern for secular achievement and one more appropriate for men of his own social background. We can perhaps see in Lindsay what may be termed the attempted "dechivalrization" of the knightly ideal, the elements of martial prowess, courtly love, and elaborate ceremonial being stripped away to leave the core concepts of justice and public service relocated in the commonweal. This may help provide an answer to what has been described as one of the central problems for the student of chivalry in the Renaissance: how to explain the metamorphosis of knight into courtier or gentleman.[26] Perhaps the most commonly cited answer to this conundrum is the influence exerted by the ideals of civic humanism. This type of thinking is clearly discernible in works such as Thomas Starkey's *Dialogue between Pole and Lupset* which, as well as celebrating Ciceronian ideas of civic responsibility for the commonweal, also draws on the traditional Aristotelian concept of society "lyvyng togydder in cyvyle lyfe accordyng to the excellent dygnyte of the nature of man every parte of thys body agreying to other."[27] However, it is equally clear that the impulse for change also lay within traditional chivalric thinking and, given Lindsay's professional position and the *mentalité* of the Scottish court, this was surely a more important influence on his political development.

The cult of chivalry had always represented a somewhat uneasy alliance between an aggressive individualism on the one hand and a sense of social responsibility on the other: The lone knight-errant in search of adventure was hardly the best guardian of public order. It is perhaps significant that in Scotland individual achievement and bravery were often downplayed in favor of Christian obligation toward the community. For Lindsay, though, this sense of social responsibility was expressed in the language of the commonweal rather than that of chivalric morality. Nowhere is this process of reorientation more clearly seen than in *The Historie of Squyer Meldrum* where heroic adventurer is gradually transformed into country gentleman. Superficially, the poem appears to fall squarely within the romantic tradition. Like any popular chivalric biography, the work is based upon allegedly real episodes but incorporates practically every traditional motif available to Lindsay. The rescue of a maiden, victory against all odds, the prophetic dream, the sleepless lover, the dawn walk, the feminine lament over the fallen hero, all demonstrate Lindsay's complete familiarity with the genre. It is, however, a genre which, as one commentator has observed, "Lindsay could no longer take quite seriously."[28] Although on one level *Squyer Meldrum* represents a sincere tribute to the memory of an old friend, admiration for the Squire was blended with an equally profound unease concerning the cultural values that inspired his adventures.

The chivalric biography, often penned—like this example—by heralds, was an important feature of the cult of knightly heroism. In many ways it represented an extension of the established canon of chivalric icons, the Nine Worthies. Latterday heroes were frequently set alongside the traditional Nine, and Scots, for example, were accustomed to viewing Robert Bruce in this context. Meldrum, however, was an incongruous figure to find in such renowned company for, unlike those authors who stressed the legendary nature of their subjects' chivalry, Meldrum's biographer was at pains to divorce romance and reality. Although dutifully recording the arms of the Nine Worthies in his Armorial Manuscript, by the time he wrote *Squyer Meldrum* Lindsay appears to have been acutely uncomfortable with the whole cult. In *The Monarche,* for example, the Old Testament heroes are favorably viewed (5656–60) and Julius Caesar accorded a certain respect (3686), but Alexander the Great (a particularly popular hero of Scottish chivalric literature) is described in damning terms:

> Quhose crueltie for to rehers,
> And saikles [innocent] blude quhilk he did sched,
> War rycht abhominabyll to be red.   (3669–71)

Lindsay also rejects an important aspect of Arthurian romance and, by implication, the "worthiness" of Arthur himself when the relationship between Lancelot and Guinevere, so often held up as the epitome of the courtly love ideal, is denounced as no more than a sordid adulterous liaison (*Squyer Meldrum,* 54). Lindsay was not alone in his criticisms. Mair for one declared himself amazed that Caesar, a tyrant who overthrew an aristocratic republic, and Alexander, a man consumed with the lust for power, should be considered "worthy."[29] Nevertheless, given Lindsay's heraldic background, his stance was striking and, if familiar to his audience, it surely did not fail to influence the reading of his work. Certainly, it warns against taking this account of knightly derring-do at face value.

The main section of *Squyer Meldrum* falls into two halves, each dealing with those aspects of chivalry with which Lindsay was least at ease, that is, with military adventure and courtly love. Felicity Riddy's very suggestive reading of the poem indicates the specific ways in which the sentiments traditionally associated with romance literature are challenged by Lindsay's earthy realism. Numerous examples could be cited here, but one, not noted by Riddy, must suffice. When Meldrum pledges himself to his Lady's cause with the cry, "That worthie Lancelot du laik / Did neuer mair, for his Ladies saik" (1079–80), recollection of Lindsay's earlier condemnation of this relationship immediately subverts the romantic atmosphere. By emphasizing the unbridgable gap between real life and literature, Lindsay forcefully suggests that the knightly ideals of love and adventure have no viable place within the context of a real society. The dismal end to Meldrum's affair with the Lady of Gleneagles underscores this point. Prosaically enough, his erstwhile love is married off elsewhere and, although her enemy, Meldrum's assailant, eventually meets a satisfactorily sticky end, his death is simply an example of the mindless violence which itself serves to intrude reality into this romantic tale of chivalric idealism. Such episodes ensure that we are struck, not by the elaborate accounts of romance and military adventure, but rather by the absence of any sense of justice or protection—in Lindsay's eyes, the two most important aspects of the chivalric code. It is no accident, therefore, that having described Meldrum's adventures on the battlefield and in the bower, he turns finally to the Squire's life in the local community. The threefold division of the poem is by no means evenly balanced; concentrating on the knightly exploits, by far the greater part deals with a relatively short period in Meldrum's life. Yet even this reinforces the "unreal" nature of a life dedicated to the chivalric ideal, and the undramatic picture of social responsibility painted by Lindsay at the end of the poem provides a potent corrective to the earlier illusory and ultimately irrelevant tales of knight-errantry. The lone adventurer who squirms out of entanglement with the Maid of Carrickfergus is gradually brought to a position in which he finds himself bound by responsibility on all sides. As Lord Lindsay's most valued household official, as Sheriff Depute, and as local doctor, he was a valued member of the Fife community:

> To euerie man [he was] an equall Iudge,
> And of the pure he wes refuge,
> And with Iustice did thame support
> And curit thair sairis with gret comfort;   (1539–42)

Significantly, the stress is upon those traditional tenets of the knightly code (justice and protection of the poor) which were so important in Lindsay's commonweal thinking. In *The Historie of Squyer Meldrum*, Lindsay is suggesting a new role for men such as his old friend, a new paradigm for the aspirations of the lesser nobility. Written at a time when Lindsay was not at court, the poem's intended audience probably comprised his own Fife-based neighbors, men who would themselves have known of Squire Meldrum and his activities in the locality.[30] Interestingly, early editions of Lindsay's work (although not specifically of *Squyer Meldrum*) clearly recognize this concern with the art of government and its implications for men of this social background. A sixteenth-century English publisher, noting Plato's observation that men are born to serve not themselves but "the common welth and countrey," considered his work edifying for "al estates but chiefly for Gentlemen, and such as ar in authoritie" (London, 1566; reprinted, 1575 and 1581).[31]

ONE OF THE MOST vexatious problems for students of sixteenth-century texts is the question of audience. We do not know and can only guess who exactly Lindsay's intended audience was. Certainly his withdrawal from court after 1543 heralded a critical change in the focus of his work. Poems such as *The Tragedie of the Cardinal* and *Squyer Meldrum* are explicitly located in the Fife locality; they speak to Lindsay's neighbors rather than to fellow courtiers. It would, however, be wrong to insist on too rigid a demarcation between court and community, "high" and "low" culture, early works and late. Indeed, Lindsay's very first extant work, *The Dreme,* displays exactly the concern for the entire country that is so characteristic of his later writing. Nor should court poetry be viewed exclusively as the preserve of the audience for whom it was originally composed. After all, even this audience is difficult to define. Fluid in terms of personnel and location, the peripatetic court was an organic creation, and many courtiers, be they great lords or simple traveling entertainers, had an existence outside its ambit. William Stewart might have composed his metrical translation at court, and for a lady of the court, but he confidently expected that "Out throw the realm the rumor wald [be rung]."[32]

Quite how this "rumor" would spread, however, is far from clear, and hazarding an explanation raises many—probably unanswerable—questions concerning the production and circulation of literary texts and the nature of the sixteenth-century reading—or listening—public. Though the use of publicly performed drama renders such questions less relevant in the case of *Ane Satyre,* they still possess important implications for Lindsay's other works. Of those published during his lifetime, only three still survive: *The Testament of the Papyngo* (London, 1538), *The Tragedie of the Cardinal* (London[?], 1548), and *The Monarche* (St. Andrews[?], 1554). However, arguments supporting the existence of lost editions of most of the other poems are generally convincing.[33] Yet by modern standards print runs were tiny, running to between 200 and 1,000 copies with many very much smaller.[34] Books were prohibitively expensive, and unsurprisingly their ownership was largely restricted to a male social elite.[35] The situation was to improve somewhat during the course of the sixteenth century and, when the Scottish printer Thomas Bassendyne died in 1577, an inventory taken of his goods included over 1,300 unbound "Psalmes of Prois" and 505 unbound "David Lyndesayis" priced at three shillings each.[36] But the fact that of all Bassendyne's editions of Lindsay only one survives is a telling indication of the difficulties involved in assessing the scale of the sixteenth-

Figure 6. "Poetry reading in the sixteenth century." Woodcut from *A Dialogue betweene Experience and a Courtier, of the miserable estate of the worlde, first compiled in the Schottishe tongue by Sir Dauid Lyndesay, Knight, (a man of great learning and science) now newly corrected, and made perfit Englishe*. London, 1566. Courtesy of the Trustees of the National Library of Scotland.

century book trade. Lindsay's incunabula may well have vanished without trace. As for manuscript versions of his work, the picture is even dimmer, and until the compilation of *The Bannatyne Manuscript* in the mid 1560s there is no concrete evidence of his works circulating in this form.

The other side of the dissemination coin is the question of literacy, if anything an even more contentious issue during this period. It has been estimated that by the mid seventeenth century between 10 and 25 percent of Scottish males were literate.[37] Nevertheless, the sixteenth century undoubtedly saw rising levels of literacy among the lay population of Scotland, and it is interesting to note that when Henry Charteris published a volume of Lindsay's work in 1568 he included an "Adhortation of all Estatis, to the reiding of thir present warkis," which urged "Craftismen and merchandis" to "Reid in this Buke, the speiche gif ye can spell."[38] Clearly, though, Lindsay and his contemporaries expected their work to reach a much wider audience than can be accounted for by a rise in literacy alone. For this they depended on oral communication (see Fig. 6). Stewart, for example, believed that his translation would enable every man "Other to reid the storie or till heir," a belief which echoes the cry of Gavin Douglas who hoped that, as a result of his translation, Virgil would "with euery gentill Scot be kend, / And to onletterit folk be red on hight / That erst was bot with clerkis comprehend."[39] While there are important distinctions between a reading and a hearing public, the paucity of both available books and those able to read them had the same consequence for both groups.[40] For each, reading was what has been described as an "intensive" rather than an "extensive" business, a small number of texts being constantly read and reread.[41] If we cannot say with certainty who it was that had access to Lindsay's works, we are perhaps on safer ground in thinking that those who did were extremely familiar with his ideas.

Further clues to the nature of Lindsay's sixteenth-century audience are provided by the texts themselves. Such evidence has to be handled with caution but, carefully sifted, it can yield results. Different "voices" are required for speaking to different audiences, and perhaps one of the most intriguing ways of identifying an author's intended audience is to consider how he chose to address them.[42] Of course this can never simply be taken at face value. The Testament of the Papyngo, for example, opens with Lindsay disowning his usual courtly listeners:

> Quharefor, because myne mater bene so rude
> Off sentence, and of Rethorike denude,
> To rurall folke myne dyting bene directit,
> Far flemit frome the sicht of men of gude.
> For cunnyng men, I knaw, wyll soune conclude
> It dowe no thyng bot for to be deictit:
> And, quhen I hair myne mater bene detractit,
> Than sall I sweir, I maid it bot in mowis [jest],
> To landwart lassis quhilkis kepith kye & yowis.   (64–72)

This is, however, more than a poetic commonplace designed to elicit a rueful smile from the audience and to prepare them for some harsh home truths. Lindsay's description of his "barbour rusticall indyte" (239) is belied both by the style and the content of the poem. The opening section (concluded by the above passage) possesses a comic tone, but its overall mood is more serious-minded; a dignified roll call of Scotland's great poets is delivered in elevated language, and the introduction to the parrot's tale continues in this vein. Indeed, the point is stressed by the use of the parrot—a traditional heraldic symbol of eloquence—to narrate the tale and proclaim its moral message. (For those unfamiliar with bestiary lore, Lindsay makes the point explicit by having the Papyngo bequeath her "Eloquence and toung Rethoricall" (1105) to the goose.) Quite clearly a courtier, the parrot lets slip the pretense that her tale is for "landwart lassis" and, the earlier dedication forgotten, she addresses her deathbed epistles to the king and her brother courtiers. Nevertheless, the opening appeal was not made pointlessly. On the contrary, Lindsay's clever use of the *vox populi vox Dei* idea does much to sharpen his polemic. The long-established notion of the poor as in some way nearer to God, as *imitatio Christi,* exercised a powerful appeal to the popular and literary imagination throughout the Middle Ages, and it appears several times in the corpus of Lindsay's work.[43] The traditional association between poverty and moral purity evoked by Lindsay's supplication to the "rurall folke" is again recalled in the second half of the poem during the Papyngo's encounter with the rapacious avian clerics. Here, the Papyngo, her moral consciousness heightened by imminent death, is credited with knowledge of "the vulgare pepyllis Iudgement" (765) and invited to explain why the clergy are held in such low esteem. At this point, the *vox populi* tradition imparts added authority to her words, allowing Lindsay to launch a vitriolic attack on the worldliness of the Church while at the same time distancing himself from the debate. And yet, this rapidly breaks down. The parrot's allegorical denunciation of corruption engendered by sensuous and material lusts may convey the gist of the "vulgare pepyllis Iudgement," but it is palpably not, as she claims, what "The commoun peple sayith" (770). Skillfully, Lindsay has conflated the voices of poet, parrot, and people to a point where it becomes impossible to separate them.

While *The Testament of the Papyngo* illustrates Lindsay's use of the *vox populi* tradition to persuade the ruling classes, in his later works, notably *Ane Satyre* and *The Monarche,* his intended audience is not so obvious. Presenting his ideas in the form of a drama for public performance surely represents a bid to attract a much more socially diverse audience. From the earl of Rothes to the unidentified Willie Cadyeoch and his wife, *Ane Satyre* itself incorporates references to many local figures, a device which relies for effect upon the audience's familiarity with these names, perhaps even from their actual presence in the assembled crowd.[44] Many of the Cupar community must have been involved in the play's production, and this community—in all its aspects—is forcefully brought into the action of the play by a variety of dramatic means including the setting, topical references, and direct address.[45]

Creating a dramatic space for the representation of "real" characters did more than unite the audience in sniggering complicity. With a character such as the Pauper—unnamed but no less real—Lindsay insinuated a much more menacing image into the minds of his audience. The Pauper appears at the end of the first part of the play in what has been misleadingly referred to as the Interlude. In fact, the introduction of this particular character and his encounter with the rascally pardoner have powerful thematic links with the rest of the action, illustrating the consequences of monarchical misrule at an individual level and paving the way for the discussion of social injustice and ecclesiastical corruption that dominates the remainder of the play. Now, in direct contrast to the allegory that has gone before, the divide between "fact" and "fiction" is less clear-cut, and the Pauper seems simply to wander into the action "out of the feild" (1931), having lost his way to the neighboring town of St. Andrews. The fact that he hails from the East Lothian town of Tranent which, as Lindsay was well aware, had but recently suffered English military action, further confuses the distinction between real person and dramatic invention. This is reinforced when the Pauper crudely dismisses the drama unfolding around him. "I wil not gif for al your play worth an sowis fart," he declares, "For thair is richt lytill play at my hungrie hart" (*Ane Satyre*, 1956–57). Gradually, however, he joins the other dramatis personae. The voice of the poor, "the greit murmell" (2538) as it is described, has elbowed its way onto the stage and demanded its say. Already the Pauper has challenged social convention by climbing on the throne vacated by Rex Humanitas, and his continued presence serves to underscore the nearness of social anarchy, pressing home the need for the type of strong government able to maintain the established order. A similar effect is achieved with the introduction of John the Commonweal, made to enter the play at the point where Diligence calls upon all those with grievances to step forward. Given Lindsay's subtle distortion of the boundary between fact and fantasy, we can easily imagine the frisson of alarm felt by the audience as one of their number boldly stood up clamoring to be heard.[46] Like the Pauper, John quickly becomes an integral character of the play, and yet there is a decidedly apprehensive note in Merchandis's request that he remain at the bar letting none but himself come near (2543–44). Fear of "that many headed monster, an unbridled populace," was of course the other side of the *vox populi* coin.[47] The idyllic notion of the poor as Christ's special flock existed uneasily in a cultural and political climate fearful of social disorder. Theoretically, the voice of the poor was the voice of the morally pure; in practice it was also the highly threatening talk of the socially delinquent, as dangerous as it was unpredictable. Both concepts were subtly deployed by Lindsay in order to exert pressure upon those in authority. However, *Ane Satyre* is rather different from his other works, for although the reforming message is aimed at the political community the "pure commouns" were also given the opportunity to view their own representative's participation in this process.

The question of audience is also important in Lindsay's final work, *The Monarche*. The opening "Epistil to the Redar" clearly directs the poem to the Governor, to his half-brother Archbishop Hamilton, and "To the faithfull Prudent Pastouris Spirituall, / To Nobyll Erlis, and Lordis Temporall" (37–

38). This appeal to the politically powerful was imperative if Lindsay's message were to have any constructive repercussions. His experiences at court in the 1530s had taught him how necessary it was to "Maik thaim requeist, quhilk hes the Gouernance, / The Sinceir word of God for tyll Auance" (73–74). Yet, the poem's appeal is much more multivalent than this might suggest, and Lindsay also asserts that "to Colyearis, Cairtis, & to Cukis / To Iok and Thome, my Rhyme sall be diractit" (549–50). His message of reform in the face of impending apocalypse was relevant to all sections of society. "Brether," he declares as if preaching to all humanity, "I counsall yow, repent" (2513).

One of the ways Lindsay attempts to convey this idea is to place himself firmly upon the side of the poor commons, referring, for example, to "ws lawid peple" (645), "ws peple of the law estait" (654), and "ws, thy pure lawid commoun populair" (4965). But, as in *The Testament of the Papyngo*, the authorial voice continues to confuse. Elsewhere in *The Monarche*, Lindsay refers to the commons as "the Bestiall rest" (1925), while works such as *Ane Satyre* make full use of the traditional comic potential of characters such as the Tailor and Sowtar (cobbler). Lindsay is clearly not of this class; even if nothing at all were known of his social background, the scholarly content of *The Monarche* sets him apart from the "lawid peple." However, unlike earlier poems, his final work represents a much more sincere claim to be writing for the people in the sense that his work was intended to instruct not only those at court but a much wider audience within the community as a whole:

> Quhowbeit that diuers deuote cunnyng Clerkis
> In Latyne toung hes wryttin syndrie bukis
> Our vnlernit knawis lytill of thare werkis,
> More than thay do the rauyng of the Rukis.   (545–48)

This, Lindsay avers, inspires the dedication of his work to humble folk, and there is a very real sense that the poem itself seeks to speak to this wider audience. An informed exposition of world history, otherwise inaccessible, is promulgated in verse, and the accounts of Christian eschatology can be seen as an attempt to plug the gap created by a lack of readily available vernacular Bibles. Lindsay's didactic intentions also extended to exposing the corrupt practices of the Church. He excuses the "simpyll peple rude" (2387) their ignorance, stressing the culpability of an inadequate and immoral ecclesiastical establishment, and he offers his own "Exclamatioun agains Idolatrie" as a corrective to the erroneous teachings of the Church (2397–705). The arguments put forward in this passage are based partly on Scripture and partly on a practical appeal to the uneducated. Can images run, he asks; can they feel, talk, or see?

Central to the question of audience and Lindsay's treatment of the common folk was his commitment to the vernacular.[48] Of course, Lindsay was not the only Scot of this period writing in his own language. Some, like the author of *The Complaynt of Scotland,* might have struggled with what they considered the limitations of their native tongue, but they were determined to speak in the "domestic scottis language maist intelligibil for the vlgare pepil."[49] *The Complaynt's* propagandist function renders this unsurprising, but the example of the humanist translators and the same drive to inform— what has been dubbed "the popularizing mood of the time"—persuaded numerous authors to turn to the vernacular.[50] It is no accident that this flowering of Middle Scots coincided with that brief period when the language of the court and of government was familiar even to the most humble member of the population.[51] Certainly, this linguistic coincidence helps explain why Lindsay felt able to address such differing audiences. If, as suggested in the previous chapter, the vernacular was central to court culture, then it was even more important—if not imperative—for those authors whose didactic intentions led them to aim at a broader audience.

Lindsay's *Monarche* incorporates a long "Exclamatioun to the Redar, Twycheyng the Wryttyng of Uulgare and Maternall Language," justifying his use of the "vulgair toung" (540):

> Tyll vnleirnit I wald the cause wer kend
> Off our most miserabyll trauell and torment,
> And quhow, in erth, no place bene parmanent.   (542–44)

Although the poem includes the same conventional pseudocondemnation of his "rurall ryme" (101) found in *The Testament of the Papyngo,* Lindsay also proclaims this much more serious work "Off Rethorike heir" (103). As this vividly suggests, it was as a language of persuasion rather than one of aesthetics that the vernacular appealed to Lindsay. Aureate descriptions of nature he considered "vnfrutful and vaine discriptioun" (203), "mater without edificatioun" (205). Not neglecting first to prove his expertise in this area, Lindsay goes on to reject an elevated style in favor of a blunter approach more suited to his proselytizing purpose, contending that poetry of this professedly despised sort—along with works of logic, astronomy, medicine, and philosophy—may be written in whatsoever language the author wishes. "Bot lat ws haif the buikis necessare," he continues, "To commoun weill, and our Saluatioun / Iustly translatit in our toung Uulgare" (678–80). Significantly, this, the only appearance of the term "commonweal" in *The Monarche,* is firmly linked to the use of the vernacular and the "education" of the population.

As well as supporting the call for a vernacular Bible and liturgy, Lindsay also advocated a greater use of Scots in the conduct of legal affairs. In *Ane Satyre,* the Pauper provides a wry reminder of popular confusion when confronted with the consistorial courts and their process of *citandum, lybellandum, opponendum, interloquendum, ad replicandum,* and *pronunciandum* (3059–78). Lindsay's desire for a more readily comprehensible system has a precise social justification: Not only will it minimize the type of bewilderment instanced by the Pauper, but by advertising its penalties it will help deter crime (*The Monarche,* 666–67), and by removing ambiguity it will eliminate the need for greedy lawyers. Thus Lindsay is moved to cry

> I wald sum Prince of gret Discretioun
> In vulgare language planelye gart translait
> The neidful lawis of this Regioun: (*The Monarche,* 650–52)

There was nothing radical in such a plea. The provision of an accessible corpus of Scottish law had been one of the principal reasons given for the establishment of the first Scottish printing press in 1507 and, indeed, Lindsay's lines forcefully recall the 1540 statute requiring the printing of all "actis safar as concernis the comoun wele."[52] This time a copy of the acts was actually produced by Thomas Davidson in February 1542, but Lindsay's demand over a decade later suggests that ignorance was still widespread. (For his publication of the *Acts,* Davidson used a woodcut of the royal arms taken from Lindsay's Armorial, and the latter's possible involvement here may have contributed to his continuing concern.) That there was still room for improvement is backed up by James Henrisoun, whose "Godly and Golden Book," written in 1548, argued that the law should be collated and "prynted in there mother tonge for there better obseruacion . . . that none shall perishe through Ignorance."[53] Such calls did much to keep alive the ideal of a codified, accessible corpus of law and, in 1553, the Clerk Register was instructed to extract from the records all acts relating to the commonweal made since the death of James V that they might be printed "swa that na persoun may pretend ignorance in time to cum."[54] The example of men like Lindsay and Henrisoun provides a telling illustration of the important role played by the vernacular—and in particular by the notion of the commonweal, itself a vernacular term—in the development of political discourse in Renaissance Scotland.

SOCIAL ANALYSIS in the later Middle Ages was constrained by a number of factors promoting what has been described as a static, nonconstructive approach to political theorizing.[55] The concept of Fortune, an arbitrary and implacable force in the affairs of men, undoubtedly inhibited a more sophisticated social analysis, but arguably the most important factor in this respect was the ethical framework within which such discussion took place. Moral failings were perceived as the cause of socioeconomic problems, and political and ethical goals were largely interchangeable. Gradually, how-

ever, the analysis shifted beyond questions of moral responsibility, hesi-
tantly turning to explanations involving impersonal forces open to investigation and thereafter to manipulation by legislation and government
action. The reasons behind this shift are various and complex, but in
sixteenth-century Scotland some of the catalysts seem to have been the
social dislocation occasioned by the Rough Wooing, the threat to Scottish
independence posed by both English and French ambitions, and the highly
charged religious situation.[56]

Lindsay's poetry provides an important indication of this process, most
tellingly illustrated by a comparison of his two "John the Commonweal"
works: *The Dreme* and *Ane Satyre of the Thrie Estatis*.[57] Just as the geographically very precise account of Scotland's plight found in *The Dreme* is set
within a much wider cosmological framework, so the condemnation of
"Unthrift, sweirness, falset, pouertie, and stryfe" (965) is set within a much
broader moral matrix. The dream-voyage through Heaven and Hell clearly
denotes the poem's concern with universal questions of sin and salvation.
This is firmly brought out in John's allegorical analysis of contemporary affairs which blames the activities of "Singulare Proffect," "Symonie," "Couatyce," "Pride," "Sensuale Plesour," and "Cowardyce" for his extremity. The
ethical theme is continued in Lindsay's "Exhortatioun to the Kyngis Grace"
which, in similar fashion, focuses upon the cardinal virtues as proper companions for the young king:

> Tak Manlie curage, and leif thyne Insolence,
> And vse counsale of nobyll dame Prudence.
> Founde the fermelie on faith and fortytude:
> Drawe to thy court Iustice and Temporance;
> And to the commoun weill haue attendance   (1064–68)

In the closely linked poem *The Complaynt,* Lindsay celebrates James's kingship by depicting royal government aided by "The foure gret verteous
Cardinalis" (379); the strictly ethical demands laid down by John as the
condition of his return to Scotland have been realized. All that is required,
such an approach implies, is the reinstatement of a virtuous monarch and,
at a stroke, violence, robbery, poverty, social degeneracy, and ecclesiastical
corruption are eradicated. Moreover, this desirable state of affairs is bound
to come about in time for, influenced by ideas of a cyclical Fortune, Lindsay
expected good rulers to follow bad as surely as "efter the nycht cumis the
glad morrow" (*The Dreme,* 999).

In *Ane Satyre,* on the other hand, Lindsay begins to explore contemporary
society with less recourse to the established relationship between sin and
social disorder and with an attempt to discern the more immediate causes of
socioeconomic breakdown. Of course, Lindsay could not step outside the

traditional framework altogether, and he does not abandon the conventional belief that the sovereign's moral rectitude is fundamental to good government. However, the demands made by John the Commonweal in *Ane Satyre* are much more specific and do not always depend upon abstract, ethical concepts. For example, complaints concerning the administration of justice are met with proposals for an extension of the system based upon the College of Justice established in 1532. The suggested endowment of a second College, based in either Elgin or Inverness, sought to overcome problems of access and communication, and the addition of two extra senators (Lindsay proposes sixteen rather than the original fourteen) would strengthen each individual institution.[58] Significantly, those who were making their careers in the law, men like Henry Balnaves, Thomas Bellenden, Robert Galbraith, and the family of James Foulis, were men with whom Lindsay had a considerable degree of sympathy, and his suggestion may have owed something to his desire to reinforce their position.[59] His proposal was accordingly well thought out. He details not only the composition of the new College but also the salaries of its members, proposing what was surely a most unrealistic—almost tenfold—increase in government expenditure (3845–56).[60] Aware no doubt of the problems already experienced in funding the system, he envisages that this should be paid for with money derived from his proposed dissolution of Scotland's nunneries, a measure clearly inspired by Henry VIII's dissolution of the monasteries, which English Reformers had originally hoped would provide for poor relief and education. The creation of a second northern college, this time in Aberdeen, was also advocated by James Henrisoun in his "Godly and Golden Book" (1548), but as this was never actually published, it is hard to claim it as the source of Lindsay's ideas.[61] What is clear, however, is that by the middle of the sixteenth century a more informed, more prescriptive debate concerning society and government in Scotland was beginning to take shape.

Another complaint made by both Henrisoun and Lindsay concerned the "endlesse abhominable consistorie lawes," which, "prolixt, corrupt and perpetuall," both oppressed and impoverished the poor.[62] At least one historian finds such charges unconvincing, and certainly the manner in which Lindsay chose to articulate them requires further comment.[63] His concern for those who, like the Pauper, found themselves the victim of an incredibly lengthy, costly, and ultimately fruitless legal process is somewhat disingenuous. It was not society's poor who sought legal redress in the consistory courts but the relatively wealthy lairds and burgesses, men rather like Lindsay himself, who had something to gain and the money to pay for it. Indeed, Lindsay himself had pursued at least two actions for the recovery of teinds in the Church courts during the 1540s and, in criticizing the system, he was motivated not by the outrage of the oppressed but by the concern of his own class.[64] Nevertheless, whatever the impulse behind his censure of the consistory courts, this type of thinking represents an essentially pragmatic approach to the question, which marks a considerable departure from the simple acclamation of justice, "hir sweird on hie" (*The Complaynt*, 381), which Lindsay had relied upon twenty years earlier.

Albeit conditioned by the demands of generic convention, Lindsay's treatment of poverty offers a highly suggestive commentary on contemporary approaches to the problem. Hitherto, looking at poverty within the traditional socioethical matrix had served to inhibit the systematic examination of its causes in terms other than those which viewed the phenomenon as the irredeemable consequence of man's fallen nature, and attempts at its alleviation had focused largely upon an exhortation to almsgiving on the one hand and upon the extirpation of idleness on the other. Christian obligation to the poor was emphasized by traditional kingship literature, and this duty was taken very seriously. In 1535, for example, James V requested his Lords of Council that "ane man of gud conscience . . . be chosen by you quhilk sallbe callit *advocatus pauperum,*" who in return for representing the poor was to receive an annual salary of ten pounds.[65] Through Veritie's opening speech, Lindsay recalls this bond between the king and his poor subjects but, as we shall see, the action taken to ensure that Veritie's strictures are met depends upon more than the personal intervention of a bounteous monarch.

Although sixteenth-century governments little understood the chronic inflation and population explosion that combined to destabilize the economy, they were only too well aware of the problems it spawned.[66] In the course of his career, Lindsay provided various explanations for the poverty he saw around him. In *The Dreme* he attributes it to the failure of justice, policy, and peace, dependent in turn upon a virtuous adult king, and in *The Tragedie of the Cardinal* it is war which impoverishes nation and individual alike. But, beyond a return to adult rule and an implied advocacy of Anglo-Scottish union, Lindsay comes up with no real solutions. In *Ane Satyre* he views poverty—like war, plague, and famine—as punishment meted out by a wrathful God (1491). (It should be noted that this idea was to form an important part of developing Protestant thought concerning God's disapproval of the Catholic faith; this may well represent the beginning of Lindsay's interest in this type of interpretation, and it may be no accident that the idea is expressed through the character Veritie.) In a more traditional vein, Lindsay continues to subscribe to the well-established and widely held theory of the "strang beggar" (2603) whose moral turpitude leads John to number him among his principal enemies.[67] This seemingly important counter to the subversive message conveyed by the characterization of the Pauper was, however, ambivalently endorsed. The idea of the "strang beggar" provided a conceptual framework for John's attack on the parasitical mendicant orders, the "idill doggis" (2621) and "weil fed hoggis" (2622) who were Lindsay's principal satirical targets. Whether the Pauper should also be considered this type of "strang beggar" is however by no means clear. Only four months before the *Satyre*'s first performance, legislation "for refraining of the multitude of maisterful and strang beggars" had stipulated that each parish should provide for its own poor, setting out punishments for those found outside the parish of their birth.[68] Provision being made to publicize the acts "swa that na man sall pretend Ignorance or allege he knew not samyn in tyme tocum," the audience must have been well aware of the official response the Pauper might expect. It is after all the royal herald, Diligence, who curses the appearance of the "vilde beggar Carle" (1933) and demands to know why he has not been driven away by the provost and bailies. But the Pauper's own description of his descent into penury and the sympathetic treatment he receives from Rex Humanitas were surely designed to elicit a more ambivalent response.

In many ways extremely conventional in its approach, *Ane Satyre* does attempt to identify some of the specific causes of poverty in Scotland with a far greater degree of precision. The poverty of the commons is, Lindsay suggests, the result of unnecessarily harsh economic exploitation by landlords both spiritual and temporal. Mails and teinds are squeezed out of the population while the practice of feuing—considerably well advanced by the mid sixteenth century despite Lindsay's description of it as "the new plague" (2573)—is viewed as a particular cause of economic hardship and social dislocation:[69]

> Thus man thay pay great ferme or lay thair steid.
> And sum ar plainlie harlit out be the heid
> And ar destroyit without God on them rew.   (2575–77)

Lindsay's argument, however, is not with feu-ferme tenure itself but with its abuse. He does in fact advocate the feuing of all temporal lands, but only to those who actually worked the land and only if a reasonable grassum, feu-duty, and augmentation were set:[70]

> Set into few your temporall lands,
> To men that labours with thair hands,
> Bot nocht to ane gearking gentil man,
> That nether will he wirk, nor can:
> Quhair throch the policy will increase   (2685–89)

> My lords conclud that al the temporal lands
> Be set in few to laboreris with thair hands,

With sic restrictiounis as sall be devysit
That thay may liue and nocht be supprysit,
With ane ressonabill augmentatioun: (2805–9)

Again this echoes Henrisoun who, lamenting the plight of "the poor la-
bourers of the grounde," argued that the lands they occupied should be "sett
to them in feu or longe taxes [tacks]" at the current price.[71] This approach
can usefully be compared to that of John Mair, addressing the problem
several decades previously.[72] Arguing that security of tenure would encourage efforts to increase productivity, Mair believed feuing capable of qua-
drupling national wealth.[73] Additionally, he considered it an effective measure for diminishing the undesirable influence exerted by great landlords
over their tenants. It is, unfortunately, not entirely clear who Mair's new
feuars were. He wrote of men who "rent their lands from the lords, but
cultivate it by means of their servants and not with their own hands," which
suggests that he envisaged a class of lesser landlords, a newly prosperous
quasi middle class capable of countering the power and pretensions of the
nobility.[74] Clearly, the ideal feuars of Lindsay and Henrisoun were not the
same as Mair's, and the vehemence with which Lindsay insisted that lands
be feued to manual laborers seems almost to represent a direct riposte to the
type of idea put forward by the theologian. Given this, we might think
Lindsay's proposals strikingly radical, but in fact they are very similar to the
measures passed in 1559 by the Scottish Church, which prohibited the
feuing of Kirk lands "save only to tenants and tillers of the same."[75] The key
issues here were security of tenure and the protection of existing tenants,
and Lindsay aims a further blow at economic abuse when he attacks the
death duties exacted by both spiritual and temporal landlords (the corspresent, upcloth, and heriot) and proposes their abolition.

Just how accurate was Lindsay's assessment of the impact that the feuing
movement had on Scotland? Undoubtedly there were evictions and cases of
individual hardship. However, by the end of the sixteenth century the
majority of feus recorded in surviving charters had been granted to sitting
tenants, most of whom were receiving their first piece of heritable property.[76] Yet, when set against the very fact of his attempted analysis, there is a
sense in which Lindsay's accuracy becomes unimportant. Of more significance is the way in which he makes a very specific call for reform, proposing
its enforcement by the estates. The forces of parliamentary legislation
brought to bear upon this issue will "the Commoun-weil . . . advance"
(3809). Again, this represents a significant evolution of the idea that the
commonweal will prosper simply by coming under the king's benevolent,
all-encompassing gaze. It is tempting to conclude that this interpretive
shift owed much to the humanist-inspired discourses of social criticism

which, it has been argued, underlay similar developments south of the border where, at least in the first half of the sixteenth century, there existed a new confidence that government policy was capable of changing the situation.[77]

The program of reform advocated by Lindsay in *Ane Satyre of the Thrie Estatis* is hardly a model of thoughtful socioeconomic analysis. Individual and quirky, it addresses those problems he considered particularly pressing. However, it is important to recognize that Lindsay was attempting a more sophisticated rationalization of social problems and, furthermore, suggesting solutions that did not rely exclusively upon moral regeneration. The increased emphasis upon the role of parliamentary legislation represents another new element in Lindsay's thinking, a development of his ideas concerning counsel. Of fundamental importance to the discussion of virtuous kingship, the idea of good counsel reaches something of a climax with *Ane Satyre*. Here Rex Humanitas is positively beset by a whole host of assorted advisors, good and bad. Finally, however, the moral conversion complete, "Gude Counsell with Lady Veritie / Ar profest with our kingis Maiestie" (3778–79). This strongly echoes the descriptions of royal government supported by the cardinal virtues that we find in earlier works although, as we shall see, Veritie is not a "virtue" in the same sense as Gude-Counsall or Chastitie but rather the representation of the living Word of God, a form of Scripture-based evangelicalism which sustains the king's newfound commitment to divine precept. This commitment is made equally to the commonweal, for it is at this point in the play that John is stripped of his tattered rags and gorgeously reclothed. "All verteous peopil now may reiosit," declares Correctioun, "Sen Common-weill hes gottin ane gay garmoun" (3773–74). However, in *Ane Satyre*, Lindsay calls on more than these allegorical royal mentors, and the dramatic introduction of a recognizable parliamentary assembly heralds a more concrete discussion of royal counsel firmly grounded in the political experiences of Renaissance Scotland. Given that the play is the earliest extant example of its kind, it is impossible to say to what extent Lindsay was working within an established literary tradition when he introduced the three estates as *dramatis personae*. It had long been common in France, and its popularity in Scotland, at least by the middle of the sixteenth century, can be seen from its adaptation in Wedderburn's *Complaynt of Scotland*.[78] Essentially, though, the estates motif had hitherto been used to convey a social vision rather than to comment upon any sort of parliamentary assembly. Something more along these lines is found in Henryson's fable, *The Trial of the Fox*, but here the animal parliament is concerned exclusively with the familiar theme of judicial punishment.[79] The fifteenth-century *Thrie Prestis of Peblis* does, it is true, incorporate a (human) parliament, but on this occasion the estates are summoned only to advise the king and not for the purposes of lawmaking. The detailed account of specific legislation found in *Ane Satyre* seems to have been something new.

The fundamental importance attached to Parliament in Lindsay's vision of reform is forcefully conveyed by Divyne Correctioun's bold assertion that he "will do nocht without the conveining / Ane Parlement of the estatis all" (1578–79). Part of the reform process was, of course, the estates' own reformation. Their dramatic entry "gangand backwart led be thair vyces" is a compelling representation of their moral and political corruption. However, as the head has been restored, so too are the members (with the notable exception of Spiritualitie), and the estates are then involved in the redress of John's grievances.

While the moral rehabilitation of Rex Humanitas in the first part of the play makes possible the political rehabilitation of John the Commonweal in the second, it is the latter, described by Diligence as "The best pairt of our Play" (1925), that really engages Lindsay's concern. Certainly it is far lengthier than the drama of moral fall and redemption that precedes it. Now the play is no longer so intently focused upon the king, and the location of authority becomes much more fragmented. As Rex Humanitas stands passively by, the problems besetting the commonweal are described by John who ponders how he should deal with them if he were king. Advice concerning society's problems is variously provided by John, Gude-Counsall, Veritie, and the two lay estates, while the king's involvement is paid only token recognition. A good example of this is Divyne Correctioun's declaration that the prelates be deprived and three learned clerks appointed in their place. He might claim that the judgment was made "With the advice of King Humanitie" (3705), but the audience assuredly remembers that the suggestion was Veritie's (3155–60). Similarly, though it is maintained that Rex Humanitas "tyll the Commoun-weil hes ay bene kynd" (2554), John's sorry tale gives patent lie to the assertion. It is for this reason that Lindsay suggests a more formal collective responsibility when it comes to maintaining the commonweal.

This becomes clear when we recall the fate of John the Commonweal in *The Dreme*. In this earlier work, John sadly quits Scotland vowing to return only when virtuous kingship is restored. In *Ane Satyre,* this has been done, yet still John plays an active and central part in the reform process, a process which culminates when the temporal estates, "The Common-weill tak be the hand, / And mak with him perpetuall band" (2715–16). In rousing tones, Temporalitie pledges "The Common-weill for till defend / From hence-forth till our lives end" (2711–12), and the dramatic scene in which Temporalitie and Merchandis embrace John powerfully symbolizes the ideals of social unity and collective responsibility for the commonweal. The idea of the commonweal had always stressed universal good above singular profit and, on one level, this is what the lay estates' commitment to John is all about, a dramatic reminder that all sections of the audience have to attend to the commonweal. But, significantly, whereas in *The Dreme* it seems that good government, being simply a question of monarchical morality, can and indeed will be restored in a matter of time, in *Ane Satyre* the audience is left with the impression that John's security rests upon more fragile foundations. Following the parliamentary business of the play, the first to respond is the Pauper, who thanks Rex Humanitas for restoring the health of the commonweal but offers a warning that harks back to the king's ill-advised slumbers in the arms of Dame Sensualitie: "It had ben als as gude ye had sleipit / As to mak acts and be nocht keipit" (3960–61). Like the unruly and irreverent sermon preached by Folly, his words are a disturbing reminder of the potential proximity of social mayhem and a clear illustration that continued good government depends on both the sustained goodwill of society's members and the effective enforcement of the new legislation.

As presented in Lindsay's *Satyre,* the commonweal ideal has become much more formalized, institutionalized even. It is no accident that the arena in which the point is made is a recognizable parliamentary assembly and the agency whereby it is enacted is the formal band, the favored Scottish method of describing allegiance. Moreover, not only is the ideal of the commonweal a guiding political principle for the whole community (symbolized by John's installation among the estates), it could, on occasion, attain a certain coercive force. The decision to dissolve the nunneries, for example, is taken not only "Becaus thay ar nocht necessair" but also because "thay ar contrair / To Iohn the commoun-weill" (3702–4).[80]

WHILE THE IDEAL of the virtuous king remained very much part of Lindsay's—and indeed of Scotland's—political thinking, it is clear that the idea of the commonweal gradually assumed an ever greater importance. Moreover, in the course of his career, the relationship between king, community, and commonweal is subtly modified by Lindsay. While in theory society had always aspired to the ideal of universal and public good, now the political community was being invited to play a much more decisive, more formal role in achieving that aim.[81] In view of the political background against which his later works were written, this shift is less than surprising. Not only was there an infant girl on the throne, but Lindsay's changing expectations of noble and lairdly achievement coupled with his personal parliamentary experiences encouraged this development. The embodiment of a principle rather than any particular class, John the Commonweal nevertheless articulated ideas that appealed particularly to men of Lindsay's position. *Ane Satyre* certainly did not demand social revolution, or even such measures as the admission of the lairds into Parliament, but arguably it was the type of thinking we see in Lindsay, the insistence that both Parliament and society—but particularly Parliament—embrace the idea of commonweal, that helped pave the way for such developments.

III

Reform and Reformation

The Church

Gett vpe, thow slepist all to lang, O Lorde,
And mak one haistie reformatioun.
—*The Monarche,* 2701–2

SEVEN

Poetry, Humanism, and Reform

The Early Works

Thocht Gawine Dowglas, Bischop of Dunkell,
In ornate meter surmount did euerilk man;
Thocht Kennedie and Dunbar bure the bell
For the large race of Rhetorik thay ran:
Yit neuer Poeit of our Scottische clan,
Sa cleirlie schew that Monstour with his markis,
The Romane God, in quhome all gyle began,
As dois gude Dauid Lyndesay in his warkis.[1]

The glowing praise heaped upon "gude Dauid Lyndesay" by his first general editor owed more to post-Reformation perceptions of his religious sympathies than to an appreciation of his poetic ability. His savage satire of a corrupt ecclesiastical establishment, his angry attack upon the papacy, and his apocalyptic vision greatly appealed to Protestant Scots of the later sixteenth and seventeenth centuries and, their appetite for his works seemingly insatiable, they did not hesitate to claim him as one of their own.[2] This confessionally inspired enthusiasm has inevitably colored subsequent interpretations of Lindsay's religious position, and his reputation as "a Calvinist of the sixteenth century" has proved remarkably long-lived.[3] Even if such descriptions are well wide of the mark, they raise important questions for any analysis of Lindsay's works, the majority of which survive only as printed after 1560 and the establishment of the Protestant Church in Scotland. At a time when the future of the new Kirk was by no means secure, sixteenth-century editors kept a close watch for any sign of theological deviance.[4] Such vigilance surely explains at least one difference between two early texts of *Ane Satyre of the Thrie Estatis* when an obviously Catholic reference to the intercessory role of the Virgin escapes the notice of Bannatyne but not of Charteris (4622–24). Elsewhere, Lindsay's publishers make desperate attempts to justify some of the regrettable "Papist" lapses found in his works. "Sic wes the ignorance of thai dayes thit men euin of scharpest iugement culd not espy all abusis," lamented Charteris in a marginal note to his 1568 edition, excusing Lindsay his references to Catholic belief with the claim that "He semis rather to elude then to allow of Purgatorie."[5] The fact that such comments were deemed necessary suggests that on the whole Lindsay's early editors printed his works much as they found them and forbore from subjecting the texts to automatic Protestant revision. In view of the hostility to the pre-Reformation Church expressed elsewhere, perhaps such details could be overlooked. Certainly, it is only on this, admittedly rather unsatisfactory, basis that Lindsay's surviving works can be used to analyze his thinking.

More recently, Lindsay's reputation as a religious radical has been challenged by an attempt to recast him in the role of orthodox reformer whose aims were at one with the contemporary impetus for reform found within the sixteenth-century Church.[6] The picture is, however, more complex than either of these interpretations suggests. Indeed, the very fact that such revisionism has been possible hints at the subtleties of the situation and the extraordinarily fluid ideological context of the pre-Reformation period. As convincingly demonstrated by recent work on the subject, the Scottish Reformation cannot be viewed as the simple confrontation of two opposing faiths, its outcome either straightforward or predetermined.[7] In the course of several decades a variety of ideas, both orthodox and heretical, were alternately taken up and discarded in a manner inimical to neat theological classification. Indeed, as we have already seen, definitions of heresy and orthodoxy were in themselves problematic. Approaching the Reformation in this less dogmatic way provides a more meaningful framework within which to locate Lindsay's works and trace the development of his thinking. The orthodox teachings of the Church, educated Christian humanism, and a thoroughgoing evangelical Protestantism might at first sight appear a bizarre combination of ideas, but this is true only if we are looking for the ordered justification of a consistently held theological position. If, on the other hand, we view Lindsay as a man groping toward understanding in an uncertain religious climate, then the complexities of his thought are more readily understandable and the contradictions in his writing easier to explain. The tensions in Lindsay's thinking may make for a more complex study than has sometimes been thought but, seen in this way, he presents a more accurate reflection of religious culture in Renaissance Scotland.

BEFORE EXAMINING Lindsay's religious position more closely, it is perhaps as well to state that his uncompromising rejection of the Lutheran doctrine of Justification *sola fides* constitutes an irrefutable commitment to the Catholic faith. It is, after all, this question of the relationship between man and God that lies at the heart of the Reformation message. At the same time, however, Lindsay was deeply concerned by the visible abuses he saw around him and, inspired by the ideas of Erasmian humanism, he was driven to launch an impassioned plea for a spiritual and moral renaissance of the religious life. More alarmingly for the Church, this was supplemented by a potentially radical political critique which took its cue from developments south of the border. Pushed into an ever more hostile position, Lindsay ended up denying some important tenets of the Catholic faith, and in places his work displays the subtle yet unmistakable influence of Protestant thinking. Though not an out-and-out Protestant, Lindsay was certainly something more than a straightforward Catholic reformer.

From the known onset of his literary career Lindsay was deeply vexed by questions of sin and salvation, of heaven and hell, and, on a more terrestrial plane, by the conduct of Church affairs (especially clerical standards) in sixteenth-century Scotland. From *The Dreme* to *The Monarche,* these issues inform most of his work. Expressing his dissatisfaction with the ecclesiastical establishment and lampooning its members, Lindsay's work was conditioned by a long tradition of religious satire teeming with familiar characters and well-worn complaints. This observation highlights one of the most serious problems facing historians who attempt to use fictional texts in order to illuminate historical reality. For it must be appreciated that literary depictions of the Church and its personnel were largely determined by the demands of generic convention, language and imagery being conditioned by traditional expectations. As we shall see, Lindsay's discussion of Church affairs relies upon several very traditional literary motifs, all of which would have been extremely familiar to his sixteenth-century audience. Indeed, they would hardly have expected him to write in any other way, and it would not be overstating the case to say that traditional poetic forms and existing stereotypes conditioned the public discussion of religion. On the other hand, for Lindsay, this conventional discourse represented a particularly apt way of articulating his ideas, not all of which were as accepted as the forms in which they were expressed.

The very fact that religious satire itself has a history is testimony to the enduring gulf between the lofty idealism that inspired the Church and the often less than laudable practices of its personnel. The discontent of Renaissance critics was of course nothing new; the history of the Church is littered with repeated attempts to admonish the slack and to promote renewed Christian zeal. But, in the first decades of the sixteenth century, the Church was particularly vulnerable to criticism, however conventionally expressed. Indeed, this was recognized by the Church itself which, even before the Council of Trent had finished framing the official response to the Protestant challenge, attempted to initiate a measure of reform. In Scotland, a series of provincial councils held between the years 1549 and 1559 sought "to restore tranquility and preserve complete unity in the ecclesiastical estate," attempting to assuage its grumbling congregations and stem the drift to heresy.[8] The deliberations of these assemblies can make lurid reading. No doubt the anguish kindled by a perceived "corruption of morals and profane lewdness of life in churchmen of almost all ranks" was in part justified.[9] Yet, despite the problems that undoubtedly existed, it is a serious mistake to overemphasize the weaknesses of the Church in early-sixteenth-century Scotland. The relative spiritual and material health of the monasteries, the many collegiate foundations of the period, numerous endowments and donations generously bequeathed (especially to the friars), and a popular enthusiasm for shrines and pilgrimages testify to the fact that, in many respects, the Kirk was a vital organization which continued to command a great deal of loyal respect among the faithful. Few of the most visible cases of abuse were new, and several probably aroused a general feeling of what is best described as tolerant irritation. Yet, in certain quarters at least, the problems of the Church provoked a new type of outrage, a new demand for increased lay participation in the religious life. As Jenny Wormald reminds us, the complaints that so disturbed sixteenth-century churchmen represent no more than the criticisms of an articulate minority.[10] But it is equally true that any chance of change lay only with this elite.

Several reasons help to explain the changing attitude of these newly vocal critics of the Church, not least the fact that, owing to increased levels of lay literacy, many were for the first time able to locate their own experiences within a wider context and to articulate their demands in a way that proved increasingly difficult to ignore. For some, calls for religious change were underpinned by potent ideological considerations, either by the ideas of humanism or by the new Protestant faith. Humanist scholarship, with its emphasis on classical language and learning, philological and textual criticism, rhetoric and history, posed a number of challenges to ecclesiastical authority. Long-accepted interpretations of Scripture were subjected to a new informed criticism, and the quest for textual fidelity was paralleled by calls for a revived spiritual purity aimed at sweeping away the abuses of the past. With ignorance and tradition blocking the path to virtue and salvation, the scholarship of Christian humanism offered the key to improved spiritual well-being. As such, it was by no means inimical to orthodox theology but, in a situation already disturbed by the gradual infiltration of Protestant opinion, it added another unsettling voice to the religious debate.

Lutheran ideas had been entering Scotland, principally via the East Coast ports, since the 1520s and, despite the government's panic legislation of 1525 and 1527 forbidding the importation of heretical literature, trade in these doctrinally suspect cargoes persisted.[11] In a letter of 1534, James V informed the Council of his concern that Lutheran tracts were being smuggled into "Leith, Edinburgh, Dundee, Sanctandrois, Montros, Abirdene and Kirkaldy," ordering them to "provid and see the scharpest way possible for the staunching thereof."[12] Of equal if not greater significance for the influx of Protestant opinion, although far harder to trace, was the influence of individuals and their personal relationships. We can perhaps guess at the impact of Protestant martyrs such as Patrick Hamilton or George Wishart, but it is much harder to assess the role played by anonymous traveling scholars and merchants or even more specific figures, men like the Cromwellian emissaries to the Scottish court, Dr. William Barlow and Sir Ralph Sadler. Significantly perhaps, English rumors alleged that attempts were made to hasten Barlow's departure "for fear he suld contaminate some of the Scottish court with this new sect."[13] If this is true, it may have been more than an expression of paranoia on the part of the Scottish government for, returning to Scotland the following year, Barlow was able to report that he had obtained secret information regarding the king's Council from "a few credyble frendys."[14]

A further problem for those attempting to chart the early faltering steps of Protestantism in Scotland relates to the "Lutheran literature" reportedly in circulation. The use of this blanket terminology makes it unclear which ideas were available and could be most readily taken up. What does seem certain is that a major part of the illicit book trade was devoted to the importation of English vernacular Bibles. An English ambassador in Antwerp in 1527 reported that English books, notably Tyndale's New Testament, were being shipped into both England and Scotland, to Edinburgh and St. Andrews in particular.[15] The impact of such literature and indeed of Lutheran opinion in general is extremely difficult to assess. Its spread seems to have been a fragmentary business possessing no real geographic or theological unity. However, whether it is true to declare the growth of Protestantism before 1540 and even later as a "far from major problem" is debatable.[16] The existence of pockets of heretical opinion within the country and at court should not be overlooked. It had put down roots which although not widespread did, in places, run deep and which, most important of all, proved difficult to weed out. Certainly the suppliers of vernacular Bibles and Lutheran texts considered that demand warranted the hazardous business of exportation, and their wares were eagerly received by a minority of Scots, some of whom—as is testified by the library of Sir John Borthwick— were influential members of society.[17] We cannot say for certain whether Lindsay had access to such literature, but at least one commentator thinks that he may have read Luther's writings, and there is enough in his work to demonstrate a degree of familiarity with Protestant opinion.[18]

Far easier to trace is the debt owed by Lindsay to scriptural sources. As has been pointed out, Lindsay's most consistent biblical source is the Vulgate, but it has been suggested that at some stage in his career he also acquired an English New Testament.[19] This would certainly accord with the vigorous support of vernacular Scripture found in his work, but it is in fact quite difficult to tell which, if any, of the available English Bibles Lindsay may have owned. A plausible candidate is that brandished by Veritie in *Ane Satyre of the Thrie Estatis,* "In Englisch toung, and printit in England" (1146). The first English Bible to merit such a description is Coverdale's translation, first printed in 1535 and issued two years later under royal license. The same year also saw the London publication of Matthew's Bible, a work which drew upon the earlier versions of both Coverdale and Tyndale. An edition of the latter's New Testament was produced in London in 1538, and in the following year the Great Bible (Coverdale's revision of Matthew's Bible) appeared.[20] It was probably this which was used by the English government in its attempted destabilization of the Scottish Borders and also, briefly, when supporting the reform policy of Arran's regency administration.[21] This perhaps is the most likely Bible possessed by an evangelical Scot such as Lindsay for, if he obtained it in the early 1540s, it would explain the increasingly intense concern with the dissemination of vernacular Scripture observable in his later works.

The ideological and religious influx that existed in the early-to-mid sixteenth century was particularly noticeable at court where a number of religious evangelicals—of whatever theological persuasion—attempted to influence the future direction of royal policy. With James himself appearing to encourage this development, it must have seemed as if the heart and mind of the king were there for the winning. Such perceptions gave rise to a keen public discussion of Church reform, evidenced most notably by the work of David Lindsay. The Epiphany drama of 1540 provides arguably the most compelling case for considering court literature as a form of evangelical persuasion but, at least a decade before this date, Lindsay was using his verse to exhort James to "haue Ee" (*The Complaynt,* 412) to the spiritual estate.

Bearing in mind the problems involved in using literary texts for such an analysis, it is still possible to show how Lindsay's early works—*The Dreme, The Complaynt,* and *The Testament of the Papyngo*—illuminate the religious debate as it was conducted within court circles. The most striking point to emerge from an examination of these poems is their debt to humanist thinking and to the type of ideas associated with Erasmus in particular. Through Lindsay's poetry, an Erasmian-inspired reforming agenda was set clearly and insistently before king and court. Typically, Lindsay's position in these early works is theologically conservative, at least so far as his fleeting references to matters of doctrine allow us to judge. But even this reticence serves to confirm that this is an essentially humanist critique.

Concerned largely with questions of moral behavior, Lindsay launches a passionate indictment of the Church's failings addressed, again in typical humanist fashion, to the king. His aggressive attack, albeit ethically oriented and highly contingent upon his chosen poetic genre, actually represented a challenge to the Church on a number of fronts: He assailed clerical standards with accusations of ignorance and immorality, he challenged the position of the Church in secular affairs (specifically its legal jurisdiction) and, by citing the example of the pure apostolic Church and with reference to Scripture, he brought into question the validity of several established aspects of the Church's teaching.

By far the most frequent and most vehement of Lindsay's complaints in these poems are those directed against standards of clerical behavior and morality. Of course, the corrupt cleric had long been the butt of medieval satirists as, pressing home the moral message, they also exploited the comic potential afforded by a familiar cast of stock characters. Clearly, this well-established literary tradition exerted a significant influence on Lindsay's work. The amusing examination of the proud bishop, the gluttonous monk, and the worldly parson found in *Ane Satyre of the Thrie Estatis* relies very heavily on three time-honored clerical stereotypes. Such examples warn us against viewing literary texts as a straightforward depiction of reality. Nevertheless, while admitting that literary convention shaped Lindsay's work to some extent, we should also note that it served as an entirely appropriate vehicle for the expression of his ideas. As has already been observed in another context, the ethical thrust of much medieval literature, the complaint genre in particular, perfectly complements the moral emphasis inherent in any humanist critique.

Like that of many humanists, Lindsay's attack upon churchmen was savage in expression, yet by no means radical in intention. Simply put, he believed that the spiritual estate no longer "mad ministratioun / Conforme to thare vocatioun" (*The Complaynt,* 414–15). The ignorance, immorality, and worldliness of the clergy he considered deplorable in themselves, but more importantly they interposed a serious barrier between the people and their salvation. Typically, Lindsay measured the failings of the sixteenth century in terms of a perceived discrepancy between it and a consciously historical vision of the early Christian Church. As the dying parrot tells her deathbed companions, "ye bene all / Degenerit from your holy prematyuis, / As testyfeis the proces of your lyuis" (*The Testament of the Papyngo,* 770–72). Something of a literary cliché, this approach was widely adopted by evangelical reformers, both humanist and Protestant, and it was eagerly seized on by Lindsay as an explanation for present decadence and a model for future conduct.[22] First employed in *The Complaynt,* the idea is most comprehensively expressed in *The Testament of the Papyngo* when the dying parrot presents an elaborate, allegorical account of the corruption of the Christian ideal. Through his mouthpiece the Papyngo, Lindsay identifies the outstanding attributes of the early Church as chastity, poverty, devotion, and evangelism, praising the humility of Spiritualitie's "peirles, prudent predicessouris" (773).

This was not, however, the first occasion on which Lindsay used his work to discuss, or rather to criticize, the clergy. Like *The Testament of the Papyngo,* both *The Dreme* and *The Complaynt* display a virulent, if hugely traditional, streak of literary anticlericalism. In all of these poems, the attack is grounded in questions of moral behavior, frequently being expressed in abstract, allegorical language. Yet there is a sense in which these three works illustrate a shift in Lindsay's thinking as he begins to use traditional forms and ideas to engage in a more precise discussion of ecclesiastical abuse. In *The Dreme,* Lindsay describes those prelates, wicked yet unnamed, who writhe in Hell; in *The Complaynt,* he satirizes the ambitious churchmen of sixteenth-century Scotland; and finally, in *The Testament of the Papyngo,* the dying parrot offers a uniquely personal insight into the consequences of clerical corruption.

Constructing a statistical analysis of Lindsay's criticisms of the Church is not as straightforward as it might seem. Many points are repeated and rephrased within the course of a few lines; some are made explicitly, others more overtly. And does the praise of virtue constitute the condemnation of its antonym? The value of such an exercise is in any case questionable, for what matters here is not whether Lindsay satirizes churchmen rather more for their lust than for their greed but the fact that such ethical considerations dominate his critique. Indeed, since the sexually immoral cleric—to name but one example—was a familiar figure of medieval satire, his appearance in Lindsay's work tells us little. Though Lindsay uses *The Dreme* to depict Hell inhabited by ecclesiastics who misappropriated their revenues to clothe their mistresses and provide for their bastards, his criticism is couched in general terms only, with none of the specifically targeted attacks found, for example, in the later *Satyre.* Thus Dame Rememberance shows the narrator the fate of those prelates whose "Couatyce, Luste, and ambysioun" (183) have condemned them to eternal damnation, while the charges levied against contemporary churchmen by John the Commonweal are conceived of in the same abstract, ethical manner. Describing how he has been driven away by "the Spiritual stait" (976), John complains that Simony "rewlis vp all that rowte" (979), that Covatice has barred him entry, that Pride has chased off Humility, that Devotion has fled, and that Sensual Pleasure has banished Chastity. His allegorical language is in keeping with the poem as a whole which presents a diagnosis of social ills in an accustomed ethical formulation and demands a moral regeneration of all elements of society in order to restore the health of the commonweal. The importance of universal moralities is paramount. Thus, in his "Exhortatioun to the Kyngis Grace," Lindsay offers no specific suggestions for Church reform but focuses instead upon an ultratraditional advocacy of the cardinal virtues.

By contrast, *The Complaynt* explicitly urges James to "haue Ee" (412) unto the spiritual estate and to suppress such allegedly superstitious practices as pilgrimages and praying to images. *The Complaynt,* the most overtly autobiographical of Lindsay's works, is also grounded much more firmly in his own experiences during the minority regimes of the 1520s. Again, however, we should be wary of accepting literary criticism as a reflection of historical reality. Even if presented by a convincingly "real" narrator identifiable from the records, the depiction of Scottish prelates during this period was not intended as a detailed account of their activities. The vain and worldly churchmen stand alongside the equally stylized courtiers, fools and flatterers concerned only with their own self-interest and the corruption of the young king. The traditions of an anticourt literature provide Lindsay with a useful, not to mention colorful, portrait of the "peruerst Prelatis" (344), underlining the moral corruption that was his real satirical target:

> The proudest Prelatis of the kirk
> Was faine to hyde thame in the myrk
> That tyme, so failyeit wes thare sycht   (309–11)

Although it has been argued that these lines refer to the deprivation of Archbishop James Beaton by Angus in 1526, the message is surely best seen as the ethically inspired criticism of those worldly and cynical churchmen whose eyes ought to have been upon higher things.[23] Nevertheless, that Lindsay chose to stress worldly ambition above any other moral failing (there is, for example, none of the usual criticism of clerical promiscuity found in his other works) is probably significant, illustrating how even formulaic denunciations of the clergy allowed Lindsay to engage in a more contemporary debate. The dual role of churchmen as spiritual pastors on the one hand and as secular landowners, statesmen, lawyers, and officials on the other had always generated some tension, but this had largely been mitigated by the fact that, in a virtually illiterate lay society, the educated clergy were the only suitable candidates for such positions. However, by the sixteenth century, the situation was changing, owing not least to the humanist program for lay education. Now that an increasing number of laymen were able to occupy positions hitherto monopolized by the Church, the nature of clerical duties was viewed more critically.

The Complaynt matches a condemnation of clerical involvement in domestic politics with an attack upon their position in the court and Session:

So blyndit is thare corporall Ene
With wardly lustis sensuall,
Takyng in realmes the gouernall,
Baith gyding court and cessioun,
Contrar to thare professioun,   (314–18)

According to Lindsay, clerical involvement in this respect should allow only for intervention in matters spiritual, "Referryng vnto lordis and kyngis / Temporall causis to be desydit" (328–29). In this way, Lindsay developed a conventional criticism of clerical worldliness into a vigorous challenge to the role of the Church in secular government. Lindsay could be sure that such a challenge would receive an appreciative response from at least certain sections of his audience. Tension between the secular and spiritual authorities seems to have been a feature of the period, surfacing, for example, in February 1539 with Foulis's claim that "hes grace nor his lordis of counsale be nocht astreynit to obey ony inhibitions fra ony judge spirituale, bot that thai may proceid in ony matter and geffe lettres conforme to justice as the use has ben in tymis bigane."[24]

As in both *The Dreme* and *The Complaynt,* the condemnation of abuses found in *The Testament of the Papyngo* benefits from being articulated by one who suffers at the hands of an immoral clerical establishment. Asked to explain why churchmen are held in such low esteem, the dying parrot offers a vivid account of the Church's corruption by Property, Riches, and Sensuality. In the same terms used by John the Commonweal in *The Dreme,* she describes how Sensuality seduced the spiritual estate and procured the banishment of Dame Chastity. However, there is in Lindsay's treatment of chastity a rather more specific discussion of the Church, namely a consideration of the female religious, specifically the Convent of Sciennes in Edinburgh. Although he criticizes "The sillye Nonnis" (908) for succumbing to the blandishment of Riches and Sensuality, he is full of praise for the virtuous sisters of Sciennes. The explanation for this is not clear; perhaps it was simply that Sciennes was a recent foundation and the nuns all ladies of rank, but, even if Lindsay looked favorably on the convents in 1530, he would in time adopt a much more hostile opinion.

Her comments on the nuns excepted, the Papyngo's criticism, like that found in both *The Dreme* and *The Complaynt,* is aimed at the top of the ecclesiastical hierarchy. Certainly, the bishops were, as Wormald terms them, the "headline-hitters" of the pre-Reformation Kirk.[25] Exemplifying some of the most conspicuous abuses in the Scottish Church, the "Lordis of Religioun" (*The Dreme,* 984) presented an obvious and, arguably, an easy satirical target. In *The Testament of the Papyngo,* however, Lindsay widens the scope of his attack, and the three birds who appear to rob the dying parrot disguise themselves as an Augustinian canon, a monk, and a friar. This poem is particularly interesting for the light it sheds upon Lindsay's ambivalent attitude to the friars. Like later criticisms of their privileges, their craven reluctance to denounce malpractice, and their idolatry, the unflattering depiction of the bird-friar owed much to a long-standing tradition of antimendicant literature.[26] Yet on other occasions Lindsay rejects this deeply ingrained, highly popular discourse and adopts a markedly less hostile tone. The reason for this may lie in the friars' place in the religious life of pre-Reformation Scotland. Active preachers in the community, the scale of donations and endowments made to them suggests they received considerable lay support, and although he believed preaching to be the duty of the secular clergy, Lindsay acknowledges mendicant achievements in this field.[27] Surely it is this that lies behind his occasional ambivalence, evidenced for example by *The Dreme,* which describes how virtue has been largely driven from the spiritual estate and "Deuotion is fled vnto the freris" (982). In *The Testament of the Papyngo,* beside the savage characterization of the false friar, admiration and criticism are more finely balanced in the observation that were it not for the preaching of the "beggyng freiris / Tynt [lost] war the faith amang the Secularis" (1036–37). Later, Lindsay's opinion hardened, and increasingly frequent and savage criticism culminates in *Ane Satyre* where, in a possibly deliberate parody of his earlier image, the "Deuotioun" who hides himself among the friars is really Flatterie under an assumed name. Lindsay's attitude toward the mendicant orders has been examined in some detail as it nicely illustrates the difficulties of attempting a categorical assessment of his opinion, especially given the literary clichés in which much of the discussion was couched. We can offer definite statements only with respect to any particular period, and even they may require careful qualification.

Focusing on the experiences of the dying parrot, *The Testament of the Papyngo* offers a more precisely targeted critique of clerical abuse, specifically of clerical avarice, which suggests its consequences not just for the general well-being of the commonweal but also for the individual. Despite the instances of saintly poverty cited as examples of virtue, Lindsay makes it clear that riches, of themselves, are not at issue. Despite the parrot's denunciation of the Donation of Constantine and her allegorical account of how Property and her daughter Riches seduced the ecclesiastical estate, she concedes that "Ryches, . . . is not to be refusit, / Prouidyng, alwaye, it be nocht abusit" (973–75). And, when the raven claims that "Lang tyme efter the kirk tuke propertie, / the Prelatis leuit in gret perfectioun" (983–84), he is not being entirely disingenuous, for Lindsay here leaves off attacking the historical endowment of the Church and concentrates instead upon those secular princes whose ill-judged ecclesiastical patronage encourages avarice and ambition.

Just how devastating the consequences of material greed can be is brutally illustrated by the deathbed encounter between the unfortunate parrot and the three feigned clerics, the pye (magpie), raven, and gled (kite). Although the three avow their concern for the Papyngo's spiritual welfare, it is immediately apparent that their only interest lies in her "gudis naturall" (658). Following her death they reveal their true carrion nature and "Full gormondlyke" (1149) fall upon the Papyngo's corpse, devouring it "Quhill scho is hote" (1151). The poem, which begins as a courtly rendition of a fall-of-princes type tragedy, the language elevated and dignified, ends on a completely different note, evoking squalid morality, physical violence, and, in the audience, revulsion and horror.

In attacking the worldly greed of the clerical establishment, Lindsay was hitting the Church in its most vulnerable spot, for arguably financial grievances did more than any other to sour clerical-lay relationships at least at a parochial level. The problem here was the system of appropriations whereby the revenues of the parish were appropriated by various religious institutions such as cathedrals, monasteries, collegiate churches, and universities. By the sixteenth century, the revenues of 86 percent of all parish churches had been appropriated, and by 1560 only 148 remained independent.[28] Arrangements to serve the appropriated parishes involved the installation of a vicar. However, failure to provide the majority of vicars with an adequate stipend meant that they were rarely of the highest caliber, and economic necessity forced many to exploit what was their most readily available source of extra income, their parishioners. Teinds (which formed part of the appropriated income) were rigorously exacted, often resulting in acrimonious litigation, and on top of this the average parishioner faced numerous and strident demands for mortuary dues and other voluntary offerings. Significantly, unlike his earlier works, *The Testament of the Papyngo* focuses its satirical attack on the parish community. "The wyffis of the village cryis, with cair" (712) at the approach of the greedy friar, and the parrot herself recalls his theft of a chicken. As we shall see, Lindsay's criticism of the Church was increasingly concerned with abuse at the grassroots level, charting its effects not only upon the body politic but also upon individual members of society.

LINDSAY'S contribution to the religious debate represented more than a traditionally articulated, humanist-inspired attack upon some of the most visible failings of the Church. His early poems also serve to promote a typically humanist program for education, preaching, and spiritual reform.

"Thame promoue that war moste sapient" (1031), advises the raven in *The Testament of the Papyngo* while, dealing with the wider problem of an uneducated clergy, he urges lay lords to ensure the education of their sons, thereby guaranteeing a new generation of learned clerics. This stress on education as the key to spiritual regeneration is typical of humanist, especially Erasmian, thinking. Ironically, although the situation is so desperate that even the raven recognizes the problem, he and his two colleagues display an ignorance of vocation and office bordering on the sacrilegious. The birds' frantic attempts to persuade the Papyngo of their sincerity only comprise such casual allusions to their offices as to suggest their utter depravity. Willing to "deuotely saye . . . / The auld Placebo bakwart" (704–5), they are prepared to minister to the parrot even if her soul "with Pluto war profest" (708). Such clerical disregard for the spiritual welfare of their flock was what really fired Lindsay's anger, and his criticisms are directed not against the "crass ignorance of literature and all the liberal arts" which concerned even the ecclesiastical establishment but against the clergy's failure to grasp the nature of their vocation.[29] As Lindsay understood it, priests had a sacred duty "To Preche with vnfenyeit intentis, / And trewly vse the Sacramentis, / Efter Christis Institutionis" (*The Complaynt*, 415–17). By 1530 the preaching of the Gospel and the administration of the sacraments according to Christ's institution were distinctive marks of the Church for Lutherans, and Lindsay seems here to echo the Confession of Augsburg formulated that same year: "The Church is the Congregation of the saints, in which the Gospel is rightly taught and the sacraments are rightly administered."[30] Although Lindsay's words are not in themselves unorthodox and hardly constitute conclusive proof of a commitment to Lutheran beliefs, they do suggest that the spirit of the Reformers was beginning to exert a subtle influence on his ideas and to inform the language in which he expressed himself.

Of the two vocational elements mentioned by Lindsay, it was preaching—arguably the key issue of the pre-Reformation period—which claimed the greater part of his attention:

> Gret plesour war to heir ane Byschope preche,
> One Dane, or Doctour in Divinitie,
> One Abbote quhilk could weill his conuent teche,
> One Persoun flowing in Phylosophie.
>
> (*The Testament of the Papyngo*, 1032–35)

In *The Dreme*, the principal issue at stake is salvation through penance, and churchmen who "did nocht instruct the Ignorant, / Prouocand thame to pennance, be preching" (190–91), languish in the "painefull poysonit pytt of hell" (189). In *The Complaynt*, however, the emphasis has been subtly shifted. Lindsay declares preaching the rightful "professioun" (325) of clerics and, echoing Isaiah, he compares those who do not preach to "Doggis that can nocht bark" (322).[31] But he no longer links his call for increased preaching with the administration of the sacraments and that particular path to salvation. His words suggest instead a more Scripture-based, evangelical conception of preaching as he attacks those priests who "may nocht thole the lycht / Off Christis trew Gospel to be sene" (312–13). Again this shows an intellectual debt to humanist, possibly even to Lutheran, ideas. While in general Lindsay's treatment of matters of doctrine in these early poems is largely conservative, it is possible to detect instances of some more radical thinking. It should of course be noted that this is not a prominent feature of these works; nor, given the nondogmatic character of the pre-Tridentine Church, would Lindsay's theological ambiguity necessarily have brought him into conflict with the clerical authorities. Nevertheless, these early flashes of a more unorthodox approach are well worth consideration.

From at least 1528, Lindsay's understanding of Purgatory seems to have been somewhat unclear. It appears in *The Dreme* as a port of call in the narrator's dream-voyage when, having described his journey through Hell, Lindsay continues with his passage through Purgatory and Limbo. But, compared to his detailed treatment of the former, these receive scant attention: Twenty-five stanzas deal with Hell, only four with both Purgatory and Limbo. Moreover, although the narrator dreams of Purgatory, he appears to question whether it is the inevitable destination of his soul. "I purpose neuir to cum heir agane," he tells Dame Rememberance but, recollecting the teachings of the Church, adds (somewhat cryptically):

> Bot, yit, I do beleue, and euer sall,
> That the trew kirk can no waye erre at all.
> Sic thyng to be gret Clerkis dois conclude;
> Quhowbeit, my hope standis most in cristis blude. (347–50)

The emphasis on Christ's suffering as the basis of hope was characteristically, although by no means exclusively, a feature of Lutheran thinking. Whether Lindsay was in fact here seriously challenging the Church along Lutheran lines is almost impossible to tell; he was of necessity highly ambiguous, and only tone of voice could reflect any intended irony in the narrator's possible repudiation of the learned clerks' scholarship. The phrase "the trew kirk" is also suggestive, for Lutherans commonly drew the distinction between the true Church, which cannot err, and that of tradition, which can. Again, however, it is hard to decide whether Lindsay is deliberately expounding a specific Protestant viewpoint or whether his language and general outlook have been more subtly informed by the ideas of the Reformation. It is, in fact, much easier to note Lindsay's ambivalence than to trace its roots. On the one hand, there were several prominent humanist thinkers who derided the mechanics of the doctrine of Purgatory, the "imaginary pardons" and laborious mathematical calculations used to tot up the time one could expect to spend there.[32] On the other hand, it is also interesting that the denial of Purgatory was one of the charges leveled against the Lutheran martyr Patrick Hamilton, being subsequently linked with the heresies associated with his teaching.[33] As such, it may have been one of the more conspicuous features of early Scottish Protestantism. However, which of these—if either—Lindsay picked up on is unclear. Whichever it was, it seems to have strengthened his understanding of the personal relationship between God and his soul, deepening his suspicions of the Church's claims in this respect.

In *The Complaynt,* Lindsay turned his attention to images and pilgrimages, but here his criticisms owe little to Protestant thinking and everything to the humanist-informed attack upon "vaine traditiounis" (418).[34] In selecting "superstitious pylgramagis" (421) and "Prayand to grawin Ymagis" (422) as his targets, it is hard to say whether Lindsay was first and foremost demonstrating, even flaunting, his familiarity with contemporary humanist concerns or whether in fact he was drawing attention to two aspects of the popular religious life in Scotland crying out for reform.[35] Certainly, given Lindsay's humanist sympathies, they appeared so to him, and he would return to both issues at greater length in later works. In *The Monarche,* for example, he presents an extended account of the "Imageis maid with mennis hand" (2282) found "in every kirk and queir / Throuch Christindome, in burgh and land" (2280–81). The list of some thirty saints popular in Scotland suggests that, whether Lindsay approved or not, these icons played an important role in popular religious life. Pilgrimages too exercised a powerful hold on the Scottish imagination. Probably owing to rising costs and to religious and political upheavals within Europe, pilgrims in the sixteenth century traveled more frequently within Scotland than outside it. Traditional Scottish devotional centers remained popular, and new shrines, like that at Loretto in Musselburgh, were founded.[36] But, if Lindsay hoped to persuade the king to put a halt to the pilgrimage industry, he was plowing stony ground. James V, like his father before him, was an enthusiastic pilgrim and a generous patron of shrines, including the much derided Loretto.[37]

Like both *The Dreme* and *The Complaynt, The Testament of the Papyngo* articulates a basically humanist critique of the sixteenth-century Church, railing at abuses but accepting the essential tenets of the Catholic faith. The portrayal of the false confessors represents an attack not upon the doctrine of the Confession but upon the corrupt practices that accompany it, and despite her misgivings the parrot makes her final confession and is shriven.

In one respect, however, *The Papyngo* does adopt a more radical position. This is the question of clerical marriage, a measure championed by Protestant rather than humanist thinkers and one which Lindsay too supported. Arguing that celibacy leads only to promiscuity and that clerical marriage was sanctioned by the apostolic Church, he calls for the marriage of prelates to be sanctioned under papal license. Until the Council of Trent made the opposing position a matter of dogma, the advocacy of clerical marriage was not, strictly speaking, a heretical act. It is, however, hard to visualize how even his qualification would have rendered Lindsay's proposal acceptable to the Church authorities. Certainly the issue appears to have been particularly contentious in Scotland during the 1530s when a number of Protestant sympathizers, said to have attended the marriage of Thomas Cocklaw, vicar of Tullibody, were executed for heresy.[38] Albeit not the sole charge against them, the marriage ceremony does seems to have been the catalyst provoking the Church to action in the matter.

Lindsay's participation in the religious debate had the dual intention of exposing corruption and inspiring reform. Typically, the agent of reform was the king. Given Lindsay's very king-centered political thinking, this is hardly surprising. Moreover, such an approach was in line with how humanist thinkers tended to address the problem and, since the Scottish king, like many of his European counterparts, had gradually accumulated a whole host of rights over the Church in his realm, the strategy was not without some justification.[39] The direct "Exhortatioun" contained in *The Dreme* does not, it is true, specifically address the question of religious reform, but the main body of the poem strongly suggests that such action is required. This is made explicit in *The Complaynt* where, giving greater force to his advice to "haue Ee" (412) to spiritual affairs, Lindsay reminds James of those biblical kings who resisted idolatry and were rewarded by God and—more tellingly perhaps—of the fates of those who did not. Although the Papyngo's "Epystyll to the Kyng" offers no specific advice concerning the ecclesiastical estate, the message benefits from being more forcefully articulated in the second part of the poem where the raven lays the blame for the avarice, worldliness, and ignorance of the clergy squarely upon princes who secure benefices for unworthy candidates. This was hardly a novel criticism. The fifteenth-century poem *The Thrie Prestis of Peblis* levied exactly the same charge against a negligent monarch who, realizing the truth of the complaint, is driven to surrender all interest in "kirk-gude" (434) and to declare that churchmen shall "have all the charge" (435). Lindsay's solution was less radical, proposing that appointments be made in consultation with "ane Congregatioun" (1019) of learned kirkmen. Whether James would have been happy with this constraint upon his ecclesiastical patronage is doubtful, but he may have been more responsive to the idea subtly suggested when the gled snatches up the Papyngo's heart, bequeathed by her to the king. The Church, such an episode implies, is avaricious to the point of robbing the crown. The corollary of this, insinuated if not openly stated, is that the king should consider remedial action and retribution. However, Lindsay here was not demanding that the king undertake a full-scale Protestant settlement. Rather, he called upon him to encourage what was essentially a program of moral regeneration along humanist lines. There is in these early works no real political element of the kind that made this type of criticism so threatening to the Church. Nor, as yet, did Lindsay envisage a role for the king that went beyond the traditional guardianship of Haly Kirk.

LINDSAY'S discussion of ecclesiastical affairs in these early poems is conditioned by an essentially personal piety focusing upon the individual's relationship with Christ rather than upon the intercessory and interpretive role of the Church. We have already seen something of this in the discussion of Lindsay's attitude toward Purgatory and his declared intention to place his hope "in cristis blude" (*The Dreme,* 350). This emphasis on Christ was probably one of the most important features of late-medieval piety, and the enormous expansion of interest in the Passion helps explain both the popularity of mysticism (a particularly flourishing tradition in fifteenth-century England) and the type of contemplative spirituality known as *devotio moderna* popular on the Continent.[40] It also informed the thinking of northern humanists such as Erasmus who criticized mechanical devotion and vulgar superstition, emphasizing instead the inner life and personal piety.

> Quharefor traist nocht in tyll auctoritie,
> My deir brother, I praye yow hartfullie,
> Presume nocht in your vaine prosperitie;
> Conforme your traist in God alluterlie;
> (*The Testament of the Papyngo,* 598–601)

As this passage illustrates, such contemplative personal spirituality often accompanied a renunciation of trust in earthly institutions. But reconciling the conflicting calls of piety and position proved difficult for Lindsay, and his early work vividly reveals the uncomfortable ideological tensions felt by a courtier who was often profoundly disturbed by his environment. As described by Lindsay, the court offers an uncertain life. Not only does the arbitrary force of Fortune pull security from under men's feet, but even basic ideals of Christian morality offer no guide. At court, the accepted moral code is twisted and perverted; self-indulgence and licentiousness flourish, corruption and depravity prosper. Of course, this type of anticourt literature was very traditional, and to a certain extent the lurid pictures of court life found in *The Complaynt* and *The Testament of the Papyngo* should be seen as part of this stylized genre. Nevertheless, Lindsay's unease appears to run deeper than this. Both his animal-courtiers, the Papyngo and Bagsche the king's hound, ultimately lament that they ever came to court in the first place, and we cannot help wondering whether this is an expression of Lindsay's own regrets. In *The Complaynt,* he considers the merits of a "quiet lyfe, and sober rent" (504), threatening to withdraw "Unto my sempyll Hermytage" (506). The context of this warning—the mock petition of a disgruntled old servant—cautions against taking it too seriously, but its juxtaposition against a particularly repellent depiction of a morally bank-rupt court does heighten its attraction. Moreover, it is perhaps significant that, pondering the same question more than twenty years later, Lindsay returns to these ideas employing exactly the same turn of phrase (*The Monarche,* 4999). The reconciliation of the court of the earthly prince and that of Christ attempted in Lindsay's early poems is an uneasy business. "Syne, serue your Prince, with enteir hart, trewlie," he writes, "And, quhen ye see the court bene at the best, / I counsall yow, than draw you to your rest" (*The Testament of the Papyngo,* 602–4). But it is hard to believe that Lindsay was satisfied with such a clumsy attempt at resolving the dichot-omy. Indeed, that he was not is, as we shall see, clear from his final work, *The Monarche,* which as well as conveying his personal struggle with this question also demonstrates its final triumphant resolution.

EIGHT

Controversy and Conflict

1530–1555

Following the composition of *The Testament of the Papyngo* in 1530, Lindsay appears to have withdrawn from the discussion of religious affairs. He was, it is true, probably involved in the 1540 Epiphany drama, but it was not until the late 1540s that he produced anything comparable to his earlier critique. Of course, there may have been such works, now lost, but it could simply be that during this period (certainly until 1543) his official duties proved increasingly time-consuming. In terms of his diplomatic activity, this period represents Lindsay's busiest, and between 1530 and 1537 he spent a total of at least two years outside Scotland. There were other reasons too why his experiences abroad may have checked Lindsay's evangelical enthusiasm, for in France and England alike he saw just how damaging its consequences could be for domestic tranquility, not to mention for those whose involvement in the debate cost them their lives. A more tangible result of the diplomacy of the 1530s—the French marriages of James V—also served to discourage debate. In 1537 James returned from France having promised action against Lutherans in Scotland, and a year later his marriage to Mary of Guise allied the Scottish royal house with one of the most staunchly orthodox families at the French court.[1] In a period when the Scottish Church was rather more on the offensive in the battle against heresy (nineteen people were executed in the decade and a half after 1528), Lindsay may have deemed it prudent to withdraw from such a public forum. Whatever the reasons for Lindsay's apparent silence, it was only with *The Tragedie of the Cardinal* that he returned to religious polemic (though, as the work of Buchanan and the activities of men such as John Borthwick demonstrate, the debate continued irrespective of Lindsay). Nevertheless, it would be wrong to consider this a fallow period insofar as the development of his thinking is concerned. On the contrary, his experiences in three key areas were to prove enormously influential. These were his travels outside Scotland, the situation at the Scottish court, and, particularly during the later 1540s, his position as a member of the Fife community.

IN THE SUMMER of 1531, Lindsay undertook his first known journey outside Scotland, and his seven-week stay at the imperial court at Brussels saw him well placed to observe some of the direct consequences of religious controversy. Arriving in the wake of the Diet of Augsburg where attempts to restore peace had not only foundered but resulted in military mobilization on both sides of the theological divide, Lindsay would have been well aware of the links between religious controversy and civil conflict. He himself reported the preparations made for an imperial expedition against the German Lutherans, and it is tempting to suggest that Lindsay's determination to encourage the authorities along the peaceful path of ecclesiastical reform arose, in part at least, from firsthand knowledge of what happened when conciliation yielded to confrontation.

Following his visit to the imperial court, Lindsay was dispatched to France, a member of the party commissioned to treat for the Franco-Scottish marriage alliance. In fact, during the course of the 1530s Lindsay visited the country no less than three times. As elsewhere in western Europe, the ideological situation in France was far from settled. Clear-cut confessions of faith were slow to emerge, and the official response to heterodoxy was less than coherent. The picture was complicated by the fact that the Sorbonne, fiercely determined to safeguard Catholic orthodoxy, viewed with suspicion any deviation from its own narrow, scholastic teaching, and consequently humanism, already regarded in a hostile light, also came under attack. This led to clashes with the French king who, although uncompromisingly antagonistic toward heresy, was anxious not to enact measures that would curb the intellectual movement his generous, if somewhat erratic, patronage had done much to foster. In the course of a nine-month stay in France, Lindsay could not have been unaware of the developing religious controversy. Indeed, much that has been identified as characteristic of early French Protestantism accords with Lindsay's own views. Its stress upon uncontroversial aspects of the Christian faith, upon inner spirituality and devotion to *l'Evangile,* echoed the concerns of his early works and occupied him greatly in later years.[2]

The impact of Reformed opinion in France was impressed upon Lindsay during his second visit two years later. This took place only a few months after a sermon preached by Nicholas Cop, the rector of the University of Paris, had created uproar in the French capital, and talk of Cop's sermon, heavily influenced by the works of Erasmus and Luther, together with his subsequent flight, still reverberated through Paris. October 1534 also witnessed a watershed in the history of the French Reformation with the "Affair of the Placards" when religious radicals posted broadsheets in Paris and other French towns attacking "les horrible, grands & importable abuz de la Messe papalle."[3] It is not clear exactly when Lindsay left France, but David Beaton, a member of the same delegation, was still in the country at this point and probably at court.[4] It seems likely, therefore, that Lindsay too was witness to the critical events of autumn 1534. The real significance of the Affair lies in the fact that it revealed a much more radical form of religious unorthodoxy than had been hitherto apparent: a militant sacramentarianism which owed more to the teaching of Huldrych Zwingli than to Martin Luther. It was this—rather than any perceived personal insult—which so alarmed Francis I and resulted in his greater willingness to condone the rigorous extirpation of heresy advocated by the Sorbonne and Parlement. The Affair initiated a wave of repression that lasted many months, and it may be no coincidence that in June 1535 the Scottish Parliament reenacted its own antiheresy legislation.[5]

The events of October 1534 probably represent Lindsay's first encounter with Zwinglian theology and sacramentarianism in particular.[6] Sporadic outbreaks of iconoclasm and the theological attacks on sacramentarianism launched at the University of St. Andrews suggest that the influence of Zwingli's teaching was already being felt in Scotland; but until the mission of George Wishart in the 1540s its impact on early Scottish Protestantism, although important, was not widespread.[7] For Lindsay, exposure to the ideas of the Swiss Reformation probably came in France, and the events of October 1534 seem to have taught him just how explosive an issue the doctrine of the Mass was. Certainly, he does not refer to it in any of his works. This raises interesting, if perhaps unanswerable, questions concerning the interpretation of Lindsay's religious position from the evidence of his works alone. Was he simply uninterested in this fundamentally important point? Or, alternatively, was it such a benchmark of Protestant opinion that it was best left alone? Interestingly, in the admittedly rather different circumstances of the early 1560s, the poet Alexander Scott showed a similar reluctance to broach the issue: "With mes nor maytnes nowayis will I mell," he wrote, "To iuge thame iustlie passis my ingyne."[8]

While assessing the effects of Linsay's French experiences remains a highly speculative business, it is much easier to trace the profound influence exerted on his thinking by developments in England. As far as is known, Lindsay's first visit to England took place in February 1532 when he arrived at court seeking safe-conduct for the embassy traveling to France of which he himself was a member. His stay was probably brief, but it occurred at a significant juncture for anyone interested in Church reform. In November 1529 the Reformation Parliament had assembled at Westminster. By the time Lindsay arrived in London, statutes had been passed reforming mortuary and probate fees, clerical pluralism, and nonresidence, and Convocation had submitted to the king's demand that he be styled "Sole Protector and Supreme Head of the English Church." Admittedly they had obtained the important qualification "as far as the law of Christ allows," but the direction of the government's thinking was becoming clear. By the time Lindsay returned to England on his journey home from France nine months later, Parliament had passed the Act in Conditional Restraint of Annates, the independence of Convocation had been quashed with the Submission of the Clergy, and the resignation of the chancellor, Thomas More, had signaled his dissent from such a program of action. When Lindsay next visited England in August 1535, the king's "Great Matter" had been settled: Anne Boleyn was queen, More and Fisher had paid for their opposition with their lives, and parliamentary legislation had all but completed the Henrician break with Rome. Ecclesiastical reform enacted by virtue of royal authority—overriding, if necessary, the interests and position of the first estate— was, as *Ane Satyre* forcefully illustrates, an idea to which Lindsay was to become greatly committed. At home, he seems to have enjoyed sympathetic contact with men such as the English ambassador Ralph Sadler and the Scotsman Sir John Borthwick, both of whom were associated with the ideals of Cromwellian reform, and his own commitment was surely inspired and fostered by the example of England.

His English experiences must also have reinforced Lindsay's belief in the key role literature could play in the dissemination of evangelical opinion. Lindsay's second visit to the English court in 1535 coincided with a vigorous evangelical propaganda campaign conducted through the media of pamphlets and sermons, and only a couple of months earlier Henry had attended a savagely anticlerical play in which the king was depicted cutting the heads off his obstinate clergy.[9] It may be true that there was no officially organized campaign of dramatic propaganda, but individuals cannot have failed to appreciate the didactic potential of plays such as John Bale's *King John,* first performed in 1538 under the patronage of Cromwell and Cranmer.[10] The notion that "players, printers, [and] preachers . . . be set up of God, as a triple bulwark against the triple crown of the pope to bring him down," was widely held among evangelical Protestants and, although not inspired by any one performance or indeed by the specifically antipapal thrust of such a vision, Lindsay's response to the general idea is vividly demonstrated by his later works.[11] The Epiphany drama of 1540 illustrates that Lindsay was not the only one to be attracted by this strategy, and the Scottish court, like its English counterpart, proved a useful forum for this type of evangelical persuasion.

ALTHOUGH no longer engaged in a public critique of Church affairs during the 1530s, Lindsay's thinking was heavily influenced by the development of religious controversy at the Scottish court in this period. As evidenced by his early works, the ideals of Christian humanism were keenly discussed in court circles and peddled, in some quarters at least, as a blueprint for ecclesiastical reform. Other ideas, however, were also in circulation and, as we have seen, there existed at court a small but by no means uninfluential group of laymen (men such as Kirkcaldy of Grange, Learmonth of Dairsie, Henry Balnaves, and Thomas Bellenden) who, at some point in the decade, embraced the Protestant faith. Essentially committed to the Catholic Church, the Scottish king was not averse to exploiting the unsettled religious climate for his own ends. His artful petitions to the pope helpfully reminded the pontiff how much easier it was to maintain a standing church than to raise a fallen, and sly references to the threat of heresy helped secure a hefty tax on the Scottish clergy.[12] As this suggests, it was the Church's wealth rather than its spiritual well-being that truly interested James V, and his success in tapping this source of revenue without recourse to schism may well have prevented him from following Henry VIII along that path.

The reasons for James's occasional sympathy for the cause of ecclesiastical reform is arguably less important than the fact of its existence, for it undoubtedly encouraged the evangelicals at court to believe that the king's support was there to be won. Certainly Lindsay's humanist critique was offered in this hope. In seeking to advance their cause with the king, evangelicals adopted a variety of strategies. The most obvious, most direct, was the straightforward appeal to the king. Thomas Bellenden's request for English papers "touching the suppression of religion, and . . . the reformation of the mysdemeanours of the clergye" was made with just such an aim in mind.[13] John Borthwick too attempted this type of forthright evangelical persuasion, and later charges against him would allege that he wrote to James urging him to seize the temporal wealth of the Church.[14] Another who wrote in support of the evangelical cause was the exiled Scot Alexander Alane, or Alesius, who pleaded with James not to take measures against vernacular Scripture (although it has to be said that Alesius was writing to defend himself from the Catholic Cochlaeus and that he was at pains to refute the suggestion that he himself was translating Luther's New Testament into Scots).[15]

A more subtle, arguably more effective, way of advancing the evangelical cause was through imaginative works. Criticisms of the ecclesiastical establishment and suggestions for reform were offered not in the form of tracts and letters but as part of the poems and plays designed for the entertainment of the court. Such an approach had several advantages over a more direct attack. Addressing what was very often a captive audience, the deft use of language and imagery also offered an author a degree of protection against hostile critics. In *The Testament of the Papyngo*, for example, Lindsay's amusing characterization of the four birds and the mock denunciation of his "rude indyte" (1176) masked the seriousness of his message and perhaps too helped dissipate the anger of his clerical audience.

Lindsay's early poems forcefully suggest that his participation in the religious debate was inspired and informed by the ideals of Erasmian humanism. Later works reveal how important this type of thinking continued to be, but it is equally clear that his attitude was also conditioned by English affairs. As illustrated by the actions of men like John Borthwick and Thomas Bellenden, the example of England offered at least some Scots an attractive model for ecclesiastical reform. *Ane Satyre of the Thrie Estatis* and *The Monarche* both demonstrate Lindsay's support for the type of Cromwellian settlement he himself had seen in England (even if, theologically speaking, he remained closer to Henry VIII than to the king's chief minister).[16] If, as seems likely, Lindsay was also involved in the 1540 Epiphany drama, this provides further evidence of his enthusiasm for such ideas.

Concluding "vpon the Declaracion of the noughtines in Religion, the Presumpcion of busshops, the collucion of the spirituall Courts . . . and mysusing of priests," the play attacked ecclesiastical exploitation of the poor, the immorality of the religious houses, and the lust of the clergy (and their habit of marrying their bastards to the aristocracy, thereby debasing noble blood). It also upheld the crown's right to the lands and wealth of the Church. The arguments it advanced were sanctioned by Scripture and, significantly, its proposed reforms endorsed by the lay estates in defiance of the clergy, a scenario which, as the audience would be aware, echoed recent events south of the border. Indeed, according to Thomas Bellenden, James himself viewed the play with reference to the English situation, threatening to send six of his proudest bishops "vnto his vncle of england" if they would not mend their ways. It has been suggested that the play "tailored its demands for reform in the Erasmian terms most likely to find favour with James V."[17] But, while this is true, it is important to grasp that in this play Lindsay—if we accept him as the author—went further than in his earlier poetry, adding to the debate a political element hitherto missing from his critique. No longer the traditional poet-observer bringing abuses to the attention of the monarch, Lindsay now acted as an informed political commentator suggesting specific—and feasible—methods for the implementation of his ideas. With the example of England so close to hand and with English agents ready to assist Scottish malcontents, his criticisms were now palpably more dangerous to the established Church, something James's response to the play, if not entirely apocryphal, made chillingly clear.

Partly in response to this newly politicized criticism, Beaton was driven to launch an offensive against suspected heretics at court when, a couple of months after the Epiphany drama, he moved against John Borthwick. Ultimately and fortuitously, Borthwick escaped to England, and the whole affair may have been arranged as a sop to Beaton's mounting anger with the king's toleration, a sacrifice seen by James as preferable to the more wide-spread persecution of influential men which the cardinal may have been soliciting. Only a few months before his accusation and just some six weeks after the performance at Linlithgow, Borthwick had been associated with Lindsay in entertaining Cromwell's ambassador, Ralph Sadler, and, as is illustrated by the charges against him, he was deeply sympathetic to the Cromwellian reform program.[18] Concerned less with theology and more with the need for a Henrician-type Reformation, he urged casting off papal authority and transferring ecclesiastical wealth to the royal Treasury. Additionally, he attacked the monasteries and demanded a vernacular New Testament. Many of his views were shared by Lindsay, whose earlier works endorsed the notions that "the Scottish nation was blinded and had not the true Catholic faith," that it was lawful for bishops to marry, and that the temporal jurisdiction of the Church should be abolished. "Speir at the monks of balmirrynoch / Gif lecherie be sin" (*Ane Satyre*, 261–62), he would later write, words which forcefully recall Borthwick's description of the monasteries as "brothel houses, swine styes and dens of discord." Similarly, Borthwick's reported cry "With what a filthy cankered stomach do these Romish swine note the New Testament with heresy?" has powerful links with the words of Flatterie who also condemns the New Testament in such terms. Lindsay did not go as far as Borthwick in demanding the complete disendowment of the Church (although the Epiphany play apparently agreed with his proposition that the crown had a right to appropriate Church wealth) and, while he bitterly denounced the sale of pardons, the attack on their efficacy was couched in more ambiguous terms. Likewise, although he lambasted the consistory courts, Lindsay, unlike Borthwick, did not declare canon law invalid. Nor did he call for the religious life to be dissolved; Lindsay refers explicitly only to the nunneries. Borthwick was also charged with denying papal supremacy and, although Lindsay never explicitly endorsed this, his description of the pope as an antichrist together with implementation of the type of reform program suggested in *Ane Satyre* brought him perilously close to such a position. The points of similarity among Borthwick, Lindsay, and the others involved in the Epiphany production illustrate that support for a Cromwellian-type settlement was more widespread, and for the Church more dangerous, than the isolated action against Borthwick might suggest.[19]

Lindsay was perhaps fortunate to escape Borthwick's fate. A number of factors may have saved him: his relationship with the king, the dignity of his heraldic office, and perhaps too, James's determination not to give Beaton his head in any antiheresy campaign. In fact, at this stage in his career, Lindsay could feel well satisfied. In June 1540, Balnaves, the Treasurer's Clerk, assigned Lindsay and his wife 1,000 merks owed to the king by Sir Walter Lundy.[20] The explanation for the windfall is unclear, but as a token of royal favor the message was plain, and it was probably this which enabled Lindsay to purchase Ovir-Prates in Fife the following year.[21] However, it was not all plain sailing for the evangelicals and, as we have seen, the last years of the reign saw a perceptible hardening of attitudes.[22]

It was probably around this time that the short poem *Kitteis Confessioun* was written. Included in Charteris's general edition of Lindsay's works with the words, "Compylit (as is beleuit) be Schir Dauid Lindesay," it seems to have been originally circulated anonymously. Lindsay's most recent general editor agrees with his first concerning the poem's authorship, claiming that "the style, particularly of the last hundred lines, is unmistakable."[23] Certainly, there is much that sounds like Lindsay. The satirical denunciation of the first curate's greed and lust and of the prurience and ignorance of the second accords well with his Erasmian criticisms of clerical behavior, while the depiction of the curate who views all "Inglis Bukis" or Bibles (21) as heresy prefigures the drama of *Ane Satyre*. The stress on the saving merits of "Christis blude" (59) and the references to the early Church, "the gude Kirk Primityue" (138), are also typical of Lindsay. Likewise, Kittie's assertion that pilgrimages lead only to immorality is found elsewhere in his writing as is the call for the use of the vernacular. However, what distinguishes *Kitteis Confessioun* from Lindsay's other works is its ridicule of the way in which confession is heard and penance prescribed. Moreover, the author goes so far as to condemn the entire sacramental practice as "nocht ellis bot mennis law" (101). In decidedly Protestant fashion, he declares

> To the greit God Omnipotent
> Confes thy Syn, and sore repent,
> And traist in Christ, as wrytis Paule,
> Quhilk sched his blude to saif thy Saule:
> For nane can the absolue bot he,
> Nor tak away thy syn frome the.   (109–14)

But whether this is Lindsay's work remains open to question. For Lindsay never returned to an attack on auricular confession, nor did he question the sacrament of penance. Indeed, his later poems reveal a commitment to the doctrine of salvation through works. It could perhaps be argued that in a period of intense religious uncertainty the ideas expressed in *Kitteis Confessioun* were indeed Lindsay's—but only briefly. However, one other point—the reference to "the Paip, the Antechriste" (108)—may be significant. As we shall see, Lindsay never describes the pope as *the* antichrist but as one antichrist among many. And, if the poem were written sometime before the end of 1542 (as the reference to the king suggests), it would represent a surprisingly early appearance of the antichrist idea in Lindsay's work. His most likely source in this respect was John Knox who, even if he did not introduce Lindsay to such ideas for the very first time, does appear to have exerted a decisive influence over his thinking on the matter. And, as Lindsay did not hear Knox preach on the subject until 1547, his authorship of *Kitteis Confessioun* is unlikely. However, although Lindsay's authorship must remain open to question, the poem sheds interesting light on ideas in the pre-Reformation period. For, if a hand other than Lindsay's penned *Kitteis Confessioun,* it usefully illustrates how many of the latter's beliefs and sympathies were being echoed elsewhere in Scotland.

FOLLOWING the death of James V in 1542, the religious situation altered with Arran's assumption of the governorship, his decision to reverse the direction of foreign policy, and his resolve to allow a measure of religious reform. For Lindsay, the most significant aspects of the early months of the regency administration were the legislation authorizing the reading of vernacular Scripture, a further visit to England and, finally, the ostracization occasioned by Arran's reconciliation with Beaton and the repudiation of the Treaties of Greenwich.

It is almost certain that Lindsay attended the 1543 Parliament where acts were passed permitting the reading of "the haly write baith the new testament and the auld in the vulgar toung in Inglis or scottis."[24] Lindsay's later works reveal his passionate support for such a measure, and he undoubtedly viewed the passage of the relevant legislation with approval. One of those sponsoring the bill was Henry Balnaves who had been with Bellenden when the latter requested details of the English Reformation and, for the evangelical Protestants at court, it must have seemed as if a Henrician-type settlement, one enacted through the estates and overriding clerical opposition—just as played out on stage three years earlier—was now a real possibility. Indeed, with the death of James V and the loss of potential royal patronage, this would seem to represent the surest, perhaps the only, way of implementing any reform program. Too much, however, still rested with the political will of the governor. His rapprochement with Beaton put an end to the hopes of the Reformers, and by December 1543 Parliament was calling for the implementation of the antiheresy legislation passed in 1525 and 1535. Nevertheless, this brief period of ascendancy proved inspirational. Not only did it encourage association with more radical Protestants such as John Rough and Thomas Guillame, the chosen preachers of the earl of Arran, but above all it suggested what could be accomplished in favorable circumstances. Significantly, when Lindsay came to write *Ane Satyre of the Thrie Estatis* some ten years later, he incorporated a scene in which Diligence was instructed to seek out "sum devoit cunning Clarks" (3159), able to "schaw the word of God vnfeinzeitlie" (3441). Such a strategy exactly mirrors the action taken by Arran who, at the height of his enthusiasm for reform, wrote to the English government explaining how he "cause[d] certane pur freris that ar weil lernit in the Haly Scripturis, preche playnly the trew Word of God, to draw the hartis of the pepill to God, and to cause thaim understand the abusion of the stait of the clergy in tymis past."[25]

Another important influence on Lindsay during this period was the action, military and evangelical, of the English government in Scotland during the invasions of 1543–50. Both *The Tragedie of the Cardinal* and *The Monarche* reveal his anguish at the miseries inflicted upon his country, miseries he might well have experienced firsthand. An English base was established at Broughty, some twenty miles from Cupar, and East Lothian—Haddington in particular—was the scene of much destructive action. Although Fife escaped relatively lightly, many of its inhabitants were involved in the conflict. According to Pitscottie, those who set off on the 1545 campaign and fought in the Battle of Ancrum Moor included "my lord Lyndsayis servandis, kin and friendis" and, with Lindsay spending much more of his time at the Mount, he would have been in closer contact with such men.[26] The English campaign, however, was not waged in the field alone; military action was accompanied by propaganda intended to convince the obstinate Scots of the folly of sustained opposition. Hoping to undermine Beaton's authority, the English administration instructed Hertford to post the taunt, "You may thank your Cardinal for this," in the areas left devastated by his troops.[27] Lindsay's work shows that at least one Scot responded to the gibes as, possibly having witnessed them himself, he resurrected a similar charge against Beaton in *The Tragedie of the Cardinal*. "I wes the rute of all that gret myscheif" (187), the ghostly prelate declares, "I wes the cause of mekle more myschance" (190).

The return of George Wishart in 1544 can probably be seen as another instance of English ideological intervention in Scotland. Wishart's charismatic personality, energetic proselytizing, and articulate message offered potential leadership and cohesion to the scattered, disparate Protestant groups within Scotland. Arriving via England from Germany and Switzerland, his theology owed more to Zurich than to Wittenberg (in 1536 he had completed an English translation of the First Helvetic Confession of Faith, published circa 1548), and his presence in Scotland indicates the increasing importance of Zwinglianism in the Scottish Reformation.[28] Other factors also support this view, as sporadic outbursts of iconoclasm and official denunciations of sacramentarianism testify.[29] Since the late 1520s, Lindsay had been vociferous in his condemnation of those who prayed "to grawin Ymagis" (*The Complaynt,* 422) and, possibly influenced by the spirit of

Wishart if not the man himself, he elaborated upon this at length in *The Monarche*. It is not known whether Lindsay ever heard Wishart preach but, given that the latter spent the autumn of 1545 in Dundee and followed this up with visits to East Lothian, Lindsay must at least have heard of his activities.[30] Indeed, the connection between Lindsay and Wishart was not just geographical for, although not closely related, Wishart's mother may well have been a Lindsay herself.[31] Certainly it seems as if the preacher's evangelical style and open-air sermons may have influenced Lindsay's own decision to address himself to a wider audience. Indeed, the poet's commitment to the evangelical cause and to Wishart in particular may have been more apparent to contemporaries than to historians, for it is surely no accident that one of the earliest editions of *The Tragedie of the Cardinal*, that published in London by John Day and William Seres (ca. 1548), is bound with an account of the trial and martyrdom of George Wishart introduced by the English Protestant Robert Burrant.[32]

One result of Wishart's execution was to illustrate that the Church, working in harness with the secular administration, possessed the means to stifle the religious debate in brutal fashion. This totally horrified Lindsay, and *The Tragedie of the Cardinal* attacks Beaton's policy of repression. With an almost barbaric frankness, the Cardinal describes how he would have

> . . . distroyit mony vther;
> Sum with the fyre, sum with the sword and kynfe;
> In speciale mony gentyll men of fyfe,
> And purposit tyll put to gret Torment
> All fauoraris of the auld and new Testament.   (213–17)

In fact, Lindsay's words reveal more about contemporary perceptions of Beaton than the actual program of persecution for, apart from Wishart's execution in St. Andrews, Fife seems to have produced few of Beaton's Protestant martyrs.[33] It is interesting to note the recurrence of this phraseology in *The Monarche* when Lindsay describes the damnation of those who persecuted "Prophetis and Prechouris, / Sum with the fyre, sum with the sworde, / Quhilk plainly prechit Goddis worde" (5807–9), for while these lines can be taken to refer to the early martyrs of the Christian Church, Lindsay could be confident that they would evoke the memory of more recent executions. His antipathy toward the government's policy of repression is also suggested by Lindsay's vigorous denunciation of the friars "Prouocand princis to shed saikles blude" (*The Monarche,* 2542). The use of the word "saikles" (innocent) here strongly conveys Lindsay's sympathy with those who had suffered persecution, and he goes on to suggest that "Christis floke, without malyce or rye, / Conuertit fragyll faltouris, . . . / Be Goddis worde, withouttin sweird or fyre" (2546–48). There is perhaps a deliberate ambiguity here, for with the use of the past tense Lindsay could be referring either to the Apostles or, more radically, to the broader church of all believers. If we accept such an interpretation, Lindsay posits a situation challenging not only the policies of persecution but also the Church's monopoly over spiritual instruction, suggesting a much greater lay involvement. This is reinforced by the passage describing how members of the congregation should play an active role in the spiritual life of the community, discreetly correcting their brothers of sin "In friendly maner" (2552) and drawing wider attention to the matter only as a last resort.

Lindsay's increasing sympathy with confessed Protestants can also be seen during the period of Beaton's murder and the subsequent siege of St. Andrews Castle. This episode provided him with material for his poem *The Tragedie of the Cardinal* but, as in earlier works, the subject matter is highly conditioned by generic convention. Nevertheless, Lindsay skillfully exploits his chosen genre to convey his message. The traditional "fall-of-princes" framework emphasizes Beaton's arrogance and worldly ambition as the Cardinal climbs ever higher, his "pridefull hart . . . nocht content at all" (62), until finally he is brought low. The appearance of Beaton's ghost to relate the tale lends added force to his pleas for reform, pleas addressed to prelates and princes alike. In keeping with the style of the poem as moral exemplar the cry is for an essentially ethical reformation. Lindsay urges prelates to attend to the souls in their cure, to preach "the auld and new testament" (318), and to leave off harlotry, gaming, and greed. As in *The Complaynt* and *The Testament of the Papyngo,* he implores princes to guarantee the learning and virtue of those they nominate to benefices:

> Quharefor I counsayle eueryilk christinit kyng
> With in his realme mak Reformatioun,
> And suffer no mo Rebaldis for to ryng
> Abufe Christis trew Congregatioun.   (421–24)

The Tragedie of the Cardinal is particularly interesting for the light it sheds on Lindsay's attitude toward the Cardinal's assassins and, by implication perhaps, toward the Castilians as a whole. In describing the murder, Lindsay names no names and, apart from conveying the suddenness of the attack, provides no details. The language he employs, however, engenders a certain moral ambivalence, even suggesting approbation of the assassins' actions. The choice of this particular poetic framework allows Lindsay to present the assassination as the destruction of a tyrant-figure, the inevitable fall of overweening pride and ambition, and Beaton attributes his death to "the hie power Divine" (139), a process which, like the defeat of Goliath, "culd not be troch mortal mannis ingyne" (140). In this way, Lindsay appears to absolve the murderers of moral responsibility for the deed, seeing them as agents of a form of divinely inspired tyrannicide. The emphasis on hubris and nemesis inherent in Lindsay's chosen literary genre effectively draws attention away from this detail. However, while others might be struck by this sense of fatalism—or perhaps by Lindsay's robust scandal-mongering—the Castilians and their sympathizers cannot have failed to appreciate this potentially subversive interpretation of their actions. Certainly this is how Robert Burrant viewed the episode. His introductory address to the reader—a vitriolic catalogue of those rulers who oppressed the godly and paid dearly for their tyranny—clearly links Lindsay's account of the Cardinal's death with the trial and execution of George Wishart.

Yet, despite an apparent sympathy with the Castilians, the rousing cry delivered by Lindsay in this poem is, in fact, for a very conservative type of reformation, a moral regeneration along Erasmian lines. The attack on Beaton, although vicious, is extremely orthodox in character. This may be explained by the circumstances surrounding the poem's composition. Although it is not known exactly when it was written or published, the reference to Beaton lying unburied for over seven months gives us an earliest possible date of January 1547 and, given that the work depends in part on its topicality, a significantly later date seems unlikely.[34] It may be that in the volatile aftermath of the assassination, Lindsay only felt safe with a reversion to the type of poetry he had written earlier in his career. Perhaps too, his traditional technique was intended as a deliberate rejection of the confrontational approach adopted by those holed up in the besieged castle. Clinging to the ideals and aspirations he had embraced in the previous decade, Lindsay provided a reminder that there were other paths to reform. Despite his subtle endorsement of Beaton's murder, the idea of resistance to monarchical or even quasi-monarchical authority clearly offended Lindsay's political and religious sensibilities. "Paul biddis ws be obedient," he writes elsewhere, "To Kyngis as the most excellent" (*The Monarche*, 4593–94). Admittedly, this citation of that much used text, Romans 13, occurs in a different context (the requirement for popes to submit to secular authority), but it does seem to express Lindsay's essential position. Faced with circumstances offering little prospect of reform, he could only counsel patience. It could perhaps be argued that such opposition to resistance is in itself evidence of Lindsay's attachment to a Lutheran position. However, Luther's own attitude shifted after about 1530 when, like many Reformers, he was forced to confront the problem of resistance.[35] Writing shortly after he himself had taken up arms against the governor, Balnaves offers a sugges-tive—if rather confused—example of Scottish thinking on the issue. Telling men to "Giue to thy prince and superiour his duetie . . . concerning temporall riches" and to "disobey him not; howbeit he bee evill and doe thee wrong," Balnaves also states that obedience is God's will "in all thinges not repugning his command."[36] The great importance Balnaves attaches to social order, stability, and hierarchy inhibits his words if not his actions. But though he may not have heeded his own advice to "Be not a perturber of the commoun weale," this type of thinking certainly struck a chord with Lindsay.

Following his deputation to the castle in an official capacity, Lindsay maintained informal links with the Castilians to the point of being present at the consultation between Balnaves and Rough which resulted in Knox's call to the ministry. He was probably also present at the new preacher's inaugural sermon when, taking as his text the seventh chapter of the Book of Daniel (which describes the prophet's vision of the four beasts or kingdoms), Knox described the destruction of the four world monarchies by "that last Beast . . . the Romane Church."[37] That the pope was an antichrist, "One contrare to Christ," Knox justified with an exposition of the false teaching of the Catholic Church: the doctrine of good works, pilgrimages, pardons, clerical celibacy, fasting, Purgatory, and the Mass. As has been pointed out, the parallels between this and *The Monarche* are, at first sight, quite striking.[38] However, although *The Monarche* makes much of Daniel's dream, it does not represent such a fundamental "blow to the root." Lindsay carefully denies the doctrine of Justification *sola fides;* he makes no mention of the Mass, and his attitude toward Purgatory is considerably more ambiguous than Knox's unequivocal rejection. However, he did agree with Knox on the question of pilgrimages, fasting, and clerical celibacy, and he too branded the pope an antichrist. (Like Knox at this stage, he used the term to refer to one—of several—who was inimical to the teachings of Christ.) This comparison of Knox's sermon and *The Monarche* illustrates the ideological links that existed between Lindsay and the Castilians. Lindsay clearly had some sympathy for a group that included men whom he would have known at court such as Balnaves, Rough, and Borthwick, together with others who were familiar figures in the local community. However, he certainly did not share their Reformed faith. Such ideological overlap as there was only serves to suggest that religious belief at this point was often, like Lindsay's, idiosyncratic, personal, and difficult to pin down. The respective actions of Lindsay and Knox reveal another crucial difference between the two. Whereas the latter committed himself to the Castilians, besieged and awaiting foreign aid, Lindsay kept aloof, clinging to a vision of reform enacted through persuasion. With reform and reconciliation as opposed to schism and confrontation on his personal agenda, Lindsay was perhaps perceived as a less dangerous threat to the establishment and hence was allowed his freedom of action and expression.

Before the composition of *Ane Satyre* and *The Monarche* and his return to the religious debate, Lindsay traveled to Denmark as a member of the

Scottish embassy dispatched to treat with Christian III in the winter of 1548–49. His encounter with the Lutheran Church in that country may also have shaped his religious beliefs, although links between Scotland and Denmark probably ensured that many Scots were familiar enough anyway with the Danish situation.[39] The Protestant Church in Denmark, as established by Parliament in 1536, placed great stress upon preaching and the proper use of tithes. Bishops and superintendents exercised no temporal authority, and ultimate control rested with the crown.[40] As illustrated by his later works, such ideas greatly appealed to Lindsay, but just how involved he was in the discussion of religious affairs in Denmark is impossible to ascertain. It is at least likely that he was in touch with some of those Scots whose beliefs had forced them to seek exile there. One such was John MacAlpine also known as Maccabeus, a Dominican friar of Perth. Obliged to flee Scotland in 1534, MacAlpine spent some time in England where he wrote in defense of clerical marriage and was Bishop Shaxton's staunch ally in imposing the vernacular Bible in Salisbury (two ideas important to Lindsay's own thinking). Arriving in Denmark via Wittenberg, he subsequently became a professor of theology at Copenhagen University.[41] The 1554 edition of *The Monarche* is credited with being "Imprentit at the command and Expensis off Doctour Machabeus in Copmanhovin," and although probably printed by John Scot in St. Andrews, these words suggest MacAlpine's interest in Lindsay's work and his acquaintance with the poet. Another Scot exiled in Denmark was John Gau, author of *The Richt Vay to the Kingdom of Heuine* (1533), essentially a translation of a work by the Danish Lutheran Christiern Pedersen. Friendly with MacAlpine, he was resident in Copenhagen at the time of Lindsay's visit and may also have met the poet.[42] Even more intriguing, but unfortunately just as speculative, is the possibility that Lindsay's Danish embassy saw renewed contact with his old acquaintance, John Borthwick. Now working for the English government, Borthwick had been dispatched to Denmark to counter the Scottish embassy of which Lindsay was part.[43] However, although the two were certainly in Denmark at the same time, whether they actually met remains unclear and, with so little known of Lindsay's Danish contacts, it is very difficult to chart their influences on the development of his thinking. It may be, however, that the events of the past two decades had been sufficient in themselves to inspire Lindsay's return to the religious fray.

IN VIEW of the caustic criticisms and occasional doctrinal ambiguity found in his later works, Lindsay's continued escape from censure and prosecution appears even more surprising than it had in the 1540s. According to his kinsman, Lindsay of Pitscottie, an act decreeing that "Schir Dawid Lyndsay's buike sould be condemnid and burnt" was passed in December 1559 and duly enforced.[44] Surviving records fail to support his assertion, but if we discount the chronology this may be a reference to the legislation passed by Parliament in February 1552 forbidding the unauthorized publication of "bukis, ballatis, fangis, blasphematiounis rymes or Tragedies outher in latine or Inglis toung."[45] It could well have been the passing of this act that encouraged Lindsay to present his ideas in the form of a publicly performed drama rather than a printed poem. Nevertheless, he was clearly aware of the dangers involved: "Speik thou of Preistis," warns Diligence, "but doubt thou will be hangit" (*Ane Satyre*, 2030). The fact that the act was aimed primarily at printers may have provided Lindsay with an escape clause, but the 1554 publication of *The Monarche*, dedicated to the governor and his half-brother and printed under the name of a Danish exile, again suggests Lindsay's caution. The political situation may have warranted such prudence, but this apart Lindsay's return to the religious debate was marked not by circumspection but by an increasingly radical, ever more urgent, critique.

NINE

Returning to the Fray

Politics and Prophecy

Some two decades after Lindsay had first called for ecclesiastical reform, *The Tragedie of the Cardinal* announced his return to the discussion of religious affairs. This work, together with *Ane Satyre of the Thrie Estatis* and *The Monarche,* resumed the excoriating critique of the Church and its personnel found in his earlier poetry. Now, however, Lindsay went much further. His final compositions exhibit an increasingly politicized approach to the problems of institutional reform along with an urgent demand for spiritual regeneration which, in terms of its sheer intensity, was something new. Indeed, writing in the last years of his life, Lindsay addressed not only the question of his own spiritual salvation but the eschatological expectations of all humanity.

In view of the renewed government offensive against heretical activity, in particular the 1552 censorship legislation, the reasons for Lindsay's return to religious polemic are not immediately obvious. Emboldened in part by the relief of domestic political tension arising from the end of eight years of intermittent Anglo-Scottish warfare, Lindsay was probably also encouraged by the Church's own initiative "to restore tranquility and preserve complete unity."[1] The Provincial Councils of 1549, 1552, and later of 1559 highlighted many of the abuses that Lindsay himself so vehemently criticized, and this may have led him to envisage a sympathetic audience for his works, confirming him in the belief that persuasion and reform still remained viable options. He may also have taken his appointment to the Danish embassy as a sign of restored official favor, fortifying his resolve to persuade the governor and his half-brother as, in a previous decade, he had attempted to persuade the king. As we have seen, Lindsay's later works were addressed to a much broader, more socially diverse audience than the court-based poems he had hitherto written. Inspired perhaps by the mission of George Wishart, he appears determined to convey his message to as large an audience as possible. Underlying this evangelical imperative was Lindsay's developing interest in the idea of the apocalypse as, convinced that world history was reaching its conclusion, the need to play an active role in the drama became increasingly urgent. The religious debate to which Lindsay returned in the 1550s was no longer an intellectual discussion at the royal court but a conflict between the forces of good and evil waged on a grand cosmological sale.

LINDSAY'S later works illustrate the development of his thought in a number of directions. Not only does his belief in the imminent End lend his work a prophetic quality, but the political element of his critique becomes much more pronounced. However, there is also much reiteration of earlier themes, and Lindsay's attitude to the Church retains a strong moralizing, Erasmian element. Blistering criticism of the personal standards of church-men remains an essential feature of his work with lust, greed, ignorance, and worldly ambition again his principal targets. In *Ane Satyre,* for example, John the Commonweal denounces clerics in familiar terms: "As for our reverent fathers of Spiritualitie," he cries, "Thay ar led be Couetice and cairles Sensualitie" (2446–47).

In articulating what was often a highly traditional literary anticlerical-ism, Lindsay also delivered some extremely pertinent gibes. The examina-tion of the bishop, abbot, and parson found in *Ane Satyre of the Thrie Estatis* relies upon conventional clerical stereotypes, but it also contains some more topical barbs. When the parson flaunts his "round bonats . . . now four nuickit" (3416), the audience would have remembered that three years earlier the Provincial Council had decreed that only round birettas were to be worn.[2] Likewise, while the council had stipulated that wool and not silk was appropriate for clerical dress, Lindsay's Prioress is revealed to be wear-ing a silk kirtle beneath her habit (3651–56).[3] The specificity of these jokes illustrates that the more sophisticated approach to socioeconomic problems seem in *Ane Satyre* was also turned upon the affairs of the Church. This is particularly striking in Lindsay's consideration of the role of nuns in Scot-tish religious life. Here Lindsay advocates marriage in preference to the convent. The Prioress curses her friends whose greed compelled her to take the veil and seek material advancement. "Marriage be my opinioun," she declares, "is better Religioun / As to be freir or Nun" (3672–74). Preference for a Christian marriage above communal celibacy was a characteristic feature of Protestant thinking, and it was one to which Lindsay had long been attracted. However, the passing of legislation supporting such action in *Ane Satyre*—the introduction of a recognizably realistic program for the implementation of specific proposals—represents an important develop-ment in his thinking.

This conceptual shift is also discernible in Lindsay's continued campaign against clerical avarice and the Church's economic exploitation of the poor.

He does not, of course, eschew the more traditional discourse altogether, and arguably Lindsay's most savage indictment of clerical greed depends on deeply familiar imagery:

> Christ did command Peter to feid his scheip,
> And so he did feid thame full tenderlye.
> Off that command thay take bot lytill keip,
> Bot Christis scheip thay spolye petuouslye,
> And with the woll thay cleith thame curiouslye.
> Lyk gormand wolfis, thay tak of thame thare fude,
> Thai eit thair flesche, & drynkis boith mylk & blude.
>
> (*The Monarche*, 4799–805)

In *Ane Satyre*, however, Lindsay goes beyond a moral castigation of avarice, making mortuary dues the subject of specific attack and, moreover, of carefully targeted parliamentary legislation. Economic grievances appear to have aroused a greater sense of contemporary outrage than did sexual immorality and, when the Church addressed the question of death duties in 1559, it was in part "to put an end to the clamour and murmurs of grumblers at morturies."[4] Lindsay too responded to this "clamour," approaching the issue in a way that extended the simple description of abuse and concomitant call for moral reform to encompass a more specific and coercive means of dealing with the problem.

As in his earlier works, Lindsay did not confine himself to the criticism of clerical vice; he also sought to encourage churchmen in their "true vocation," exhorting them to preach the Word of God and live in accordance with it. Churchmen of all ranks are condemned for their failure in this respect.[5] "Sir God nor I be stickit with ane kynfe / Gif ever Persoun preichit in all his lyfe" (*Ane Satyre*, 2938–39), the poor man exclaims, but in general it is the bishops whom Lindsay attacked for their failure to preach, claiming that this was the reason "the peple now abhor thame" (*The Monarche*, 4494). This was throwing down the gauntlet to many sixteenth-century ecclesiastics. The lack of active preachers was recognized by the three Provincial Councils, and a series of acts was passed aimed at raising the intellectual standards of the clergy with stress laid upon the necessity of preaching, "seing that the preaching of the Gospel is no less necessary to Christian commonwealth than lecturing thereon."[6] This particular statute described preaching as "the principal duty of the bishops," but in recognition of the existing situation it permitted prelates to entrust the duty to "fit persons." Ten years later, however, the Council insisted that bishops preach in person at least four times a year, only elderly clerics over the age of fifty and "not hitherto . . . accustomed to preach" being allowed to delegate the responsibility.[7] Such a solution had been suggested by Lindsay in *The Monarche* when he argued that if bishops could not fulfill this responsibility they should pay for a suffragan until their death enabled the appointment of "ane perfyte precheour" (4861). Shared by Catholic reformers, Protestant evangelicals, and those—like Lindsay—whose religious sympathies cannot be so easily defined, concern about preaching was clearly one of the key issues of the pre-Reformation period.[8] And, as shown by the similar approaches adopted by Lindsay and the Church authorities, it would be wrong to insist upon too rigid a confessional demarcation among those who addressed the problem during this period.

In other respects, however, Lindsay did advance some rather more radical ideas. In *The Monarche,* for example, he goes so far as to claim that preaching ability should be seen as the precondition of "Spiritual Auctoritie" (4839). And, mindful perhaps of the way in which the Danish Church stressed the proper use of tithes, Lindsay explicitly linked the provision of teinds with preaching: "The law is plaine: our teinds suld furnish teichours" (*Ane Satyre,* 2936). Such declarations represent an aggressive assertion of lay interest in ecclesiastical affairs. Men such as Lindsay clearly felt they had more than a spiritual stake in the concerns of the Kirk, and more than ever before they expected their demands to be met.

Although Lindsay's enthusiasm for preaching was shared by many within the ecclesiastical hierarchy, it does seem as if his conception of the sermon and its importance for the spiritual life became, to some extent, informed by Protestant thinking on the matter. In emphasizing the importance of preaching, the Provincial Council of 1549 described how preachers were to explain the true use of the Church's ceremonies and to prohibit, confute, and denounce false opinion.[9] Preaching viewed in this way is essentially a didactic action, with true spiritual knowledge of Christ being fully obtained through the agency of the sacraments, viewed by the Catholic Church as the "instrumentis of goddis mercy and grace in our iustificatioun."[10] For Protestants, however, preaching was of central importance; the Word of God was viewed as a spiritual force in which and through which the Holy Spirit worked. As Luther expressed it, "Christ can not be known except through his word."[11] To use an oft-cited metaphor, the pulpit rather than the altar assumed center stage in the spiritual life. In *Ane Satyre of the Thrie Estatis* this was quite literally the case when a pulpit was set up before the audience and "ane schort sermon" (3441) preached.

Conceiving of the Word of God in this way, Lindsay's characterization of Veritie becomes extremely significant. Veritie should not be equated simply with the virtue of that name but also with a Scripture-based evangelism or even the Word of God itself. Her close association with the New Testament and her own speech serve to underscore this allegorical meaning.[12] Defending the Testament she carries, Veritie declares:

> Forsuith my friend ye have ane wrang iudgement,
> For in this Buik thair is na heresie:
> Bot our Christs word, baith dulce and redolent,
> Ane springing well of sinceir veritie.   (1148–51)

This covert association with Reformation thought is reinforced by the accusations of heresy hurled against her and by Veritie's own reference to her travels over "many stormie sey" (1072). Indeed, it may not be too fanciful to suggest that Veritie's very performance on stage reflects the spiritual force of the spoken Word. Her participation in the action of the play, in the moral rehabilitation of Rex Humanitas and the work of the estates, illustrates its dynamic power, its capacity first to alter and then to sustain lives.

The characterization of Veritie also has implications for the kingship of Rex Humanitas. Although Lindsay's belief that ecclesiastical reform should be undertaken by the king dates at least to the late 1520s, it is in his later works that it receives fullest expression. Both *Ane Satyre* and *The Monarche* were intended to awaken the potential power of the secular authorities to promote a program of Church reform, and in these works, notably *Ane Satyre*, Lindsay offers a much more specific critique concerning the nature of royal intervention in Church affairs. Of course, it had long been accepted that the king had a responsibility for the welfare of the Kirk. Royal duty to the Church was a common theme of traditional kingship literature, and periodic legislation reaffirmed "that the honor and fredome of halikirk and priuilege grantit it thereto be obseruit."[13] Recast by the Reformers, this essentially protective partnership offered the prince a more significant role. Luther might have despaired of finding such a paragon, but he nevertheless placed the Church under the direct control of the godly prince.[14] A Scottish example of this ideal is found in Henry Balnaves's treatise on Justification and, though Lindsay could not have known this particular work, he was probably well enough acquainted with the author's ideas. In Balnaves's work, some of the traditional ideals of kingship—justice, wisdom, and humility—are recast in the language of a Protestant evangelical. The stress is upon the importance of Scripture which, like Veritie in *Ane Satyre,* should guide the prince's every action:

Therefore, humblie and lowly submit thy selfe in the handes of thy God, and take thought of him, being gouerned by his Word. Begin at him, and set forth the true and perfite worshipping of God in thy kingdome. Restore the true, pure, and syncere Christian religion; abolish, destroye and put downe all false worshippinges and superstitions, contrare the Word of God. . . . This is thy vocation, in the which thou shouldest walke and orderly proceed in guiding of thy people, as thou art taught by the Worde of God.[15]

Lindsay's work suggests a growing enthusiasm for this type of idea, and the image of the godly prince ruling in strict accordance with Scripture is evocatively conveyed when Divyne Correctioun installs Veritie as one of Rex Humanitas's principal counselors: "Blist is the Realme that hes ane Prudent King, / Quhilk dois delyte to heir the veritie" (3780–81). As we shall see, the legislative action of *Ane Satyre* diminishes papal authority in Scotland almost out of existence, and clearly the evangelical rule of Rex Humanitas is intended to be—like that in England and Denmark—one that brooks no external interference. In the words of Divyne Correctioun, the king is "the head . . . of this congregation, / Preordinat be God omnipotent" (3329–30).

The changing character of the Church–crown relationship is also suggested by the first act passed by the three estates:

> It is devysit be thir prudent Kingis,
> Correctioun and King Humanitie,
> That thair Leigis induring all thair Ringis,
> With the avyce of the estatis thrie,
> Sall manfullie defend and fortifie
> The Kirk of Christ and his Religioun,
> Without Dissimulance or hypocrisie:
> Vnder the paine of thair punitioun.   (3791–800)

While this recalls the type of legislation habitually passed in defense of "Haly Kirk," the traditional formula with its stress on the rights and privileges, immunities and freedoms, enjoyed by the Church and its personnel differs markedly from the simple defense of "The Kirk of Christ and his Religioun." Indeed, given royal manipulation of ecclesiastical privileges and procedures, Lindsay's reference to hypocrisy and dissimulation becomes particularly pointed. Such a discussion of godly kingship was, however, at odds with the political realities of mid-sixteenth-century Scotland, and while Lindsay pinned his hopes on a monarchically led reform program, his attitude toward royal authority inhibited any response other than a stoic acceptance of the present situation:

> I traist to se gude reformatione
> From tyme we gett ane faithfull prudent king
> Quhilk knawis the trueth and his vocatione
> All Publicanis, I traist, he wyll doun thring,
> And wyll nocht suffer in his realme to ring
> Corrupit Scrybis, nor fals Pharisiens
> Agane the treuth quhilk planely doith maling:
> Tyll that kyng cum we mon tak paciens.
>
> (*The Monarche*, 2605–12)

That Lindsay's understanding of the Word of God is informed, partially at least, by Protestant theology is suggestively articulated through the iconography of *Ane Satyre*. Inextricably associated with the book she carries, the character of Veritie assumes particular significance. A long-established symbol of learning or sanctity, the image of the book or Bible was frequently reappropriated by Protestants to signify the Word of God. As such, it was often placed in the hands of the temporal ruler, thereby denoting his headship of the Church and signaling a rejection of the interpretive and intercessory role of the Church. Uniting ecclesiastical and secular authority in the person of the godly monarch, the Bible became an increasingly important feature of English Protestant royal iconography, what has been described as "the fundamental and most oft repeated pictorial symbol for Edward [VI]'s government as a zealous ruler."[16] By installing Bible-brandishing Veritie as one of Rex Humanitas's new counselors, Lindsay reinforces the idea of evangelical, godly kingship; of a divinely sanctioned, scripturally modeled monarchy such as that evoked by English iconographers. To some in the audience, Veritie's imprisonment by the three Vices and her subsequent liberation by the reformed Rex Humanitas may even have recalled the pageantry staged during Edward's coronation and the tableau depicting Justice, Faith, and "ancient Truth, which long Time was suppressed / With Heathen Rites and detestable Idolatrye," bound by "Abuses" until rescued by Henry VIII.[17] Even if not a direct allusion to this particular piece of Protestant image building, the allegorical import of Veritie's predicament delivered a similar message to Lindsay's Scottish audience.

Of almost equal symbolic importance in the nascent Protestant iconography, particularly as it emerged in England, was the image of the sword. As well as being an ancient symbol of secular regal authority, St. Paul's description of the Sword of the Spirit as the Word of God (Ephesians 7:17) rendered it a potent symbol of the Bible itself. Also associated with the martyrdom of St. Paul, the author of the crucial distinction between Faith and Works, the sword was doubly qualified for absorption into the Protestant iconographic tradition. Evoking the presence of the most important Protestant saint and linking the authority of God's Word with the regal authority of the king, the image of the sword, like that of the book, was a resonant symbol of godly kingship. The two images acquired added potency when brought together, and it may be no coincidence that while Veritie carries a Bible Divyne Correctioun wields a sword (1508). Of course, the sword was a long-established symbol of judicial authority, but Correctioun's status as divine emissary and his juxtaposition with Veritie suggest that—for those cognizant with the type of symbolism circulating south of the border—his sword could be seen as something more than the traditional sword of justice. In this way, the use of symbolic stage props in *Ane Satyre of the Thrie Estatis* may have delivered a subtly encoded message concerning the nature of Rex Humanitas's new rule which, bound by the Word of God, was inspired by the example of England.

LINDSAY'S discussion of religious affairs is marked by considerable thematic continuity, in terms of not only the moral failings of clerics but also some of the practices upheld by the Church. Pilgrimages and the use of images, two themes already dealt with in earlier works, are again the object of his attack. However, Lindsay's later treatment of these topics illustrates a greater debt to Protestant thinking than the essentially Erasmian tone of *The Complaynt*. In *The Monarche,* he launches a two-pronged assault on pilgrimages, denouncing them as occasions "Off fornicatioun and Idolatyre" (2369). The former charge is the more mundane, a simple criticism of the sexual promiscuity of the pilgrims. Lindsay was not alone in such complaints, and in 1558 one of the charges leveled against the heretic Walter Myln was his declaration that "there is no greater whoredome in no places, then at your pilgramages, except it be in common brothels."[18] Likewise, the anonymous author of *Kitteis Confessioun* had also described pilgrimages as "The verray way to wantouness" (80). However, in the eyes of the Church, Lindsay's most damaging criticism related not to the sexual conduct of pilgrims but to the object of their devotions: the shrines, their images and relics. "Quhy," he asks the prelates, "thole ye thame to ryn frome toun to toun, / In Pylgrammage tyll ony Ymageris, / Hopand to gett, thare, sum Saluatioun, / Prayand to thame deuotlye on thare kneis?" (*The Monarche,* 2649–52).

In *The Monarche,* the discussion of images and idolatry is developed by Lindsay at some length. Relating how the practice was first invented by Ninus and later sustained by the greed of both craftsmen and priests, Lindsay turns to the "Imageis vsit amang Cristin men," offering a vivid insight into the multiplicity of saints commonly invoked in pre-Reformation Scotland. In traditional enough fashion, he acknowledges that images serve as the religious literature of the illiterate, but he categorically denies that they should be the object of veneration. "Quharefor, brether, I counsall yow, repent," Experience exhorts the Courtiour, "Gyff no honour to caruit stock nor stone" (2513–14). This advice was at odds with the official teaching of the Church, expressed for example by the Provincial Council of 1559 which declared that "The images of Christ and the saints are lawful for the representation of the same and in order to their imitation; and the said images are to be treated with reverence, and not subject to derision and jeerings."[19] Lindsay, it is true, fell short of advocating iconoclasm or even "derision and jeerings," but repeated attempts by the Church to enforce respect for images and to deal with image breakers suggest that this was perceived as a problem.[20]

Although the two could easily be confused, a refusal to honor images did not necessarily constitute a denial of the efficacy of prayer to the saints themselves. However, though Lindsay is careful never to reject explicitly the intercessory power of the saints and makes a conventional enough reference to it in both *Ane Satyre* (4622–24) and *The Monarche* (5690–94), in acknowledging the value of an image for the "vnleirnit" (2327) he stresses the value of saints as moral exemplars and not as potential mediators between God and man:

> For, quhen lauid folk vpone thame luikis,
> It bringith to rememberance
> Off sanctis lyuis the circumstance;
> Quhow the faith for to fortifye,
> Thay sufferit pane rycht pacientlye.
>
> (*The Monarche*, 2328–32)

Only God, Lindsay asserts, should be the object of man's prayer and devotion: "Geue laude and glore to God Omnipotent / Allanerlie" (2525–16).

During the early 1550s, this was a matter of some dispute. Controversy arose when the English Dominican Richard Marshall preached a sermon at St. Andrews declaring that the Lord's Prayer should be addressed only to God.[21] This was vigorously attacked by those who maintained, as was commonly held, that it might also be said to the saints. The ensuing squabble severely damaged the Church's reputation, and the unseemly wrangle was extinguished only when the 1552 Provincial Council promised to address the problem in its planned Catechism, a simple statement of faith designed to be read in Church once a week for the education of clergy and laity alike. However, when printed eight months later, *Hamilton's Catechisme* failed to resolve the issue. In a discussion of how men should keep the Sabbath, it somewhat casually included the words, "thai suld say thair Pater Noster to God," but in the section dealing specifically with the Lord's Prayer, the exposition is followed by "Ane declaratioun schawand to quhem we suld pray, and for quhom," which instructs people to pray to God, to good men and women that their prayers may help obtain grace, and also to the saints for "no man suld dout, bot that sanctis pray for our saluatioun."[22] Lindsay was clearly aware of this controversy and, in *Ane Satyre*, Folly refers to the quarreling friars unable to agree "To quhom thay sall say thair Pater Nosters" (4604). Writing only a few months after the *Catechisme*'s publication, Lindsay rejects the ambiguous approach of the authorities and, referring to the Pater Noster, he writes:

The quhilk is nocht directit, I heir say
To Iohne, nor Iames, to Peter nor to Paull,

Nor nonne vther of the Apostlis twelf,
Nor to no Sanct, nor Angell in the Hewin
Bot onely tyll our Father, God hym self.

(*The Monarche*, 2627–31)

His words rebuke those who "Doith wyrschip all thir Ymagereis; / In Kirk, in Queir, and in the closter, / Prayand to thame our Pater Noster" (2314–16). The fact that Lindsay urged Archbishop Hamilton to this more radical position may reflect a belief that his stance was backed by a degree of popular opinion. Aware that the Pater Noster controversy had done little to strengthen the authority of the Church, Lindsay seized upon the opportunity of undermining it still further.

As well as holding that the Lord's Prayer should be directed only to God, Lindsay firmly believed that it should be said in the vernacular, a view that also extended to the Ave Maria and Creed. In a highly practical fashion, one designed to appeal to his popular audience, Lindsay points out that the ancients simply wrote in their own languages, that the Commandments were given to Moses in his native tongue, and that the saints and apostles used the vernacular: Had Jerome lived in Argyll, "In to Yrische toung his bukis had bene done compyle" (*The Monarche*, 628). When *The Monarche* was written in 1553, *Hamilton's Catechisme* had already provided a vernacular exposition of the Creed, Ave Maria, and Lord's Prayer. But the fact that Lindsay was still calling for such translations is a pointed criticism of their availability, for although the *Catechisme* was to be regularly read in church, access to the text was restricted to clerics and a few laymen whom the Church ordinaries considered virtuous, discreet, and of good faith.

Although the Church authorized the vernacular exposition of the Lord's Prayer, Ave Maria, Creed, sacraments, and Ten Commandments, access to vernacular Scripture was less clear-cut. The parliamentary act of March 1543 was, it is true, never repealed, but calls for the enforcement of existing legislation led to the renewed persecution of Protestants, and the widespread enthusiasm for Scripture reading noted by John Knox swiftly evaporated.[23] The *Catechisme* of 1552 contained no specific injunction against reading Scripture in the vernacular, but whether this signified recognition of a fait accompli or whether it was simply an oversight is unclear.[24] Vernacular prayers, however, were definitely not sanctioned. When in 1559, the lay lords submitted a petition (which subsequently formed the basis of the ecclesiastical statutes of that year), their call for public prayer in the vernacular was denied.[25] Had he still been alive at this date, Lindsay would undoubtedly have supported their position:

> It wer als plesand to thare spreit, in deid,
> God have mercy on me, for to say thus,
> As to say *Miserere Mei, Deus*. (*The Monarche*, 619–21)

Lindsay's deliberate reference at this point to "Childreyng, and Ladyis of honouris" (615), the most insignificant members of society, suggests that he intended a much more universal access to the vernacular than would ever be sanctioned by the authorities. Henry VIII's 1543 Act for the Advancement of True Religion, which effectively limited access to Scripture to an upper-class, male elite, was much more typical of contemporary attitudes. Sadler reported that this legislation greatly offended those Scots "such as do pretend . . . to be professors of God's Word."[26] But the Scottish act of the same year had sanctioned only the possession and reading of Scripture, and the careful reaffirmation of government opposition to disputation and heresy underlined official fears of what might happen should the Bible become widely discussed.

As with the early works, there is little discussion of theological points of doctrine in either *Ane Satyre* or *The Monarche*. Whether this reflects Lindsay's personal attitude to religious faith or whether it was conditioned by simple prudence is difficult to assess. Certainly, Lindsay was well aware of the Church's ability to smother dissent and, given the background of suspicion and persecution against which he wrote, it is not all that surprising that he is all but silent upon some of the specific controversial doctrinal issues of the day. However, while Lindsay's poetry understandably lacks the method of a theological treatise, it clearly suggests the general character of his piety.

With regard to the sacraments, Lindsay has very little to say. Quite possibly, broaching the issue, and the Eucharist in particular, was, as his French experiences had demonstrated, simply too hazardous. Indeed, following Wishart's mission of the 1540s and the attendant spread of Zwinglian ideas, the ecclesiastical authorities were particularly keen to crack down upon those who "are becumin Sacramentis."[27] *The Monarche*, however, offers a tantalizing suggestion that Lindsay was at least aware of Protestant arguments concerning the saving power of the seven sacraments. Declaring that preachers should "Tyll all vertew thare hartis inclyne" (4845), Lindsay goes on to outline their duties in more detail: "In speciall, to preche with trew intentis, / And minister the neidfull Sacramentis" (4846–47). Lindsay's choice of the word "neidfull" is very suggestive in this context. Although he might simply be affirming the necessity of all seven sacraments, his unusual, tautological phrasing does beg the question which—if indeed any—of the sacraments he considered "nonneedful."[28] Unfortunately, this ambiguity, if such it is, is all we have to suggest that Lindsay was at least intrigued by contemporary discussion of the issue.

Belief in the necessity of the sacraments is, of course, determined by one's conception of the relationship between God and mankind, of salvation attained by the latter and of grace granted by the former. This was the crux of the Reformation divide. Luther and his successors offered people a new understanding of that relationship, and the idea that man can be justified by faith alone represents the cornerstone of Reformation theology. To consider Lindsay's attitude to this position is to reach the heart of his religious faith, and it is clear that, despite his many sympathies with Protestant thought and his tolerance of confessed Protestants, his faith was that of the Catholic Church. Lindsay's later works, particularly *The Monarche,* incorporate a vigorous challenge to the Protestant doctrine of Justification *sola fides.* Asked what faith is, Experience tells the Courtiour, "Faith without Hope and Charitie / Aualit nocht, my Sonne" (482–83); "Quyk faith but cheretabyll werkis / Can neuer be, as wryttis Clerkis" (490–91). Of course, Protestants did not deny works any value. Faith and charity are found together and, in the words of the Lutheran martyr Patrick Hamilton, "he that hath faith can not displease God."[29] Yet Lindsay's words cannot be considered a subtle endorsement of the Protestant position, for while the above passages stress the need for faith *and* works, elsewhere the emphasis is upon the latter:

> Geue charitie in to the failis,
> Thy faith nor Hope no thyng auailis.   (494–95)
>
> Do all the gude that may be wrocht
> But Caritie, all aualis nocht.   (498–99)

Lindsay's discussion of faith again recalls *Hamilton's Catechisme* and the argument that it is not sufficient only to have faith but that "This faith is alwayis ionit with hoip and cheritie, and werkis throw lufe."[30] Like Lindsay, *The Catechisme* cites James 2, noting that even the Devil might have faith but that he wants hope and charity. The role assigned to faith in *The Catechisme* and endorsed by Lindsay in *The Monarche* is not entirely in line with that promulgated at Trent some five years earlier and is, arguably, slightly Protestant in tone.[31] Whether this represents a deliberate doctrinal compromise is unclear, but it does seem as if the formula, whether by accident or design, was acceptable to men such as Lindsay who, in other respects, were more responsive to Protestant ideas.

Lindsay himself, while not accepting Luther's teaching on the matter of Justification, did tend to downplay the role of the Church in the process of winning salvation. He stressed the importance of an individual's good works rather than the sacraments of the Church and, above all, he emphasized the saving merits of Christ's suffering: "in Christis Blude sett all thy hole confort" (*The Monarche,* 6275). This type of personal, contemplative piety was also a feature of Lindsay's earlier work as, inspired by Christ's Passion, he expressed his desire for a more spiritual, introspective existence. While, as we have seen, Lindsay was at first unable to square this ideal with his service at the royal court, writing in his old age he appears firmly committed to the renunciation of worldly ambition. Warning the Courtiour not to trust in earthly rewards, Experience explains, "There is no warldly thyng at all, / May satisfie ane mannis Saull" (5042–43). This message is hammered home in the final "Exhortatioun" which, stressing that "the tyme is verray short" (6274), urges men to consider the miseries of the world, to fix their eyes upon approaching death, and "In erthlye materis tak . . . no more cummer" (6299). In similar terms, *The Monarche* offers its audience what can only be described as a personal prayer for salvation:

> Grant ws to be, Lorde, of the chosin sort
> Quhame of thy mercy superexcellant,
> Did puriffy, as scripture doith report
> With the blude of that holy Innocent
> Iesu, quhilk maid hym self Obedient
> On to the deth and steruit on the Rude
> Lat ws, O Lorde, be purgit with that blude.   (6232–38)

Passages such as this provide the key to Lindsay's own inner faith which, contemplative and highly personal in nature, was acutely sensitive to Protestant criticisms of the Church's monopoly on salvation and its attendant claims. Thus Lindsay was not only unsympathetic to the Church's personnel, its economic exploitation of the poor, and its independence from royal control, he was also increasingly suspicious of its claims regarding the remittance of sin.

In *Ane Satyre,* Lindsay launches a damning attack on the sale of indulgences, papal remissions of sin that reduce time spent in Purgatory.[32] In the first instance, his satire is directed against the rapacious and ignorant pardoner, Sir Robert Romeraker. There is, in fact, little evidence for the activity of pardoners in early-sixteenth-century Scotland, and it has been suggested that Lindsay's creation was influenced by Chaucer or, alternatively, by the French work *La farce d'un Pardonner.*[33] However, if pardoners were a rare sight, Sir Robert's appearance in *Ane Satyre* at the point where allegory gives way to topical discussion cannot be accidental. For if he failed to evoke personal memories for the audience, Lindsay's pardoner would have recalled, for some at least, Friar Tetzel and the controversy that sparked the Lutheran Reformation. Having exposed the pardoner as nothing but a greedy charlatan, Lindsay builds upon his indignant moral criticisms, calling into question the legitimacy of the pardons themselves and implying that they are as worthless as the fake relics Sir Robert hawks from town to town. From the outset, the utter irreligiosity of the pardoner is made clear. He enters cursing "This vnsell wickit New-Testament, / With them that it translaitit" (2051–52). Not only does he condemn the Reformers Luther, Bullinger, and Melanchthon, but he also goes so far as to lament the birth of St. Paul. The audience's expectations of this papal representative are further confounded by the unnatural, not to mention illegal, "divorce" ceremony over which he presides.[34] Instructing the Sowtar and his soon-to-be-former wife to kiss one another on the arse may have provided the audience with much scatological amusement but, more sinisterly, it conjures up visions of the diabolic pact, worthy indeed of "Baliels braid blissing" (2179).

Not without humor, Lindsay fashions a Scottish context for the purposes of illustrating the type of unease that existed regarding the practice of selling indulgences when, in a comic scene, the Pauper looks in bewilderment—and in vain—for his purchase. The belief that "It is mere human talk to preach that the soul flies out [of Purgatory] immediately the money clinks in the collection box" (even, suggests Lindsay, the talk of the Devil) was not exclusively Lutheran.[35] Many humanists, notably Erasmus, were hostile to such mechanical devotions, bitterly denouncing careful mathematical calculations regarding "the paying off of sin."[36] This attitude may also have found sympathy with Scottish Catholic reformers; on the question of indulgences, *Hamilton's Catechisme,* for example, is silent.[37] Again, it is impossible to tell whether Lindsay was influenced more directly by the arguments of orthodox reformers or by confessed Protestants. Arguably, however, this is relatively unimportant, for the significance of Lindsay's work is to illustrate the penetration of such ideas not just among an educated elite but among the more socially diverse audience laughing at the Pauper's discomfiture.

While *Ane Satyre* presents a savage yet amusing attack on the sale of indulgences, *The Monarche* offers a more complex and critical discussion. Here, Experience refers to the pope's power to remit sin, declaring disingenuously:

> It doith transcend my rude Ingyne
> His Sanctitude for tyll defyne,
> Or to schaw the auctoritie
> Pertenyng to his Maiestie.   (4345–48)

His sardonic account of a God in thrall to the papal command—another inversion of the natural order—serves to underscore the perversity of the idea that

Quhame euer he byndis by his mycht,
Thay boundin ar in Goddis sycht.
Quhame ever he lowsis in erth heir doun,
Ar lousit be God in his Regioun.   (4353–56)

What made indulgences such an important issue was, of course, the doctrine of Purgatory. Although the Pauper confidently expects his "sillie soule will pas to Purgatorie" (*Ane Satyre*, 2277), in *The Monarche* Lindsay is, as in earlier works, much more ambiguous. Discussing the revenue raised by the sale of indulgences, he wonders at "That maruelous monstour callit Purgatorye," wryly noting "Howbeit tyll ws it is not amyable, / It hes to thame bene veray profytable" (4775–77). Whether it is the aggressive abuse (that is, the rapacious sale of pardons) that is "not amyable" or whether it is the doctrine of the "maruelous monstour" itself is, deliberately perhaps, left unclear. Similarly, when Lindsay writes, "For Peter, Androw, nor Iohn culde neuer gett / So profytable ane Fysche in to thare nett" (4790–91), we cannot tell whether he is claiming that the Apostles did not sell indulgences or, more radically, that they did not suscribe to the idea of Purgatory. Certainly, the lines could have evoked current Protestant arguments that Purgatory was but a creation of the Roman Church for which there was no apostolic foundation. Other evidence also supports the idea that Lindsay was delivering a circumspect critique of Purgatory, in particular his accounts of the soul's experiences after death. "Thy spreit sall passe, but tarying," he writes, "Strauait way tyll Ioye Inestimabyll / Or to strange pane Intollerabyll" (5164–67). While the words "strange pane" may allude to Purgatory, the phrases "but tarying" and "Strauait way" strongly suggest that Hell rather than Purgatory is to be inferred from this passage. That Purgatory had no place in Lindsay's vision of the afterlife is perhaps confirmed by a similar turn of phrase when he notes that those who die leave a troubled world, passing on "Tyll Ioy and euirlestand lyfe" (5145). It seems, therefore, that over a period of some thirty years Lindsay's attitude toward Purgatory grew increasingly hostile. And with belief in Purgatory being made an article of faith in 1559, it seems as if such attitudes were a growing problem for the Scottish Church.[38]

As we have seen, Lindsay's attack on indulgences was bound up with his attitude toward the papacy. Historians have tended to suggest that in the early decades of the sixteenth century the question of papal authority was, if anything, hardly debated in Scotland.[39] But there is evidence for important, albeit small and scattered, pockets of antipapal sentiment. One orthodox aspect of this was the attack on excessive claims to papal authority put forward by conciliarist theorists such as John Mair: It could be but a short step from the rejection of the *ius divinum* of the papacy to rejection of the office as a whole. Indeed, two early Scottish Protestants, Hamilton and Alesius, both seem to have made this step having first been Mair's pupils.[40] Outside the universities, there were at least a few antipapalists at court, most notably John Borthwick.[41] English emissaries such as Dr. William Barlow and Sir Ralph Sadler attempted to encourage such sentiment, and it is surely significant that, only months after the death of James V, Parliament was prepared to sanction diplomatic alliance and dynastic union with a schismatic nation. Writing in 1543, Sadler, dubious about Scottish commitment to the Reformed faith, noted that "such as pretend to favour God's word, do like chiefly that part which confuteth the primacy of the bishop of Rome."[42] There are also examples of antipapalism on a more humble level, and among the religious refugees in England in 1537 were four Ayrshire Scots who declared that the bishop of Rome was not the pope.[43] They would undoubtedly have appreciated those *Gude and Godlie Ballatis* which offered a colorful attack on both the person and the authority of the pontiff. While such sentiments may have derived, like many of the songs themselves, from Germany (where popular antipapalism was more prevalent), and while such songs as *The Paip, that Pagane full of Pryde* possess a crude brutality untypical of the collection as a whole, they may (if circulated in uncensored form before 1565) have helped prepare for the reception of antipapal feeling within Scotland.[44] The well-noted fact that *Hamilton's Catechisme* fails to make any reference to the authority of Rome may reflect what was, by this date, not so much Scottish indifference to the question but official awareness of a growing antagonism toward the papacy. Lindsay, influenced by his visits to England and his contact with John Knox, was extremely responsive to such feeling and, indeed, his own ferocious satires must have contributed to the growth of Scottish antipapalism in the sixteenth century.

Lindsay's attitude to the papacy, however, was not one of straightforward hostility. Historical and institutional continuity were important to him and, believing the papacy to have apostolic foundation, he could not repudiate it entirely. Instituted by Christ, "be the vertew of his wourde" (4380), it was still to be viewed as reformable. However, beyond an implied plea for moral regeneration, Lindsay offers no specific suggestions for reform.[45] Concentrating instead upon the corruption to which he believed the papacy had succumbed, he is driven into an ever more hostile position. This, combined with his enthusiasm for a monarchically led reform process, fostered an attitude bordering upon the schismatic; although desperate to maintain the possibility of reform, the very reforms he demands amount to a virtual rejection of Rome.

Of Lindsay's later works, *The Monarche* offers the most comprehensive criticism of the actions and authority of the pope. However, *Ane Satyre* also offers, somewhat more obliquely, a damning rejection of papal authority. In the first part of the play, Lindsay effectively establishes the moral corruption of the papacy, satirizing the Roman court as the resort of Sensualitie, "the lemand lamp of lechery" (238). (Significantly, such an attack suggests that Lindsay felt there was sufficient antipapalism in his Cupar audience for his words to generate an appreciative response.) In the second part of the play, Lindsay develops his assault, moving from questions of morality to those of authority. Here, the statutes enacted by the three estates loosen ties with Rome arguably to the point of schism. This is equally apparent from the dramatic action of the play. For example, Spiritualitie's opposition to the forcible removal of his servants, Couetice and Sensualitie, is accompanied by a threat to complain to the pope, which by its total ineffectiveness further exposes the sham of papal authority in Scotland. Something similar can be seen with regard to the abolition of corspresent. Initially, Temporalitie recommends that the king seek papal permission for this measure, but within minutes the legislation has been enacted without any reference to Rome at all.[46] The import of papal approval (which would surely have been unforthcoming) is unambiguously depicted as irrelevant to Lindsay's vision of a secularly guided reform process. Other statutes also assist the dissolution of papal influence in Scotland. Pluralism, a practice requiring papal dispensation, is abolished; the dispatch of moneys to Rome for benefices other than great archbishoprics was forbidden (although there was, in fact, nothing new about this type of barratry legislation); and the proposed institution of clerical marriage can only be viewed as a defiant rejection of papal authority.

An even more explicit attack on the papacy is found in *The Monarche,* which includes a lengthy and extremely hostile "Discriptioun of the Court of Rome" (4743–973). Here Lindsay again rejects papal influence in Scotland, repeating the common grouse that "Preistis suld no more our substance so consume, / Sendyng, yeirlye, so gret ryches to Rome" (4769–70). In more general terms, he attacks papal pretensions to power over secular rulers. "Peter, be my Opinioun," he writes, "Did neuer vse sic Dominioun" (4605–6). In temporal affairs, Lindsay believed the spiritual authority should be subject to the secular, rendering to Caesar what is rightfully his. In startling, extravagant terms, he describes the degeneracy of the court of Rome:

> Ane horribyll vaill of euerilk kynd of vyce,
> Ane laithlye Loch of stynkand Lychorye,
> Ane curssit Coue, corrupt with Couatyce,
> Bordourit aboute with pryde and Symonye,
> Sum sayis, ane systerne full of Sodomye,
> Quhose vyce in speciall, gyff I wald declair,
> It wer aneuch for tyll perturbe the air. (4946–52)

Pushing his attack to the very limit, Lindsay must nevertheless have antici-
pated a less than hostile response, not only from the more obvious antipapalists in his audience but even from the Church authorities. This is, after
all, extraordinary language to find in a work ostentatiously dedicated to a
Catholic archbishop, one in whose hands his own fate as an accused heretic
might lie.

Lindsay did not only attack the moral depravity of the papacy. Arguing
that such practices as clerical celibacy, dietary restrictions, the sale of indulgences, even indulgences themselves, were all the invention of the Church,
he suggests that not only the personnel but also the practices of the Roman
Church had become hopelessly corrupt. While accepting that the papacy
embodied a desirable link with the apostolic Church, Lindsay was appalled
by its enslavement to sensuality and materialism and the consequent corruption of its ideals and practices. Typically, the pathway to reform is left
open (just), but the thrust of Lindsay's argument is unmistakably geared
toward a dissolution of the ties that bound Scotland to Rome.

LINDSAY'S antipapalism was closely bound up with his apocalyptic interpretation of history, and in *The Monarche,* arguably the most antipapal of all
his works, he offers his audience nothing less than a fully fledged apocalypse.[47] This functions partly as didactic instruction, partly as a call to
repentance, but, in the first instance, as an explanation for the miserable
condition of the contemporary world and the personal wretchedness of the
narrator.[48] Morbid as this might sound to the modern mind, it was in fact
an optimistic ideology, explaining the apparently inexplicable and enabling
Lindsay to meet death with equanimity. His exegesis over, Experience
comforts the Courtiour, "Dreid nocht to dee" (6300).

Since the emergence of apocalypticism two to three centuries B.C., the
idea of a revealed or prophesied truth embodied in the historical process had
become well established in western consciousness. The Jewish belief in
God's direct involvement in human history was readily absorbed into the
Christian tradition, and apocalypticism underpinned historical and eschatological thinking throughout the Middle Ages and beyond.[49] The
medieval apocalyptic tradition (or rather traditions) received a further stimulus in the form of the ideas of the Reformation.[50] For many Reformers, the
Apocalypse appeared to speak directly to them. By explaining history, it
legitimated their own often bewildering experiences, locating them firmly
within the matrix of revealed history. In this way, such otherwise incomprehensible phenomena as suffering, persecution, and the entire existence of
the Roman Church attained meaning. Consequently, Protestant writers
became increasingly concerned with apocalyptic themes and, by the time

Lindsay wrote *The Monarche*, there existed a number of possible sources upon which he could draw.

Lindsay's apocalypticism appears to have been derived from the emergent Protestant tradition as developed both in England and on the Continent. The preaching of John Knox, who seems to have derived his ideas principally from English sources—or at least English translations of continental works—may well have been Lindsay's first encounter with such thinking.[51] Knox himself was convinced that he had opened the eyes of his Scottish audience and, although notoriously prone to exaggerate the importance of his own actions, he was probably correct in thinking that his type of Reformed apocalypticism was new to the majority of Scots.[52] Much easier to trace is Lindsay's debt to continental sources: In *The Monarche*, the important German apocalypse, *Carion's Chronicle*, is expressly cited no less than five times (3521, 3616, 3621, 4506, and 5286).[53] A world history framed with reference to Daniel's vision of the four monarchies and brought up to the sixteenth century, *Carion's Chronicle* was first issued around 1531, after which it appears to have passed to Melanchthon and his colleagues for comment and correction. A number of Latin versions of Carion's work were published; one such was translated into English, and French versions also followed. Although it is difficult to tell which edition Lindsay was familiar with, his reliance upon the work—cited in preference to other named texts—constitutes a self-confident declaration of his familiarity with contemporary European scholarship.[54] We must, however, beware of seeing this as exclusive to Protestant sympathizers as the undoubtedly Catholic author of *The Complaynt of Scotland* also refers to Carion for the purposes of historical periodization.[55] Clearly, Scots could be impressed and influenced by the scholarship of Protestant apocalypticism without necessarily sharing the faith that inspired it. Nevertheless, the work of Lindsay and Wedderburn together with Knox's first sermon suggests that by the mid sixteenth century apocalyptic ideas conditioned by Protestant thinking were gaining ground in Scotland.

Fundamental to all apocalyptic thinking is the idea of history and historical change. That God works in history and through history is the heart of the apocalyptic message. The traditional idea of history as a divinely structured progress, cosmic in scope and linear in orientation, was grounded in the work of early Christian writers such as Eusebius, Augustine, and Orosius.[56] This view existed alongside the classical view of a cyclical history, frequently presided over by the goddess Fortuna idly toying with her wheel. While Lindsay makes conventional enough use of this image, most notably in *The Testament of the Papyngo* and *The Tragedie of the Cardinal*, *The Monarche* reveals his rejection of what was, for him, a profoundly unsatisfactory way of comprehending man's place in the world. Following patristic world histories and their vision of a divinely ordered cosmos, he cites both Eusebius and Orosius as sources.[57] Indeed, Orosius's title *De Miseria Mundi* was borrowed by Lindsay for his own work, "Off the Miserabyll Estait of the Warld."

In *The Monarche*, history is employed in a number of different ways. First, Lindsay presents a narrative version of history from Creation to Judgment; second, he uses history to illustrate a moral message concerning the exercise of power; and third, history is used as apocalypse, to explain not only the past but the present and future also. Of course, these different functions frequently overlapped. The stories of Ninus, Semaramis, and Sardanapalus, for example, represent traditionally articulated warnings against the vices of pride, ambition, and lust. At the same time, however, Lindsay makes it clear that it is God's intervention in the world that is under discussion. Writing of the death of Semaramis, he notes various suggestions as to why she was murdered, yet concludes, "None vther cause I can defyne, / Except punissioun deuyne" (3221–22). Biblical episodes such as the Flood, the destruction of Sodom and Gomorrah, the fate of Lot's wife, the Egyptian plagues, and the twice-over destruction of Jerusalem also introduce a moral lesson while simultaneously suggesting God's action in history. Indeed, the entire history of the four world monarchies is presented in this light:

> Thir Monarcheis, I vnderstand,
> Preordinat wer by the command
> Off God, the Plasmatour of all,
> For to doun thryng and to mak thrall
> Undantit Peple vitious
> And als for to be gratious
> To thame quhilk vertuous wer and gude,
> As Daniell, heth done conclude
> At length, in tyll his Propheseis,   (3724–32)

Although God's action was everywhere apparent in history, it was not generally believed that the past could be used to predict God's will for the future. Nevertheless, this privileged information had been revealed to a few chosen individuals and, as this passage illustrates, scriptural prophecies were eagerly scanned by those seeking a framework within which to fix both contemporary and future events.[58] The prophetic tradition was multifaceted, being derived in the first instance from three principal biblical sources: the Book of Daniel which described the passage of four world empires, the Book of Revelation which traced the history of the Church, and the prophecy of Elijah which, with its tripartite division of history, effectively described the duration of the world. As this suggests, periodization is the crucial factor in imparting prophetic potential to a work, and in the Middle Ages there existed at least two other important historical periodizations which, as articulated by Augustine, proved extremely influential in the development of apocalyptic thinking. First, there was the idea of the three stages of salvation—in effect, a Christianization of the Talmudic prophecy of Elijah—which split world history into a period before Moses (*ante legum*), a period under the Law (*sub lege*), and a period under the Grace of Christ (*sub gratia*). Alongside this stood the Six World Ages or "Cosmic Week" theory which divided history into six millennia followed by a seventh thousand-year period, a chronological macrocosm of the six days of Creation and the Sabbath. This interpretation was often complicated by virtue of being conflated with the twentieth chapter of Revelation which predicted a period when Satan would be bound for a thousand years while the saints ruled with God. Although this could give rise to a powerful chiliastic hope (the expectation of experiencing this Sabbath period on earth), Augustine's insistence that it was not to be taken literally but as a metaphor for the period *sub gratia* emerged as the standard interpretation of the Middle Ages.[59] This nonmillenarian view, typical of early Protestant apocalypticism, was central to Lindsay's *Monarche*.

For his own apocalypse, Lindsay draws upon more than one of these traditional chronologies. Like Carion, Lindsay's basic historical framework is supplied by the four world monarchies prophesied by Daniel but, again like Carion, he also incorporates the prophecy of Elijah into his history:

> The worlde shall stande syxe thousand yeres and after shall it fall,
> Two thousande yeares wythout the lawe.
> Two thousande yeares in the lawe
> Two thousande yeares the tyme of Christ
> And yf these yeares be not accomplyshed our sinnes shall be the
> cause, whyche are great and many.[60]

It being commonly accepted that Creation could be dated to 4000 B.C., the six-thousand-year span of history was therefore shared by Elijah's prophecy and the Cosmic Week interpretation. Nevertheless, Lindsay takes care to attribute his periodization to his German source, making clear his ideological allegiance to "cunnyng Maister Carioun" (5288) and the emerging tradition of Protestant apocalypticism.[61]

As Lindsay calculates, this type of periodization leaves men with several centuries yet in hand: "And so remains to cum, but weir / Four hundreth, with sewin and fourtye yeir" (5301–2). However, the problem for mankind was that human sin would cause the final period of history to be cut short by an unspecified number of years. Like most early Reformers, Lindsay denies that any exact calculation concerning the duration of future time can be made: "perturbe nocht thine intent / To knaw day, hour, nor moment," Experience tells the Courtiour; "To God allone the day bene knawin, / Quhilk neuer was to none Angell schawin" (5264–67). However, despite this uncertainty, Lindsay shared the conviction of many Protestant thinkers that the End was imminent. Not only was the prophecy of Elijah nearing fulfillment, but various other signs existed to presage the end of the historical process. Disturbances in nature, violations of the social order, and general moral decadence were all traditionally understood to herald the End, and in the mid sixteenth century men did not have to look far for such phenomena. *Carion's Chronicle* includes many marvelous omens, and Lindsay too, although much less lurid and comparatively unspecific, locates contemporary disasters within an apocalyptic scheme:

> Tokynnis of darth, hunger, and pestilence,
> With cruell weris, boith be sey and land,
> Realme aganis realme with mortall violence,
> Quhilkis signifyis the last day ewin at hand.   (4238–41)

A further harbinger of the End was the perceived corruption of the spiritual estate and, following certain unnamed "cunnyng clerkis" (5334), Lindsay construes the darkening of the sun, moon, and stars described in the Gospels as the decay of church, prince, and people.[62] The corruption of the Roman Church was a major theme of the developing Protestant apocalyptic tradition, with the pope increasingly identified as the antichrist prophesied in the Book of Revelation. In support of this, Protestants also cited the Book of Daniel, which describes a period after the four world monarchies characterized by the rule of a wicked king who persecutes the godly. According to more traditional exegesis, this period had not yet arrived, for the fourth empire (that of Rome) still survived in the form of the Holy Roman Empire. Lindsay, however, had no doubt but that the four empires had run their course:

> Now is the warld of Irne myxit with clay,
> As Daniell at lenth hes done indyte.
> The gret Impyris ar meltit clene away;
> Now is the warld of dolour and dispyte.   (4231–34)

In addition to supplying a further sign that the world "is drawand to ane end" (4237), this interpretation also allowed Lindsay to locate the prophesied fifth empire in his own times. Furthermore, he too identifies the fifth empire, that of the antichrist, with the Roman papacy. Found in Luther and subsequently developed by other Protestant thinkers, this idea had been expounded in England as early as February 1536 when Cranmer argued that the fourth empire was in ruins, "that the pope was the true antichrist and none other need be looked for."[63] Lindsay may have been influenced by such ideas, but he did not share the decidedly Protestant belief that the pope was the *only* antichrist. Although he believed that no further incarnations of the antichrist need be looked for in history (5234–37), he saw around him numerous and various antichrists:

> The warld is drawand neir ane end.
> For legionis ar cum, but doute,
> Off Antechristis, wer thay soucht out.   (5313–15)

As this suggests, the medieval antichrist tradition was far from monolithic. It was, in fact, essentially threefold although the different motifs could and did overlap. First, there had developed an elaborate mythology designed to identify a specific individual antichrist by means of his birth and career, a fantastical, demonic parody of the life of Christ.[64] In *The Monarche,* the Courtiour refers to this "wyckit man, from sathan sent" (5175), only to have Experience to reject the legend:

> My Sonne (said he) wryttis Iohne,
> There sall nocht be one man allone,
> Hauyng that name in speciall.
> Bot Antechristis in generall
> Hes bene, and now ar, mony one.   (5192–96)

This owes more to the second traditional view of the antichrist as a spiritual opposition to Christ existing throughout history. As illustrated by *The Monarche,* this was frequently conflated with the third aspect of the antichrist which cast the Turks (occasionally the Jews) in this role:

> All Turkis, Sarazenis, and Iowis,
> That in the sonne of God nocht trowis
> Ar Antechristis, I the declare,
> Because to Christ thay ar contrare.   (5208–11)

However, it is clear that Lindsay's anxiety about the rule of antichrist was stimulated largely by his perceptions of the papacy, a new and highly terrifying antichrist whose appearance presaged nothing less than the End of the world. As evidence that he is living in the "latter aige" (4905), Lindsay recalls Pauline prophecies concerning a ruler who would forbid "the band of Mariage" (4907) and the eating of meat. For Lindsay, the "man of Iniquity" (5226) sitting in "the holy sait" (5228) is clearly a reference to the pope. The prophesied final monarchy of the latter days is the corrupt temporal authority of the papal see, and Rome, once "ane brycht Hierusalem" (4940), has become the Babylon of the Apocalypse. This unnatural sense of disorder and perversion is strengthened by Lindsay's depiction of papal authority as a parody of secular kingship, a parody which operates simultaneously as a parody of Christian values. The pope is portrayed as a ruthless temporal ruler with officials in his dominion lands who, in order to implement his authority, wield both fire and sword. The papal diadem is set against the Crown of Thorns, and a series of comparisons between the humility and poverty of Christ and the pride and materialism of the pope serves to illustrate how far removed the latter is from the Christian ideal.

Equating the pope with antichrist had important implications for those who stood in opposition to the papacy, helping to explain a major problem of Reformation theodicy: Why were those of the True Faith forced to suffer for that faith? The persecution of Veritie in *Ane Satyre* emotively recalls the suffering of early Protestants, and Veritie herself draws attention to the apocalyptic import of her predicament:[65]

> The Prophesie of the Propheit Esay
> Is Practick alace, on me this day:
> Quha said the veritie sould be trampit doun
> Amid the streit, and put in strang presoun.
> His fyue and fyftie chapter quha list luik,
> Sall find thir wordis written in his Buik.
> Richt sa Sanct Paull wrytis to Timothie
> That men sall turn thair earis from veritie.   (1176–83)

Veritie, however, expresses confidence that God will vindicate her suffering and judge her oppressors. Envisaging the torments awaiting those who presently torment her, she is able to face her ordeal confidently, and her words here prefigure those used by Lindsay in *The Monarche:*

> Bot in my Lord God I haue esperance,
> He will prouide for my deliverance.
> Bot ye Princes of Spiritualitie,
> Quha suld defend the sinceir veritie
> I dreid the plagues of Iohnes Revalatioun
> Sall fall vpon your generatioun.   (1184–89)

Lindsay's stress upon the punishment awaiting those who persecute the godly, the apocalyptic adaptation of the traditional biblical theme of retribution, acts to fortify faith in difficult circumstances. There is no doubt in Lindsay's writing that persecutors—referred to as "Unmerciful memberis of the Antichrist" (2573)—shall be judged and the faithful triumphantly vindicated:

> The Innocent blude that day, sall crye,
> One loude vengeance, full peteouslye
> On those creuell bludy bouchouris,
> Martyeris of Prophetis and Prechouris,

Sum with the fyre, sum with the sworde,
Quhilk plainly prechit Goddis worde.
That day thay sall rewardit be,
Conforme to thare Iniquitie.   (*The Monarche*, 5804–11)

Lindsay's work strongly suggests that the experiences of suffering and persecution, participation in the final cosmic struggle between the forces of good and evil, was a vital component of the drama of the latter days. His uncompromising belief that the End was near undoubtedly inspired a sense of involvement in what was widely perceived as the last chapter in world history. This feeling of personal involvement was vital in mitigating what might otherwise have been a very passive approach to the affairs of a world that had anyway run its course. Although we might expect the renunciation of worldly ambition in favor of spiritual contemplation to emasculate Lindsay's stirring social and political criticisms, his apocalyptic convictions gave his pleas for reform an added urgency. With "The plaiges of Iohnis Reuelatioun" (*The Monarche*, 4958) poised to fall on the ungodly, repentance and reform were more vital than ever.

This is made clear in the final portion of *The Monarche* where Lindsay takes his world history up to and beyond "the day Iugement" (5445) when Christ will descend to earth above Mount Olivet and "All Prophesie thare salbe compleit" (5567). With history having reached the end of its progress through time, the poem moves into a suprahistorical era to consider Judgment, Heaven, and Hell. Lindsay describes a literal resurrection of the dead and the immortalization of the living. He portrays Christ's separation of the sheep and the goats, listing at length those who will be damned. Although clerics of all ranks teem in Hell, this passage, like Falset's final speech in *Ane Satyre*, represents a call for the repentance of all of society. In particular, though, it articulates Lindsay's final desperate plea for Church reform: "On thame gret sorrow salbe sene, / Without that thay thare lyfe amend / In tyme" (5923–25). Faced with an impossible task—the attempted description of a glory "non in erth may comprehend"—Lindsay does not attempt anything too ambitious but relies instead upon an appeal to familiar sensations (6160). Heaven means the end of physical suffering and the enjoyment of "sensuall plesouris delectabyll" (6130). This down-to-earth approach was calculated to appeal to the broad audience to whom he addressed the poem. By fixing in his readers' minds a vision of Heaven as comprehensible as it was inspirational, Lindsay helped to strengthen their faith, calling them to repentance and preparing them to meet death with fortitude.

IT IS NOT too fanciful to suggest that *The Monarche* addresses not only Lindsay's fellow countrymen but also the poet's own fears and uncertainties.

Lindsay's suggestive use of the first person, the elderly courtier-narrator, helps render a very public discourse intensely personal. When the Courtiour returns home to record his encounter with Experience, the reader is put in mind of Lindsay returning to the Mount to record his thoughts on a life spent in royal service, on the problems besetting the contemporary world, and finally on the hope of spiritual salvation to come. Significantly, the meeting between Experience and the Courtiour over, Lindsay resumes the evocative description of the natural environment found at the beginning of the poem. Now, however, dawn is turned to dusk, and the twilight of the day effectively suggests not only that the poem is at an end but also that the days of the poet's life and, indeed, of the very world itself are drawing to a close.

CONCLUSION

When Henry Charteris published his 1568 edition of Lindsay's works, he noted that it was customary to include a description of the author, his background, appearance, and character. However, given that Lindsay had been dead only thirteen years and that many readers still entertained vivid memories of him, Charteris felt it "not greitlie neidful to tary . . . thairon."[1] While eloquent testimony to Lindsay's sixteenth-century reputation, this decision to dispense with the usual formalities can only be a cause of deep regret, not to mention intense frustration, for modern readers. The work of Lindsay's more recent editors has done much to compensate for their predecessor's ill-judged assumption, but there are still many details of Lindsay's life that remain unknown today. Though surviving records enable the reconstruction of the basic outline of Lindsay's life and career, it is clear that such sources will never be able to plug all the gaps. The best way to flesh out these rather bare bones and perhaps the only way to construct anything like a recognizable biography is to pay much greater attention to the context—the political and cultural milieu—in which Lindsay lived and wrote. The attractions—and some of the limitations—of such an approach have been amply illustrated by this particular study. Although piecing together Lindsay's career to form any sort of coherent whole involves much conjecture and guesswork, it is nevertheless possible to draw some conclusions concerning the activities in which he was engaged and the attitudes he both encountered and expressed. If nothing else, it has been possible to identify some of the most intriguing features of the period, pointing the way to future study.

Perhaps the most important point to emerge is that Lindsay was first and very often foremost a courtier. Although noting this basic fact, standard accounts of Lindsay's life rarely acknowledge its significance. Too often Lindsay's modern popular reputation (based largely and erroneously upon *Ane Satyre of the Thrie Estatis*) has obscured the fact that the majority of his works are court poems. Simply recognizing Lindsay's position as a court poet does not, however, go far enough. For, as this study has shown, the office—if such it can be called—was by no means straightforward. Court poets occupied an ill-defined niche, offering a service over and above that of their fellow courtiers, making a special bid for attention, but receiving no official financial reward for their efforts. Despite this, they enjoyed a uniquely privileged position. As exponents of a well-established literary tradition, they were able to advise and criticize their royal masters to a quite exceptional degree, while over and above this, their work also helped shape a king's reputation and even, it could be argued, his very identity.

Lindsay's long service at the courts of James IV and James V is important for much more than his development as a court poet. Clearly, his personal situation stimulated an acute and enduring interest in questions of kingship, service, and good government. Although his presence at court meant that Lindsay was attuned to a variety of ways in which political issues were conceived and discussed, it has rarely been appreciated just how political a writer he was. Unsurprisingly, he was strongly attached to a highly conventional view of kingship derived in the first instance from classical authorities, enlarged upon by patristic writers, and augmented and hammered home by generations of medieval and Renaissance authors, both Scottish and European. The time-honored ideal of a king supported by the twin pillars of personal virtue and good counsel, charged with the defense of his realm and the equitable administration of justice within it, is vigorously upheld in Lindsay's writing. However, although in many respects deeply conservative, Lindsay's discussion of kingship is not without its own distinctive elements. These are of particular interest when considered in relation to the emerging humanistic court culture associated with the period and the more established value system embodied in the traditional cult of chivalry.

The very fact that Lindsay was at court during the 1530s is of fundamental importance when we consider the debts he owed to humanist thinking. Although the identification of humanists at court is still in its early stages, it seems fair to conclude that they existed in sufficient number to contribute a distinctive strand—although by no means the only one—to the multifaceted cultural milieu we conveniently label court culture. Certainly Lindsay's work bears the imprint of humanist ideas, illustrated, for example, by his discussion of the education appropriate to a prince, an education in which learning is deemed to hold the key to that personal virtue which guarantees political success. However, while an emerging humanistic court culture appears to have exercised a significant influence on Lindsay, it may be a mistake to overemphasize its impact at court more generally. Important but relatively limited in its effect is probably a more accurate assessment. As we have seen, it existed alongside much more familiar value systems, and traditional attitudes continued to matter long after humanism had first announced its presence on the Scottish stage. One of the most important conclusions to emerge from this study has been the great sense of cultural diversity that characterized the ethos of the Scottish court. Humanism contributed to this, existing as it did alongside a taste for more bawdy entertainment, for sensitive religious verse and expressions of individual piety, for ballads and love lyrics, for chivalric romances, for knightly jousts and Renaissance ceremony. Despite this rich blend of influences, it still seems appropriate to talk of a recognizable court culture. As is vividly demonstrated by Lindsay's work, the presence of the king conditioned much of what went on at court. The courtly arts—from literature to jousting, from music to architecture—were profoundly concerned with enhancing the status of the crown, and it does not seem too far-fetched to conclude that it was a cult of kingship (particularly as seen in the reigns of James IV and his son) which bound the disparate strands of court culture together.

A firmly established *mentalité* of the period, and one intimately associated with ideas of kingship, was that expressed by the cult of chivalry. Of course, as herald and later Lyon King of Arms, this was particularly pertinent to Lindsay's thinking. Again, while Lindsay's heraldic status is universally remarked upon, its significance has been too readily overlooked by historians. However, examining the nature of heraldic office in the sixteenth century is an extremely rewarding exercise for anyone interested in Lindsay more generally. Not only does it shed light upon some of his specific activities (his embassies abroad, his participation in occasions of public spectacle, and his involvement in the administration of the law of arms), but it also provides a further conceptual framework for the formulation of his political and social attitudes. Lindsay's use of the traditional precepts of chivalric ideology—variously endorsed, rejected, or adapted—is highly suggestive. It reveals that while the knightly creed continued to exercise a powerful attraction for many sixteenth-century Scots, not least for the Stewart monarchs James IV and James V, others, notably Lindsay himself, were less tolerant of its assumptions.

This was especially so in the case of kingship. For many, the concepts of the ideal king and the ideal knight were largely inseparable, the virtues of the latter being particularly necessary in a sovereign duty-bound to preserve the freedom of his realm. But, although some of Lindsay's early poetry makes this conventional identification, it was one which aroused his growing unease. Lindsay's attitude here, in part the product of his humanist sympathies, was reinforced by personal experience of the disastrous effects of war. His conviction that peace was an essential prerequisite for Scottish well-being was strengthened by the savage English incursions of the 1540s, but it is clear that his consternation was rooted in the early days of his career. For Lindsay, the Battle of Flodden was, in retrospect at least, a major calamity leading to a period of national misfortune. He was, therefore, extremely anxious to play down—although not to abandon entirely—the idea that the king was chiefly the defender of his kingdom. Every one of his works dealing with kingship concentrates not upon the defense of the realm but almost exclusively upon the royal obligation to ensure the administration of justice within it. Lindsay's work, therefore, offered an important alternative to the more traditional vision of Scottish kingship, which stressed the character of the king as armed defender of the nation's political and military independence. Although undoubtedly more timeworn, this was far from irrelevant to Scots in the sixteenth century, and indeed it received possibly its most stirring evocation in the work of the humanist Hector Boece. Lindsay's was of course neither the only nor the first voice raised against this perspective. Arguably, however, he did more than most to popularize such ideas and, unquestionably, in the period of the Rough Wooing when Scotland had faced minority rule, enemy invasion, and virtual semioccupation, Boece's confident exposition of Scottish kingship—indeed, of the Scottish national identity—would have rung very hollow. Lindsay's on the other hand offered a more realistic, arguably more compelling, expression of the ideals of government. Moreover, in spite of a deep-seated reluctance to jettison the king from his political thinking, Lindsay's vision of society and kingship after 1542 took account of the fact that Scotland no longer had an adult male king, or the prospect of one for some time to come. Although *Ane Satyre of the Thrie Estatis* forcibly illustrates the well-established association between the personal virtue of the monarch and the good government of his realm, Rex Humanitas is gradually pushed to the political margins, and the three estates—formally bound to John the Commonweal and guided by Veritie, the Word of God—have a correspondingly more important role to play.

Lindsay's unease with traditional chivalric tenets extended beyond his analysis of kingship. This is hardly surprising. After all, the mores of chivalry were almost universally upheld among the secular elite of western Europe. That Lindsay was anxious to play down the chivalric—specifically the martial—elements of a training for social leadership is most clearly conveyed in *The Historie of Squyer Meldrum*. Of particular interest here is the way in which he chose not to reject the chivalric ideology out of hand but to incorporate some of its fundamental concepts (notably that of service in and for the community) into a new understanding of social responsibility. This development (possibly inspired by English chivalric sources) offered Scots an alternative manner of viewing and expressing traditional notions of service. No longer was the stress upon duty to a military overlord (or even to the lady of chivalric romance); in Lindsay's work heroes were to be found in the local community, administering justice, dispensing charity, and generally ensuring public well-being. Another important point to emerge is that this new lay servant of the commonweal is (as Squyer Meldrum illustrates) not necessarily nobly born. This is especially interesting as, of course,

Lindsay's social origins were very similar to those of his old friend. Indeed, not only Lindsay but several lay, nonaristocratic household and government officials were making their way in the service of the commonweal at this time. Although it is certainly premature to talk of the eclipse of the aristocracy in government either national or local, Lindsay's work suggests that the ideological foundations for the rise of the "men of the middling sort," the lairds, lawyers, and ministers of the seventeenth century, were laid several generations previously.[2]

Lindsay's ideas concerning service chimed in very naturally with the idea of the commonweal, an idea to which sixteenth-century Scots were growing increasingly accustomed. When Lindsay's character, John the Commonweal, made his first appearance in 1526, the idea of the commonweal was a relative newcomer to Scottish political discourse. By the middle of the century and the performance of *Ane Satyre,* he was sufficiently well established for Lindsay to accord him only the briefest of introductions to what appears to have been a socially mixed audience, one whose political sophistication must have varied quite considerably. Lindsay's work provides an excellent source for this process of familiarization. Indeed, it is tempting to go further and conclude that it was his work that did much to consolidate the commonweal's claim to a preeminent place in the political vocabulary of Renaissance Scotland. The care and defense of the commonweal, a word that evoked not only local well-being but also in some respects the nation itself, was, according to Lindsay, the most solemn duty of the three estates. Given Lindsay's personal convictions, it is ironic that the idea of the commonweal was to emerge as one of the most potent rallying calls for those aiming to rouse their fellow countrymen to take up arms against the representative of sovereign authority.[3]

As we have seen, war represented a grievous affront to Lindsay's political sensibilities, but given that the conflicts of the early sixteenth century were largely the result of Anglo-Scottish hostility, perhaps we ought to consider whether Lindsay's beliefs derived in fact from a pro-English, rather than a purely pacifist, stance. In any case, the influence of England on many of Lindsay's attitudes (particularly in the religious sphere) is so important that it is well worth analysis. With regard to the problems of warfare, it seems fair to conclude that the graphic descriptions of national misgovernment, social dislocation, and individual suffering presented by Lindsay confirm the argument that it was war itself, irrespective of the adversary, which he found so abhorrent. Peace, it should be recalled, was the cornerstone on which Dame Rememberance's vision of a thriving nation was built. Nevertheless, there is unquestionably something to be said for the idea that Lindsay favored a pro-English foreign policy. Strongly critical of the abrogation of the Treaties of Greenwich, he went so far as to support some form of dynastic union, believing it not only possible but essential if centuries of hostility were to be brought to an end. His Armorial Manuscript (completed significantly enough in 1542), to which Boece's account of the racial origins of some of Scotland's leading families is added, may also have been designed to show his fellow countrymen that conflict between Englishman and Scot contradicted a common heritage and a shared ancestry.

Although Lindsay's support of dynastic union may have been in part a response to the problems of female minority rule, it was his support for the religious settlement established by Henry VIII that lay at the heart of his commitment to the English cause.[4] Admittedly, a call for religious reform led by secular authority is found in Lindsay's work even before the 1530s. It is, however, in *Ane Satyre of the Thrie Estatis* (1552) that the idea is most comprehensively worked out, and here Lindsay takes his cue very much from developments south of the border. *Ane Satyre* introduces to its Scottish audience an important political element (clearly derived from England) to what had hitherto been a largely Erasmian call for moral reform and improved clerical standards. Not only are proposals for reform articulated much more precisely (for instance, the specific complaints against feuing and the consistory courts, the abolition of death duties, and the institution of clerical marriage), but Lindsay also suggests how they might be put into practice. As the presence of Divyne Correctioun and Veritie makes plain, the process of reform is sanctioned by God and by Scripture. It requires no further authority and, like the Reformation settlements in England and in Denmark, it tolerates no external—that is, papal—interference. It is obvious that Lindsay was fully aware of the novel elements he was bringing to the religious debate and that his suggestions went appreciably further than anything hitherto proposed (such as, for example, the measures enacted by the reforming provincial councils of the Church under the direction of Archbishop Hamilton). As Spiritualitie is driven to exclaim, "For quhy sic reformatione as I weine / Into Scotland was never hard nor seine" (*Ane Satyre*, 3721–22).

The introduction of a new politicized critique was not Lindsay's only contribution to Scottish religious opinion in the pre-Reformation period. The vehement antipapal sentiment found in his later work (most notably the lurid description of moral putrefaction at the papal court in *The Monarche*) points to a rising tide of antipapalism in Scotland. Such evidence as we have suggests that in the first half of the sixteenth century antipapalism, although present in patches, was not particularly widespread. Lindsay's work, however, suggests that by the 1550s there was an eager audience for scurrilous antipapal material, and he himself may have done much to reinforce such sentiments. Another area in which Lindsay's work (again chiefly *The Monarche* but also to a lesser extent *Ane Satyre*) helped disseminate new ideas was with regard to apocalyptic thinking. Although Lindsay was not the only or indeed the first Scot of his generation to be influenced by the type of Protestant apocalypticism developing in England and on the Continent, he was one of its most noteworthy proponents. Arguably, *The Monarche* played a crucial role in preparing the Scottish psyche for the reception of the apocalyptic ideas which, as Arthur Williamson has shown, were to be so decisive in shaping political and theological convictions in the years to come.[5]

Lindsay's work has long been recognized as a fruitful source for the investigation of Scottish religious culture in the pre-Reformation period. What this study has shown is that the religious situation was more complex than has sometimes been appreciated. In Lindsay, for example, we can see the importance of traditional expressions of piety, of orthodox programs for reform, of the politicoreligious attractions of schism, and of Protestant apocalypticism. As we have seen, it makes little sense to think of Lindsay as some sort of litmus test either for the advance of Protestant opinion in sixteenth-century Scotland or for the collapse of the established Church. The long-running debate concerning Lindsay's precise confessional affinity is in many respects a red herring. What we do find in Lindsay's work, however, is intriguing evidence of a process of enquiry, discussion, and debate. It suggests too something of the character of that debate. His early poems, *The Dreme, The Complaynt,* and *The Testament of the Papyngo,* vividly illustrate the preoccupation with religious affairs found at the Scottish court while, following the death of James V, Lindsay's experiences in his own locality proved the decisive influence on his religious development. Unlike John Knox and his fellow Castilians, Lindsay could not sanction the violent call for reform embodied in the premature putsch of 1547, and his later works again offered Scotland an alternative perspective, this time a return to the process of debate and persuasion in which he had participated during the previous decade. Now, however, the call for repentance and reform was given added urgency by the rapid approach of the Day of Judgment.

These ideas are most clearly articulated in *The Monarche,* an enormously important source for religious attitudes on the eve of the Reformation. Of course, what it presents is essentially the vision of one individual, but it is tempting to conclude that the poem offers a more wide-ranging view of Scottish spirituality in the pre-Reformation period. In a final creative burst, Lindsay drew together many of the themes that characterize his other compositions. In this, the most personal of all his poems, Lindsay also explored—and finally satisfied—his own spiritual needs. It is indeed fitting to describe it as his swan song: a last moving lament for his church and his country which, by virtue of its power and passion, inspires author and audience alike.

APPENDIX I

A SUMMARY OF LINDSAY'S WORKS

The Dreme of Schir Dauid Lyndesay of the Mount, Familiar Seruitour to our Souerane Lord Kyng Iames the Fyft (The Dreme)

Date: 1526? See Chapter 1.
Length: 1,134 lines.

The Dreme falls into four main sections, the third being further subdivided. The first part, "The Epistil," establishes that this is an advice-to-princes type poem addressed to James V by one who has served the king since the latter's childhood. Having laid out the personal background to the poem, Lindsay then sets the scene to provide the poetic framework within which he discusses his political ideas. This, "The Prolong," describes a bleak January night when the narrator, unable to sleep, takes a walk along the seashore. His encounter with Dame Flora, "in dule weid dissagysit" (78), prompts an eloquent lament for the joys of summer which recalls more traditional descriptions. In somber mood, the narrator hides himself in a cave where eventually he falls asleep and dreams. The traditional genre of the dream voyage incorporating both a physical journey and an advance in learning is successfully exploited by Lindsay as a framework for his ideas concerning kingship.

The narrator recounts his meeting with Dame Rememberance and their subsequent voyage through the cosmos. Passing first to Hell, he sees among the damned representatives from the whole of society. Querying the reasons for their perdition, he learns of the vicious acts of prelates, princes, queens, and "Comoun peple" (303). Following a brief visit to Limbo, the pair pass through the four elements, the planets, the moon, and the sun, arriving finally in Heaven. Acknowledging human inadequacy in the face of such divine majesty, the poet-narrator describes the angelic hierarchy, the Virgin, the saints, and blessed Trinity. Reluctantly, he is dragged back to earth which Dame Rememberance agrees to show him "all at one sycht" (624). Two short sections entitled "The Qvantitie of the Erth" and "The Deuision of the Eirth" list the physical dimensions of the world and its most important kingdoms, and "Of Paradice" discloses the location and nature of Eden. After this education in cosmology, the focus of the poem becomes much more specific with the narrator asking to be shown Scotland. Confused as to why a country so "gude and fair" (807) should suffer such miserable poverty, he turns to Dame Rememberance for an explanation. She ascribes the situation to the "Wantyng of Iustice, polycie, and peace" (860), which in turn is the result of poor government.

At this point, they catch sight of a ragged fleeing figure—John the Commonweal—who, when pressed as to the reasons for his plight, delivers "The Complaynt of the Comoun Weill of Scotland." His confrontations with a whole host of vices effectively suggest the moral degeneracy of the nation, particularly of society's leaders. Vowing not to return until the accession of "ane gude auld prudent Kyng" (1005), John leaves the country. This is the signal for another farewell as Dame Rememberance leads the narrator back to his nook in the rocks. Finally, awakened by the cannon of a passing ship, he hurries home to pen the details of his vision. The poem ends with "The Exhortatioun to the Kyngis Grace," a traditional yet heartfelt discussion of kingship which urges James V to cleave to the cardinal virtues, to seek good counsel, and to attend to the welfare of his soul.

The Complaynt of Schir Dauid Lindesay (The Complaynt)

Date: 1530. This is suggested by the reference to "Auld Willie Dile" (85) last recorded Christmas 1529, ER, 15:458.
Length: 510 lines.

In *The Complaynt,* Lindsay combines an amusing petition for royal favor with some serious comments on the nature of good government. The poem opens with Lindsay bemoaning his lack of advancement at court. He does not blame James for, unlike others, he has not raised his voice in flattery but instead has quietly devoted himself to the service of the king. He recalls past duties caring for the infant James and his confident hope of reward. His dreams were however shattered by the events of the minority. Chronologically fairly accurate, Lindsay's account of the regency administrations is highly colored. In vivid, alliterative language, he describes his own dismissal, rails against the termination of James's education, and recalls how the king was seduced into vicious living by immoral and irresponsible courtiers who cared only for their own material advancement. A change of administration (when the earl of Angus assumed control) proved even worse. The Church in particular suffered as prelates, blinded by worldly ambition, meddled in secular affairs and neglected their spiritual vocation. The nation was rent by civil war, and the court became the resort of traitors, oppressors, murderers, and thieves. Eventually, however, the Douglases were driven from Scotland, and James's assumption of personal authority allows Lindsay to offer a reiteration of the advice provided in *The Dreme.* Here, however, he paints a picture of James already ruling with "The foure gret verteous Cardinalis" (379), having restored order to the kingdom. Only the Church still awaits attention. At this point, Lindsay launches upon a scathing attack of the clergy, calling on James to put a stop to such practices "As superstitious pylgramagis, / [And] Prayand to grawin Ymagis" (421–22). Finally, Lindsay returns to his earlier petition. Although his tone is at first much lighter—the mock request for a loan with fantastical terms of repayment—he ends on a more serious note, urging James to recall his responsibilities before God and reminding him of God's judgment of wicked rulers.

The Testament and Complaynt of our Souerane Lordis Papyngo, Kyng Iames the Fyft, quhilk lyith sore woundit, and may not dee, tyll euery man haue hard quhat he sayis. Quharefor, gentyll redaris, haist yow, that he wer out of paine (The Testament of the Papyngo)

Date: 1530. The colophon of the 1538 edition claims the work was completed in
    December 1530.
Length: 1,185 lines.

Lindsay begins this poem pondering what he might have written had he "Ingyne Angelicall" (1) and recalling those poets, past and present, who excelled at their art. Lamenting that they have exhausted the store of eloquence and subject matter, he describes his tale of a wounded parrot as matter "rude" (64), fit only for "rurall folk" (66). The "Complaynt" that follows opens with a proverb—"Quho clymmis to hycht, perforce his feit mon faill" (73)—which immediately proclaims this a fall-of-princes type morality tale. In some detail, Lindsay describes the parrot and the balmy morning on which she meets her death as, ignoring her keeper's warnings, she climbs to the very top of a tree from where she is blown to the ground. There is some comedy in the contrast between Lindsay's extravagant grief and the picture of a fat parrot falling from a twig, but the essential seriousness of the moral message is reasserted by the parrot herself who repents her unnatural ambition and realizes how fickle a mistress Fortune is.

In his grief, the poet fancies he hears the Papyngo speak to both the king and "Hir brether of courte." Her advice is presented in two epistles, the first of which, to James V, is almost a mini-mirror-for-princes. This describes the education and pursuits proper for a king. In addition, the parrot urges James to rule himself well, to work with good counsel, and to treat his barons with mercy and justice. To her fellow courtiers, the parrot stresses the lesson to be learned from her own fall. The uncertainties of political fortune are illustrated by the careers of past Scottish kings and nobles, of figures such as James Beaton, Cardinal Wolsey, and Francis I. Though the parrot urges her colleagues to fix their eyes only on the court of Christ, this renunciation of worldly care sits uneasily in the poem as a whole. Only the dying parrot is able to bid farewell to actual courts, recalling the various royal residences in which she has lived.

At this point, the poem changes tack, and Lindsay embarks upon a virulent satire of some of the abuses found in the Scottish Church. This is focused on three birds, a pye (magpie), a raven, and a gled (kite) who, disguised as a canon regular, a monk, and a friar, arrive to attend to the dying parrot. It is soon clear, however, that they care not for her eternal soul but for her material goods. During the exchange between the Papyngo and her confessors, the Papyngo is asked why clerics are generally held in such low esteem. Her perspicacity heightened by imminent death, the parrot delivers a long allegory illustrating the corruption of the Church by property, riches, and sensuality. In response to this, the raven draws attention to the culpability of princes who distribute benefices among unworthy candidates. He calls for improved education and a greater devotion to preaching. Finally, her end near, the parrot distributes her goods and makes her last confession. At this point, the avarice and duplicity of the avian clerics become clear. With no thought for her bequests, they fall upon her body, devouring it "Quhill scho is hote" (1151). The final two stanzas reintroduce the authorial voice, but the reiteration of the mock belief in the poem's crudity only underlines that it is the immorality of the clerics—not the bluntness of the poet—which is so shocking.

The Complaint and Publict Confessioun of the Kingis Auld Hound, callit Bagsche, directit to Bawte, the Kingis best belouit Dog, and his companyeonis (The Complaint of Bagsche)

Date: 1530–42.
Length: 224 lines.

Like *The Testament of the Papyngo,* this amusing yet nevertheless seriously intended beast fable offers a commentary on the fickleness and unpleasantness of a life spent at court. It takes the form of advice given by an old, once-favored, royal hound to the younger dogs who currently enjoy good fortune. Bagsche's description of his career is characterized by aggression, brutality, and ingratitude; yet these are the very qualities that bring him to the king's attention and secure his advancement. Eventually, however, he goes too far but, although condemned to hang, his old age procures a pardon from an overindulgent monarch. Yet, as an outcast, Bagsche finds life far from easy as his foes are out "to fang" (68) and "doun dang" him (69). Offering his own experiences as a moral exemplar, he urges his fellow hounds to mend their lives, to curb their ambition, and to refrain from wrongdoing.

The Answer quhilk Schir Dauid Lindesay maid to the Kingis Flyting (The Flyting)

Date: ante 1537. References to a future French marriage date the poem before 1537.
Length: 70 lines.

Traditionally, flyting was a form of poetic duel characterized by vigorous alliteration and insult. The poem begins with a reference to James's opening sally (probably a real composition) which allows Lindsay to praise the king's poetic gifts and denigrate his own. He also pours scorn on his own performance as a lover, a reject from the court of Venus. Yet, it soon becomes clear that this is no fault, for the amorous antics he describes are not noble but simply sordid. Using imagery heavily reliant upon the battlefield, artillery in particular, Lindsay emphasizes James's intemperance and profligacy. The account of an unseemly coupling with a kitchen maid suggests not only that his conduct is undignified but also that it might lead to physical disease. Finally, having proved his skill in the field, Lindsay modestly denies that he can flyte, he offers a final warning against promiscuity, and, ending on an optimistic note, he refers to the rumor that a shield able to withstand James's "dintis" (69), that is, a wife able to curb his sexual excesses, may soon arrive from France.

The Deploration of the Deith of Quene Magdalene (The Deploratioun)

Date: 1537. Madelaine died July 1537.
Length: 203 lines.

The Deploratioun is a tribute not just to the dead French queen but also to French literary culture. Typically the deploration was used for obituary verse, to honor the dead and press home a moral message. Lindsay's deploration, less latinate and high-flown than most French examples, seems more designed for Scottish tastes. As well as being a tribute to Madelaine, the poem also celebrates the kingship of James V, casting him in the role of chivalric hero. *The Deploratioun* opens with a lament for Madelaine's death (particularly as she died without issue). It recalls the love that existed between the royal couple, comparing them to such legendary figures as Leander and Hero. Casting his mind back to their wedding, Lindsay provides a detailed description of both of the celebrations that accompanied James's entry into Paris and of those that should have greeted his bride on her arrival in Scotland. Now, however, bright clothes are exchanged for sable; songs of welcome are turned to dirges. Again, this offers Lindsay the opportunity to muse on the inconstancies of worldly fortune and the necessity of nourishing religious faith. Nevertheless, the poem ends on a more hopeful note. Not only will poets immortalize Madelaine and thereby conquer death, but her memory shall serve to "Keip ay twa Realmes, in Peice and Amite" (203).

The Iusting betuix Iames Watsoun and Ihone Barbour, seruitouris to King Iames the Fyft (The Iusting)

Date: 1538–40.
Length: 68 lines.

In this short poem written for the entertainment of the court, Lindsay uses specific and recognizable figures within a highly traditional comic genre (Watson was a barber in the king's service; Barbour, described as a leech and a gentleman of the chamber, appears in the records in the latter capacity). The mock tournament is described according to the conventions of a poetic genre that includes, inter alia, William Dunbar's *Turnament*. The joust takes place in St. Andrews on Whitmonday before the king, queen, and assembled court, and it is probable that Lindsay produced this poem to entertain those assembled there for tournaments in 1538, 1539, or 1540. The racy meter and alliterative language make this a lively work and, though it may have been partly malicious in intention, the clumsy antics of the two unsuitable combatants serve principally to entertain. Indeed, the final line establishes the essentially good-humored tone of the poem, thanking God that no blood was shed.

Ane Suplication Directit frome Schir Dauid Lyndesay, Knycht, to the Kyngis Grace, in Contemptioun of Syde Tallis (In Contemptioun of Syde Tallis)

Date: 1537–42. A reference to the queen (157) places it after James's marriage.
Length: 176 lines.

This comic petition, directed against fashion—specifically long gowns that trail in the dust—is designed as a piece of court entertainment. The subject matter is traditional but amusingly presented. The comedy arises from a combination of the lively language, the disparity between the poet's outrage and the trivial nature of its source, and the individual scenes he describes. These include a nun who to protect her tails hoists her gown up above her "lillie quhyte hois" (58), men who reel from the dirty thighs of their sweethearts, and the collection of rubbish gathered up by such gowns (which, Lindsay asserts, could easily provide supper for a sow). The false modesty that prohibits showing an inch of ankle (it is, Lindsay suggests, nothing more than the Devil's own pride) is also responsible for ladies covering their faces, another practice he roundly condemns. Confident of the support of all but the most "wantoun glorious hure" (172), he ends by urging James to issue a proclamation outlawing such practices.

The Tragedie of the Umquhyle Maist Reverend Father Dauid, be the Mercy of God, Cardinale and Archibyschope of Sanctandrous. And of the haill Realme of Scotlande Primate, Legate, and Chancelare, and Administrator of the Byschoprik of Merapoys in France. And Commendator perpetuall of the Abay of Aberbrothok (The Tragedie of the Cardinal)

Date: post 1547. A reference to the Cardinal lying unburied for over seven months (267) makes the earliest possible date of composition January 1547.
Length: 434 lines.

The Tragedie of the Cardinal falls into four separate sections. "The Prolog" opens with a description of the author reading quietly in his study. His book, Boccaccio's *De Casibus Virorum Illustrium,* comes alive when a ghostly wounded figure appears before him and introduces himself as David Beaton. "The Tragedie" is related to the author by Beaton himself who describes his career in the Church and how, driven by pride and ambition, he attained effective power in the kingdom. But it is soon clear that Beaton's "actis honorabyll" (73) were in fact no such thing. He recounts how, to display his liberality, he would gamble at cards and dice, how he sabotaged hopes of Anglo-Scottish amity by dissuading James from meeting Henry VIII at York, how this resulted in war, dearth, hunger, and even the melancholy death of the king. *The Tragedie of the Cardinal* also provides the first published reference to Beaton's alleged forgery of James's will. Recalling his captivity in the early months of the regency administration, Beaton explains that, far from instilling a sense of humility, this only served to fire his ambition yet further. When released, he raised havoc throughout the kingdom, riding against the governor, bringing over Lennox simply to discomfort him, and forcing the abrogation of the treaty with England. The resultant wars he acknowledges as entirely his fault. He also confesses that all his actions were dictated by loyalty to the king of France, that he deceived the earl of Arran and imprisoned his son, that he plotted against Angus and his brother, and that he persecuted "All fauoraris of the auld and new Testament" (218). Although Beaton believed his position impregnable, his allies, his riches, and even his enormously fortified castle offered no protection against his downfall. Retribution when it came was swift, with the assassination being presented as akin to an act of God. The final description of Beaton's "ded and deformit Carioun" (216) displayed as a public spectacle sets the seal on his humiliation.

The poem ends not with a return to the author but with two pieces of advice (of roughly equal length) directed "To the Prelates" and "To the Prencis." Beaton urges his fellow clerics to consider his example and mend their ways. He stresses the need to return to the simple practices of the early Church, to care less for temporal possessions, to renounce gambling and whoring, and, above all, to preach the Word of God. He remembers his own ignorance and failure and begs his colleagues to take heed of his example.

Princes are castigated by Beaton for providing unsuitable candidates to benefices. He stresses the need to promote the learned and virtuous rather than the ill-educated and immoral, pointing out that he himself rose to eminence as a result of such practices. Freely confessing his own ignorance of spiritual matters, he acknowledges that he and his like have "done the warld abuse" (405), and he repents of ever becoming a churchman. After a critical dig at nuns who are no better than whores, Beaton bids farewell with a rousing call for reformation directed to "eueryilk christinit kyng" (421).

The Historie of ane Nobil and Wailyeand Squyer, William Meldrum, umquhyle Laird of Cleische and Bynnis (The Historie of Squyer Meldrum)

The Testament of the Nobil and Vailyeand Squyer Williame Meldrum of the Bynnis

Date: 1550. Meldrum died 1550; last recorded in July 1550, *RMS*, 4:490.
Length: 1,594 lines. *The Testament,* printed distinct from *The Historie,* numbers 253 lines.

By introducing the life history of his old friend, Squire Meldrum, with reference to more celebrated accounts of knightly heroes, Lindsay draws attention both to the chivalric content of the poem and to its uneasy relationship with the realities of life. The Squire's career falls into two distinct sections, dealing first with his military achievements and then with his romantic involvement with the Lady of Gleneagles. Four episodes are chosen to illustrate the Squire's exploits in the field. The first of these is the naval expedition against England launched in 1513. It is during the sack of Carrickfergus that Meldrum witnesses an assault on a young woman. Although he repulses her attackers with ease, he finds it harder to deflect the love of the grateful young girl, whom he ultimately abandons in spite of accepting her ring. From Ireland, Meldrum travels to northern France, the site of the campaign led by Henry VIII. When the English champion, Master Talbart, issues a challenge to the assembled French and Scottish troops, it is Meldrum who accepts it and who, despite the disparity in age and experience, wins the combat. Meldrum's third adventure also takes place in France when he repels a gang of Englishmen who attack the house of "Our worthie Scottis" (632). Although his exploits earn him renown throughout the country, Meldrum determines to return to Scotland. However, en route, his ship is attacked by an English galleon and a bloody fight ensues.

The magnanimity the victorious Meldrum shows toward his defeated foe recalls his earlier treatment of Master Talbart, underlining the chivalrous character of the squire-hero.

With Meldrum's return to Scotland, the poem changes direction, describing his encounter with the Lady of Gleneagles and their subsequent love affair. Although Lindsay employs many of the motifs found in romance literature, the descriptions of the physical consummation of their love and the cozy intimacy of their domestic life offer a more realistic picture. However, the couple's happiness is destroyed by a neighboring knight who, determined to marry the Lady to a gentleman of his choosing, ambushes Meldrum. On this occasion, sheer force of numbers overcomes the valiant Squire who is left for dead. The governor's lieutenant, a former comrade of Meldrum's, has his assailants thrown into prison. However, his own murder paves the way for their release, and when they finally meet their end their murder is simply another example of anarchic violence. Reality intrudes again when the Lady of Gleneagles (despite her supposed passion) leaves the Squire and is married off elsewhere. Meldrum himself learns from the doctors who dress his wounds and charitably uses his newfound skills in the care of the poor.

Lindsay ends his *Historie* by offering a corrective to the romantic tales of chivalric adventure, describing instead how Meldrum spends the rest of his life in the service of the Lord of the Byres, dispensing justice and charity to the community. The biographical account of the Squire's life is followed by what is almost a separate work, *The Testament of the Nobil and Vailyeand Squyer Williame Meldrum of the Bynnis*. Here, Meldrum himself is allowed to speak as he makes the arrangements for his death. Lindsay the poet becomes instead the friend entrusted with the funeral arrangements. In some considerable detail, *The Testament* describes an elaborate chivalric interment, the pomp of which seems to contradict Meldrum's statement that he never cared for riches or rent. Similarly, the piety that commends his spirit to God is set against a ceremony that evokes Mars, Venus, and Mercury. Bidding farewell to his companions, particularly Lord Lindsay, to the ladies of France, the Maid of Carrickfergus, and the Lady of Gleneagles, the Squire offers a prayer for his soul, and with this, equally his own prayer, Lindsay ends a work that combines an affectionate tribute to an old friend with a more subtle critique of the chivalric lifestyle he enjoyed in his youth.

Ane Pleasand Satyre of the Thrie Estatis in Commendatioun of Vertew and Vituperatioun of vyce (Ane Satyre of the Thrie Estatis)

Date: 1552. This is suggested by references to the Pater Noster quarrel (November 1551), and to the Schmalkaldic War (1550–52). *The Cupar Banns* refer to a performance on Tuesday, 7 June, which again points to 1552.

THE CUPAR BANNS

Length: 277 lines.

This short piece, known only from *The Bannatyne Manuscript,* announces the play, the time and place of its performance, and something of its content. In addition, the audience is entertained by a motley yet comical collection of stock characters: the henpecked husband; Finlaw of the Futband, a braggart and coward in the *miles gloriosus* tradition; the fool; and an old man cuckolded by his youthful wife.

ANE SATYRE OF THE THRIE ESTATIS

Length: 4,630 lines.

The earliest complete specimen we have of a Scottish play, *Ane Satyre* is also our only example of Lindsay's work as a dramatist. The text survives in two forms, as preserved in *The Bannatyne Manuscript* and as printed by Robert Charteris in 1602. The relationship between the two texts and indeed to what Lindsay actually wrote is highly problematic. Charteris's is the lengthier, probably more complete, certainly more standardized, version, and his is the text (as edited by Hamer) used here.

The play is introduced by the herald Diligence who indicates what the audience may expect and urges them not to take offense at what they will see. The drama is divided into two parts of unequal length. The first is an allegorical morality tale centered around the character of Rex Humanitas. Although filled with noble aspirations, the young king is easily corrupted. In the first instance he is led astray by his ignorant, yet not fundamentally evil, courtiers (Wantonnes, Placebo, and Solace) who introduce him to the promiscuous Dame Sensualitie. Though the onstage action focuses on the sexual corruption of the king, it is important to grasp that the allegory is much wider in its implications, and what we are seeing here is nothing less than the complete subjugation of reason to appetite.

The arrival of Gude-Counsall, of late an exile from Scotland, suggests the prospect of better rule, but such hopes are dashed by the entrance of the three Vices: Flatterie, Falset, and Dissait. Disguising themselves as clerics they perform a blasphemous mock baptism, emerging as Sapience, Devotioun, and Discretioun respectively. Under these names, they are taken on by Rex Humanitas and, secure in his favor, they are able to prevent Gude-Counsall from gaining an audience with the king. Gude-Counsall is not, however, the only one seeking Rex Humanitas. As the latter lies in debauched sleep, Veritie enters with words of advice concerning the importance of justice and moral rectitude. Fearful lest they be exposed, the Vices approach the lords of Spiritualitie and persuade them to apprehend Veritie as a heretic. This they are eager to do as she bears with her an English New Testament which they consider evidence of her Lutheranism. Refusing to recant her position, Veritie is consigned to the stocks. At this point, Chastitie arrives seeking shelter, only to be turned away by the ladies of religion, the lords of Spiritualitie, and, in an amusing scene, by the wives of the craftsmen who had agreed to lodge her. When she finally appeals to Rex Humanitas, the animosity of his paramour lands her too in the stocks. Although the Vices appear to have triumphed, news of the imminent arrival of Divyne Correctioun causes them to flee, hiding themselves among churchmen, merchants, and craftsmen. Their parting act is to steal the royal treasure, but there is little honor among these thieves, and they swiftly fall out over the division of the spoils.

The arrival of Divyne Correctioun, the self-proclaimed emissary of God, inaugurates the reform of both the king and his kingdom. Ordering the release of Veritie and Chastitie, he rouses the king from his lust-induced slumber, reminds him of God's judgment of wicked rulers, and casts out Dame Sensualitie (who seeks refuge with Spiritualitie). The courtiers are rebuked but pardoned their ignorance and the king disabused concerning the identity of his false counselors. In their stead, Divyne Correctioun installs Gude-Counsall, Chastitie, and Veritie and bids Rex Humanitas call a parliament. The first part of the play ends with Diligence summoning the three estates and announcing a break in the proceedings.

Before the action resumes with the arrival of the estates, there is a series of episodes centering on a poor man and a pardoner. Here, in contrast to the allegory that has gone before, Lindsay introduces a new sense of realism. Treated by Diligence like a member of the audience, the Pauper sustains this impression by explaining that he is on his way to the neighboring town of St. Andrews. Describing how the deaths of his parents and his wife have left him destitute, with both landlord and vicar demanding mortuary dues from him, the Pauper hopes to seek recompense at law—a prospect that Diligence greets pessimistically. At this point, the pardoner, Sir Robert Romeraker, enters. Clearly no spiritual man, he roundly condemns not only the translators of the New Testament but also St. Paul and the Gospel itself. The crude and distinctly secular relics he has for sale arouse a suspicion (later verified) which also extends to the pardons and dispensations he is hawking. This is confirmed when he performs a divorce for the Sowtar (cobbler) and his wife which is not only illegal and physically obscene but also carries diabolic associations. Encountering the Pauper, Sir Robert swindles him out of his last groat, selling him an indulgence he neither wants nor believes in.

At this point, Diligence announces the arrival of the three estates who—in a dramatic representation of their corruption—enter the stage "gangand backwart led by their vyces." Despite Spiritualitie urging the parliament's postponement, all those with grievances are invited to present their bills. At this point, John the Commonweal steps up and, leaping into the play area, becomes one of the play's central characters. Making clear the implications Rex Humanitas's corruption had for the whole realm, John presents a sorely neglected appearance. He identifies the Vices who led the three estates in their unnatural procession as Couetice and Sensualitie (Spiritualitie), Publik Oppressioun (Temporalitie), and Falset and Dissait (Merchandis). Flatterie too lurks among them. Despite Spiritualitie's loud complaints, the Vices are led to the stocks. The lay estates, however, prove much more amenable to reform and call for the assistance of Gude-Counsall. He stresses the need to care for the commonweal and points out how the commons are impoverished both by war and by the Church (particularly the feuing movement). John the Commonweal joins in the complaint, attacking the thieves who oppress loyal laborers (especially in the Borders), idle beggars (including friars), and judicial corruption (both spiritual and temporal). Divyne Correctioun orders all lands to be set in feu to those who work them and, while Spiritualitie attempts to wriggle out of this injunction, the temporal estates pledge themselves to defend the commonweal. Invited to complain further against Spiritualitie, John overcomes his initial fear to attack the overrigorous exploitation of mortuary dues, to condemn those who exact teinds but do not preach, and to criticize promiscuous prelates. Further complaints concerning the flow of Scottish money to Rome and abuse of pluralism also result in legislation. The discussion then turns to the question of preaching, which is revealed as woefully inadequate. Indeed, when challenged, Spiritualitie confesses never to have read the New Testament. Enraged by this assault, Spiritualitie rounds on John with accusations of heresy. These are rejected when Divyne Correctioun proclaims himself satisfied with John's homely creed in which he repudiates the abuses of bishops and friars. As a result of this debate, legislation is drawn up stipulating that kings should dispense benefices only to worthy candidates able to preach. Further complaints against Spiritualitie include a gripe about the interminable and incomprehensible proceedings of the consistory courts, the ignorance of clerics, and the huge dowries they offer to marry off their bastard daughters. In response to this, Diligence is instructed to seek out learned clerics skilled at preaching.

The serious business of parliament is here interrupted by the arrival of Thift, alarmed at the reported arrival of a justice-dispensing monarch, and in a highly comic episode peppered with local references Thift is beguiled by his master, Oppressioun, into taking his place in the stocks. The action now reverts to the attack on the Church as Diligence returns with three learned clerics. Their sober demeanor contrasts forcibly with the worldly ambition and licentiousness displayed by Spiritualitie. This is underlined by the response to the sermon preached by the Doctour of divinity, a simple statement of Christian faith which they can in no way comprehend. Diligence too receives something of a spiritual education as the other divines point out the contradiction between the poverty of Christ and the worldliness of the Church. This leads to a verbal attack on friars paralleled by the apprehension of one, revealed beneath his hood as Flatterie. (Similar rough treatment of the Prioress reveals her to be wearing a forbidden silk kirtle beneath her habit.) In exchange for his freedom, Flatterie offers to help hang his fellow Vices. Spiritualitie's garments are transferred to the three wise clerics and, unrecognized even by their own servants, they quit the stage. John too is reclothed and in his "gay garmoun" (3774) is installed at the heart of parliament where the fifteen acts composing the legislative action of the play are proclaimed by Diligence. These cover:

1. the defense of Christ's Kirk
2. the enforcement of laws passed by the previous parliament
3. the feuing of temporal lands "Till verteous men that labours with thair handis" (3812)
4. the punishment of lords who offer protection to thieves and arrangements for the compensation of their victims
5. the establishment of Colleges of Justice in Edinburgh and Aberdeen
6. the dissolution of the nunneries to pay for the above
7. the strict separation of temporal and spiritual jurisdiction
8. the granting of benefices only to worthy candidates
9. the requirement for bishops to preach

10. the abolition of pluralism (royalty excepted)
11. the abolition of mortuary dues (clerical and secular)
12. the prohibition of absenteeism
13. the prevention of money flowing to Rome
14. the introduction of clerical marriage
15. the prohibition of marriage between offspring of the first and second estates

With the hanging of the Vices (Flatterie not included) it might seem as if the play were over, but at this point Lindsay introduces the character of Folly. The comic account of his pursuit by a sow and his wife's rumbling bowels gives way to an amusing but much more serious sermon which, in contrast to the controlled modesty of the Doctour's homily, paints a picture of widespread folly which serves to remind the audience of the nearness of disorder and the importance of the action that has gone before. It is fitting that the play should finish on this humorous yet serious note before finally being brought to a close by the herald Diligence.

Ane Dialog betuix Experience and Ane Courteour, Off the Miserabyll Estait of the Warld (The Monarche)

Date: 1554. The poem refers to the 447 years remaining until the end of the world (5301–2) which, given that this was commonly expected in the year 2000, dates the poem to 1554.
Length: 6,338 lines.

This, Lindsay's final and most important work, consists of four parts or "bukes" (variously subdivided) flanked on the one hand by an "Epistil" and "Prolog" and on the other by an "Exhortatioun." The first of these introduces the poem—a "Lytil quair of mater miserabyll" (1)—with a stylized mock modesty that also suggests its title and subject matter. Lamenting the absence of a Scottish king, Lindsay dedicates his work to the governor, the earl of Arran, and to Archbishop Hamilton, hoping too that all of society's leaders (both lay and clerical) will heed the warnings that both the poet and a wrathful God give to a nation living with no regard for divine precept. The themes of sin and misery are carried over into the "Prolog" where they prey upon the mind of the poet-narrator. Unable to sleep, he takes a walk through a delightful landscape bathed in a glorious dawn. Dismissing such eloquent passages of description as "vnfrutful and vaine" (203), Lindsay renounces the pagan muses and prays to God for his inspiration. Calvary not Parnassus casts its shadow over this work.

In the first buke of *The Monarche*, the poet-narrator encounters an old man, Experience, with whom he shares his distaste for a life spent at court. Experience tells him that his desire for earthly happiness is a fool's dream; life is a constant struggle, for misery proceeds from sin. Asked to explain the origins of this sin, he recounts the story of the Fall—but also that of the Resurrection which offers the promise of redemption through Christ. This leads to a discussion of the nature of faith which includes an uncompromising rejection of the Protestant idea of Justification by Faith Alone and an emphatic endorsement of the doctrine of Good

Works. When the Courtiour enquires how Adam broke God's commandment, Experience urges him to read the Bible (although he will give as good an account as he is able). This prompts Lindsay's lengthy interjection entitled "Ane Exclamatioun to the Redar, Twycheyng the Wryttyng of Uulgare and Maternall Language," in which he rededicates *The Monarche* to the unlearned that they might know of such "heycht mater" (540). Arguing that languages such as Hebrew, Latin, and Greek were all originally vernaculars, comprehensible to the meanest members of society, he calls for the production of vernacular Scripture, prayers, and, in a more secular vein, vernacular law books. Returning to the main narrative, Experience delivers accounts of "The Creation of Adam and Eve" (notable for its evocative—and very sensuous—description of the joys of Eden) and "Of the Miserabyll Transgressioun of Adam" (which includes a vehement denunciation of female rule). The world history continues with Cain's murder of Abel, the corruption of Seth's blood with the seed of Cain, and an account of how Noah escaped the flood sent to punish an idle people seduced into sin by Satan.

The second buke opens with the Courtiour interrogating Experience about the origins of such misfortunes as war and idolatry. This paves the way for the history of Nimrod, the builder of Babylon. Drawing on Josephus and Orosius, Lindsay provides a detailed account of the Tower he built, before God, punishing Nimrod for his pride, introduced different languages and so caused the project to fail. Nimrod too is held responsible for the establishment of idolatry, and Experience describes how a constantly burning fire, originally made as sacrifice to God, was worshiped by the people. Turning to war (in the course of which the Courtiour offers a moving and eloquent account of its horrors), Experience explains that its origins lie in the "Pryde, Couatyce, and vaine glore" (2013) of the first emperor of the Assyrian monarchy, King Ninus. Ninus also devised the first image, a golden statue of his father Bellus, which he ordered all under his authority to worship. Sustained by the greed of craftsmen and priests, imagery spread throughout the world. The section entitled "Off Imageis Vsit Amang Christin Men" provides a lively account of those common in sixteenth-century Scotland, suggesting the numerous saints important in the popular religious life. While acknowledging that images are useful to the illiterate, Experience makes clear that to pray to them is no less than idolatry. This leads to an "Exclamatioun Aganis Idolatrie" which calls for repentance, especially from churchmen who encourage such practices. The section also includes a passage proposing how those who offend against the teaching of the Church should be treated and calling for the repentance of those who currently oppress the professors of Christ's Word. Experience trusts to see "gude reformatione / From tyme we gett ane faithfull prudent king" (2605–6) but, until that time comes, he counsels patience. Lindsay also launches an attack on pilgrimages, occasions "Off Fornicatioun and Idolatrye" (2669), before ending the interpolation with a final prayer for reformation. Returning to the narrative, Experience continues his account of the reign of Ninus with a description of the construction of Ninevah (the dimensions given according to Diodorus), of the war against Zoroastes, of his marriage to Semiramis, and the story of how she tricked him out of his authority and his life. Lindsay continues to use the example of Assyrian monarchs to offer advice concerning the nature of good government when he describes how Semiramis, in many ways an admirable ruler, was undone by her lust. The dreadful slaughter arising from her campaign against Stabrobates of India is also described at some length. Semiramis's downfall again allows Lindsay to make an impassioned denunciation of gynecocracy. Women should not ape men and, similarly, men should not be effeminate. This latter precept is illustrated by the career of Semiramis's son, Sardanapalus, whose eventual death brings to a close the 1,240-year-long Assyrian monarchy.

The third buke opens with a brief account of some of the events contemporaneous with the Assyrian monarchy: the destruction of Sodom and Gomorrah, the Exodus of the Israelites, the Trojan War, and the foundation of Rome. Lindsay then turns to the remaining three monarchies which he considers in much less detail. Indeed a single section is entitled "Ane Schort Discriptioun of the Secund, Third, and Ferd Monarche." This describes the establishment of the Persian Empire by King Cyrus, the conquest of the Greek Empire by Alexander the Great, and, finally, the building of the Roman Empire by Julius Caesar. The history of the four monarchies not only illustrates the transience of worldly power but also possesses an important providential function. Allowing the punishment of sinners and reward of the godly, it was also prophesied by Daniel, whose vision is explained here at some length. In response to the Courtiour's query as to the most miserable misfortune experienced in the world during the fourth monarchy, Experience delivers a long and extremely powerful account of the twice-over destruction of Jerusalem. This also incorporates a stirring depiction of the Crucifixion. Again Experience stresses the unreliability of worldly ambition and the impermanence of worldly authority. God uses tyrants and emperors to scourge a wicked people and then casts his wand into the fire. Now, "The gret Impyris ar meltit clene away" (4223), and dearth, pestilence, and war herald that the world is drawing to its end. The poem's central message is once again repeated: Fix your eyes on God, "And mend thy lyfe, quhil thow hes tyme & space" (4244). Asking whether there is no contemporary equivalent of the past empires, the Courtier learns that there is indeed one in the form of the papacy. The authority of the pope is described in a manner that parodies both the authority of secular rulers and that of Christ. The papacy has usurped the power of God while riches and sensuality have corrupted the pure apostolic Church. The neglect of Christ's instructions has led to a whole string of false practices, among them clerical celibacy and fasting. At this point, Lindsay devotes a whole section to "Ane Discriptioun of the Court of Rome," which vehemently attacks the sale of indulgences (and possibly the whole doctrine of Purgatory). Calling for priests to preach and administer the sacraments, Lindsay urges the repeal of all laws contrary to Christ's teaching. He recalls Pauline prophecies and the text of Revelation and begs God to kindle repentance in the hearts of both churchmen and those "Now lauboryng in to the Kirk Militant / That we may, all, cum to thy kirk Tryumphant" (4972–73).

Finally, Experience sums up his answer to the Courtiour's original question concerning how he might best reconcile himself to the miseries of this life. He must keep God's commandments, renounce his trust in earthly authority, and fix his eyes upon the Four Last Things: Death, Judgment, Heaven, and Hell. It is this eschatological vision which forms the basis of the fourth and final buke of *The Monarche*. "Off the Deith" is a particularly gloomy passage, the sonorous rhythm and repetition suggesting the inevitability of death. This is followed by "Ane Schorte Discriptioun of the Antechriste," the antichrist being expected to appear prior to the Day of Judgment. Refuting the traditional legend of the antichrist, Experience explains that there are already many antichrists "Makand Lawis contrar to Christe" (5246). In reply to the Courtiour's question, he explains that although the timing of Judgment Day cannot be known it is undoubtedly imminent. In order to support his contention, Experience—citing Carion—refers to the prophecy of Daniel, to Elijah's periodization of world history, and to such other tokens as the corruption of the spiritual estate. In vivid language, he gives an account of the expected end of the world, depicting a literal resurrection of the dead and the immortalization of the living. This is followed by an explanation of "The Maner quhow Christ sall cum to his Iugement" and the separation of the saints and sinners. By representing all ranks of society—but particularly churchmen—in this latter category, Lindsay is able to make a final plea for repentance and reform. Turning finally to the prospect of Heaven, Lindsay, despite acknowledging the difficulty of depicting divine bliss, attempts to convey something of the joys of the life to come. Like his earlier description of Eden, this relies heavily on the evocation of the type of physical delights his audience could most readily comprehend.

Having completed his history up to and indeed beyond the end of time, Lindsay ends *The Monarche* with "Ane Exhortatioun Gyffin be Father Experience vnto his sone the Curteour." This reiterates the poem's central message, focusing on the miseries of the world, the need to relinquish worldly ambition, to live quietly, and to look forward to everlasting bliss. Finally, Experience takes leave of the Courtiour who returns home to record his wisdom. At this point, Lindsay returns to his description of the natural environment. Now, however, dawn is turned to dusk as the poem, the life of the narrator, and indeed the world itself draw to a close.

THE LINDSAY FAMILY TREE

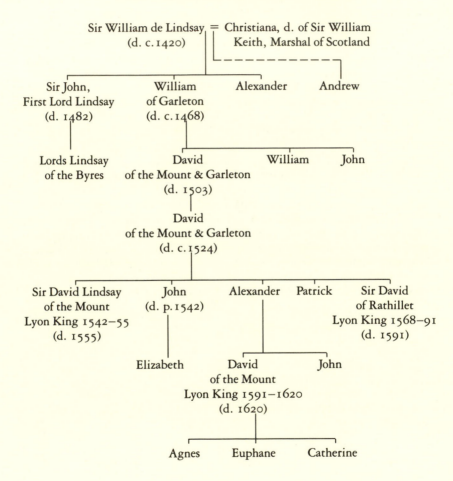

Sir William de Lindsay = Christiana, d. of Sir William
(d. c. 1420)   Keith, Marshal of Scotland

Sir John,   William   Alexander   Andrew
First Lord Lindsay of Garleton
(d. 1482)   (d. c. 1468)

Lords Lindsay   David   William   John
of the Byres   of the Mount & Garleton
                        (d. 1503)

                        David
                  of the Mount & Garleton
                     (d. c. 1524)

Sir David Lindsay   John   Alexander   Patrick   Sir David
of the Mount   (d. p. 1542)   of Rathillet
Lyon King 1542–55   Lyon King 1568–91
(d. 1555)   (d. 1591)

                  Elizabeth   David   John
                           of the Mount
                           Lyon King 1591–1620
                           (d. 1620)

                  Agnes   Euphane   Catherine

NOTES

INTRODUCTION

1. R. Pitcairn, ed., *The Autobiography and Diary of Mr James Melville, minister of Kilrenny, in Fife, and professor of theology in the University of St Andrews* (Edinburgh, Woodrow Society, 1842), 18–19.

2. R. W. J. Evans, "The Court: A Protean Institution and an Elusive Subject," in *Princes, Patronage, and the Nobility: The Court at the Beginning of the Modern Age, c.1450–1650,* ed. Ronald G. Asch and Adolf M. Birke (Oxford, 1991), 486.

3. Perez Zagorin, *The Court and the Country: The Beginning of the English Revolution* (London, 1969).

4. Geoffrey Elton, *The Tudor Revolution in Government* (Cambridge, 1953); *Reform and Reformation: England, 1509–1558* (London, 1977); *Studies in Tudor and Stuart Politics and Government,* 4 vols. (Cambridge, 1974–92), esp. vol. 3.

5. Christopher Coleman and David Starkey, eds., *Revolution Reassessed: Revisions in the History of Tudor Government and Administration* (Oxford, 1986); David Starkey, ed., *The English Court from the Wars of the Roses to the Civil War* (London, 1987).

6. Linda Levy Peck, ed., *The Mental World of the Jacobean Court* (Cambridge, 1991), 3.

7. Ronald G. Asch, "Introduction: Court and Household from the Fifteenth to the Seventeenth Centuries," in *Princes, Patronage, and the Nobility,* ed. Asch and Birke, 2.

8. Roger Chartier, *The Cultural Uses of Print in Early Modern France,* trans. Lydia G. Gochrane (Princeton, 1987), 11.

9. Lauro Martines, *Society and History in English Renaissance Verse* (Oxford, 1985).

10. Kevin Sharpe, *Criticism and Compliment: The Politics of Literature in the England of Charles I* (Cambridge, 1987).

11. See, for example: Quentin Skinner, "Meaning and Understanding in the History of Ideas," *History and Theory* 8 (1969): 1–53; Peter Laslett, W. G. Runciman, and Quentin Skinner, *Philosophy, Politics, and Society* (Oxford, 1972); James Tully, ed., *Quentin Skinner and His Critics* (Cambridge, 1988). See too Skinner's own work, especially *The Foundations of Modern Political Thought,* 2 vols. (Cambridge, 1978), and J. G. A. Pocock's *Virtue, Commerce, and History* (Cambridge, 1985).

12. The term "New Historicist" was first coined by Stephen Greenblatt with whose work the approach is particularly associated; for example, *Learning to Curse: Essays in Early Modern Culture* (New York and London, 1990). For a discussion of New Historicist criticism, see Jean E. Howard, "The New Historicism in Renaissance Studies," *English Literary Renaissance* 16 (1986): 13–43. This stimulating article has subsequently been reprinted in two collections of essays, both of which admirably illustrate the approaches it describes: *Renaissance Historicism: Selections from English Literary Renaissance,* ed. Arthur F. Kinney and Dan S. Collins (Amherst, 1987); *New Historicism and Renaissance Drama,* ed. Richard Wilson and Richard Dutton (London and New York, 1992).

13. Joanne S. Norman, "A Postmodern Look at a Medieval Poet: The Case of William Dunbar," and Deanna Delmar Evans, "Bakhtin's Literary Carnivalesque and Dunbar's *Fasternis Evin in Hell,*" both in *SSL* 26 (1991): 343–53 and 354–65.

14. The benefits of being able to accept a variety of positions—and the similarities

between them—are provocatively discussed by Laurence Lerner, "Against Historicism," *New Literary History* 24 (1993): 273–92.

15. H. G. Aldis, *A List of Books Printed in Scotland before 1700: including those Printed furth of the Realm for Scottish Booksellers: with Brief Notes on the Printers and Stationers* (Edinburgh, 1970).

16. *The Poetical Works of Sir David Lyndsay of the Mount,* ed. George Chalmers, 3 vols. (London, 1806); *The Poetical Works of Sir David Lyndsay,* ed. David Laing, 3 vols. (Edinburgh, 1879).

17. *The Works of Sir David Lindsay of the Mount, 1490–1555,* ed. Douglas Hamer, 4 vols. (Edinburgh, STS, 1931–36).

18. J. E. H. Williams, "The Poetry of Sir David Lyndsay: A Critical Study" (Ph.D. diss., Australian National University, 1978). Dr. Williams has since published a number of articles on Lindsay and is currently preparing a new edition of his selected works. Details of these articles can be found in the Bibliography, as can the numerous studies of Lindsay's religious position, discussed more fully in Chapter 7. The work of Professor James K. Cameron in this field has been particularly suggestive; see, in particular, "Aspects of the Lutheran Contribution to the Scottish Reformation," *RSCHS* 22 (1984): 1–12; "Humanism and Religious Life," in *Humanism in Renaissance Scotland,* ed. John MacQueen (Edinburgh, 1990): 161–71.

19. John Durkan, "The Cultural Background in Sixteenth Century Scotland," in *Essays on the Scottish Reformation, 1513–1625,* ed. David McRoberts (Glasgow, 1962), 292.

ONE. BACKGROUND AND BEGINNINGS

1. The family tree (App. 2) illustrates the relationship between the two branches of the family and also Lindsay's own immediate progenitors. The accuracy of this genealogy has been the subject of debate; cf. Sir Thomas Innes of Learney, "Sir David Lindsay of the Mount," *Scottish Notes and Queries* 13 (1935): 145; Chalmers, *Lyndsay,* 1:3; Laing, *Lyndsay,* 1:ix; and Hamer, *Works,* 4:283.

2. *The Testament of Squyer Meldrum,* 205–9. Concerning the relative importance of blood ties and physical interaction, see Jenny Wormald, *Lords and Men in Scotland, 1442–1603* (Edinburgh, 1985), 80–83.

3. Those Lords Lindsay contemporaneous with Lindsay were Patrick, the fourth lord (d. 1526) and his grandson, John, the fifth lord (d. 1563). Both were important figures at court and in the locality. For further genealogical and biographical information, see Sir James Balfour Paul, *The Scots Peerage,* 9 vols. (Edinburgh, 1904–14), 5:396–98. The Mount had been in the Lindsay family at least since 1467 when a "David Lindissay de Mont" first appears in the records. He was probably the first to hold both the Mount and Garleton in conjunction; *RMS,* 2, no. 911; *HMC Report on the MSS of the Earl of Hume* (London, 1891), 142–43. In the sixteenth century, David Lindsay and his wife held the Mount from David Petblado of that Ilk; *RMS,* 3, nos. 1761, 2748; *RSS,* 2, no. 1633.

4. *RMS,* 3, nos. 1761, 2748; *RSS,* 2, no. 1633 (Lindsay and his wife confirmed in the lands of the Mount and Garleton held from David Petblado and Lord Lindsay respectively); *RMS,* 3; no. 2256 (John, Lord Lindsay, confirmed in his lands including Garleton held from the crown).

5. George Buchanan, *The History of Scotland from the Earliest Period to the Regency of the Earl of Moray,* ed. and trans. James Aikman, 6 vols. (Glasgow, 1845), 1:30.

6. Margaret H. B. Sanderson, *Cardinal of Scotland: David Beaton, c. 1494–1546* (Edinburgh, 1986), 7.

7. We know of Lindsay's brothers, John, Alexander, Patrick, and a second David, from Lindsay's arrangements for the inheritance of his lands, *RMS,* 3, nos. 2529, 2748.

8. The traditionally accepted birthdate, 1490, first proposed in 1806 by George Chalmers, was based upon the entry "Da. Lindesay" among the incorporated students of St. Andrews University for the year 1508 or 1509. Arguing that Lindsay would have matriculated three years earlier at the age of fifteen, Chalmers arrived at a birthdate of 1490; *Lyndsay*, 1:4; *Early Records of the University of St Andrews, 1413–1579*, ed. James Maitland Anderson (Edinburgh, SHS, 1926), 208. However, university records do not necessarily provide an accurate indication of the age of students embarking upon study, nor is there any conclusive evidence that this reference is in fact to David Lindsay of the Mount. Hamer tentatively suggests that Lindsay was born "a little before October 19 1486"; *Works*, 4:ix. This is based on a charter of 19 October 1507, granted by Patrick, Lord Lindsay of the Byres, confirming "dilecto nostro consanguineo David Lindesay filio et heredi apparenti David Lindesay de Month nostri eciam consanguinei" in the lands of Garleton-Alexander. Unfortunately, the charter in question, quoted by Laing and accepted by Hamer, is only partially reproduced and inadequately referenced; Laing, *Lyndsay*, 1:ix. If it may be accepted as evidence, it does suggest that Lindsay—who must have been of age by this date—was born at least before October 1486.

9. John Mair, *A History of Greater Britain as well England as Scotland (1521)*, ed. and trans. Archibald Constable (Edinburgh, SHS, 1892), 48.

10. John Durkan, "Education, the Laying of Fresh Foundations," in *Humanism in Renaissance Scotland*, ed. MacQueen, 124.

11. John Durkan, "Education in the Century of the Reformation," in *Essays on the Scottish Reformation*, ed. McRoberts, 152.

12. *ER*, 13:127.

13. *Early Records of the University of St Andrews*, 203–4.

14. Although once so styled (*APS*, 2:429), such references are so scarce as to suggest clerical error.

15. Durkan, "Education in the Century of the Reformation," 153.

16. The charter refers to "quas terras de Garmiltoun cum pertinen. quondam David Lindesay consanguineus noster AVUS DICTI DAVID habuit hereditaire et de nobis tenuit &c." Dated 19 October 1507 and the sasine 6 April 1508; Laing, *Lyndsay*, 1:ix. As already mentioned, there are difficulties in accepting this charter. It certainly seems that Lindsay's grandfather was dead by 1503 when his (second?) wife, Janet Shaw, lodges an action against Lindsay's father concerning her terce, *Acts of the Lords of Council, 1501–1503*, ed. Alma B. Calderwood (Edinburgh, 1993), 216.

17. *RMS*, 3, no. 1781.

18. *TA*, 4:169.

19. Ibid., 313.

20. Ibid., 441.

21. Thus one John Wilson acquired the sasine of a tenement on the south side of the High Street "in the name of David Lindsay of Garmylton"; *Protocol Book of John Foular*, 3 vols. (Edinburgh, SRS, 1930–53), 1, no. 886; noted by R. J. Lyall, ed., in *Sir David Lindsay of the Mount: Ane Satyre of the Thrie Estatis* (Edinburgh, 1989), xv.

22. Although the records are by no means complete, it seems that the king and queen had separate accounts at least by 1508 for which year (25 January–4 August) there is a separate account relating specifically to Margaret's household. This includes the payment to the groom Lindsay in the prince's stable; *ER*, 13:lxxvi–lxxx.

23. *TA*, 4:268, 5:199, 310, 438.

24. Ibid., 4:321.

25. Norman Macdougall, *James IV* (Edinburgh, 1989). For a discussion of *The Testament of the Papyngo* and Lindsay's assessment of James's court, see 293–95.

26. John Leslie, *The History of Scotland from the Death of King James I in the year 1436 to the year 1561* (Edinburgh, Bannatyne Club, 1830), 78; Robert Lindesay of Pitscottie, *The History and Chronicles of Scotland*, ed. AE. J. G. Mackay, 3 vols. (Edinburgh, STS, 1899–1911), 1:242–44.

27. Pitscottie, *Chronicles*, 1:244.

28. Ibid., 259. Although often unreliable, Pitscottie's relationship with Lindsay and the fact that the latter was his probable source for the episode make it worthy of consideration.

29. Buchanan, *History of Scotland*, 2:190.

30. That he spent some time at Linlithgow is suggested by the payment of six shillings he received in 1513 for the construction of a door in the north tower; *TA*, 4:523.

31. Laing suggests it was a scheme initiated by Margaret; *Lyndsay*, 1:xiv. A similar idea is advanced by R. L. Mackie, *King James IV of Scotland: A Brief Survey of His Life and Times* (Edinburgh and London, 1958), 243–44. According to Macdougall, there may be some merit in this interpretation; *James IV*, 265. With no evidence to support his contention, Hamer maintains that, if it was a trick, then "Lindsay was not a party to it"; *Works*, 4:xi.

32. Macdougall, *James IV*, 265–66.

33. *TA*, 5:127, 112; *ER*, 14:242; *RSS*, 1, no. 3164; *TA*, 5:196; *ER*, 14:462, 15:44.

34. Lindsay is described as "The Kingis master of household" (*TA*, 5:160); Argyll as "*magistro hospitii domini regis*" (*ER*, 14:194).

35. *TA*, 5:196; *ER*, 14:462, 15:44.

36. "Ordinance for the Keeping of James V," in *HMC Report on the MSS of the Earl of Mar and Kellie* (London, 1904), 11.

37. *The Letters of James V*, ed. R. K. Hannay and Denys Hay (Edinburgh, SHS, 1954), 388. James's recollection is confirmed by Dunbar's first recorded appearance in his service in February 1517; *TA*, 5:111.

38. The author of this statement, David Paniter, is quoted by D. E. Easson, *Gavin Dunbar, Chancellor of Scotland, Archbishop of Glasgow* (Edinburgh and London, 1947), 4. Buchanan judged him "upright and learned but rather deficient in political knowledge"; *History of Scotland*, 2:239.

39. "Ordinance for the Keeping of James V."

40. It may also be significant that the 1522 entry in the *Exchequer Rolls* recording Lindsay's payment occurs immediately below one to the king's preceptor; *ER*, 14:462.

41. Ibid., 350 (1518), 459 (1522), 15:89 (1524).

42. The heart that appears in Lindsay's arms is an allusion to the well-known Douglas device, and the fact that Lindsay was able to quarter Janet's arms does suggest she was reasonably well born; Hamer, *Works*, 4:xii.

43. *TA*, 5:196.

44. Although in a letter of March 1525 Margaret referred to Dunbar as "master to the Kyng" in the past tense, in January 1526 he was recorded by the English ambassador as being continually about the king; *SP Henry VIII*, 4:343, 429. He probably lost his influence under Angus whose political opponent he was; *L&P Henry VIII*, 4, no. 4728.

45. *SP Henry VIII*, 4:368.

46. Ibid., 243.

47. My own account of the minority is highly indebted to the pioneering study by W. K. Emond, "The Minority of King James V, 1513–28" (Ph.D. diss., St. Andrews University, 1988).

48. Ibid., 423.

49. *RSS*, 1, no. 3267. Although Margaret did not remarry until 1526, she had been contemplating divorce from Angus as early as 1517.

50. *APS*, 2:300.

51. *ER*, 15:116, 229.

52. *TA*, 5:310.

53. *ER*, 15:395, 473.

54. For example, W. Murison, *Sir David Lyndsay, Poet and Satirist of the Old Church in Scotland* (Cambridge, 1938), 8.

55. Lindsay maintains that it was James's generosity and personal intervention that ensured the continued payment of his pension (*The Complaynt*, 266–67), but this is probably best read as flattery of the king's munificence.

56. Emond, "The Minority of King James V," 558.

57. Hamer, *Works*, 3:12.

58. Janet Williams has argued that each of these nursery stories "has been chosen to make its own contribution to a well-devised educational scheme, which offered James exemplary counsel, inspiring forecasts of his future role, and jocular portraits of his kingdom in ancient times." This interpretation usefully brings out the important didactic function of these tales and of *The Dreme* itself, but it does not necessarily follow that they were original compositions; "Lindsay's 'Antique' and '"Plesand' Stories," in *A Day Estivall: Essays on the Music, Poetry, and History of Scotland and England and Poems Previously Unpublished in Honour of Helena Mennie Shire*, ed. A. Gardner-Medwin and J. E. H. Williams (Aberdeen, 1990), 163.

59. He cites as an authority "The Auctour of the Speir" (639), almost certainly a reference to Sacro Bosco's *Sphaera Mundi*. In addition, he probably also drew upon the *Chronica Chronicarum Abbrege*.

60. *The Dreme*, 182, 170, 166, 175; *Orpheus and Eurydice*, 222, 200, 226, 223. See *The Poems of Robert Henryson*, ed. G. Gregory Smith, 3 vols. (Edinburgh, STS, 1906–14), 3:28–65. These similarities have been noted by Hamer, *Works*, 3:16.

61. Cf. *The Dreme*: "Phebus brycht, / That lustie lampe and lanterne of the heuin" (421–22), "As Roye royall, . . . / . . . into his golden chair" (426–27), Venus, "sumtyme constant and sumtyme variabyll," with "hir blenkis amorous" (411, 407), and *The Testament of Cresseid*: "fair Phebus lanterne of light" (197), "As king Royall he raid vpon his Chair" (204), Venus, "in hir face seemit gret variance, / Quhyles perfyte truth and quhyles Inconstance" (223–34), "with blenkis amorous" (226); *The Poems of Robert Henryson*, 3:3–24.

62. *The Poems of William Dunbar*, ed. John Small, 3 vols. (Edinburgh, STS, 1893), 2:9.

63. Chalmers, *Lyndsay*, 1:54; Hamer, *Works*, 3:1–2.

64. Hamer, straining to maintain his position, comments, "although this is spoken of as in the present, Lindsay must be referring not to the fighting of 1526 but to the cleaning up of the country in 1528 after the flight of the Douglases"; *Works*, 3:1–2.

65. Cf. Sandra Cairn's argument that *The Dreme* represents a subtle piece of court propaganda praising the policies of the new administration; "Sir David Lindsay's *Dreme*: Poetry, Propaganda, and Encomium in the Scottish court," in *The Spirit of the Court: Selected Proceedings of the Fourth Congress of the International Courtly Literature Society*, ed. Glyn S. Burgess and Robert A. Taylor (Woodbridge and Dover, NH, 1985), 110–19.

66. Hamer, *Works*, 3:47–49.

67. Ibid., 64–67.

TWO. A HERALDIC CAREER

1. Innes of Learney, "Sir David Lindsay of the Mount," 171; Hamer, *Works*, 4:288–89.

2. *ER*, 5:116, 229.

3. George Seton, *The Law and Practice of Heraldry in Scotland* (Edinburgh, 1863), 480; *TA*, 5:377.

4. *TA*, 5:431; *ER*, 16:12.

5. Chalmers, *Lyndsay*, 1:11–12; Laing, *Lyndsay*, 1:xxii; Hamer, *Works*, 4:288–90.

6. Hamer suggests that Pettigrew may have been a Douglas appointee who fled with his patrons to England and was out of the country for most of the period in question; *Works,* 4:289. However, given the participation of the Lyon King in the Parliament of 1528 (when the Douglases were forfeited), this seems unlikely; *APS,* 2:324–27.

7. *L&P Henry VIII,* 9:151, 165; *TA,* 6:423.

8. *RPC,* 1:568 (April 1569).

9. J. H. Stevenson, *Heraldry in Scotland,* 2 vols. (Glasgow, 1914), 1:38.

10. W. Croft Dickinson, "Courts of Special Jurisdiction," *Introduction to Scottish Legal History* (Edinburgh, Stair Society, 1958), 397. See *RPC,* 1:658–60, where the Council praises the appointment of officers made by Lindsay of Rathillet and orders no further changes to be made.

11. *RPC,* 1:660. The Lyon King in 1569 was David Lindsay of Rathillet who is generally considered to be Lindsay's brother. Given that he lived until 1591 and could only have been an infant on his father's death, there must have been a considerable gap between the two brothers. The assumption that they were at least half-brothers is based on a letter of 1561 written by Thomas Randolph to William Cecil in which he recommends Lindsay, Rothesay Herald and brother of "the notable David Lyndsaye, Kynge of Armes"; *Selections from Unpublished Manuscripts in the College of Arms and British Museum illustrating the Reign of Mary Queen of Scots* (Glasgow, Maitland Club, 1837), 92.

12. Chalmers, *Lyndsay,* 1:39.

13. *APS,* 3:449.

14. In 1569 there were eighty-three minor officers; *RPC,* 1:658–60.

15. The Scottish officers of arms were never "incorporated," as happened, for example, in fifteenth-century England, a process which would have led (as it did south of the border) to their virtual separation from the royal household; Sir Thomas Innes of Learney, "The Style and Title of the Lord Lyon King of Arms," *Juridical Review* 44 (1932): 198.

16. Maurice Keen, *Chivalry* (New Haven and London, 1984), 125.

17. Richard Firth Green, *Poets and Princepleasers: Literature and the English Court in the Late Middle Ages* (Toronto, Buffalo, and London, 1980), 168–72. A well-known example of this is the account penned by Somerset Herald recording the marriage of Margaret Tudor to James IV; John Leland, "Account of the Marriage between James IV and Margaret Tudor," in *Johannis Lelandi Antiquarii de Rebus Britannicis Collectanea,* 6 vols. (London, 1774), 4:265–300.

18. E. Beveridge, ed., *Fergusson's Scottish Proverbs* (Edinburgh, STS, 1924), 116.

19. A. R. Wagner, *Heralds and Heraldry in the Middle Ages* (Oxford, 1956), App. F.

20. *Gilbert of the Hayes Prose Manuscript,* ed. J. H. Stevenson, 2 vols. (Edinburgh, STS, 1901–14), vol. 1, "The Buke of the Lawe of Armys" or "The Buke of Bataillis." A revised edition of Hay's prose works is currently being prepared for the Scottish Text Society by Jonathan A. Glenn.

21. Two surviving Scottish examples of sixteenth-century heraldic manuscripts are "John Scrymgeour's Heraldic Collection," dating from the first half of the century, NLS, Adv. MS 31.5.2, and "Sir David Lindsay of Rathillet's Heraldic Collection," NLS, Adv. MS 31.3.20. Both are derived from the late-fifteenth-century Loutfut Manuscript, prepared by the Scottish pursuivant, Adam Loutfut, BL, Harleian MS 6419. This is the subject of a forthcoming Scottish Text Society publication, *The Deidis of Armorie,* ed. L. A. J. R. Houwen.

22. Green, *Poets and Princepleasers,* 170.

23. Fig. 1, "Habit of a Herald," is taken from the late-sixteenth-century Seton Armorial, NLS, ACC. 9309, fol. after 23. *The Deploratioun* refers to the "burneist siluer wandis" borne by the heralds which, as shown here, recalled the staff of Mercury, messenger of the gods.

24. For example, *APS,* 3:193.

25. *APS*, 3:554.

26. Ibid.

27. NLS, Adv. MS 31.6.5.

28. Sir Thomas Innes of Learney, *Scots Heraldry,* 2nd ed. (Edinburgh and London, 1956), 13, 234.

29. It has been asserted that earlier in his career Lindsay visited Italy; for example, Innes of Learney, "Sir David Lindsay of the Mount," 146. This is based on a passage in *The Monarche* where the Courtiour refers to seeing Pope Julius II wage war against Louis XII (5422–24), an allusion to the Siege of Mirandola, 1511. However, there is no real reason to view the Courtiour in this strictly autobiographical fashion, and given Lindsay's position at court in 1511 an Italian journey seems unlikely. In fact, the idea hardly seems worth mentioning but for the fact that it has proved remarkably long-lived and is still being uncritically accepted; for example, R. D. S. Jack, *The Italian Influence on Scottish Literature* (Edinburgh, 1972), 31.

30. *Letters of James V*, 191, 193–94. It has been suggested that Lindsay accompanied the embassy of Sir John Campbell; for example, Murison, *Sir David Lyndsay*, 10. Pitscottie makes the same error. These letters disprove this point.

31. *Letters of James V*, 204–5; *L&P Henry VIII*, 5:443; Pitscottie, *Chronicles*, 1:354.

32. *Letters of James V*, 215–16.

33. Edmond Bapst, *Les Mariages de Jacques V* (Paris, 1889), 180; *TA*, 6:44, 46.

34. *Letters of James V*, 215–16.

35. Ibid., 226.

36. *SP Henry VIII*, 8:385.

37. *Letters of James V*, 257–58.

38. *TA*, 6:232; Bapst, *Les Mariages de Jaques V*, 210.

39. Sanderson, *Cardinal of Scotland*, 258.

40. *Letters of James V*, 294–95, 303–4.

41. At the ceremony, Lindsay received plate worth twenty pounds; *L&P Henry VIII*, 9, no. 151. Lindsay's participation here reflects the ceremonial and symbolic importance attached to his office. His role, however, was not entirely symbolic, and he was also charged with securing a safe-conduct for the bishop of Aberdeen who was shortly to travel through England to France; *SP Henry VIII*, 5:30.

42. *L&P Henry VIII*, 9, no. 178. (The installation is mistakenly dated 24 August.)

43. *TA*, 6:455, 456, 7:16.

44. Pitscottie, *Chronicles*, 1:358. This unlikely tale is confirmed; *L&P Henry VIII*, 11, no. 631.

45. Sanderson, *Cardinal of Scotland*, 64. For contemporary accounts of the proceedings, see *Relations Politiques de la France et de l'Espagne avec L'Ecosse au XVIe Siècle*, ed. Alexander Teulet, 5 vols. (Paris, 1862), 1:106–8.

46. *TA*, 7:16.

47. Donald E. Queller, *The Office of Ambassador in the Middle Ages* (Princeton, 1967), 60.

48. *SP Henry VIII*, 7:385.

49. *TA*, 6:46.

50. BL, Cotton MS Caligula BI, fol. 313. A facsimile can be found in Laing, *Lyndsay*, 1:xxiv. Laing provides a transcript of Lindsay's letter, as does Hamer, *Works*, 4: 255.

51. Sanderson, *Cardinal of Scotland*, 66–67.

52. Leland, "Account of the Marriage between James IV and Margaret Tudor," 295.

53. Pitscottie, *Chronicles*, 1:379. Royal entries are discussed more fully in Chapter 5.

54. Ibid., 381. For evidence relating to the tournament, see *Accounts of the Master of Works, 1529–1615*, ed. Henry M. Paton, (Edinburgh, 1957), 221–22.

55. Hamer, *Works*, 3:140.

56. *Extracts from the Records of the Burgh of Edinburgh, 1528–1557* (Edinburgh, SBRS, 1871), 89.

57. For details on Foulis, see John Durkan, "The Beginnings of Humanism in Scotland," *Innes Review* 4 (1953): 7–8.

58. John A. Inglis, *Sir Adam Otterburn of Redhall* (Glasgow, 1935), 117–18.

59. *L&P Henry VIII*, 13, pt. 2, no. 30.

60. *RSS*, 2, no. 4910. There is no record of Lindsay bearing the title Sir David before this date.

61. Stevenson, *Heraldry in Scotland*, 1:62.

62. NLS, Adv. MS 31.4.3 (bound with later material). Figs. 2 and 3 are taken from Lindsay's Armorial as reproduced under the title *Facsimile of an Ancient Heraldic Manuscript Emblazoned by Sir David Lyndsay of the Mount, Lyon King of Armes, 1542* (Edinburgh, 1822).

63. See Chapter 5.

64. *Discours Particulier d'Escosse, 1559/60*," ed. Peter G. B. McNeill, in *Miscellany II* (Edinburgh, Stair Society, 1984), 119. This is a document on the government of Scotland prepared at the command of Mary of Guise for the French administration.

65. NLS, Adv. MS 31.4.3, fol. 53.

66. *APS*, 2:361.

67. NLS, Adv. MS 31.4.3, fol. 111.

68. *The Chronicles of Scotland Compiled by Hector Boece Translated into Scots by John Bellenden (1531)*, ed. R. W. Chambers and Edith C. Batho, 2 vols. (Edinburgh, STS, 1938–41), 2:169. Boece contains the same passage; *Scotorum Historiae* (Paris, 1527), fol. 266v.

69. R. Dickson and J. P. Edmond, *Annals of Scottish Printing from the Introduction of the Art in 1507 to the Beginning of the Seventeenth Century* (Cambridge, 1890), 109. See too Hamer, *Works*, 4:18.

70. Stevenson, *Heraldry in Scotland*, 1:42.

71. Evidence relating to the Scottish coronation ritual during this period is scanty. BL, Add. MS 35844, fols. 191r–192v, which purports to be "Ane Form of the Coronatioun of the Kinges of Scotland" (sixteenth century), was actually penned by the second earl of Hardwicke who, unfortunately, does not give his source. For an account of a seventeenth-century ceremony, see that of Sir James Balfour of Denmilne, NLS, Adv. MS 32.2.26, fols. 36r–42v, collated with two English sources and printed in *The Manner of the Coronation of King Charles I of England* (London, Henry Bradshaw Liturgical Text Society, 1892), 94–106. The available evidence is assessed by R. J. Lyall, "The Medieval Scottish Coronation Service: Some Seventeenth Century Evidence," *Innes Review* 28 (1977): 3–21. See too Chapter 5.

72. Lyall, "The Medieval Scottish Coronation Service," 7; Stevenson, *Heraldry in Scotland*, 1:42.

73. *A Dialogue against the Feuer Pestilence by William Bullein from the edition of 1578 collated with the earlier editions of 1564 and 1573*, ed. M. W. Bullein and A. H. Bullein (London, EETS, 1888). This description only appears in the 1564 edition. Bullein's reliability is, however, questionable. He claims the lion on Lindsay's breast was white when it was surely red, but he did come from the north of England and his account was written less than ten years after Lindsay's death.

74. *APS*, 2:284. The forfeiture passed in 1515 was rescinded the following year.

75. This seems demonstrated by Pettigrew's continued tenure despite obvious incapacity. For brief biographical accounts of the Lyon Kings, see F. J. Grant, *Court of the Lord Lyon, 1318–1945* (Edinburgh, SRS, 1946).

76. *The Warkis of the Famous and Worthie Knicht Schir Dauid Lyndesay of the Mont . . . Imprentit by Iohne Scot at the expensis of Henrie Charteris* (1568), fols. 3v, 4v. Reproduced in Hamer, *Works*, 1:399, 401.

THREE. SUCCESS AND SURVIVAL

1. *Letters of James V,* 241, 252, 260–61, 273–74 (June 1533–August 1534).

2. James K. Cameron discusses the first two periods in "Faith and Faction: Conflicting Loyalties in the Scottish Reformation," in *States, Countries, Provinces,* ed. Michael Hurst (Bourne End, 1986), 72–92.

3. Most recently, Maria Dowling, *Humanism in the Age of Henry VIII* (London, 1986), and Joseph S. Block, *Factional Politics and the English Reformation, 1520–1540* (Woodbridge, 1993).

4. Block, *Factional Politics,* 7.

5. This is particularly associated with the work of Paul Oscar Kristeller, for an introduction to which see Michael Mooney, ed., *Renaissance Thought and Its Sources: Paul Oscar Kristeller* (New York, 1979).

6. The idea of "vernacular humanism" is suggested by Priscilla Bawcutt's use of the term in her assessment of Gavin Douglas, who clearly fits into this important category; *Gavin Douglas: A Critical Study* (Edinburgh, 1976), 36.

7. Exactly how humanism is understood determines any assessment of Lindsay's humanist reputation. For Hamer, the fact that Lindsay knew no Greek or Hebrew meant that he was no humanist (*Works,* 4:xli), whereas MacQueen, adopting a more uncritical approach, ranks him alongside such humanist luminaries as Mair, Boece, Buchanan, and Napier ("Conclusion," *Humanism in Renaissance Scotland,* 178). The concept of vernacular humanism provides a meaningful way of addressing this problem.

8. Important works on Scottish humanism include: John Durkan, "The Beginnings of Humanism"; idem, "The Cultural Background in Sixteenth Century Scotland," in *Essays on the Scottish Reformation,* ed. McRoberts, 274–331; idem, "Early Humanism and King's College," *Aberdeen University Review* 48 (1980): 259–79; idem, "Giovanni Ferrerio, Humanist: His Influence in Sixteenth Century Scotland," in *Religion and Humanism,* Studies in Church History 17, ed. K. Robbins (Oxford, 1981), 181–94; John MacQueen, "Some Aspects of the Early Renaissance in Scotland," *Forum for Modern Language Studies* 3 (1967): 201–22, and edited by the same author, *Humanism in Renaissance Scotland;* Bawcutt, *Gavin Douglas;* Leslie J. Macfarlane, *William Elphinstone and the Kingdom of Scotland, 1431–1514* (Aberdeen, 1985); I. D. McFarlane, *Buchanan* (London, 1981); Ian B. Cowan and Duncan Shaw, eds., *The Renaissance and Reformation in Scotland* (Edinburgh, 1983).

9. Durkan, "Early Humanism and King's College," 261.

10. Whitelaw's Latin oration delivered to Richard III in 1484 has been described as "the earliest extant piece of extended humanist prose delivered by a Scot"; MacQueen, "Some Aspects of the Early Renaissance in Scotland," 207.

11. For this information and further details concerning Ferrerio, see Durkan, "Giovanni Ferrerio, Humanist."

12. *ADCP,* 430, 459; Durkan, "The Beginnings of Humanism," 10.

13. Durkan, "The Beginnings of Humanism," 7.

14. Lindsay's reference is perhaps to Sir Thomas Galbraith, a chaplain of the Chapel Royal. Not only was this Galbraith responsible for the magnificently illuminated marriage settlement of 1503, he is also recorded as singing ballads to James IV along with the King of Bean; *TA,* 2:350, 1:184.

15. *Livy's History of Rome, the First Five Books translated into Scots by John Bellenden, 1533,* ed. W. A. Craigie, 2 vols. (Edinburgh, STS, 1901–3); *Virgil's Aeneid translated into Scottish Verse by Gavin Douglas,* ed. David F. C. Coldwell, 4 vols. (Edinburgh, STS, 1957–64).

16. *TA,* 5:434, 6:37, 97, 98, 208.

17. McFarlane, *Buchanan,* 21, 48; Durkan, "The Beginnings of Humanism," 6; *Letters of James V,* 271.

18. It is worth noting here the debate concerning possible links among humanism, patronage, and government in Tudor England. See, for example, James McConica, *English Humanists and Reformation Politics under Henry VIII and Edward VI* (Oxford, 1965), and Arthur J. Slavin, "Profitable Studies: Humanists and Government in Early Tudor England," *Viator* 1 (1970): 307–25. Maintaining the need for a strict definition of humanism, Alistair Fox has recently challenged the conventional idea that the advancement of learned, literary men was due to their humanist background; "Facts and Fallacies: Interpreting English Humanism," in Alistair Fox and John Guy, *Reassessing the Henrician Age: Humanism, Politics, and Reform, 1500–1550* (Oxford and New York, 1986), 17. He goes on to argue that although humanism was influential in certain areas, notably the religious life and education, it was not a direct influence upon politics. He refutes McConica's hitherto influential thesis that the Henrician reform program was underwritten by an Erasmian ideology and suggests that any contribution to English political life was made by a very different, more pragmatic, brand of English humanism; "English Humanism and the Body Politic," in Fox and Guy, *Reassessing the Henrician Age*, 34–51.

19. McFarlane, *Buchanan*, 67.

20. *SP Henry VIII*, 5, pt. 4:154.

21. James Kirk usefully demonstrates the preponderance of clerics among the early Reformers; "The Religion of Early Scottish Protestants," in *Humanism and Reform: The Church in Europe, England, and Scotland, 1400–1643: Essays in Honour of James K. Cameron,* ed. Kirk (Oxford, 1991), 361–412.

22. For details of Borthwick's career, see John Durkan, "Scottish 'Evangelicals' in the Patronage of Thomas Cromwell," *RSCHS* 21 (1983): 127–56.

23. McFarlane, *Buchanan*, 42–67; Kirk, "Early Scottish Protestants," 383–84.

24. Euan Cameron, "The Late Renaissance and the Unfolding Reformation in Europe," in *Humanism and Reform,* ed. Kirk, 19.

25. *Sir James Melville's Memoirs* (Edinburgh, Bannatyne Club, 1827), 65; David Calderwood, *History of the Kirk of Scotland,* ed. T. Thomson and D. Laing, 8 vols. (Edinburgh, Wodrow Society, 1842–49), 1:140.

26. F. J. Grant, *The Faculty of Advocates in Scotland, 1532–1943* (Edinburgh, SRS, 1944), 10.

27. *SP Henry VIII*, 5, pt. 4:169–70.

28. *TA,* 5:276–77. For Eure's "Nootes" of the play, see BL, Royal MS 7.C.xvi, fols. 137–39; printed in Hamer, *Works,* 2:2–6.

29. Greg Walker, "Sir David Lindsay's *Ane Satire of the Thrie Estatis* and the Politics of the Reformation," *SLJ* 11 (1989): 6–9; McFarlane, *Buchanan*, 53–54.

30. For a further discussion of this, see Joanne Spencer Kantrowitz, *Dramatic Allegory: Lindsay's "Ane Satyre of the Thrie Estaitis"* (Lincoln, NB, 1975), 11–22. This is not to suggest that the Epiphany performance was an early performance of *Ane Satyre* or even a prototype version. The two seem sufficiently distinct for them to be reckoned as separate works.

31. *Letters of James V,* 187, 200.

32. D. E. R. Watt, ed., *Scotichronicon by Walter Bower,* 9 vols. (Aberdeen, 1987–), 8:316–18.

33. *Hamilton Papers,* 1, no. 33.

34. Buchanan, *History of Scotland,* 2:259. See too Chapter 7.

35. *Hamilton Papers,* 1, no. 73; rpt., *L&P Henry VIII,* 16, no. 990 (my italics). Craig is generally accounted a supporter of Cardinal Beaton—a probable mistake on Eure's part.

36. *L&P Henry VIII,* 15, no. 249; rpt., *State Papers of Sir Ralph Sadler,* ed. A. Clifford, 3 vols. (Edinburgh, 1809), 1:46–49, 47 (hereafter cited as Sadler, *Papers*).

37. *L&P Henry VIII,* 15, no. 248; rpt., Sadler, *Papers,* 1:17–45.

38. Sanderson, *Cardinal of Scotland*, 89, 87.

39. Ibid., 91.

40. *The Works of John Knox,* ed. D. Laing, 6 vols. (Edinburgh, Wodrow Society, 1846–64), 1:81–82 (hereafter cited as Knox, *Works*); Sadler, *Papers,* 1:94.

41. Knox, *Works,* 1:82.

42. Pitscottie, *Chronicles,* 1:392. For an account of Hamilton's career see Charles McKean, "Hamilton of Finnart," *History Today* (January 1993): 42–47.

43. Sanderson, *Cardinal of Scotland,* 149.

44. Significantly, Buchanan too describes the episode in this religious/factional context; *History of Scotland,* 2:260.

45. *L&P Henry VIII,* 11, no. 248.

46. Pitscottie, *Chronicles,* 1:387–93, 392.

47. *Hamilton Papers,* 1, no. 85.

48. Ibid., no. 275.

49. *SP Henry VIII,* 5, pt. 4:14.

50. *Hamilton Papers,* 2, no. 63; Sadler, *Papers,* 1:316.

51. *APS,* 2:370–71.

52. Sanderson, *Cardinal of Scotland,* 149.

53. *RMS,* 3, nos. 2529, 2748. The second charter drawn up in August 1542, describing in much greater detail the arrangements for the inheritance of his estates, suggests that Lindsay, acknowledging he would die childless, was concerned to tidy up his affairs.

54. The charter of 1542 (*RMS,* 3, no. 2748) is the last recorded appearance of both Janet Douglas and John Lindsay. Exactly when each died is not clear, but both were certainly dead by 1555 when Janet is referred to as deceased (ibid., 4, no. 1006) and the Mount is inherited by Alexander Lindsay; see App. 2.

55. *Hamilton Papers,* 1, no. 340.

56. Ibid., no. 264.

57. *HMC 11th Report* (London, 1887), 119–20.

58. Sadler, *Papers,* 1:138.

59. *CSP Scot,* 1:43.

60. *APS,* 2:415.

61. *SP Henry VIII,* 4:262–65. For a discussion of Lindsay's attendance at parliaments, see Hamer, *Works,* 4:285–88. With regard to 1543, Hamer writes, "Certainly at this parliament as at others, there was a 'Dauid Lindsay *pro cupro.*' This may or may not have been the poet but, as Lyon King he would have had an *ex officio* seat, sitting at the foot of the throne in personal attendance."

62. *L&P Henry VIII,* 18, pt. 1, no. 37.

63. *SP Henry VIII,* 4:270; Sadler, *Papers,* 1:63.

64. Hamer, *Works,* 4:269.

65. *TA,* 8:340; *L&P Henry VIII,* 19, pt. 1, no. 435.

66. *SP Henry VIII,* 4:262–65.

67. For a detailed account of this period, see Sanderson, *Cardinal of Scotland,* 160–76.

68. An analysis of the signatories is provided by Sanderson who argues that it was something less than a broad-based resistance; ibid., 167–68. Jenny Wormald on the other hand views it as illustrative of widespread opposition to the government; *Mary Queen of Scots* (London, 1988), 50–51.

69. For details of Beaton's actions, see Sanderson, *Cardinal of Scotland,* 174.

70. *Hamilton Papers,* 2, no. 116.

71. Knox, *Works,* 1:105–6. Details of the episode (which Knox probably obtained from Balnaves) were picked up and repeated by both Calderwood and Spottiswoode (Calderwood,

History of the Kirk, 1:161; John Spottiswoode, *History of the Church of Scotland, 1639,* 10 vols. [Edinburgh, Bannatyne Club, 1847–50], 1:144, 192). That Lindsay was among those purged from court is rejected by Hamer: "He did not quit official service, and the statement that Lindsay retired from court during the regency is certainly untrue, except in so far as there was a great closing down of court activities after the death of James V"; *Works,* 4:xxix. However, as we have seen, the period following James's death was marked by intense diplomatic activity (activity, moreover, in which Lindsay was directly involved), and he was certainly at the hub of the arrangements for the royal funeral.

72. *Hamilton Papers,* 2, no. 131.

73. Reported by Bute Pursuivant in the Parliament of December 1543; *APS,* 2:429, 438, 441; *TA,* 8:275.

74. *Hamilton Papers,* 2:716.

75. *ER,* 18:17, 23.

76. *TA,* 8:403.

77. See Chapter 8.

78. *L&P Henry VIII,* 19, pt. 1, no. 350; *SP Henry VIII,* 4:377.

79. *APS,* 2:472.

80. Sanderson, *Cardinal of Scotland,* 229.

81. Durkan, "Scottish 'Evangelicals,' " 153; *RPC,* 1:43; *CSP Scot,* 1, no. 14.

82. *RPC,* 1:28.

83. *SP Henry VIII,* 4:581–82.

84. *RPC,* 1:28.

85. Knox, *Works,* 1:186.

86. Brother Kenneth, "Sir David Lindsay—Reformer," *Innes Review* 1 (1950): 79–91. See also Chapter 8.

87. Details of this episode are best obtained from the Danish sources examined by Thorkild Lyby Christensen, "The Earl of Rothes in Denmark," in *Renaissance and Reformation in Scotland,* ed. Cowan and Shaw, 60–74. For Lindsay's expenses, see *TA,* 9:259 (December 1548), 347 (October 1549, some months after his return). SRO, RH 2/7/6, fol. 142, is an incomplete eighteenth-century copy of his instructions.

88. T. L. Christensen, "Scoto-Danish Relations in the Sixteenth Century: The Historiography and Some Questions," *SHR* 48 (1969): 80–97, and "Scots in Denmark in the Sixteenth Century," *SHR* 49 (1970): 125–45.

89. See Chapter 8.

90. Christensen, "The Earl of Rothes," 69.

91. *TA,* 10:84–85.

92. A precise dating (Tuesday, 7 June 1552) is possible owing to a reference in *The Cupar Banns.* This short piece, designed to announce the performance, is found in W. Tod Ritchie, ed., *The Bannatyne Manuscript,* 4 vols. (Edinburgh, STS, 1928–34), 3:87–100; rpt., Hamer, *Works,* 2:10–32. The debate concerning dating is summarized by Lyall, *Ane Satyre,* ix–xiv.

93. StA, B 13/10/1; Anna Jean Mill, *Medieval Plays in Scotland* (Edinburgh and London, 1927), 168.

94. Hamer, *Works,* 4:140–43.

95. Charteris, *The Warkis,* fol. 2v; rpt., Hamer, *Works,* 1:396. For this dating of the manuscript, see Alisdair A. MacDonald, "The Bannatyne Manuscript—A Marian Anthology," *Innes Review* 37 (1986): 36–47.

96. *Extracts from the Records of the Burgh of Edinburgh, 1528–1557,* 196–97; *City of Edinburgh Old Accounts,* 2 vols. (Edinburgh, SBRS, 1899), 1:110.

97. *RMS,* 4, no. 1006.

FOUR. KINGS AND KINGSHIP

1. For a discussion of the links between subject and subjectivity, see Antony J. Hasler, "William Dunbar, the Elusive Subject," in *Brycht Lanternis: Essays on the Language and Literature of Medieval and Renaissance Scotland*, ed. J. Derrick McClure and Michael R.G. Spiller (Aberdeen, 1989), 194–208.

2. Found in *The Complaint of Bagsche, The Deploratioun*, and *The Flyting*, respectively.

3. It is generally accepted, writes Agnes Muir Mackenzie, that Rex Humanitas is "a candid but kindly sketch of James V"; *Ane Satyre of the Thrie Estatis*, ed. J. Kinsley (London 1954), 20. In fact, it is not generally accepted at all, and indeed its acceptance can have disastrous consequences. It forces John MacQueen into the untenable argument that *Ane Satyre* was first performed before a Cupar audience in the early 1530s. His obsession with historical topicality also leads MacQueen to suggest that Dame Sensualitie is a portrait of James's mistress, Margaret Erskine; "*Ane Satyre of the Thrie Estatis*," *SSL* 3 (1966): 129–43. For a convincing rebuttal of this, see Anna Jean Mill, "The Original Version of Lindsay's *Satyre of the Thrie Estatis*," *SSL* 6 (1968): 67–75.

4. The richness and importance of the Scottish tradition have been fully demonstrated by Sally Mapstone's substantial study, "The Advice to Princes Tradition in Scottish Literature, 1450–1500" (Ph.D. diss., Oxford University, 1986).

5. Rebecca W. Bushnell, *Tragedies of Tyrants: Political Thought and Theater in the English Renaissance* (Ithaca and London, 1990), 10–11.

6. *The Education of a Christian Prince, by Desiderius Erasmus*, ed. and trans. Lester K. Born (New York, 1965), 173.

7. *Ane Satyre*, 1878, and *The Complaynt*, 499; *The Testament of the Papyngo*, 268, 255, and 256. Although Lindsay did not use them in such a way, the terms "officer" and "governor" could have less conservative implications, suggesting, for example, conditional tenure of the office. For Mair's use of the terms, see Roger A. Mason, "Kingship, Nobility, and Anglo-Scottish Union: John Mair's *History of Greater Britain (1521)*," *Innes Review* 41 (1990): 207–8.

8. "The Buke of the Governaunce of Princis (1456)," in *Gilbert of the Hayes Prose Manuscript*, 1:145. The importance attached to this obligation was one of the central features of the advice-giving tradition; Mapstone, "The Advice to Princes Tradition," 95–97.

9. For a further discussion of this dual obligation and its dependence upon a conflation of Aristotelian and biblical vocabulary, see Roger A. Mason, "Kingship, Tyranny, and the Right to Resist in Fifteenth Century Scotland," *SHR* 66 (1987): 138–39.

10. Ian H. Stewart, *The Scottish Coinage* (London, 1955), 78, 81.

11. Granting remission for crimes without sufficient grounds (or in exchange for payment) is a complaint regularly found in kingship literature. Mapstone has argued that this type of specific legalistic language and imagery was a distinctive feature of Scottish kingship literature; "The Advice to Princes Tradition," 451.

12. For example, Jennifer M. Brown, "The Exercise of Power," in *Scottish Society in the Fifteenth Century*, ed. J. M. Brown (London, 1977), 35–65.

13. The term "patriotic conservatism" is used by Roger Mason to describe a *mentalité* that set a high premium on the traditionally articulated principles of good government and, above all, on loyalty to the crown; "Kingship, Tyranny, and the Right to Resist" and, more recently, "Chivalry and Citizenship: Aspects of National Identity in Renaissance Scotland," in *People and Power in Scotland: Essays in Honour of T. C. Smout*, ed. Roger Mason and Norman Macdougall (Edinburgh, 1992), 59.

14. A group of three poems in *The Bannatyne Manuscript* all lament the youth of James V: *Iesus Christ that deit on Tre, Now is our King in Tendir Aige, Rolling in my Remembrance*, in

Bannatyne Manuscript, ed. Ritchie, 2:245–51. An interesting exception to this general consensus is the author of *The Complaynt of Scotland* whose support for Mary of Guise's administration prevented him from identifying minority government as one of Scotland's problems. He even went so far as to explain why, despite the words of Isaiah, Mary's youth was not a scourge of God. Youth, he argued, was to be taken in the sense of ignorance or inconstancy. Cicero's injunction to look to virtue not age was more relevant to the Scots; *The Complaynt of Scotland by Robert Wedderburn (c.1550),* ed. A. M. Stewart (Edinburgh, STS, 1979), 23–24.

15. This problem is discussed by Constance Jordan, "Women's Rule in Sixteenth Century British Political Thought," *Renaissance Quarterly* 40 (1987): 421–51.

16. *Bannatyne Manuscript,* ed. Ritchie, 2:108.

17. This is particularly true with respect to Lindsay's earlier poetry. His later works, notably *Ane Satyre,* demonstrate a more informed response to specific sociopolitical problems but, as we shall see, this discussion was rather uneasily married to a highly conventional presentation of kingship.

18. Bellenden, *Chronicles of Scotland,* 1:19.

19. *The Dreme,* 1107; *Squyer Meldrum,* 1501–2; *The Monarche,* 2847–48, 5873.

20. *Meroure of Wyssdome: Composed for the Use of James IV, King of Scots, by Johannes de Irlandia,* vol. 3, ed. Craig McDonald (Edinburgh, STS, 1990).

21. *Ane New Yeir Gift to the Quene Mary, Quhen Scho Come First Hame* (25), in *The Poems of Alexander Scott,* ed. James Cranstoun (Edinburgh, STS, 1896), 1–8; also *Bannatyne Manuscript,* ed. Ritchie, 2:235–41.

22. *Bannatyne Manuscript,* ed. Ritchie, 2:228–31.

23. See too the anonymous *On Princlie Liberalitie,* in *The Maitland Folio Manuscript,* ed. W. A. Craigie, 2 vols. (Edinburgh, STS, 1919–27), 1:207–9.

24. P. Hume Brown, *George Buchanan: Humanist and Reformer* (Edinburgh, 1890), 252.

25. One volume of this type was Thomas Hoccleve's *Regiment of Princes,* printed in Frederick J. Furnival, ed., *Hoccleve: Works* (London, EETS, 1887). Hamer has noticed the striking similarity between the opening lines of this and of *The Monarche* (*Works,* 3:255), and further echoes of Hoccleve's work can be found in Lindsay's writing; cf. *Regiment of Princes,* 2553–54, and *The Testament of the Papyngo,* 290–91. It is, therefore, probable that Lindsay knew Hoccleve's work, but this could equally be a reference to the *De Regimine Principum* surviving in various manuscripts, including the *Liber Pluscardensis,* printed by Chepman and Millar as *The Buke of Gude Counsale to the King,* in *Maitland Folio Manuscript,* ed. Craigie, 1:115–25; 2:74–91. This is, in many respects, very similar to Lindsay.

26. The importance of these lines is illustrated by their repetition—omitting line 312—in *Ane Satyre* (1896–98). Here, Lindsay mentions the legendary line of Scottish kings descended from Fergus I, claiming that James V was the one hundred and fifth of this line. This accords with the most detailed biographical account of the dynasty, Boece's *Scotorum Historiae.* However, Lindsay's assertion that fifty-five kings had been killed is not in line with Boece. Why the disparity? We know from his Armorial Register that Lindsay had a detailed knowledge of the work, at least by 1542. However, he was writing here in 1530, only four years after Boece had completed his work and before Bellenden's translation (begun in 1531). Clearly, at this stage of his career, Lindsay knew of the work but not its details—a comment perhaps on the stir it caused at court.

27. Madelaine Pelner Cosman, *The Education of the Hero in Arthurian Romance* (Chapel Hill, 1965), 202.

28. Frank Manley and R. S. Sylvester, eds. and trans., *Richard Pace, De Fructu Qui ex Doctrina Percipitor (1517)* (New York, 1967), 14.

29. Mair, *A History of Greater Britain,* 47.

30. Ibid., 183.

31. *Precelland Prince,* 3–8, in *Bannatyne Manuscript,* ed. Ritchie, 2:231–32.

32. Bellenden, *Chronicles of Scotland,* 1:255.

33. Ibid., 306.

34. John Mair for one dwelt more on "the lives of men who were famed for their piety . . . than those of warriors, to end that the reader may feel his heart grow warm within him and strengthen himself with this spiritual marrow"; *A History of Greater Britain,* 94.

35. Ben Lowe, "War and the Commonwealth in Mid-Tudor England," *Sixteenth Century Journal* 21 (1990): 171–91, 171. See too Chapter 6.

36. As discussed in Chapter 6, Lindsay did not reject all aspects of the chivalric ideology. Indeed, some of them underpinned his thinking with regard to the commonweal.

37. James was similarly flattered in *The Complaynt* (456), although on this occasion the compliment may be intended ironically.

38. This is discussed in greater detail in Chapter 6.

39. The author here was Walter Bower, noted by Mason, "Kingship, Tyranny, and the Right to Resist," 132–33.

40. For a discussion of this proverb, ultimately derived from biblical authority but generally misquoted, see Curt F. Büller, "Wirk alle thyng by Conseil," *Speculum* 24 (1949): 410–12.

41. Bellenden, *Chronicles of Scotland,* 1:16. Buchanan is perhaps the most obvious of such writers but, for a more recent endorsement of the popular character of the Scottish monarchy, see Matthew P. McDiarmid, "The Kingship of the Scots in Their Writers," *SLJ* 6 (1979): 5–18.

42. T. D. Robb, ed., *The Thrie Prestis of Peblis, How Thai Told Thar Talis* (Edinburgh, STS, 1920), 797–98.

43. An introduction to the genre is provided by Sydney Anglo, "The Courtier: The Renaissance and Changing Ideals," in *The Courts of Europe: Politics, Patronage, and Royalty, 1400–1800,* ed. A. G. Dickens (London, 1977), 33–53.

44. This was the explanation for the origins of knighthood found in Ramon Lull's influential *The Book of the Ordre of Chyvalry, translated and printed by William Caxton,* ed. A. T. P. Byles (London, EETS, 1926). A version of this, "The Buke of the Ordre of Knychthede," was translated by Gilbert Hay for Scottish consumption; *Gilbert of the Hayes Prose Manuscript,* 2:1–70.

45. Mair, *A History of Greater Britain,* 46.

46. Bellenden, *Chronicles of Scotland,* 1:36.

47. S. J. Gunn, "The Courtiers of Henry VII," *EHR* 108 (1993): 23–49. For a contemporary discussion of a courtier's duty to offer counsel, see Balthazar Castiglione, *The Book of the Courtier,* trans. G. Bull (London, 1967), 285.

48. For an analysis of the changing interpretations of Cicero's political thought from the stress upon withdrawal and seclusion to its influence upon civic humanism, see Hans Baron, "Cicero and the Roman Civic Spirit in the Middle Ages and the Early Renaissance," in *Lordship and Community in Medieval Europe,* ed. Fredric L. Cheyette (New York, 1968), 291–314.

49. Skinner, *Foundations,* 1:222.

50. Joanne S. Norman, "William Dunbar, Grand Rhetoriquer," in *Brycht Lanternis,* ed. McClure and Spiller, 179–93.

FIVE. COURTLY VISIONS

1. J. W. Sherborne, "Aspects of English Court Culture in the Later Fourteenth Century," in *English Court Culture in the Later Middle Ages,* ed. V. J. Scatterwood and J. W. Sherborne (London, 1983), 1.

2. Ranald Nicholson, *Scotland: The Later Middle Ages* (Edinburgh, 1974), 576–94; Joan Hughes and W. S. Ramson, *Poetry of the Stewart Court* (Canberra, 1982), 1–21; Norman Macdougall, "The Kingship of James IV of Scotland: 'The Glory of all princely governing'?" *History Today,* Nov. 1984, 30–36; and, for a still useful look at the king's day-to-day patronage of the arts, see Mackie, *King James IV,* 113–28.

3. Jenny Wormald, *Court, Kirk, and Community: Scotland, 1470–1625* (London, 1981), 56.

4. *The Poems of William Dunbar,* 2:220–22.

5. Such references are too numerous to list in full, but see, for example, payments to potingaris (apothecaries), *TA,* 3:205, 208, 380; to painters, 506; lapidaries (jewelers), 114, 149, 174, 201, 360, 388; to the glass wright, Thomas Peebles, 85, 162, 183, 297, 355, 368; to ten named goldsmiths, 4:614; also 4: App. 1, shipbuilding accounts; App. 2, the accounts for artillery and works on Edinburgh Castle including payments to gunners, masons, and smiths.

6. John Purser, *Scotland's Music: A History of the Traditional and Classical Music of Scotland from Early Times to the Present Day* (Edinburgh and London, 1992), 82. Although she also acknowledges that poetry "undoubtedly flourished" at James IV's court, it is worth noting Priscilla Bawcutt's reservations concerning the king's literary patronage; *Dunbar the Makar* (Oxford, 1992), 79–80. For a still more cautious assessment of the court literature of previous reigns, see Sally Mapstone, "Was There a Court Literature in Fifteenth Century Scotland?" *SSL* 26 (1991): 410–22.

7. Mill notes only two items related to court revels in the period of the minority; *Medieval Plays,* 330. Admittedly, there are large gaps in the records, but this is still strikingly few in comparison to more settled times. For the financial background, see Athol L. Murray, "Financing the Royal Household: James V and His Comptrollers, 1513–43," in *Renaissance and Reformation in Scotland,* ed. Cowan and Shaw, 41–59.

8. Hughes and Ramson, *Poetry of the Stewart Court,* viii.

9. *This Hindir Nicht, Iesu Chryst that Deit on Tre, Now is our King in Tendir Aige, Rolling in my Rememberance,* in *Bannatyne Manuscript,* ed. Ritchie, 2:228–31, 245–51.

10. *The Bannatyne Miscellany,* 3 vols. (Edinburgh, Bannatyne Club, 1827–55), 2:1–8; Durkan, "The Beginnings of Humanism," 8. It has been suggested that the *Strena* was composed for a royal welcome; L. O. Fradenburg, "Narrative and Capital in Late Medieval Scotland," in *Literary Practice and Social Change in Britain, 1380–1530,* ed. L. Patterson (Berkeley, Los Angeles, and Oxford, 1990), 294.

11. The *Accounts of the Master of Works* for the period 1529–41 show expenditure to have exceeded £26,000; Donaldson, *James V to James VII* (Edinburgh, 1965), 57–58. For James's building, see Stewart Cruden, *The Scottish Castle* (Edinburgh and London, 1960), 146–48, 196; and for the humanist input, Martin Kemp and Clare Farrow, "Humanism in the Visual Arts, *circa* 1530–1630," in *Humanism in Renaissance Scotland,* ed. MacQueen, 34.

12. See, for example, *TA,* 5:432, 433 (Robin Hood, 1531), 6:37 (Christian Rae, Queen of the Bean, 1531).

13. The source is Thomas Wode, compiler of an anthology of part music, often referred to as the St. Andrews Psalter, put together over the years 1562/66 to 1590; Helena Mennie Shire, *Song, Dance, and Poetry of the Court of Scotland under King James VI* (Cambridge, 1969), 23–25.

14. *Letters of James V,* 170; Purser, *Scotland's Music,* 81–87.

15. *TA,* 6:255. Payment was also made for "ane play coit for the Kingis son"; ibid., 186. James IV also participated in court dramas, and in 1507 seven ells of gray cloth were purchased "to be ane mummyng goun to the King"; ibid., 3:249.

16. On such mock kings, see Sandra Billington, *Mock Kings in Medieval Society and*

Renaissance Drama (Oxford, 1991). BL, Royal MS 7.C.xvi, fols. 138–39, printed in Hamer, *Works*, 2:4–6.

17. For references to Wantonness, see *TA*, 3:369, 372, 377, 379, 4:314, 316, 318, 332, 342, 349; and to Diligence, see ibid., 1:51, 69.

18. Ibid., 2:102, 129, 131, 141, 351, 367, 382, 412, 472, 3:132, 160, 164, 171, 190, 206.

19. Ibid., 1:176, 183, 307, 330, 378, 2:132, 475, 3:192, 339, 373, 412, 412, 4:402.

20. Green, *Poets and Princepleasers*.

21. George Watson, ed., *The Mar Lodge Translation of the History of Scotland by Hector Boece* (Edinburgh, STS, 1946), 3–13.

22. The pension upon which Dunbar seems to have been wholly dependent was authorized until such time as a suitable benefice should become vacant; *RSS*, 3, no. 563. For payments to Beuenden, see *TA*, 5:434, 6:37, 97, 98, 206.

23. *TA*, 4:313.

24. Ireland, *Meroure of Wyssdome, Book VII*, 164.

25. J. E. H. Williams, "'Althocht I beir nocht like ane baird': David Lyndsay's *Complaynt*," *SLJ* 9 (1982): 5–20.

26. *The Poems of William Dunbar*, 2:48–51. For a more general discussion, see R. J. Lyall, "The Lost Literature of Medieval Scotland," in *Brycht Lanternis*, ed. McClure and Spiller, 33–47.

27. Short biographical accounts (so far as known) are provided by Hamer, *Works*, 3:68–75.

28. Although referring specifically only to Douglas and Dunbar, surely Denton Fox is correct to argue that what distinguishes Middle Scots court poetry is its diversity; "Middle Scots Poets and Patrons," in *English Court Culture in the Later Middle Ages*, ed. Scatterwood and Sherborne, 109–27.

29. Hamer, *Works*, 3:78; *RSS*, 1, nos. 769, 847, 3757; *RMS*, 3; no. 705; *TA*, 6:37, 207 (1532 and 1534); *ER*, 15:292, 382, 386, 461, 534, 546, 566, 16:135, 174, 294, 348, 393.

30. *Bannatyne Manuscript*, ed. Ritchie, 2:242–45. The fact that the poem was about James V supports Kidd's credentials as court poet.

31. *ER*, 16:370; *RMS*, 3, nos. 435, 762, 996, 1938.

32. Listed by Hamer, *Works*, 3:76–77.

33. Ibid., 3:77; *ER*, 15:158, 456; *RMS*, 3, no. 1866.

34. *Bannatyne Manuscript*, ed. Ritchie, 2:231–32, 228–31. Although anonymous in Bannatyne, the latter is ascribed to "williame stewart" in Maitland, *Maitland Folio Manuscript*, ed. Craigie, 1:353–55. *This Hindir Nicht* should not be confused with Dunbar's poem sometimes referred to by this title, or alternatively as *Musing allone; Bannatyne Manuscript*, ed. Ritchie, 2:156. If Stewart did write these two poems, he seems a probable author for another minority piece, *Rolling in My Rememberance*, attributed simply to Stewart; *Maitland Folio Manuscript*, ed. Craigie, 1:370–72.

35. William Stewart, *The Buik of the Croniclis of Scotland; or, A Metrical Version of the History of Hector Boece*, ed. William B. Turnball, 3 vols. (London, Rolls Series, 1858), 1:x. Possible references to Stewart include *TA*, 5:321, 328, 384, 309, 6:39, 92, 95, 97, 203, 205, 207, 210, 7:16, 455, 8:373, 375, 411.

36. *The Baner of Peetie* is printed in *The Bannatyne Manuscript*, ed. Ritchie, 2:3–8.

37. *TA*, 5:434, 6:37, 97; for payments for "the translatioune of Titus Livius," see 6:98, 206.

38. Durkan, "The Beginnings of Humanism," 7. This may be the Robert Galbraith referred to in *TA*, 5:293, 402.

39. *TA*, 1:184, 270, 2:350, 383, 416; Michael R. Apted and Susan Hannabus, eds., *Painters in Scotland, 1301—1700: A biographical Dictionary* (Edinburgh, SRS, 1978), 40—41.

40. Stewart, *A Metrical Version of the History*, Prologue, 112—15.

41. *Relations politiques de la France et de l'Espagne avec L'Ecosse*, ed. Teulet, 1:108.

42. Bellenden, *Chronicles of Scotland*, 1:337.

43. John Rolland, *The Seuin Seages*, ed. G. F. Black (Edinburgh, STS, 1931); also published by the Bannatyne Club, *The Sevin Sages in Scottish Metre by John Rolland of Dalkeith* (Edinburgh, 1837).

44. Knox, *Works*, 1:261—62.

45. *Bannatyne Manuscript*, ed. Ritchie, 2:254—55. References to Margaret Tudor (d. Oct. 1541) date the poem to 1541.

46. Glenn D. Burger, "Poetical Invention and Ethical Wisdom in Lindsay's *Testament of the Papyngo*," *SSL* 24 (1989): 166—67.

47. Hay, "The Governaunce of Princis," 85.

48. James actually owned a dog called Bagsche (*TA*, 7:96), and entries to the king's hounds occur throughout the accounts. For a full list, see Hamer, *Works*, 3:111—12. For a detailed literary criticism of the poem, which seeks to decode some of Lindsay's intentions, see J. E. H. Williams, "The Lyon and the Hound: Sir David Lyndsay's *Complaint and . . . Confessioun of . . . Bagsche*," *Paregon* 31 (1981): 3—12. She argues that Lindsay was writing about a political struggle centered around the discovery of a courtier in the pay of England and in support of her case cites the fact that the name of the hound recalls the "bagcheke" (the unflattering term given to the English groat depicting Henry VIII) and the fact that the royal arms of England are supported *dexter* by a hound. However, the existence of a real-life Bagsche makes this subtle message unlikely, whatever the truth concerning the poem's topical meaning.

49. I. D. McFarlane, *A Literary History of Renaissance France, 1470—1589* (London and New York, 1974), 33—34.

50. For the classic exposition of the decadence of chivalry, see J. Huizinga, *The Waning of the Middle Ages*, trans. and ed. F. Hopman, (1924; rpt., London, 1965). A similar argument is advanced by Arthur B. Ferguson, *The Chivalric Tradition in Renaissance England* (Washington, London, and Toronto, 1986). For an alternative view, see Malcolm Vale, *War and Chivalry: Warfare and Aristocratic Culture in England, France, and Burgundy at the End of the Middle Ages* (London, 1981), and Keen, *Chivalry*.

51. For the 1507 tournament, see *TA*, 3:393—97; for that of 1508, 4:117—25; see also 2:388—89, 1:262—64.

52. Ibid., 7:165, 517.

53. *Accounts of the Master of Works*, 1:221.

54. BL, Cotton MS Caligula BI, fol. 313.

55. Aldis, *List of Books Printed in Scotland*. Presumably this represents only a fraction of the total material printed but no longer extant.

56. Eric Stair-Kerr, *Stirling Castle: Its Place in Scottish History*, 2nd ed. (Stirling, 1928), 151—52.

57. This is repeated, for example, by the fifteenth-century traveler, William of Worcester; John H. Harvey, ed., *William Worcestre: Itineraries* (Oxford, 1969), 7.

58. D'Arcy Jonathan Dacre Boulton, *The Knights of the Crown: The Monarchical Orders of Knighthood in Later Medieval Europe, 1325—1520* (Woodbridge, 1987), 13. Gilbert Hay's popular translation listed the holding of a "round table" among the accomplishments of the ideal knight; "The Buke of the Order of Knychthede," 23.

59. Leslie, *History of Scotland*, 78. Macdougall suggests that this, plus the naming of James's elder brother, Arthur, was intended to recall not so much the Round Table romances

but the deceased prince of England and, hence, to draw attention to James IV's closeness to the English throne; *James IV*, 295.

60. *TA*, 5:381, 411, 412, 418, 6:225; *Accounts of the Master of Works*, 1:227, 228, 289.

61. Vale, *War and Chivalry*, 33–62.

62. Boulton, *The Knights of the Crown*, xvii–xxi; *TA*, 5:394. A target was an ornament in the shape of a shield, generally worn in one's hat.

63. Boulton, *The Knights of the Crown,* 399. Boulton considers it a "Cliental Pseudo-Order"; ibid., xx.

64. For background to the offer (the attempted sabotage of a proposed Scoto-imperial marriage alliance), see *Letters of James V,* 285, 297.

65. *L&P Henry VIII,* 8, nos. 429, 430.

66. Priscilla Bawcutt, "Dunbar's Use of the Symbolic Lion and Thistle," *Cosmos* 2 (1986): 83–97; Charles Burnett, "The Development of the Royal Arms to 1603," *Journal of the Heraldry Society of Scotland* 1 (1977–78): 9–19. The Book of Hours is currently housed in the Austrian National Library, Vienna (Codex. Lat. 1897). For an informative and generously illustrated discussion of the manuscript, see Leslie Macfarlane, "The Book of Hours of James IV and Margaret Tudor," *Innes Review* 2 (1960): 3–21.

67. R. J. Malloch, "The Order of the Thistle," *Journal of the Heraldry Society of Scotland* 1 (1977–78): 37–38.

68. Bawcutt, "Dunbar's Use," 93.

69. *Royal Commission on Ancient and Historic Monuments of Scotland: Midlothian and West Lothian* (Edinburgh, 1929), 220.

70. Roy Strong, *Art and Power: Renaissance Festivals, 1450–1650,* 2nd ed. (Woodbridge, 1984), 11.

71. Leland, "Account of the Marriage between James IV and Margaret Tudor," 288–91.

72. *The Poems of William Dunbar,* 2:251–53.

73. Frances A. Yates, *Astraea: The Imperial Theme in the Sixteenth Century* (London and Boston, 1975), 127–48; Penny Richards, "Rouen and the Golden Age: The Entry of Francis I, 2 August 1517," in *Power, Culture, and Religion in France, c.1350–c.1550,* ed. C. T. Allmand (Woodbridge, 1989), 117–30.

74. For illustrations of French triumphal arches, see Lawrence M. Bryant, *The King and the City in the Parisian Royal Entry Ceremony: Politics, Ritual, and Art in the Renaissance* (Geneva, 1986), figs. 3, 5, 8 (1549), 20, 21, 27, 28, 36 (1571); Yates, *Astraea,* plates 18a–19b.

75. *Extracts from the Records of the Burgh of Edinburgh, 1528–1557,* 91.

76. This is not to suggest that Scottish pageantry was hitherto devoid of any classical content. Margaret's Edinburgh entry of 1503, for example, depicted the Judgment of Paris. Mill views this as the earliest British instance of the introduction of the classical element into pageantry; *Medieval Plays,* 81. The 1566 fete is examined by Michael Lynch, "Queen Mary's Triumph: The Baptismal Celebrations at Stirling in December 1566," *SHR* 69 (1990): 1–21.

77. *A Diurnal of Remarkable Occurents that have passed within the country of Scotland since the death of King James the Fourth till the year 1575* (Edinburgh, Bannatyne Club, 1833), 22; *Extracts from the Records of the Burgh of Edinburgh, 1528–1557,* 89–91.

78. *Extracts from the Records of the Burgh of Edinburgh, 1528–1557,* 89.

79. *A Diurnal of Remarkable Occurents,* 22.

80. Pitscottie, *Chronicles,* 1:379.

81. Ibid., 1:244; Mary M. Bartley, "A Preliminary Study of the Scottish Royal Entries of Mary Stuart, James VI, and Anne of Denmark, 1558–1603" (Ph.D. diss., University of Michigan, 1981), 67–68, 108, 167.

82. Yates, *Astraea,* 28.

83. In *The Dreme*, Lindsay alludes to James's "hie Imperial blude" (1) and addresses him as "Excellence" (6, 50), and in *The Complaynt*, mention is made of his "power Imperyall" (116). *The Deploratioun* describes James and Madelaine as "Discendit boith of blude Imperiall" (41).

84. *TA*, 7:254, 285–86, 294, 280, 297, 487, 347, 282, 302.

85. *Accounts of the Master of Works*, 1:288.

86. For the repairs, see *TA*, 6:25, 73, 179; for the new crown, 7:278, 285. Further gold was needed for the crowns of both king and queen in June 1542; ibid., 8:82.

87. *Papers Relative to the Royal Regalia of Scotland* (Edinburgh, Bannatyne Club, 1829), 21–22; BL, Add. MS 45133, fol. 46v; "James IV Book of Hours," fols. 14v, 24v, show James at prayer and wearing such a crown.

88. SRO, E 31/8; reproduced in *The Queen and the Scots: Life in 16th Century Scotland* (SRO Exhibition Text 21), doc. 4.

89. NLS, Adv. MS 31.4.3, fol. 2. So too are all the crowns shown on the arms of Scotland's queens; only those of St. Margaret, Madelaine, and Mary of Guise are styled after the imperial fashion.

90. Ralph E. Giesey, *The Royal Funeral Ceremony in Renaissance France* (Geneva 1960).

91. For (English) heraldic funerals, see Clare Gittings, *Death, Burial, and the Individual in Early Modern England* (London and Sydney, 1984), 167–87, and Vale, *War and Chivalry*, 90–93.

92. Detailed accounts of the funerals of Henry VIII and Francis I (1547) can be found in Gittings, *Death, Burial, and the Individual*, 216–20, and Giesey, *The Royal Funeral Ceremony*, respectively.

93. "James IV Book of Hours," fol. 141v; Macfarlane, "The Book of Hours of James IV," 12. For the funeral of James V, see *TA*, 8: 141–44.

94. Ernst Kantorowicz, *The King's Two Bodies: A Study in Medieval Political Theology* (Princeton, 1957), 423.

95. Giesey, *The Royal Funeral Ceremony*, 85.

96. Ibid., 121; Kantorowicz, *The King's Two Bodies*, 427.

97. Bower, *Scotichronicon*, ed. Watt, 5:288. Neither does the "James IV Book of Hours" depict an effigy but, as noted above, this was not a depiction of Scottish ceremonial.

SIX. COMMUNITY AND COMMONWEAL

1. J. Schwend, "The Scottish Kirk in Medieval and Renaissance Literature," in *Brycht Lanternis*, ed. McClure and Spiller, 281. See too the description of the "stirring and democratic truth" conveyed by *Ane Satyre;* Roderick Watson, *The Literature of Scotland* (Basingstoke and London, 1984), 86.

2. Julian Goodare, "Parliament and Society in Scotland, 1560–1603" (Ph.D. diss., Edinburgh University, 1989), 58.

3. This is the primary meaning given by both *OED* and *DOST*. *OED* cites fourteenth- and fifteenth-century examples of the term while *DOST* has nothing earlier than the sixteenth.

4. Mason, "Chivalry and Citizenship," 59.

5. *APS*, 2:268.

6. Mason, "Chivalry and Citizenship," 59.

7. Roger Mason, "Covenant and Commonweal: The Language of Politics in Reformation Scotland," in *Church, Politics, and Society: Scotland, 1408–1929*, ed. Norman Macdougall (Edinburgh, 1983), 108.

8. Mair, *A History of Greater Britain*, 41.

9. James Henrisoun, "Ane Exhortacion to the Scottes to conforme themselfes to the honorable, Expedient, & godly Union betweene the two Realmes of Englande & Scotland"

(London, 1547), printed in Robert Wedderburn, *The Complaynt of Scotland,* ed. James A. H. Murray (London, EETS, 1872), 207–36. A second tract known as "The Godly and Golden Book," composed by Henrisoun in 1548 but never in fact published, makes a similar point; PRO, SP 50/4, fols. 128–37, largely reproduced in *CSP Scot,* 1:140–45.

10. Bullein, *A Dialogue against the Feuer Pestilence,* 17–18.

11. Inglis, *Sir Adam Otterburn,* 75–76.

12. *Hamilton Papers,* 1, no. 272.

13. Ireland, *Meroure of Wyssdome, Book VII,* 125.

14. Ben Lowe, "Peace Discourse and Mid-Tudor Foreign Policy," in *Political Thought and the Tudor Commonwealth: Deep Structure, Discourse, and Disguise,* ed. Paul A. Fideler and T. F. Mayer (London and New York, 1992), 112. See too Lowe's "War and the Commonwealth."

15. Lowe, "Peace Discourse," 112.

16. For example, Wedderburn, *The Complaynt of Scotland,* ed. Stewart, 57.

17. *The Complaynt,* 407; *The Testament of the Papyngo,* 541. The word "upland" signifies a rural environment, and in these examples John Upland is associated with appropriately rustic concerns. Critics who view these figures as interchangeable with John the Commonweal are surely mistaken; for example, Hamer, *Works,* 3:61; R. W. M. Fulton, "Social Criticism in Scottish Literature, 1480–1560" (Ph.D. diss., Edinburgh University, 1972), 146, 152, 155.

18. Underpinning the Aristotelian definition of a tyrant (one who rules for his own ends rather than for the good of the people), it was a common motif of kingship literature; Mapstone, "The Advice to Princes Tradition," 14.

19. *The Dreme,* 909–10; *The Complaynt,* 129–30; *The Testament of the Papyngo,* 381–83. Mason considers the relationship between common profit and commonweal and the implications this had for ideas of civic responsibility; "Chivalry and Citizenship," 58–59.

20. Mapstone, "The Advice to Princes Tradition," 89.

21. Hay, "The Buke of Knychthede," 28.

22. Printed in *The Book of the Ordre of Chyvalry,* ed. Byles, 113.

23. See Chapter 2, n. 11.

24. "To ane knycht appertenis that he be lover of the comon weil for be the commonalte of pepill was the cheualrie fundin & stablished and the comon weil is gritar & mair necessary than propir gude & special"; NLS, Adv. MS 31.5.2, fol. 95v. "To ane knight appertenis that he be lover of the comoun weill for be the commumitie of peple was chevalrie fundin and established. And the commoun weill is grittar & mair necessary than propir gude and speciall"; NLS, Adv. MS 31.3.20, fol. 78v.

25. Hay, "The Buke of Knychthede," 68.

26. Sydney Anglo, ed., *Chivalry in the Renaissance* (Woodbridge, 1990), xi.

27. Thomas F. Mayer, ed., *Thomas Starkey: A Dialogue between Pole and Lupset* (London, Camden Series, 1989), 40.

28. Felicity Riddy, "*Squyer Meldrum* and the Romance of Chivalry," *Yearbook of English Studies* 4 (1974): 26. Much of what follows owes a great deal to Riddy's very suggestive interpretation.

29. Mair, *A History of Greater Britain,* 83–84.

30. W. Croft Dickinson, ed., *The Sheriff Court Book of Fife, 1515–1522* (Edinburgh, SHS, 1928), 206, 226, 234, 250, 255, 258–59, 260–61, 265–66, 269–70.

31. *A Dialogue betweene Experience and a Courtier, of the miserable estate of the worlde, first compiled in the Schottishe tongue, by Sir Dauid Lyndesay, Knight, . . . now newly corrected, and made perfit Englishe* (London, 1566), Preface.

32. Stewart, *A Metrical Version of the History,* Prologue, 116.

33. Hamer, *Works*, 4:15–26.

34. Elizabeth Eisenstein, *The Printing Press as an Agent of Change: Communications and Cultural Transformations in Early Modern Europe*, 2 vols. (Cambridge, 1979), 1:11.

35. R. A. Houston, *Literacy in Early Modern Europe: Culture and Education, 1500–1800* (London and New York, 1988), 185–87.

36. Dickson and Edmond, *Annals of Scottish Printing*, 290. (A shilling more would have purchased one of his five bound copies.)

37. R. A. Houston, *Scottish Literacy and the Scottish Identity: Illiteracy and Society in Scotland and Northern England, 1600–1800* (Cambridge, 1985), 105.

38. Reprinted in Hamer, *Works*, 1:403–5. Grant G. Simpson discusses the rising level of sixteenth-century literacy in *Scottish Handwriting, 1150–1650* (Aberdeen, 1977), 10–14.

39. Stewart, *A Metrical Version of the History*, Prologue, 119; Bawcutt, *Gavin Douglas*, 93. As Bawcutt says, though Douglas hoped for such readings, his main intended audience comprised gentle-born laymen such as his patron, Lord Sinclair.

40. Eisenstein, *The Printing Press as an Agent of Change*, 1:129–36.

41. Robert Darnton discusses this notion—and suggests his own reservations—in "First Steps towards a History of Reading," *Journal of Australian French Studies* 23 (1986): 12–14.

42. For a discussion of what she terms Lindsay's various "poetic voices," see Janet H. Williams, " 'Thus Euery Man Said for Hymself': The Voices of Sir David Lyndsay's Poems," in *Brycht Lanternis*, ed. McClure and Spiller, 258–72.

43. John Peter, *Complaint and Satire in Early English Literature* (Oxford, 1956), 54.

44. Hamer provides a full list of all such references together with the results of his (largely fruitless) attempts to identify the characters in question; *Works*, 4:144–48.

45. Claude Graf, "Audience Involvement in Lindsay's *Satyre of the Thrie Estatis*," in *Scottish Studies: Scottish Language and Literature, Medieval and Renaissance*, ed. Deitrich Straus and Horst W. Drescher (Frankfurt, Berne, and New York, 1986), 427.

46. Lyall makes a similar point with regard to the intervention of the Pauper; *Ane Satyre*, xxix.

47. Mair, *A History of Greater Britain*, 302.

48. An introduction to the vernacular during this period is provided by Gordon Donaldson, "Foundations of Anglo-Scottish Unity," in *Elizabethan Government and Society: Essays Presented to Sir John Neale*, ed. S. T. Bindoff, J. Hurtsfield, and C. H. Williams (London, 1961), 287–95.

49. Wedderburn, *The Complaynt of Scotland*, ed. Stewart, 13.

50. Bawcutt, *Gavin Douglas*, 94.

51. Alex Agutter, "Middle Scots as a Literary Language," in *The History of Scottish Literature: Origins to 1660*, ed. R. D. S. Jack (Aberdeen, 1988), 22. Only recently the language of government had been Latin, and after 1603 the use of English would distinguish popular and elite culture.

52. *APS*, 2:379.

53. Henrisoun, "Godly and Golden Book," fol. 130.

54. *RPC*, 1:228–29.

55. Arthur B. Ferguson, *The Articulate Citizen and the English Renaissance* (Durham, NC, 1865), 33.

56. Writing of fifteenth-century England, Ferguson stresses the importance of altering conceptions of historical progress, changing economic relationships, and civil war; ibid., 133.

57. For a discussion of the different poetical genres of "rhetorical modes" Lindsay employed in the process, see R. J. Lyall, "Complaint, Satire, and Invective in Middle Scots Literature," in *Church, Politics, and Society*, ed. Macdougall, 55–56.

58. The original College constituted seven lay senators and seven clerics plus a clerical chancellor; *APS*, 2:335–36.

59. Although Lindsay refers to them as "cunning Clarks" (3853), he is surely not proposing an all-clerical institution. This certainly would not accord with his desire to reserve spiritual judgment for matters spiritual. Gordon Donaldson discusses the social background of lay lawyers (the majority of whom were drawn from lairdly families) in "The Legal Profession in Scottish Society in the Sixteenth and Seventeenth Centuries," *Juridical Review* 21 (1976): 1–20.

60. Judicial salaries were to be paid for with £1,400 raised from clerical taxation. Lindsay proposed salaries of 500 merks for the senators, 1,000 for the chancellors (£12,666 8d).

61. Henrisoun, "Godly and Golden Book," fol. 131.

62. Ibid., fol. 133; Lindsay, *Ane Satyre,* 2666.

63. Simon Ollivant, *The Court of the Official in Pre-Reformation Scotland* (Edinburgh, Stair Society, 1982), 143, 146. Although the diets were as numerous as Lindsay alleges, Ollivant demonstrates that they were by no means as lengthy.

64. Ibid., 142; SRO, CH 5/2/1, "Sentence Book of the Official Principal of St. Andrews, 1541–1533," fols. 39v, 54r.

65. *ADCP,* 434–35.

66. Population growth and inflation are discussed by Robert A. Dodgshon, *Land and Society in Early Scotland* (Oxford, 1981), 133–39.

67. *The Monarche* argues that the idleness of man was the occasion of his corruption by Satan and eventual punishment by God, the moral implications of idleness being made clear by the lines "wykitnes / Genereth, throw sleuthful ydilnes" (1263–64).

68. *APS,* 2:487; Lyall, *Ane Satyre,* ix.

69. A good introduction to feu-ferm tenure is provided by Margaret H. B. Sanderson, *Scottish Rural Society in the Sixteenth Century* (Edinburgh, 1982), 64–168.

70. The grassum was the down payment for a feu charter; augmentation was an increase in rent as the result of feuing reckoned as distinct entity in annual feu-duty.

71. Henrisoun, "Godly and Golden Book," fol. 133.

72. Mair's well-known statement on feuing is found in his *History of Greater Britain,* 47, but, as J. H. Burns points out, he also deals with land tenure in other works, notably *Quartius Sententiarum;* "The Scotland of John Major," *Innes Review* 2 (1951): 66–67.

73. Burns, "The Scotland of John Major," 67. Dodgshon shows that feuing did indeed lead to improvements; *Land and Society,* 101–2.

74. This is more fully discussed by Mason, "Kingship, Nobility, and Anglo-Scottish Union," 200–202.

75. *Statutes of the Scottish Church,* ed. David Patrick (Edinburgh, SHS, 1907), no. 282.

76. Sanderson, *Scottish Rural Society,* 105; see also 153–68 for a discussion of what she terms "The Dark Side" of feuing.

77. Paul A. Fideler, "Poverty, Policy, and Providence: The Tudors and the Poor," in *Political Thought,* ed. Fideler and Mayer, 194–222.

78. Anna Jean Mill, "The Influence of the Continental Drama on Lyndsay's *Satyre of the Thrie Estatis,*" *Modern Language Review* 25 (1930): 437–41. Perhaps Lindsay picked up on this during one of his French visits; possibly he knew of the tradition as transmitted to Scotland. Alain Chartier's *Quadrilogue Invectif* (1422), in which clergy, nobles, and commons each defend themselves, was known in Scotland at least from the date of the author's visit in 1428.

79. *The Poems of Robert Henryson,* 2:60–85.

80. The principle is also invoked to override Spiritualitie (3090–92).

81. From the evidence of parliamentary language, the respective roles of the king and the

estates in framing legislation do not appear to have been an issue. A wide variety of formulas is used to introduce acts of Parliament. Perhaps the most common was the simple "It is statuit and ordanit," but others included "The king and the haill parliament has statute and ordanit," "The parliament has statute and ordanit" (both 1432), "Our Souerane lord with auise, and auctoritie of the thre Estatis of his realm," "The kingis grace with auise and consent of the thre estatis of his realm" (both 1526), and "It is statute and ordanit be the Quenis Maiestie and the thre Estatis in Parliament" (1563); *APS*, 2:20, 22, 306, 307, 539.

SEVEN. POETRY, HUMANISM, AND REFORM

1. "Ane Adhortatioun of All Estatis, To the Reiding of Thir Present Warkis," 17–24, *The Warkis* (Edinburgh, 1568); rpt., Hamer, *Works,* 1:403–5.

2. Between his death and the end of the seventeenth century, at least twenty-five editions of his work were published in Scotland; Aldis, *List of Books Printed in Scotland.*

3. John Nichol, *Sir David Lyndesay's Works: Part V, Minor Poems* (London, EETS, 1871), liii.

4. Protestant revision of Catholic authors is discussed by Alasdair A. MacDonald, "Poetry, Politics, and Reformation Censorship in Sixteenth Century Scotland," *English Studies* 64 (1983): 410–21.

5. Another marginal note exclaims, "Quhat horribill torment of consciens was this auricular confessioun," next to Lindsay's reference to this particular sacrament; Hamer, *Works,* 3:18–19.

6. Brother Kenneth, "Sir David Lindsay—Reformer." This view was expounded at length by William Robinson Barclay, "The Role of Sir David Lindsay in the Scottish Reformation" (Ph.D. diss., University of Wisconsin, 1956). More recently, James K. Cameron has emphasized Lindsay's position within the traditions of Erasmian humanism; "Humanism and Religious Life," 161–77.

7. Some of the most important contributions to Scottish Reformation history include: Ian B. Cowan, *The Scottish Reformation: Church and Society in Sixteenth Century Scotland* (London, 1982); Gordon Donaldson, *The Scottish Reformation* (Cambridge, 1960); James Kirk, *Patterns of Reform: Continuity and Change in the Reformation Kirk* (Edinburgh, 1989); Michael Lynch, *Edinburgh and the Reformation* (Edinburgh, 1981); McRoberts, ed., *Essays on the Scottish Reformation;* Sanderson, *Cardinal of Scotland;* Wormald, *Court, Kirk, and Community.*

8. Patrick, *Statutes,* "Preamble," 84.

9. Ibid.

10. Wormald, *Court, Kirk, and Community,* 89.

11. *APS,* 2:295.

12. *ADCP,* 432. This was followed up by parliamentary legislation; *APS,* 2:341–42.

13. *L&P Henry VIII,* 8, no. 429.

14. *SP Henry VIII,* 5, pt. iv:36. Other evidence suggests that Barlow felt himself to be plowing stony ground when it came to evangelizing the Scots; ibid., 17–19, 36–38, 47–49.

15. *L&P Henry VIII,* 4, pt. ii, no. 2903.

16. Ian B. Cowan, "Regional Aspects of the Scottish Reformation," Historical Association Pamphlet (London, 1978), 8, 19. Discussing this problem, in particular the difficulties in assessing the available evidence, Sanderson concludes that "The extent of commitment to Lutheranism . . . is simply not quantifiable"; *Cardinal of Scotland,* 79.

17. Borthwick's library is discussed by Durkan, "Scottish 'Evangelicals,'" 132. The risks attendant on the trade in proscribed literature were high; in 1527, for example, one M. de la Tour was executed in Paris on the charge of distributing heretical books into Scotland; Gotthelf Wiedermann, "Martin Luther versus John Fisher: Some Ideas concerning the

Debate on Lutheran Theology at the University of St Andrews, 1525–30," *RSCHS* 22 (1984): 13.

18. Cameron, "Aspects of the Lutheran Contribution," 2.

19. According to Hamer, "There are renderings from one of Tyndale's English translations, as in the use of the word 'congregation' as a translation of 'ecclesia' in line 2556 [of *The Monarche*]"; *Works*, 3:245. However, see too the suggestion that Cranmer's 1539 Bible is a possible source (339). Hamer states that in an action brought after Lindsay's death disputing the ownership of his goods there is a reference to "ane byble in Inglis" (4:276). He cites as his source the *Register of Acts and Decreits*, 15, fols. 78v–79v, but I have been unable to locate the action in this volume.

20. A. S. Herbert, *A Historical Catalogue of Printed Editions of the English Bible, 1525–1961* (London and New York, 1968), 15–26.

21. *Hamilton Papers*, 1, no. 299.

22. Euan Cameron suggests that this idea, impractical and inaccurate, may in fact have wrought considerable damage to the reputation of the Church and the morale of its personnel; *The European Reformation* (Oxford, 1991), 46–48.

23. Chalmers, *Lyndsay*, 1:269. Lindsay deals explicitly with Beaton's fall in *The Tragedie of the Cardinal* where it is cited as an example of the fickleness of Fortune.

24. *ADCP*, 479.

25. Wormald, *Court, Kirk, and Community*, 83.

26. *Ane Satyre*, 774–76; *The Tragedie of the Cardinal*, 313; *Ane Satyre*, 750–52; *The Monarche*, 2589. The history of antimendicant literature is discussed by Penn R. Szittya, *The Antifraternal Tradition in Medieval Literature* (Princeton, 1986).

27. *The Tragedie of the Cardinal*, 310; *The Monarche*, 2598, 4493.

28. Ian B. Cowan, "Some Aspects of the Appropriation of Parish Churches in Medieval Scotland," *RSCHS* 13 (1959): 203. He also points out that as these independent parishes were particularly coveted by pluralists they were not necessarily any better served; *The Scottish Reformation*, 65.

29. Patrick, *Statutes*, 84.

30. E. G. Rupp and Benjamin Drewery, *Martin Luther* (London, 1970), 145.

31. He also uses this image in *Ane Satyre*, 3887–88, and *The Monarche*, 5364–67.

32. Erasmus, *Praise of Folly*, trans. B. Radice with notes by A. H. T. Levi (London, 1971), 126–27.

33. For the charges against Hamilton, see Knox, *Works*, 1:16, and for the argument that denial of Purgatory occupied a place in what he calls the "Hamilton tradition," see Wiedermann, "Martin Luther versus John Fisher," 25.

34. Hamer considers this to mark the first appearance of Lindsay the Reformer (*Works*, 4:xvii), but Cameron seems more accurate in his assessment of the inspiration as "probably more Erasmian than Lutheran" ("Humanism and Religious Life," 169). Cameron also notes "that the king should aim to end such practices is defended from the Old Testament and not, . . . as with Luther, on the basis of the doctrine of the priesthood of all believers"; "Aspects of the Lutheran Contribution," 4. However, it is also interesting to note that Balnaves's Lutheran "Treatise on Justification," written in 1548, urges kings to "put downe all false worshippinges and superstition" and cites examples from the Old Testament to support his case; printed as revised by Knox, in Knox, *Works*, 3:528.

35. Erasmus for one was a critic of both pilgrimages and misplaced prayers to images; John C. Olin, *Christian Humanism and the Reformation: Desiderius Erasmus* (New York, 1965), 337–38.

36. Cowan, *The Scottish Reformation*, 7–9.

37. *RMS*, 3, no. 1403; *TA*, 6:200–201, 299, 7:24. The shrine of Loretto at Musselburgh

was a notable target of Scottish reformers. Lindsay attacked it several times in his work: *Ane Satyre*, 4270–71; *The Monarche*, 2664. Alexander, earl of Glencairn, also wrote a satirical verse ridiculing the Hermit of Loretto, Thomas Doughty; printed in Knox, *Works*, 1:72–75. If Knox is correct in his dating of 1542, Glencairn's work may have directly inspired Lindsay.

38. Calderwood, *History of the Kirk*, 124–25. A modern account is provided by Sanderson, *Cardinal of Scotland*, 83–84.

39. The opportunity for royal patronage was the result of the papal indult of 1487, which had allowed Scottish kings eight months in which to nominate a successor when a vacancy occurred in a major benefice or abbey. In 1535 James V inveigled the pope into extending the period of nomination to a year.

40. Popular spirituality in the later Middle Ages is discussed, inter alia, by A. N. Galpern, "The Legacy of Late Medieval Religion in Sixteenth Century Champagne," in *The Pursuit of Holiness in Late Medieval Religion*, ed. Charles Trinkaus and Heiko A. Oberman, *Studies in Medieval and Renaissance Thought*, 10 (Leiden, 1974), 141–76; Christopher Harper-Bill, *The Pre-Reformation Church in England, 1400–1530* (Harlow and New York, 1989); R. N. Swanson, *Church and Society in Late Medieval England* (Oxford, 1989).

EIGHT. CONTROVERSY AND CONFLICT

1. Sanderson, *Cardinal of Scotland*, 64.

2. Mark Greengrass, *The French Reformation* (Oxford, 1987), 12–13.

3. Ibid., 24–27; R. J. Knecht, *Francis I* (Cambridge, 1982), 248; Donald R. Kelley, *The Beginning of Ideology: Consciousness and Society in the French Reformation* (Cambridge, 1981), 13–19.

4. Sanderson, *Cardinal of Scotland*, 77.

5. *APS*, 2:341–42.

6. Zwinglian doctrine on the Eucharist is discussed by Gottfried W. Locher, *Zwingli's Thought: New Perspectives*, Studies in the History of Christian Thought 25 (Leiden, 1981), 22–23, 325.

7. Duncan Shaw, "Zwinglian Influences on the Scottish Reformation," *RSCHS* 22 (1986): 119–39.

8. Scott, *Ane New Yeir Gift to the Quene Mary*, in *The Poems of Alexander Scott*, ed. Cranstoun, 1–8.

9. John Guy, *Tudor England* (Oxford, 1990), 136–37; *L&P Henry VIII*, 8, no. 949.

10. Greg Walker, *Plays of Persuasion: Drama and Politics at the Court of Henry VIII* (Cambridge, 1991), 195.

11. The words are John Foxe's, quoted by John N. King, *English Reformation Literature: The Tudor Origins of the Protestant Tradition* (Princeton, 1982), 277. Sydney Anglo examines calls for this type of antipapal drama; "An Early Tudor Programme for Plays and Other Demonstrations against the Pope," *Journal of the Warburg and Courtauld Institutes* 20 (1957): 176–79. Lyall has suggested that if *Ane Satyre* has a model then it is the English Protestant morality play, *Lusty Iuventus*; *Ane Satyre*, xxvi; Helen Scarborough Thomas, ed., *An Enterlude Called Lusty Iuventus: Liuely describyng the frailitie of youth: of nature, prone to vyce: by grace and good councell traynable to vertue by R Wever* (New York and London, 1982). However, this probably dates from the mid 1540s, and certainly it carries none of the political overtones that so distinguish *Ane Satyre*.

12. *L&P Henry VIII*, 13, pt. ii, no. 417; *APS*, 2:335. Extracting the right to tax the clergy, ostensibly for the purpose of endowing the College of Justice, James initially demanded a sum of £10,000 per annum. Successfully resisting this demand, the clergy finally

agreed to pay a lump sum of £72,000 over four years followed by an annual contribution of £1,400. Collection of the tax proved troublesome, and much of what was raised simply furnished James's extravagant architectural program.

13. *SP Henry VIII*, 5, pt. iv:169–70.

14. The charges against Borthwick are listed in the account of the reversal of his sentence in 1561, "The Ordour and Process deducit in the Declarator gevyn agains Schyr Jhon Borth-wick of Cenerie, knycht, be umquhill Dauid, Cardinall," *Bannatyne Miscellany*, 1:255–63. Based on these articles and incorporating parts of the defense Borthwick later made of his position as preserved by Foxe is *L&P Henry VIII*, 15, no. 714.

15. *Letters of James V*, 260–61.

16. Lindsay's theological position is discussed in Chapter 9.

17. Walker, "Sir David Lindsay's *Ane Satire*," 13.

18. "The Ordour and Process . . . agains Schyr Jhon Borthwick," 255–63; *L&P Henry VIII*, 15, no. 714. In the memorable phrase of John Durkan, Borthwick sought to "Cromwellize" Scotland; "Scottish 'Evangelicals,' " 132.

19. Interestingly, the notary instructed to extract the sasine of Borthwick's forfeited lands from his protocol book refused to do so. Unfortunately, the reason for his obstinacy is not recorded, but it may be reflective of a more widespread support for Borthwick's position; *ADCP*, 504.

20. Ibid., 488; *TA*, 8:315.

21. *RMS*, 3, no. 2529. Possibly the gift marked the birth of a royal heir in May 1540.

22. See Chapter 3.

23. Hamer, *Works*, 3:147.

24. *APS*, 2:415.

25. *Hamilton Papers*, 1, no. 303.

26. Pitscottie, *Chronicles*, 2:37.

27. *L&P Henry VIII*, 19, pt. i, no. 188.

28. Locher, *Zwingli's Thought*, 371.

29. *ADCP*, 528; *RPC*, 1:63; Patrick, *Statutes*, 123. The 1541 legislation commanding that the sacraments be honored may have been a response to simple irreverence, or it may reflect a rising incidence of sacramentarianism; *APS*, 2:370. Iconoclasm was sometimes, as Cowan argues, economically motivated (*The Scottish Reformation*, 100–101), but it also seems to have been inspired by genuine spiritual outrage (Shaw, "Zwinglian Influences," 122–23).

30. Wishart's activities are discussed more fully by Sanderson, *Cardinal of Scotland*, 206–12.

31. I am grateful to Dr. John Durkan for this suggestion and for many helpful conversations concerning George Wishart.

32. *The Tragical death of D. Beaton, Bishoppe of Sainct Andrewes in Scotland: Wherunto is joyned the martyrdom of maister G. Wysehart . . . for whose sake the aforesaid bishoppe was not long after slayne: Wherein thai maist learne what a burnynge charitie they shewed not only towardes him: but vnto al suche as come to their handes for the blessed Gospels sake*, ed. with an address by Robert Burrant (London, 1548).

33. Sanderson's list of 174 suspected heretics mentions only one executed in Fife, an unnamed man burned at Cupar, 1539; *Cardinal of Scotland*, 284.

34. Hamer speculates that it was printed by John Scot in March 1547 and that as a result his arrest was sought by the authorities. He also thinks that this poem was burned by the ecclesiastical authorities in 1549; *Works*, 3: 152.

35. Cynthia Grant Shoenberger, "The Development of the Lutheran Theory of Resistance, 1523–1530," *Sixteenth Century Journal* 8 (1977): 61–76.

36. Balnaves, "Treatise on Justification," in Knox, *Works,* 3:540. Although probably familiar with many of Balnaves's ideas, Lindsay would not have known his treatise, which, although written in 1548, was not printed until 1584.

37. The text of the sermon can be found in Knox, *Works,* 1:189–92.

38. Brother Kenneth, "Sir David Lindsay—Reformer."

39. Gordon Donaldson, "The Example of Denmark in the Scottish Reformation," in his *Scottish Church History* (Edinburgh, 1985), 63–63.

40. Ibid., 62–63.

41. Durkan, "Scottish 'Evangelicals,' " 139–40, 151–52.

42. John Gau, *The Richt Vay to the Kingdom of Heuine,* ed. A. F. Mitchell (Edinburgh, STS, 1888), xxiv.

43. Christensen, "The Earl of Rothes," 68; Durkan, "Scottish 'Evangelicals,' " 153.

44. Pitscottie, *Chronicles,* 2:141.

45. *APS,* 2:488–89.

NINE. RETURNING TO THE FRAY

1. Patrick, *Statutes,* "Preamble," 84.

2. Ibid., no. 176.

3. Ibid., no. 180.

4. Ibid., no. 281.

5. *Ane Satyre,* 2745–50; *The Monarche,* 4438–47, 4477–80, 4687–94.

6. Patrick, *Statutes,* no. 253.

7. Ibid., nos. 274, 275.

8. Lack of preaching was one of the complaints made by John Gau in his "Epistle to the Noble Lords and Barons of Scotland," appended to his *Right Vay to the Kingdom of Heuine,* 104–5,

9. Patrick, *Statutes,* no. 192.

10. *The Catechisme, that is to say, ane Comone and Catholik Instructioun of the Christian People in materis of our Catholik Faith and Religioun, quhilk na gude Christin man or waman suld misknaw. Set furth be the maist Reverend Father in God Johne Archbischop of Sanct Androus, . . . in his Prouincial Counsale haldin at Edinburgh the XXVI Day of Januarie, the Yeir of our Lord 1551* (St. Andrews, 1552), fol. 121v.

11. Quoted by Paul Althaus, *The Theology of Martin Luther,* trans. Robert C. Shultz (Philadelphia, 1966), 35.

12. Kantrowitz suggests that Lindsay's use of what she calls "plain 'godlie' rhetoric" suggests a debt to Protestant thinking; *Dramatic Allegory,* 65. But there is more to the characterization than this alone.

13. *APS,* 2:294. For other examples during this period, see ibid., 266–67, 282, 286, 301, 310, 341, 358, 492.

14. Skinner, *Foundations,* 2:14–16.

15. Knox, *Works,* 3:528.

16. John N. King, *Tudor Royal Iconography: Literature and Art in an Age of Religious Crisis* (Princeton, 1989), 95.

17. "The Procession of King Edward the VIth from the Tower to his Pallace at Westminster, and the Solempnitie of the Coronation," in Leland, *Collectanea,* 4:321.

18. Knox, *Works,* 1:553.

19. Patrick, *Statutes,* no. 276.

20. *APS,* 2:371; Patrick, *Statutes,* no. 225.

21. Kantrowitz, *Dramatic Allegory,* 17–21.

22. Hamilton's *Catechisme,* fols. 28v, 36r, 196v.

23. Knox, *Works*, 1:100.

24. Cameron, "Humanism and Religious Life," 162.

25. Patrick, *Statutes*, no. 258.

26. Sadler, *Papers*, 1:265.

27. *RPC*, 163. See also Patrick, *Statutes*, nos. 225, 258, 276.

28. Hamilton's *Catechisme* consistently refers to "the seuin sacraments" and does not use the term "needful." Neither does it appear to be common among the Reformers; it does not occur, for example, in the relevant section of *The First Book of Discipline*, ed. James K. Cameron (Edinburgh, 1972), 90–93.

29. Patrick Hamilton, *Patrick's Places*, in James Edward McGoldrick, *Luther's Scottish Connection* (London and Toronto, 1989), 82.

30. Hamilton's *Catechisme*, fol. 94r.

31. Cowan, *The Scottish Reformation*, 82.

32. Indulgences and their Scottish context are discussed by Annie I. Dunlop, "Remissions and Indulgences in Fifteenth Century Scotland," *RSCHS* 15 (1966): 153–68.

33. Cowan, *The Scottish Reformation*, 9; Lyall, *Ane Satyre*, 192.

34. As Lyall points out, his action was highly irregular. The right to grant divorce was restricted to the ecclesiastical courts and even then was granted only on very restricted ground; *Ane Satyre*, 194.

35. This was the twenty-seventh of Luther's *Ninety-five Theses;* Rupp and Drewery, *Martin Luther*, 20.

36. Erasmus, *Praise of Folly*, 126–27.

37. The authorities may have been awaiting the Tridentine decree on the subject, not issued until 1563.

38. Patrick, *Statutes*, no. 276.

39. Wormald, *Court, Kirk, and Community*, 79; Cameron notes that on those few occasions when the question was considered the response was generally hostile; "Aspects of the Lutheran Contribution," 10.

40. Wiedermann, "Martin Luther versus John Fisher," 26–27.

41. *L&P Henry VIII*, 12, pt. i, no. 496.

42. Sadler, *Papers*, 1:265.

43. *L&P Henry VIII*, 12, pt. i, no. 703.

44. A. F. Mitchell, ed., *A Compendious book of Godly and Spiritual Songs, Commonly Known as the Gude and Godlie Ballatis* (Edinburgh, STS, 1897), 204–7. These songs, collected sometime before 1560 by James and John Wedderburn of Dundee, were published in this form only after 1565. Alasdair MacDonald is currently preparing a copy of the 1565 edition for publication by the Scottish Text Society.

45. The closest he comes is his call for reform by the pope, "With aduyse of his counsall generall" (*The Monarche*, 4835), an interesting pointer to the influence of the conciliarist tradition on his thinking and, perhaps, more widely within pre-Reformation Scotland.

46. According to Lyall, "Lindsay here acknowledges explicitly the authority of the pope in ecclesiastical matters since his consent is a prerequisite for the abolition of death duties"; *Ane Satyre*, 196–97. But, as the subsequent enactment of the legislation shows, the very opposite is true.

47. For an examination of the confusing and often confused terminology associated with apocalypses, apocalypticism, and eschatological expectation, see Paul Christianson, *Reformers and Babylon: English Apocalyptic Visions from the Reformation to the Eve of the Civil War* (Toronto, 1978), 7; John J. Collins, *The Apocalyptic Imagination: An Introduction to the Jewish Matrix of Christianity* (New York, 1984), 4; Bernard McGinn, "Early Apocalypticism: The Ongoing Debate," in *The Apocalypse in English Renaissance Thought and Literature*, ed. C. A.

Patrides and Joseph Wittreich (Manchester, 1984), 2–39. The term "apocalypse" here is taken to refer to a literary genre, "the Apocalypse" generally refers to biblical apocalyptic literature, and "apocalypticism" refers to the attempted discernment of a message, of a revealed or prophesied truth, within the historical process and with reference to eschatological expectations.

48. The function of apocalypse as response to crisis, its ability to counter frustrated expectations and bridge the gulf between expectation and reality, is suggestively explored by Adela Yarboro Collins, *Crisis and Catharsis: The Power of the Apocalypse* (Philadelphia, 1984).

49. The medieval tradition incorporated mainstream commentaries on the Apocalypses, the Joachimist tradition, and the legend of the antichrist; Richard Bauckham, *Tudor Apocalypse: Sixteenth Century Apocalypticism, Millenarianism, and the English Reformation: From John Bale to John Foxe and Thomas Brightman* (Oxford, 1978), 17–22; Marjorie Reeves, *The Influence of Prophecy in the Later Middle Ages: A Study in Joachimism* (Oxford, 1969).

50. Despite Luther's original doubts concerning the status of Revelation in the New Testament canon, he grew to appreciate its value as a means of explaining papal corruption, and his letters reveal a growing conviction that the pope was the prophesied antichrist; Jaroslav Pelikan, "Some Uses of the Apocalypse in the Magisterial Reformers," in *The Apocalypse in English Renaissance Thought and Literature,* ed. Patrides and Wittreich, 83–85.

51. Katherine Firth has offered some tentative suggestions as to the precise identity of these sources, including George Joye's *Exposition of Daniel* (1545), Frith's translation of Luther's *De Antichristo* (1529), and possibly Barnes's *Vitae Romanorum Pontificum* (1535); *The Apocalyptic Tradition in Reformation Britain, 1530–1645* (Oxford, 1979), 116–17,

52. Knox, *Works,* 1:192.

53. *Carion's Chronicle: The Thre Bokes of Cronicles &c. gathered wyth great diligence of the best authors; whereunto is added an appendix by John Funke of Nurenborough* (London, 1550).

54. The original German was probably beyond Lindsay's linguistic scope, and the earliest French version, produced by Jean le Blond in 1553, was available too late to be of use. Basing his case on some unconvincing verbal parallels, Hamer maintains that Lindsay's source was the 1550 English translation, and noting that references to Carion occur in the last half of the poem, he concludes that Lindsay used it "not as a primary source book . . . but to supply illustrations and facts additional to those provided by other authorities"; *Works,* 3:241. However, Lindsay's use of cited authorities in *The Monarche* is by no means evenhanded, and it makes more sense to argue that Lindsay utilized Carion where it best suited. Certainly, it seems too fundamental a source to be included simply as an afterthought. Lindsay's use of Carion is also discussed by Alisdair M. Stewart, "Carion, Wedderburn, Lindsay," *Aberdeen University Review* (1972): 271–74.

55. Wedderburn, *The Complaynt of Scotland,* ed. Stewart, 28–29.

56. C. A. Patrides, *The Grand Design of God: The Literary Form of the Christian View of History* (London, 1972), 1–34.

57. Lindsay's edition of Eusebius, a fourth-century work subsequently enlarged upon by a succession of authors including St. Jerome, was that compiled by Palmerius of Florence, continuing up to 1511 (*The Monarche,* 4557). Orosius, or at least the sixteenth-century French translation used by Lindsay (1747), appears to have been a more important source, being cited by him no less than five times (1240, 1644, 1745, 1815, and 3485).

58. As Christianson comments, "not all prophets espoused an apocalyptic framework, but all apocalyptic thinkers acted, to a greater or lesser degree, as prophets"; *Reformers and Babylon,* 6.

59. McGinn, "Early Apocalypticism," 28.

60. *Carion's Chronicle,* fol. 6v.

61. Lindsay explicitly rejects the authority of The *Fasciculus* (a history of the world since

the Creation, first printed in 1474) and the *Cronica Cronicarum* (according to Hamer probably a French version of an abridgment of the *Fasciculus* printed in Paris in 1521 and 1532); *Works,* 3:449.

62. Matthew 24:29; Mark 13:24–25.

63. *L&P Henry VIII,* 12, pt. i, no. 843.

64. The legend is discussed in detail by Bauckham, *Tudor Apocalypse,* 91–93.

65. David Reid has also drawn attention to the apocalyptic undertones of Veritie's speech referring to the Last Judgment (1605–8); "Rule and Misrule in Lindsay's *Satyre* and Pitcairn's *Assembly,*" *SLJ* 11 (1984): 10.

CONCLUSION

1. Charteris, *The Warkis,* fol. 2v; Hamer, *Works,* 1:397.

2. The emergence of this class is discussed by Michael Lynch, *Scotland: A New History* (London, 1991), 247–62. Lynch argues that although the political and social (as opposed to the financial) status of the nobility was undiminished the circumstances of the Wars of the Covenant provided the stimulus for the emergence of the "middling sort." It does seem, however, that for the opportunity to be grasped there must have been at least some ideological preparation.

3. Mason, "Covenant and Commonweal," 110.

4. Of course, these policies altered over time, and Lindsay's sympathy varied accordingly.

5. A. H. Williamson, *Scottish National Consciousness in the Age of James VI: The Apocalypse, the Union, and the Shaping of Scotland's Public Culture* (Edinburgh, 1979).

SELECT BIBLIOGRAPHY

PRIMARY SOURCES

MANUSCRIPTS

British Library (BL)
"Eure's Letter and Nootes of the Epiphany drama." In Royal MS 7.C.xvi, fols. 137–39.
"Ane Forme of the Coronation of the Kinges of Scotland." In Hardwicke Papers: Historical Collections for Scotland, 1031–1620. Add. MS 35844, fols. 191–92.
Lindsay's Letter from Antwerp. In Cotton MS Caligula BI, fol. 313.
Loutfut Manuscript. Harleian MS 6419.
Wriothesley Collections. Add. MSS 45133.

National Library of Scotland (NLS)
Sir James Balfour of Denmilne's Manuscript Collection. Adv. MS 32.2.26.
Early Sixteenth-Century Heraldic Manuscript. Adv. MS 31.6.5
Sir David Lindsay's Armorial Manuscript. Adv. MS 31.4.3.
Sir David Lindsay of Rathillet's Heraldic Collection. Adv. MS 31.3.20.
John Scrymgeour's Heraldic Collection. Adv. MS 31.5.2
Seton Armorial. ACC. 9309.

Public Record Office (PRO)
James Henrisoun. "The Godly and Golden Book." SP 50/4, fols. 128–37.

St. Andrews University Library (StA)
Cupar Burgh Court Book. B 13/10/1.

Scottish Record Office (SRO)
"Lindsay Instructions, 1548." RH 2/7/6, fol. 142.
"Sentence Book of the Official Principal of St Andrews, 1541–1553." CH 5/2/1.

RECORD COLLECTIONS (PUBLISHED)

Accounts of the King's Pursemaster, 1539–40. Edited by A. L. Murray. In *Miscellany X.* Edinburgh, SHS, 1965.
Accounts of the Lord High Treasurer of Scotland. Edited by T. Dickon and Sir James Balfour Paul. 12 vols. Edinburgh, 1877–1916.
Accounts of the Master of Works, 1529–1615. Edited by Henry M. Paton. Edinburgh, 1957.
Acts of the Lords of Council, 1501–1503. Edited by Alma B. Calderwood. Edinburgh, 1993.
Acts of the Lords of Council in Public Affairs, 1501–54: Selections from the Acta Dominorum Concilii. Edited by R. K. Hannay. Edinburgh, 1932.
The Acts of Parliament of Scotland. Edited by T. Thomson and C. Innes. 12 vols. Edinburgh, 1814–75.
Calendar of Letters and Papers, Foreign and Domestic, Henry VIII. Edited by J. S. Brewer et al. 21 vols. London, 1864–1932.
Calendar of State Papers Relating to Scotland and Mary, Queen of Scots, 1547–1603. Edited by Joseph Bain et al. 13 vols. Edinburgh, 1898–1969.

261

Calendar of State Papers Relating to Scotland, 1509–1603. Edited by M. J. Thorpe. 2 vols. London, 1858.

Calendar of State Papers, Domestic, Edward VI, Mary, Elizabeth I, and James I. Edited R. Lemon et al. 12 vols. London, 1856–72.

Calendar of State Papers, Foreign, Edward VI. Edited by W. B. Turnball. London, 1861.

City of Edinburgh Old Accounts. 2 vols. Edinburgh, SBRS, 1899.

Discours Particulier d'Escosse, 1559/60. Edited by Peter G. B. McNeil. In *Miscellany II.* Stair Society Publication 35. Edinburgh, 1984.

The Douglas Book. Edited by Sir William Fraser. 4 vols. Edinburgh, 1885.

Early Records of the University of St Andrews. Edited by J. M. Anderson. Edinburgh, SHS, 1926.

The Exchequer Rolls of Scotland. Edited by G. Burnett et al. 23 vols. Edinburgh, 1878–1908.

Extracts from the Records of the Burgh of Edinburgh, 1528–1557. Edinburgh, SBRS, 1875.

Foreign Correspondence with Mary of Lorraine . . . 1548–1557. Edited by Marguerite Wood. 2 vols. Edinburgh, SHS, 1923–25.

The Hamilton Papers. Edited by Joseph Bain. 2 vols. Edinburgh, 1890–92.

HMC Report on the MSS of the Duke of Hamilton. London, 1887.

HMC Report on the MSS of the Earl of Hume. London, 1891.

HMC Report on the MSS of the Earl of Mar and Kellie. London, 1904.

The Letters of James IV, 1503–1513. Edited by R. K. Hannay and R. L. Mackie. Edinburgh, SHS, 1953.

The Letters of James V. Edited by R. K. Hannay and Denys Hay. Edinburgh, SHS, 1954.

Papers Relative to the Royal Regalia of Scotland. Edinburgh, Bannatyne Club, 1829.

Register of the Privy Council of Scotland. Edited by J. H. Burton et al. 36 vols. Edinburgh, 1877–1933.

Registrum Magni Sigilli Regum Scotorum. Edited by J. M. Thomson et al. 11 vols. Edinburgh, 1882–1914.

Registrum Secreti Sigilli Regum Scotorum. Edited by M. Livingstone et al. 8 vols. Edinburgh, 1908–.

Relations Politiques de la France et de L'Espagne avec L'Ecosse au XVIe Siècle. Edited by Alexandre Teulet. 5 vols. Paris, 1862.

Scottish Correspondence of Mary of Lorraine, 1543–1560. Edited by Annie I. Cameron. Edinburgh, SHS, 1927.

The Sheriff Court Book of Fife, 1515–1522. Edited by W. Croft Dickinson. Edinburgh, SHS, 1928.

State Papers of Henry VIII. 11 vols. London, 1830–52.

State Papers of Sir Ralph Sadler. Edited by A. Clifford. 3 vols. Edinburgh, 1809.

Statutes of the Scottish Church, 1225–1559. Edited by David Patrick. Edinburgh, SHS, 1907.

LITERATURE, HISTORIES, AND CHRONICLES (PUBLISHED)

Amours, F. J., ed. *Scottish Alliterative Poems.* Edinburgh, STS, 1897.

The Bannatyne Miscellany. 3 vols. Edinburgh, Bannatyne Club, 1827–55.

Byles, A. T. P., ed. *The Book of the Ordre of Chyvalry translated and printed by William Caxton together with Adam Loutfut's Scottish Transcript.* London, EETS, 1926.

Bellenden, John. *Livy's History of Rome, the First Five Books translated into Scots by John Bellenden, 1533.* Edited by W. A. Craigie. 2 vols. Edinburgh, STS, 1901–3.

————. *The Chronicles of Scotland Compiled by Hector Boece Translated into Scots by John Bellenden (1531).* Edited by R. W. Chambers and Edith C. Batho. 2 vols. Edinburgh, STS, 1938–41.

Boece, Hector. *Scotorum Historiae.* Paris, 1527.

Brosse, Jacques de la. *Two Missions of Jacques de la Brosse: An Account of the Affairs of Scotland in the year 1543 and the Journal of the Siege of Leith, 1560.* Edited by G. Dickinson. Edinburgh, SHS, 1942.

Buchanan, George. *The History of Scotland from the Earliest Period to the Regency of the Earl of Moray.* Edited and translated by James Aikman. 6 vols. Glasgow, 1845.

Bullein, William. *A Dialogue against the Feuer Pestilence by William Bullein from the edition of 1578 collated with the earlier editions of 1564 and 1573.* Edited by M. W. Bullein and A. H. Bullein. London, EETS, 1888.

Calderwood, David. *History of the Kirk of Scotland.* Edited by T. Thomson and D. Laing. 8 vols. Edinburgh, Wodrow Society, 1842–49.

Carion, Johan. *The Thre Bokes of Cronicles &c. gathered wyth great diligence of the best authors; whereunto is added an appendix by John Funke of Nurenborough.* London, 1550.

The Catechisme, that is to say, Ane Comone and Catholik Instruction of the Christin People in materis of our Catholik Faith and Religioun, quhilk na gud Christin man or woman suld misknaw. Set furth the maist Reverend Father in God, Johne Archbischop of Sanct Androus Legatnait and Primat of the Kirk of Scotland, in his Prouincial Counsale haldin at Edinburgh the XXVI Day of Januarie, the Yeir of our Lord 1551. St. Andrews, 1552.

Craigie, W. A., ed. *The Maitland Folio Manuscript.* 2 vols. Edinburgh, STS, 1919–27.

———, ed. *The Maitland Quarto Manuscript.* Edinburgh, STS, 1920.

———, ed. *The Asloan Manuscript.* 2 vols. Edinburgh, STS, 1923–25.

Cranstoun, J., ed. *Satirical Poems of the Time of the Reformation.* 2 vols. Edinburgh, STS, 1891–93.

A Diurnal of Remarkable Occurents that have passed within the country of Scotland since the death of King James the Fourth till the year 1575. Edinburgh, Bannatyne Club, 1833.

Douglas, Gavin. *The Poetical Works of Gavin Douglas.* Edited by John Small. 4 vols. Edinburgh and London, 1874.

———. *Virgil's Aeneid translated into Scottish Verse by Gavin Douglas.* Edited by David F. C. Coldwell. 4 vols. Edinburgh, STS, 1957–64.

———. *The Shorter Poems of Gavin Douglas.* Edited by Priscilla Bawcutt. Edinburgh, STS, 1967.

Dunbar, William. *The Poems of William Dunbar.* Edited by John Small. 3 vols. Edinburgh, STS, 1893.

Erasmus, Desiderius. *The Education of a Christian Prince.* Edited and translated by Lester K. Born. New York, 1965.

———. *Praise of Folly.* Translated by B. Radice with notes by A. H. T. Levi. London, 1971.

Gau, John. *The Richt Vay to the Kingdom of Heuine.* Edited by Arthur F. Mitchell. Edinburgh, STS, 1888.

Hay, Sir Gilbert. *Gilbert of the Hayes Prose Manuscript.* Edited by J. H. Stevenson. 2 vols. Edinburgh, STS, 1901–14.

Henryson, Robert. *The Poems of Robert Henryson.* Edited by G. Gregory Smith. 3 vols. Edinburgh, STS, 1906–14.

Ireland, John. *Meroure of Wyssdome: Composed for the Use of James IV, King of Scots, by Johanne de Irlandia.* Vol. 3. Edited by Craig MacDonald. Edinburgh, STS, 1990.

Knox, John. *The Works of John Knox.* Edited by David Laing. 6 vols. Edinburgh, Wodrow Society, 1846–64.

Leland, John. *Johannis Lelandi Antiquarii de Rebus Britannicis Collectanea.* 6 vols. London, 1774.

Leslie, Bishop John. *The History of Scotland from the Death of King James I in the year 1436 to the year 1561.* Edinburgh, Bannatyne Club, 1830.

Lindsay, Sir David of the Mount. *The Tragical death of D. Beaton, Bishoppe of Sainct Andrewes in Scotland: Wherunto is joyned the martyrdom of maister G. Wysehart . . . for whose sake the aforesaid bishoppe was not long after slayne: Wherein thai maist learne what a burnynge charitie they shewed not only towardes him: but vnto al suche as come to their handes for the blessed Gospels sake.* Edited with an address to the reader by Robert Burrant. London, 1548.

————. *Ane Dialogue betuix Experience and ane Courteour, Off the miserabill estait of the warld. Compilit be Schir Dauid Lyndesay of the Mont Knycht, Alias Lyone Kyng of Armes.* Paris, 1558.

————. *A Dialogue betweene Experience and a Courtier, of the miserable estate of the worlde, first compiled in the Schottishe tongue by Sir Dauid Lyndesay, Knight, (a man of great learning and science) now newly corrected, and made perfit Englishe.* London, 1566.

————. *The Warkis of the Famous and Worthie Knicht Schir Dauid Lyndesay of the Mont, Alias Lyoun King of Armes. Newly correctit and vindicate from the former errouris quhairwith thay war befoir corruptit: And Augmentit with sindry warkis quhilk was not befoir imprentit.* Edinburgh, 1574.

————. *Ane Satyre of the Thrie Estatis, in Commendation of Vertew and Vituperation of Vyce. Maid be Sir Dauid Lindesay of the Mont, alias Lyon King of Armes.* Edinburgh, 1602.

————. *The Poetical Works of Sir David Lyndsay of the Mount.* Edited by George Chalmers. 3 vols. London, 1806.

————. *The Works of Sir David Lindsay.* Edited by J. H. Murray. 5 vols. London, EETS, 1865–71.

————. *The Poetical Works of Sir David Lyndsay.* Edited by David Laing. 3 vols. Edinburgh, 1879.

————. *The Works of Sir David Lindsay of the Mount, 1490–1555.* Edited by Douglas Hamer. 4 vols. Edinburgh, STS, 1931–36.

————. *Ane Satyre of the Thrie Estatis.* Edited by J. Kinsley. London, 1954.

————. *Sir David Lindsay of the Mount: Ane Satyre of the Thrie Estatis.* Edited by R. J. Lyall. Edinburgh, 1989.

Mair, John. *A History of Greater Britain as well England as Scotland (1521).* Edited and translated by Archibald Constable. Edinburgh, SHS, 1892.

Mitchell, A. F., ed. *A Compendious Book of Godly and Spiritual Songs, Commonly Known as the Gude and Godlie Ballatis.* Edinburgh, STS, 1897.

Pitscottie, Robert Lindsay of. *The History and Chronicles of Scotland.* Edited by AE. J. G. Mackay. 3 vols. Edinburgh, STS, 1899–1911.

Ritchie, W. Tod, ed. *The Bannatyne Manuscript.* 4 vols. Edinburgh, STS, 1928–34.

Robb, T. D., ed. *The Thrie Prestis of Peblis, How Thai Told Thar Talis.* Edinburgh, STS, 1920.

Rolland, John. *The Seuin Seages translatit out of prois in Scottis meter be Iohne Rolland in Dalkeith.* Edited by G. F. Black. Edinburgh, STS, 1931.

Scott, Alexander. *The Poems of Alexander Scott.* Edited by J. Cranstoun. Edinburgh, STS, 1896.

Spottiswoode, John. *History of the Church of Scotland, 1639.* 10 vols. Edinburgh, Bannatyne Club, 1847–50.

Stewart, William. *The Buik of the Croniclis of Scotland; or, A Metrical Version of the History of Hector Boece.* Edited by William B. Turnball. 3 vols. London, Rolls Series, 1858.

Wedderburn, Robert. *The Complaynt of Scotland.* Edited by James A. H. Murray. London, EETS, 1872.

————. *The Complaynt of Scotland by Robert Wedderburn (c.1550).* Edited by A. M. Stewart. Edinburgh, STS, 1979.

SECONDARY SOURCES

BOOKS

Aitken, A. J., et al., eds. *Bards and Makars: Scottish Language and Literature, Medieval and Renaissance.* Glasgow, 1977.

Aldis, H. G. *A List of Books Printed in Scotland before 1700: including those Printed furth of the Realm for Scottish Booksellers: with Brief Notes on the Printers and Stationers*. Edinburgh, 1970.

Allmand, C. T. *War, Literature, and Politics in the Late Middle Ages*. Liverpool, 1976.

————, ed. *Power, Culture, and Religion in France, c.1350–c.1550*. Woodbridge, 1989.

Anglo, Sydney. *Spectacle, Pageantry, and Early Tudor Policy*. Oxford, 1969.

————, ed. *Chivalry in the Renaissance*. Woodbridge, 1990.

Asch, Ronald G., and Adolf M. Birke, eds. *Princes, Patronage, and the Nobility: The Court at the Beginning of the Modern Age, c.1450–1650*. Oxford, 1991.

Balfour Paul, Sir James. *Heraldry in Relation to Scottish History and Art*. Edinburgh, 1900.

Bapst, Edmond. *Les Mariages de Jaques V*. Paris, 1889.

Bauckham, Richard. *Tudor Apocalypse: Sixteenth Century Apocalypticism, Millenarianism, and the English Reformation: From John Bale to John Foxe and Thomas Brightman*. Oxford, 1978.

Bawcutt, Priscilla. *Gavin Douglas: A Critical Study*. Edinburgh, 1976.

————. *Dunbar the Makar* (Oxford, 1992).

Bennet, H. S. *English Books and Readers*. 3 vols. 2nd ed. Cambridge, 1969.

Billington, Sandra. *Mock Kings in Medieval Society and Renaissance Drama*. Oxford, 1991.

Bingham, Caroline. *James V, King of Scots, 1512–1542*. London, 1971.

Block, Joseph S. *Factional Politics and the English Reformation, 1520–1540*. Woodbridge, 1993.

Booty, John E., ed. *The Godly Kingdom of Tudor England: Great Books of the English Reformation*. Wilton, CT, 1981.

Boulton, D'Arcy Jonathon Dacre. *The Knights of the Crown: The Monarchical Orders of Knighthood in Later Medieval Europe, 1325–1520*. Woodbridge, 1987.

Brown, J. M., ed. *Scottish Society in the Fifteenth Century*. London, 1977.

Bryant, Lawrence M. *The King and the City in the Parisian Royal Entry Ceremony: Politics, Ritual, and Art in the Renaissance*. Geneva, 1986.

Burgess, Glyn S., and Robert A. Taylor, eds. *The Spirit of the Court: Selected Proceedings of the Fourth Congress of the International Courtly Literature Society*. Woodbridge and Dover, NH, 1985.

Bushnell, Rebecca W. *Tragedies of Tyrants: Political Thought and Theater in the English Renaissance*. Ithaca and London, 1990.

Cameron, Euan. *The European Reformation*. Oxford, 1991.

Christianson, Paul. *Reformers and Babylon: English Apocalyptic Visions from the Reformation to the Eve of the Civil War*. Toronto, 1978.

Clan Lindsay Society. 4 vols. Edinburgh, 1901–36.

Cosman, Madelaine Pelner. *The Education of the Hero in Arthurian Romance*. Chapel Hill, 1965.

Cowan, Ian B. *The Scottish Reformation: Church and Society in Sixteenth Century Scotland*. London, 1982.

Cowan, Ian B., and Duncan Shaw, eds. *The Renaissance and Reformation in Scotland*. Edinburgh, 1983.

Dickson, R., and J. P. Edmond. *Annals of Scottish Printing from the Introduction of the Art in 1507 to the Beginning of the Seventeenth Century*. Cambridge, 1890.

Dodgshon, Robert A. *Land and Society in Early Scotland*. Oxford, 1981.

Donaldson, Gordon. *The Scottish Reformation*. Cambridge, 1960.

————. *James V to James VII*. Edinburgh, 1965.

————. *Scottish Church History*. Edinburgh, 1985.

Dowling, Maria. *Humanism in the Age of Henry VIII*. London, 1986.

Dowling, Maria, and Peter Lake, eds. *Protestantism and the National Church in Sixteenth Century England*. London, New York, and Sydney, 1987.

Dunkley, E. H. *The Reformation in Denmark*. London, 1948.

Durkan, John, and Anthony Ross. *Early Scottish Libraries*. Glasgow, 1961.

Easson, D. E. *Gavin Dunbar, Chancellor of Scotland, Archbishop of Glasgow*. Edinburgh and London, 1947.

Eisenstein, Elizabeth. *The Printing Press as an Agent of Change: Communications and Cultural Transformations in Early Modern Europe*. 2 vols. Cambridge, 1979.

Ferguson, Arthur B. *The Indian Summer of English Chivalry: Studies in the Decline and Transformation of Chivalric Idealism*. Durham, NC, 1960.

———. *The Articulate Citizen and the English Renaissance*. Durham, NC, 1965.

———. *The Chivalric Tradition in Renaissance England*. Washington, London, and Toronto, 1986.

Fideler, Paul A., and T. F. Mayer, eds. *Political Thought and the Tudor Commonwealth: Deep Structure, Discourse, and Disguise*. London and New York, 1992.

Firth, Katherine R. *The Apocalyptic Tradition in Reformation Britain, 1530–1645*. Oxford, 1979.

Forbes, Leith W. *Pre-Reformation Scholars in Scotland in the Sixteenth Century*. Glasgow, 1915.

Fox, Alistair. *Politics and Literature in the Reigns of Henry VII and Henry VIII*. Oxford, 1989.

Fox, Alistair, and John Guy. *Reassessing the Henrician Age: Humanism, Politics, and Reform, 1500–1550*. Oxford and New York, 1986.

Fradenburg, Louise O. *City, Marriage, Tournament: Arts of Rule in Late Medieval Scotland*. Madison, WI, 1992.

Gardner-Medwin, A., and J. E. H. Williams, eds. *A Day Estivall: Essays on the Music, Poetry, and History of Scotland and England and Poems Previously Unpublished in Honour of Helena Mennie Shire*. Aberdeen, 1990.

Giesey, Ralph E. *The Royal Funeral Ceremony in Renaissance France*. Geneva, 1960.

Gittings, Clare. *Death, Burial, and the Individual in Early Modern England*. London and Sydney, 1984.

Goodman, Anthony, and Angus MacKay, eds. *The Impact of Humanism on Western Europe*. London and New York, 1990.

Grant, I. F. *The Social and Economic Development of Scotland before 1603*. Edinburgh and London, 1930.

Grant, Sir Francis James. *The Faculty of Advocates in Scotland, 1532–1943*. Edinburgh, SRS, 1944.

———. *Court of the Lord Lyon, 1318–1945*. Edinburgh, SRS, 1946.

Green, Richard Firth. *Poets and Princepleasers: Literature and the English Court in the Late Middle Ages*. Toronto, Buffalo, and London, 1980.

Greengrass, Mark. *The French Reformation*. Oxford, 1987.

Guy, John. *Tudor England*. Oxford, 1988.

Herbert, A. S. *A Historical Catalogue of Printed Editions of the English Bible, 1525–1961*. London and New York, 1968.

Hindman, Sandra, ed. *Printing the Written Word: The Social History of Books, circa 1450–1520*. Ithaca and London, 1991.

Houston, R. A. *Scottish Literacy and the Scottish Identity: Illiteracy and Society in Scotland and Northern England, 1600–1800*. Cambridge, 1985.

———. *Literacy in Early Modern Europe: Culture and Education, 1500–1800*. London and New York, 1988.

Hughes, Joan, and W. S. Ramson. *Poetry of the Stewart Court*. Canberra, 1982.

Hume Brown, P. *George Buchanan: Humanist and Reformer*. Edinburgh, 1890.

Inglis, John A. *Sir Adam Otterburn of Redhall*. Glasgow, 1935.

Innes of Learney, Sir Thomas. *Scots Heraldry*. 2nd ed. Edinburgh and London, 1956.

Jack, R. D. S., ed. *The History of Scottish Literature: Origins to 1660*. Aberdeen, 1988.

Jones, Michael, and R. L. Storey, eds. *Gentry and Lesser Nobility in Late Medieval Europe.* Gloucester and New York, 1986.

Jones, Richard Foster. *The Triumph of the English Language: A Survey of Opinions Concerning the Vernacular from the Introduction of Printing to the Restoration.* Stanford, 1953.

Kantorowicz, Ernst. *The King's Two Bodies: A Study in Medieval Political Theology.* Princeton, 1957.

Kantrowitz, Joanne Spencer. *Dramatic Allegory: Lindsay's "Ane Satyre of the Thrie Estatis."* Lincoln, NB, 1975.

Keen, Maurice. *Chivalry.* New Haven and London, 1984.

Kelley, Donald, R. *The Beginning of Ideology: Consciousness and Society in the French Reformation.* Cambridge, 1981.

King, John N. *English Reformation Literature: The Tudor Origins of the Protestant Tradition.* Princeton, 1982.

—————. *Tudor Royal Iconography: Literature and Art in an Age of Religious Crisis.* Princeton, 1989.

Kirk, James. *Patterns of Reform: Continuity and Change in the Reformation Kirk.* Edinburgh, 1989.

—————, ed. *Humanism and Reform: The Church in Europe, England, and Scotland, 1400–1643: Essays in Honour of James K. Cameron.* Oxford, 1991.

Knecht, R. J. *Francis I.* Cambridge, 1982.

Kratzman, Gregory. *Anglo-Scottish Literary Relations, 1430–1558.* Cambridge, 1980.

Laslett, Peter, W. G. Runciman, and Quentin Skinner. *Philosophy, Politics, and Society.* Oxford, 1972.

Levi, A. H. T., ed. *Humanism in France at the End of the Middle Ages and in the Early Renaissance.* Manchester, 1970.

Lives of the Lindsays; or, A Memoir of the Houses of Crawford and Balcarres. 4 vols. Wigan, 1840.

Locher, Gottfried W. *Zwingli's Thought: New Perspectives.* Studies in the History of Christian Thought 15. Leiden, 1981.

Lynch, Michael. *Scotland: A New History.* London, 1991.

McClure, J. Derrick, and Michael R. G. Spiller, eds. *Brycht Lanternis: Essays on the Language and Literature of Medieval and Renaissance Scotland.* Aberdeen, 1989.

McConica, James. *English Humanists and Reformation Politics under Henry VIII and Edward VI.* Oxford, 1965.

Macdougall, Norman, ed. *Church, Politics, and Society: Scotland, 1408–1929.* Edinburgh, 1983.

—————. *James IV.* Edinburgh, 1989.

McFarlane, I. D. *A Literary History of Renaissance France, 1470–1589.* London and New York, 1974.

—————. *Buchanan.* London, 1981.

Macfarlane, Leslie J. *William Elphinstone and the Kingdom of Scotland, 1413–1514.* Aberdeen, 1985.

McGoldrick, James Edward. *Luther's Scottish Connection.* London and Toronto, 1989.

Mackie, R. L. *King James IV of Scotland: A Brief Survey of His Life and Times.* Edinburgh and London, 1958.

MacMillan, Duncan. *Scottish Art, 1460–1990.* Edinburgh, 1990.

MacQueen, John, ed. *Humanism in Renaissance Scotland.* Edinburgh, 1990.

McRoberts, David, ed. *Essays on the Scottish Reformation, 1513–1625.* Glasgow, 1962.

Mattingly, G. *Renaissance Diplomacy.* London, 1955.

Mayer, Thomas F. *Thomas Starkey and the Commonweal: Humanist Politics and Religion in the Reign of Henry VIII.* Cambridge, 1989.

Mill, Anna Jean. *Medieval Plays in Scotland.* Edinburgh and London, 1927.

Mohl, Ruth. *The Three Estates in Medieval and Renaissance Literature.* New York, 1933.

Mooney, Michael, ed. *Renaissance Thought and Its Sources: Paul Oscar Kristeller.* New York, 1979.

Murison, W. *Sir David Lyndsay, Poet and Satirist of the Old Church in Scotland.* Cambridge, 1938.

Nicholson, Ranald. *Scotland: The Later Middle Ages.* Edinburgh, 1974.

Norbrook, David. *Poetry and Politics in the English Renaissance.* London, 1984.

Ollivant, Simon. *The Court of the Official in Pre-Reformation Scotland.* Edinburgh, Stair Society, 1982.

Patrides, C. A. *The Grand Design of God: The Literary Form of the Christian View of History.* London, 1972.

Patrides, C. A., and J. Wittreich, eds. *The Apocalypse in English Renaissance Thought and Literature.* Manchester, 1984.

Purser, John. *Scotland's Music: A History of the Traditional and Classical Music of Scotland from Early Times to the Present Day.* Edinburgh and London, 1992.

Queller, Donald E. *The Office of Ambassador in the Middle Ages.* Princeton, 1967.

Rabil, Albert, ed. *Renaissance Humanism: Foundations, Forms, and Legacy.* 3 vols. Philadelphia, 1988.

Robbins, K., ed. *Religion and Humanism.* Studies in Church History 17. Oxford, 1981.

Rogers, Charles. *The Life of George Wishart the Scottish Martyr with His Translation of the Helvetian Confession and a General History of the Family of Wishart.* Edinburgh, 1876.

Salmon, J. H. M. *Society in Crisis: France in the Sixteenth Century.* London, 1975.

Sanderson, Margaret H. B. *Scottish Rural Society in the Sixteenth Century.* Edinburgh, 1982.

————. *Cardinal of Scotland: David Beaton, c.1494–1546.* Edinburgh, 1986.

Scatterwood, V. J., and J. W. Sherbourne, eds. *English Court Culture in the Later Middle Ages.* London, 1983.

Seton, George. *The Law and Practice of Heraldry in Scotland.* Edinburgh, 1863.

Shire, Helena Menni. *Song, Dance, and Poetry of the Court of Scotland under King James VI.* Cambridge, 1969.

Shuger, Deborah K. *Habits of Thought in the English Renaissance: Religion, Politics, and the Dominant Culture.* Berkeley and Oxford, 1990.

Simpson, Grant G. *Scottish Handwriting, 1150–1650.* Aberdeen, 1977.

Skinner, Quentin. *The Foundations of Modern Political Thought.* 2 vols. Cambridge, 1978.

Smith, Janet M. *The French Background of Middle Scots Literature.* 2nd ed. Edinburgh, 1934.

Spearing, A. C. *Medieval Dream Poetry.* Cambridge, 1976.

Stevenson, J. H. *Heraldry in Scotland including a Recension of the Law and Practice of Heraldry in Scotland by the Late George Seton, Advocate.* 2 vols. Glasgow, 1914.

Straus, Dietrich, and Horst W. Drescher, eds. *Scottish Studies: Scottish Language and Literature, Medieval and Renaissance.* Frankfurt, Berne, and New York, 1986.

Stringer, K. J., ed. *Essays on the Nobility of Medieval Scotland.* Edinburgh, 1985.

Strong, Roy. *Art and Power: Renaissance Festivals, 1450–1650.* 2nd ed. Woodbridge, 1984.

Szittya, Penn R. *The Antifraternal Tradition in Medieval Literature.* Princeton, 1986.

Vale, Malcolm. *War and Chivalry: Warfare and Aristocratic Culture in England, France, and Burgundy and the End of the Middle Ages.* London, 1981.

Wagner, A. R. *Heralds and Heraldry in the Middle Ages.* Oxford, 1956.

Walker, Greg. *Plays of Persuasion: Drama and Politics at the Court of Henry VIII.* Cambridge, 1991.

White, Helen C. *Social Criticism in the Popular Religious Literature of the Sixteenth Century.* New York, 1944.

Williamson, A. H. *Scottish National Consciousness in the Age of James VI: The Apocalypse, the Union, and the Shaping of Scotland's Public Culture.* Edinburgh, 1979.
Wormald, Jenny. *Court, Kirk, and Community: Scotland, 1470–1625.* London, 1981.
———. *Mary Queen of Scots.* London, 1988.
Yates, Frances A. *Astraea: The Imperial Theme in the Sixteenth Century.* London and Boston, 1975.

ARTICLES

Note: Articles appearing as chapters in any of the books listed above are not cited below.
Anglo, Sydney. "The Courtier: The Renaissance and Changing Ideals." In *The Courts of Europe: Politics, Patronage, and Royalty, 1400–1800,* edited by A. G. Dickens, 33–53. London, 1977.
Bald, M. A. "Vernacular Books Imported into Scotland, 1500–1625." *SHR* 23 (1926): 254–67.
Baron, Hans. "The Secularization of Wisdom and Political Humanism in the Renaissance." *Journal of the History of Ideas* 21 (1960): 131–50.
Bawcutt, Priscilla. "Dunbar's Use of the Symbolic Lion and Thistle." *Cosmos* 2 (1986): 83–97.
Baxter, J. H. "Alesius and Other Reformed Refugees in Germany." *RSCHS* 5 (1934): 92–104.
Bennet, H. S. "The Production and Dissemination of Vernacular MS in the Fifteenth Century." *Library* 3–4 (1946–47): 167–78.
Bense, Walter F. "Paris Theologians on War and Peace, 1521–29." *Church History* 41 (1972): 168–85.
Bentley, Cranch D. "Effigy and Portraiture in Sixteenth Century Scotland." *Review of Scottish Culture* 4 (1987): 9–23.
Brother Kenneth. "Sir David Lindsay—Reformer." *Innes Review* 1 (1950): 79–91.
Brown, A. L. "The Scottish Establishment in the Later Fifteenth Century." *Juridical Review* 23 (1978): 89–105.
Burger, Glenn D. "Poetical Invention and Ethical Wisdom in Lindsay's *Testament of the Papyngo.*" *SSL* 24 (1989): 164–80.
Burleigh, J. H. S. "The Scottish Reforming Councils, 1549–1559." *RSCHS* 11 (1953): 189–211.
Burnett, Charles. "The Development of the Royal Arms to 1603." *Journal of the Heraldry Society of Scotland* 1 (1977–78): 9–19.
Burns, J. H. "The Scotland of John Major." *Innes Review* 2 (1951): 65–76.
———. "John Ireland and *The Meroure of Wyssdome.*" *Innes Review* 6 (1955): 77–98.
———. "The Political Ideas of the Scottish Reformation." *Aberdeen University Review* 36 (1955–56): 251–68.
———. "The Conciliarist Tradition in Scotland." *SHR* 42 (1963): 89–104.
Cameron, James K. "Catholic Reform in Germany and in the pre-1560 Church of Scotland." *RSCHS* 20 (1979): 105–17.
———. "Aspects of the Lutheran Contribution to the Scottish Reformation." *RSCHS* 22 (1984): 1–12.
———. "Faith and Faction: Conflicting Loyalties in the Scottish Reformation." In *States, Countries, Provinces,* edited by Michael Hurst, 72–90. Bourne End, 1986.
Carlson, David R. "Royal Tutors in the Reign of Henry VII." *Sixteenth Century Journal* 20 (1991): 253–80.
Christensen, T. L. "Scoto-Danish Relations in the Sixteenth Century: The Historiography and Some Questions." *SHR* 48 (1969): 80–97.

———. "Scots in Denmark in the Sixteenth Century." *SHR* 49 (1970): 125–45.

Clebsch, William A. "The Earliest Translations of Luther into English." *Harvard Theological Review* 56 (1963): 75–86.

Cowan, Ian B. "Regional Aspects of the Scottish Reformation." Historical Association Pamphlet. London, 1978.

———. "Some Aspects of the Appropriation of Parish Churches in Medieval Scotland." *RSCHS* 13 (1959): 203–22.

Darnton, Robert. "First Steps towards a History of Reading." *Journal of Australian French Studies* 23 (1986): 5–30.

Donaldson, Gordon. "The Legal Profession in Scottish Society in the Sixteenth and Seventeenth Centuries." *Juridical Review* 21 (1976): 1–20.

Dunlop, Annie I. "Remissions and Indulgences in Fifteenth Century Scotland." *RSCHS* 15 (1966): 153–68.

Durkan, John. "George Buchanan: Some French Connections." *Bibliotheck* 4 (1963): 66–72.

———. "Early Humanism and King's College." *Aberdeen University Review* 48 (1980): 259–79.

———. "Scottish 'Evangelicals' in the Patronage of Thomas Cromwell." *RSCHS* 21 (1983): 127–56.

Ferguson, J. Wilson. "James V and the Scottish Church." In *Actions and Conviction in Early Modern Europe,* edited by T. K. Rabb and J. E. Seigel, 52–76. Princeton, 1969.

Ferrie, H. "Some Pre-Reformation Scots in Denmark." *Innes Review* 3 (1952): 130–37.

Hale, J. R. "War and Public Opinion in the Fifteenth and Sixteenth Centuries." *Past and Present* 22 (1962): 18–35.

Harward, Vernon. "*Ane Satyre of the Thrie Estatis* Again." *SSL* 7 (1970): 139–46.

Head, David M. "Henry VIII's Scottish Policy: A Reassessment." *SHR* 61 (1982): 1–24.

Hexter, J. H. "The Education of the Aristocracy in the Renaissance." *Journal of Modern History* 22 (1950): 1–20.

Innes of Learney, Sir Thomas. "The Style and Title of Lord Lyon King of Arms." *Juridical Review* 44 (1932): 197–220.

———. "Sir David Lindsay of the Mount." *Scottish Notes and Queries* 13 (1935): 145–48, 170–73, 180–83.

James, Mervyn. "English Politics and the Concept of Honour." *Past and Present,* Supp. 3 (1978).

Jamieson, Ian. "Some Attitudes to Poetry in Late Fifteenth Century Scotland." *SSL* 15 (1980): 28–42.

Jordan, Constance. "Women's Role in Sixteenth Century British Political Thought." *Renaissance Quarterly* 40 (1987): 421–51.

Lang, Andrew. "The Cardinal and the King's Will." *SHR* 3 (1906): 410–22.

Lowe, Ben. "War and the Commonwealth in Mid-Tudor England." *Sixteenth Century Journal* 21 (1990): 171–91.

Lyall, R. J. "Politics and Poetry in Fifteenth and Sixteenth Century Scotland." *SLJ* 3 (1976): 5–27.

———. "The Medieval Scottish Coronation Service: Some Seventeenth Century Evidence." *Innes Review* 28 (1977): 3–21.

———. "The Court as a Cultural Centre." *History Today,* Sept. 1984, 27–33.

McDiarmid, Matthew P. "Sir David Lindsay's Report of the Sack of Carrickfergus, 1513." *SSL* 9 (1971): 40–47.

———. "The Kingship of the Scots in Their Writers." *SLJ* 6 (1979): 5–18.

MacDonald, Alisdair A. "Poetry, Politics, and Reformation Censorship in Sixteenth Century Scotland." *English Studies* 64 (1983): 410–21.

———. "The Bannatyne Manuscript—A Marian Anthology." *Innes Review* 37 (1986): 36–47.

Macfarlane, Leslie. "The Book of Hours of James IV and Margaret Tudor." *Innes Review* 2 (1960): 3–21.

McKean, Charles. "Hamilton of Finnart." *History Today* (Jan. 1993): 42–47.

MacQueen, John. *"Ane Satyre of the Thrie Estatis."* SSL 3 (1966): 129–43.

———. "Some Aspects of the Early Renaissance in Scotland." *Forum for Modern Language Studies* 3 (1967): 201–22.

Malloch, R. J. "The Order of the Thistle." *Journal of the Heraldry Society of Scotland* 1 (1977–78): 37–45.

Mapstone, Sally. "Was There a Court Literature in Fifteenth Century Scotland?" *SSL* 26 (1991): 410–22.

Mason, Roger A. "Kingship, Tyranny, and the Right to Resist in Fifteenth Century Scotland." *SHR* 66 (1987): 125–50.

———. "Kingship, Nobility, and Anglo-Scottish Union: John Mair's *History of Greater Britain (1521)." Innes Review* 41 (1990): 182–222.

———. "Chivalry and Citizenship: Aspects of National Identity in Renaissance Scotland." In *People and Power in Scotland: Essays in Honour of T. C. Smout,* edited by Roger Mason and Norman Macdougall, 50–73. Edinburgh, 1992.

Merriman, Marcus. "War and Propaganda during the Rough Wooing." *Scottish Tradition* 9–10 (1979–80): 20–30.

Mill, Anna Jean. "The Influence of the Continental Drama on Lyndsay's *Satyre of the Thrie Estatis." Modern Language Review* 25 (1930): 425–42.

———. "The Original Version of Lindsay's *Satyre of the Thrie Estatis." SSL* 6 (1968): 67–75.

Müller, G. "Protestant Theology in Scotland and Germany in the Early Days of the Reformation." *RSCHS* 22 (1984): 103–17.

Murray, A. L. "Exchequer and Council in the Reign of James V." *Juridical Review* 5 (1960): 209–25.

Patrides, C. A. "Renaissance and Modern Thought on the Last Things: A Study in Changing Conceptions." *Harvard Theological Review* 51 (1958): 169–86.

Reeves, Marjorie. "History and Eschatology: Medieval and Early Protestant Thought in Some English and Scottish Writings." *Medievalia et Humanistica* 4 (1973): 99–123.

———. "History and Prophecy in Medieval Thought." *Medievalia et Humanistica* 5 (1974): 51–75.

Reid, David. "Rule and Misrule in Lindsay's *Satyre* and Pitcairn's *Assembly." SLJ* 11 (1884): 5–24.

Reid, W. S. "Lutheranism in the Scottish Reformation." *Westminster Theological Journal* 7 (1944–45): 91–111.

Riddy, Felicity. *"Squyer Meldrum* and the Romance of Chivalry." *Yearbook of English Studies* 4 (1974): 26–36.

Rupp, G. "Protestant Spirituality in the First Age of the Reformation." In *Popular Belief and Practice: Studies in Church History VIII,* edited by G. J. Cuming and Derek Baker, 155–70. Cambridge, 1972.

Sanderson, Margaret H. B. "Some Aspects of the Church in Scottish Society in the Era of the Scottish Reformation." *RSCHS* 17 (1970): 81–98.

———. "The Feuars of Kirklands." *SHR* 52 (1973): 117–36.

Shaw, Duncan. "Zwinglian Influences on the Scottish Reformation." *RSCHS* 22 (1986): 119–39.

Shuffleton, Frank. "An Imperial Flower: Dunbar's *The Golden Targe* and the Court Life of James IV of Scotland." *Studies in Philology* 72 (1975): 193–207.

Slavin, Arthur J. "Profitable Studies: Humanists and Government in Early Tudor England." *Viator* 1 (1970): 307–25.

Stewart, Alisdair M. "Carion, Wedderburn, Lindsay." *Aberdeen University Review* (1972): 271–74.

Walker, Greg. "Sir David Lindsay's *Ane Satire of the Thrie Estatis* and the Politics of the Reformation." *SLJ* 11 (1989): 5–17.

Wiedermann, G. "Martin Luther versus John Fisher: Some Ideas concerning the Debate on Lutheran Theology at the University of St Andrews, 1525–30." *RSCHS* 22 (1984): 13–34.

Willard, C. C. "The Concept of True Nobility at the Burgundian Court." *Studies in the Renaissance* 14 (1967): 38–48.

Williams, A. M. "Sir David Lindsay, 1490–1555." *SHR* 12 (1915): 166–73.

Williams, J. E. H. "The Lyon and the Hound: Sir David Lyndsay's *Complaint and . . . Confessioun of . . . Bagsche*." *Paregon* 31 (1981): 3–12.

———. " 'Althocht I beir nocht lyke ane baird': David Lyndsay's *Complaynt*." *SLJ* 9 (1982): 5–20.

———. "James V, David Lyndsay, and the Bannatyne Manuscript Poem of the Gyre Carling." *SSL* 26 (1991): 164–71.

THESES

Barclay, William Robinson. "The Role of Sir David Lindsay in the Scottish Reformation." Ph.D. diss., University of Wisconsin, 1956.

Bartley, Mary Margaret. "A Preliminary Study of the Scottish Royal Entries of Mary Stuart, James VI, and Anne of Denmark, 1558–1603." Ph.D. diss., University of Michigan, 1981.

Chalmers, Trevor M. "The King's Council, Patronage, and the Governance of Scotland, 1460–1513." Ph.D. diss., Aberdeen University, 1982.

Emond, W. K. "The Minority of King James V, 1513–28." Ph.D. diss., St. Andrews University, 1988.

Fulton, R. W. M. "Social Criticism in Scottish Literature, 1480–1560." Ph.D. diss., Edinburgh University, 1972.

Goodare, Julian. "Parliament and Society in Scotland, 1560–1603." Ph.D. diss., Edinburgh University, 1989.

Mapstone, Sally. "The Advice to Princes Tradition in Scottish Literature, 1450–1500." Ph.D. diss., Oxford University, 1986.

Mason, R. A. "Kingship and Commonweal: Political Thought and Ideology in Reformation Scotland." Ph.D. diss., Edinburgh University, 1983.

Williams, J. E. H. "The Poetry of Sir David Lyndsay: A Critical Study." Ph.D. diss., Australian National University, 1978.

INDEX